# Mexico City

**JULIE MEADE**

# Contents

**Welcome to Mexico City** .. 5
- 10 Top Experiences ......... 7
- Planning Your Trip .......... 16
  - Daily Reminders ......... 19
  - What's New? ............. 22
- Best of Mexico City ........ 26
  - Best People-Watching .... 28
- Mexico City with Kids ...... 33
- Mexico City's
  Pre-Columbian Past...... 38
  - Best Murals ............. 40
- A Day of Design ........... 44
- Saturday Shopping
  in the Roma ............ 46
  - Where to Eat ............ 48

**Centro Histórico** ....... 50
**Alameda Central** ....... 86
**Paseo de la Reforma** .... 112
**Chapultepec
and Polanco** ........ 140
**Roma and Condesa** ..... 172
**Insurgentes
Sur-Narvarte** ....... 204

## Neighborhood Walks

Centro Histórico Walk. . . .54

Paseo de
la Reforma Walk ....... 116

Chapultepec Walk..... 144

Roma and
Condesa Walk........ 176

Coyoacán Walk. . .224

**Coyoacán** ............. 220
**Greater Mexico City** .. 244
**Where to Stay** ........ 264
**Day Trips** ............ 278
**Background** .......... 299
**Essentials** ........... 330
**Index** ............... 361

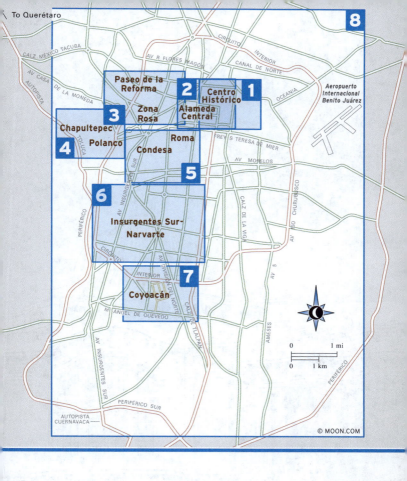

# MAPS

- 1 Centro Histórico . . . . 52-53
- 2 Alameda Central . . . 88-89
- 3 Paseo de la Reforma . . . . . . . 114-115
- 4 Chapultepec and Polanco . . . . . . 142-143
- 5 Roma and Condesa . . 174-175
- 6 Insurgentes Sur-Narvarte . . . . 206-207
- 7 Coyoacán . . . . . . . 222-223
- 8 Greater Mexico City . . . . . . 246-247

the Palacio de Bellas Artes and Torre Latinoamericana

# WELCOME TO
# Mexico City

Mexico City occupies a piece of land that seems destined to hold a grand place in history. Blanketing a broad alpine valley, it was once Tenochtitlan, an island city that was the most populous in the Americas—and by some estimates, the world—during the 15th century. Razed after the Spanish conquest, Tenochtitlan's ruins lie beneath the modern metropolis, which covers 1,480 sq km (571 sq mi) and has a population of over 21 million.

Amid the urban sprawl, there are lovely residential enclaves, architectural landmarks, and a multitude of cultural treasures, from dazzling pre-Columbian artifacts to artist Frida Kahlo's childhood home, now a museum. For those who love to eat, there is no better place to explore Mexico's varied palate. The city's famous food scene runs the gamut from relaxed street-side taco stands to elegant fine dining.

Mexico City defies expectations. Baroque palaces rise above streets noisy with traffic, generic convenience stores stand beside old-fashioned coffee shops filled with seniors sipping café con leche, and contemporary art galleries adjoin hole-in-the-wall bakeries and auto repair shops. Many of the descriptors most closely associated with the capital—crime, pollution, poverty—belie a city that is beguilingly low-key and friendly, rarely gruff, and invariably worth the effort it takes to explore. In this and every way, Mexico City is a place you must experience to understand. Come expecting one city and you'll likely find another. The contrasts, both jarring and delightful, define this mad metropolis, one of the most singular and marvelous places on earth.

fountain in Jardín Centenario, Coyoacán

1 Visiting the **Templo Mayor** archaeological site (page 66).

**2** Admiring art and architecture at the **Palacio de Bellas Artes** (page 94).

**3** Delving into pre-Columbian culture at the **Museo Nacional de Antropología** (page 148).

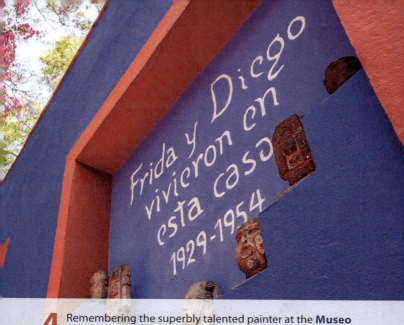

**4** Remembering the superbly talented painter at the **Museo Frida Kahlo** (page 228).

**5** Enjoying the atmosphere at **traditional cantinas** (page 196).

**6** Marveling at the pyramids of **Teotihuacán** (page 280).

**7** Eating lots of **tacos** from street stands and the city's top restaurants (page 186).

**8** Acquiring a taste for **pulque,** a fermented beverage made from the sap of the maguey cactus (page 103).

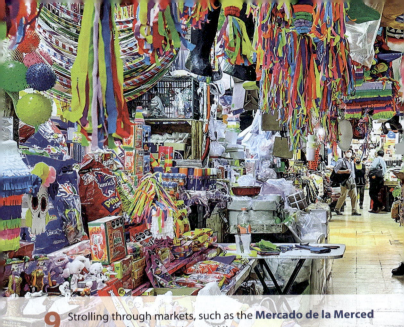

**9** Strolling through markets, such as the **Mercado de la Merced** and **Mercado Sonora** (page 111).

**10** Seeing **contemporary art** at the multitude of excellent galleries and museums (page 162).

# Planning Your Trip

## Mexico City Neighborhoods
### Centro Histórico
The oldest district in the capital, the Centro Histórico is a place of tremendous history and culture, built around a central plaza, or Zócalo, that was once at the center of the pre-Columbian city of Tenochtitlan. Today, the neighborhood is vibrant, eclectic, and urban, known for its many museums, splendid colonial-era architecture, and old-fashioned restaurants.

### Alameda Central
The magnificent Palacio de Belles Artes, a multifaceted cultural institution, sits on the eastern edge of Mexico City's oldest urban park, the Alameda Central. There are interesting sights to the north and south of these landmarks, including the busy commercial zone around the Mercado San Juan and the archeological site at Tlatelolco to the north.

### Paseo de la Reforma
The grand boulevard known as the Paseo de la Reforma is bordered by historic neighborhoods to the north and south, including the San Rafael and Santa María La Ribera, burgeoning arts districts with a laid-back urban vibe. The chic Juárez is following closely on the heels of the Roma and the Condesa as a top dining, shopping, and nightlife destination.

### Chapultepec and Polanco
The Bosque de Chapultepec, Mexico City's largest urban park, is a recreational and cultural destination. Home to the spectacular Museo Nacional de Antropología, many excellent museums, and unique landscape architecture, it is currently undergoing a massive renovation and expansion. Beside Chapultepec, Polanco is a handsome upscale neighborhood where many of the city's most famous fine dining restaurants are located.

### Roma and Condesa
These adjoining residential neighborhoods are among the coolest, greenest, and most attractive spots in central Mexico City. A popular destination for foreign visitors and expatriates, the Roma and the Condesa are the places to go to experience the city's celebrated dining and nightlife scene.

### Insurgentes Sur-Narvarte
There are fewer sights in the expansive residential neighborhoods south of the Viaducto; what you'll find here are parks, cafés, taquerias, and restaurants that cater to a local crowd and a smattering of expatriates.

## Coyoacán

There are two historic plazas at the heart of this colonial-era neighborhood, which retains a romantic small-town feel despite its big city location. In addition to the charming scenery, there are several excellent museums and cultural institutions here, notably the natal home of artist Frida Kahlo, now a beloved museum chronicling her life and work.

## Greater Mexico City

In this metropolis of millions, there are a multitude of neighborhoods, restaurants, and sights outside the well-known central neighborhoods. Head south of the city center to visit the art-and-architecture-filled campus of the Universidad Nacional Autónoma de México, the charming colonial-era district of San Ángel, or the historic farmland and canals in the southern neighborhood of Xochimilco.

# When to Go

There is no high season or low season for travel to Cuidad de México (CDMX), Mexico's capitol city. At over 2,200 m (7,200 ft) above sea level, the city's altitude tempers its tropical latitude, creating a mild and sunny climate almost all year long. May-June are the warmest months (sometimes uncomfortably so), before the start of the short **summer rainy**

the busy, historic street Madero in the Centro Histórico

**season** (June-Oct.), which brings short and often spectacular thunderstorms afternoon and evening. Normally bustling and traffic-clogged, the city is noticeably quieter during **Semana Santa** (the Easter holidays) or **Christmas,** when many locals leave town. Note that during these weeks, many restaurants, bars, and attractions also close.

## Entry Requirements

All foreign nationals visiting Mexico must have a valid **passport.** For citizens of the United States, Canada, and many other countries, a 180-day travel permit, known as the forma migratoria multiple (FMM), is issued automatically upon entry. FMMs are either stamped directly into your passport or issued electronically at one of the new self-service kiosks in the Mexico City airport. For electronic FMMs, use the QR code provided to generate an electronic copy of your visa, which you'll use at departure. When entering or leaving Mexico, children must be accompanied by their parents or, if unaccompanied or traveling with another adult, present an officially notarized and translated letter from their parents authorizing the trip.

### Transportation

Most foreign visitors arrive in Mexico City via the **Aeropuerto Internacional de la Ciudad de México (AICM),** also known as the Aeropuerto Internacional Benito Juárez, the city's main airport. The smaller **Aeropuerto Internacional Felipe Ángeles (AIFA),** in the state of Mexico, opened in 2022 and offers service to and from destinations in Mexico and Texas; ground transportation to AIFA is still more limited than to AICM, making AICM a more convenient choice.

Getting around Mexico City on public transportation is cheap, easy, efficient, and generally safe. Easy-to-use transportation options include buses, microbuses, Metro, Metrobús, and light rail, though most visitors find the **Metro** and **Metrobús** systems are all they need to get everywhere they want to go. Ride-hailing service Uber is an easy and inexpensive way to get around, as are radio taxis. Within each neighborhood, walking is the best way to see everything. Given the accessibility of public transit, driving is not recommended for short trips within the city.

### Reservations
#### CULTURAL SIGHTS AND MUSEUMS

It is generally not necessary (or even possible) to make reservations for cultural sights and museums in Mexico City. During regular weekday hours, most museums have no wait. A few important exceptions are the **Casa Luis Barragán,** which can only be visited via prebooked appointment, and the **Museo Frida Kahlo,** which often sells out weeks in advance.

# Daily Reminders

- **Monday:** Most public museums and cultural sights close, including Chapultepec park. This makes Monday a good day to stroll in the Roma and Condesa, visit markets like La Merced and the Mercado San Juan, take a day trip to the pyramids at Teotihuacán, or visit one of the few museums that are open, like the Museo del Juguete Antiguo, Casa Pedregal, or Papalote Museo del Niño.

- **Wednesday:** The last Wednesday of every month, dozens of museums and cultural centers extend their hours as a part of the Noche de Museos event. Many offer free admission and special events like concerts or movie screenings.

- **Saturday:** The punk-rock music market Tianguis Cultural del Chopo takes place every Saturday in the Santa María la Ribera. San Ángel's popular Bazaar Sábado craft market also takes place on Saturday, as does the Mercado de Cuauhtémoc, in the Roma, a small but excellent outdoor vintage market.

- **Sunday:** Many museums and cultural centers are free on Sunday (free entry may be limited to Mexican nationals). As a result, the most famous museums often fill to capacity. In the Centro, the Lagunilla art and antiquities market takes place on Sunday, and the central stretch of the Paseo de la Reforma closes to car traffic 8am-2pm, making it a great day to stroll this historic avenue. On the last Sunday of the month, the Paseo de la Reforma and several other major avenues close to create bike paths throughout the city as part of the Ciclotón.

**Above:** San Ángel's Bazaar Sábado

Reservations are also required at the wonderful contemporary art space **LAGO/ALGO** in Chapultepec, though, unlike the Casa Luis Barragán and Museo Frida Kahlo, entry to LAGO/ALGO is free.

## EATING OUT

Reservations for the city's most famous **restaurants** are a must. For well-known restaurants like **Pujol** or **Máximo Bistrot Local,** book as early as possible—at least a month before you plan to go. Newer restaurants and bars generating a lot of buzz often require advance reservations as well, particularly on weekends. Call or send a WhatsApp at least a few days ahead. Note that comida, the midday meal, is considered the most important meal of the day in Mexico, so a 2pm reservation on Saturday or Sunday can be one of the toughest to get.

Many popular **bars** accept reservations and they are strongly recommended for popular spots like **Ticuchi** and **Licorería Limantour.** Increasingly, both bars and restaurants throughout the city accept reservations through WhatsApp or Instagram, sometimes exclusively. If you don't have it on your phone, it's useful to download WhatsApp before arriving in Mexico City.

a line outside Museo Frida Kahlo

## ACCOMMODATIONS

If you are flexible about where you're staying (and especially if you are planning to stay in a budget hotel), it's fine to make **hotel reservations** a week or two before your arrival. However, if you want to stay in the Roma or the Condesa, and especially if you have your heart set on one of the popular small hotels in those areas (like **Condesa DF** or the **Red Tree House**), book your hotel reservation as soon as you plan your trip. It's also worth planning ahead if you will be visiting during a major holiday like Independence Day, popular vacation seasons like the winter holidays, or during international events like the 2026 FIFA World Cup.

### Passes and Discounts

With little exception, museums and cultural institutions in Mexico City have low admission prices. On top of that, museums often offer discounted or free admission on Sunday, and some have permanent discounts for children, seniors, educators, and people with disabilities. Increasingly, discounted admission, including free Sunday admission, applies only to Mexican nationals. There are no citywide passes for cultural centers, museums, or transportation.

### Guided Tours
#### BUS TOURS

**Turibus** (www.turibus.com.mx; Mon.-Fri. US$8, Sat.-Sun. US$10) makes frequent circuits through the city's major neighborhoods on bright red double-decker buses, with the most popular circuit running from the Zócalo to the Auditorio Nacional via the Paseo de la Reforma, passing many of the city's important sites and museums.

Also offering double-decker bus tours but taking different routes through the city is **Capitalbus** (http://capitalbus.mx; 9am to 6pm daily; US$12). Your ticket is good for 24 hours, during which time you can ride any of the three lines and get on and off the bus at official stops as often as you like.

#### FOOD TOURS

No one will give you a more engaging taste of the city than woman-owned and operated **Eat Like a Local Mexico** (https://eatlikealocal.com.mx), which runs street food and markets tours for small groups. Long-running groups **Eat Mexico** (www.eatmexico.com) and **Club Tengo Hambre** (https://clubtengohambre.com) also offer excellent guided tours of street food, markets, and taquerías. For food and cultural tours of the Roma neighborhood, reach out to writer Lydia Carey of **Mexico City Streets** (https://mexicocitystreets.com); she can also arrange tours of Xochimilco's quieter canals and farmland.

# What's New?

- **Updated green space:** The city's largest urban park, the **Bosque de Chapultepec** (page 166), is currently undergoing an ambitious restoration and expansion project. To make the park more accessible to pedestrians, a new system of footbridges, designed by famed Mexican artist Gabriel Orozco, has made the second section of Chapultepec—and all its wonderful sights—much easier to access from the first section. In 2024, the new Cuarta Sección (Fourth Section) of the park opened to the public.

- **More park attractions:** In addition to revitalized green spaces in Chapultepec, the 1960s-vintage **Museo de Historia Natural** (page 164) has been beautifully updated and restored, while the Chapultepec Park's long-running amusement park has reopened as **Aztlán** (page 167) and features a new 85-m (279-ft) Ferris wheel, **Aztán 360,** which opened in the spring of 2024.

- **More murals:** In September 2024, the former headquarters of the Secretaría de Educacion Pública reopened as the **Museo Vivo del Muralismo** (page 60), which includes an extensive series of murals by Diego Rivera, alongside work by other 20th-century masters. The Diego Rivera murals in the **Palacio Nacional** (page 68) are on view again after a multiyear closure.

- **More eats:** Mexico's City celebrated restaurant and nightlife scenes continue to grow at an astonishing clip, with new hot spots and interesting projects opening across the city, from an exotic weekly menu at culinary heritage project **Fogones** (page 184) to niche concepts like Baja California-style Chinese cuisine at the Roma's **Cantón Mexicali** (page 188).

- **New culinary stars:** Mexico City's reputation as a food capital has been duly established, and the arrival of Michelin in 2024 only sealed that reputation. Two famed Mexico City restaurants, **Pujol** (page 152)

LAGO/ALGO

and **Quintonil** (page 153), were given two stars by the prestigious French critics, and many more were awarded with stars and Bib Gourmand designations, including some taquerías!

- **Amazing art spaces:** There are several notable newcomers in Mexico City's thriving contemporary art scene, particularly the gorgeous **LAGO/ALGO** (page 159), a unique gallery space overlooking the Lago Mayor in the Segunda Sección de Chapultepec, which opened in 2022, and **Olivia Foundation** (page 198) in the Roma, which opened in 2024.

- **New windows into history:** Archaeological discoveries in the Centro Histórico continue to reveal the size and scope of the Mexica city of Tenochtitlan, atop which the modern-day metropolis was built. In 2022, the **Zona Arqueológica and Museo del Templo Mayor** (page 66) opened a new "subterranean museum" showcasing the Templo de Ehécatl and part of a pre-Columbian ball court.

- **More beer:** The craft beer scene is flourishing in Mexico City, with city-made brews like **Cosaco, Cru Cru, Yeccan,** and **Flaco Cara de Perro,** among others, appearing on bar and restaurant menus throughout the city, along with a spate of new taprooms.

- **New spirits:** Mezcal is now joined by lesser known Mexican spirits like **bacanora** and **sotol** at bars like **Tlecan** in the Roma (page 195).

- **More expats:** Remote workers and digital nomads from the United States and other foreign countries are flooding the city, changing the flavor and affecting the prices, particularly in the Roma, the Condesa, and the Juárez neighborhoods. Concerns about gentrification, the effects of Airbnb and other vacation rentals on the local housing market, and the imperiled survival of longtime small businesses are major topics of conversation in Mexico City today.

Día de Nuestra Señora de Guadalupe in Mexico City

## CULTURAL TRIPS

The Mexican government's **Instituto Nacional de Antropología e Historia** (INAH), or National Institute of Anthropology and History, offers guided tours of the city sights in Spanish as well as cultural trips to destinations around central Mexico. The trips, operated under the name Paseos Culturales INAH, usually include a Spanish-speaking guide and entrance fees. For more information, visit the INAH office in the Museo Nacional de Antropología (tel. 55/5553-2365 or 55/5215-1003; https://paseosculturales.inah.gob.mx).

# Calendar of Events
## February

For art lovers, consider a visit during **Art Week Mexico,** when Mexico City's biggest contemporary art fair, **Zsona MACO** (México Arte Contemporáneo; www.zsonamaco.com), is held over five days in the Centro Citibanamex in the Lomas de Sotelo. Several smaller art fairs run at the same time, and there are countless exhibitions and events at galleries throughout the city.

## March and April

**Semana Santa** (Holy Week, the week before Easter) officially begins on Domingo de Ramos, or Palm Sunday, when handwoven palm crosses are sold outside the city's churches, and runs through Easter Sunday. The main reason to visit (or avoid) Mexico City during the Easter holidays is to experience a notably quieter metropolis. Traffic is subdued, museums are nearly empty, and you'll rarely need restaurant reservations—though a large number of shops, restaurants, and bars close for the week.

## September

Mexico commemorates its independence from Spain on September 16; however, the main **Día de la Independencia** festivities in Mexico City take place on the evening of September 15, when thousands of revelers crowd the Zócalo. At 11pm, the president of the republic appears on the balcony of the Palacio Nacional, reenacting Miguel Hidalgo's cry for independence, including "Viva México!"—also known as El Grito. Fireworks and parties follow. There is a military parade through the Centro and along the Paseo de la Reforma the next day.

## December

The Virgin of Guadalupe miraculously appeared to Saint Juan Diego on the hill of Tepeyac on December 12, 1531. Today, the **Día de Nuestra Señora de Guadalupe** is one of the most important religious holidays across Latin America. On the days leading up to the 12th, pilgrims walk through the city toward the Basílica de Santa María de Guadalupe in northern Mexico City, often setting off fireworks as they go.

Independence Day parade on the Paseo de la Reforma

# Best of Mexico City

## Day 1
**The Centro Histórico**
**Metro:** *Zócalo*
### MORNING

Mexico City's **Zócalo,** one of the largest public squares in the world, was once an open plaza at the center of the Mexica city of Tenochtitlan, the remains of which lie beneath the modern metropolis. After the conquest, the Zócalo became the heart of the new Spanish city, and was called the Plaza Mayora throughout the colonial era. Take a moment to feel the power and history of this grand plaza, then head north to visit the remains of the city of Tenochtitlan's holiest site at the fascinating and recently expanded **Museo del Templo Mayor.** Here, the base of the twin temple-pyramid that adjoined Tenochtitlan's central plaza has been excavated; it was destroyed by the Spanish in the 16th century and then buried for centuries beneath the colonial city. Its base was uncovered in the 1970s, along with hundreds of artifacts now held in the on-site museum.

### AFTERNOON

Have lunch at **El Cardenal,** just a block from the Zócalo, widely considered one of the best traditional Mexican restaurants in the city. After lunch, loop back to the Zócalo to see the awe-inspiring murals by Diego Rivera that cover the central patio and staircase of the **Palacio Nacional.** Rivera's detailed rendering of the city of Tenochtitlan is particularly moving following a visit to the Templo Mayor.

From the Palacio, head west along the bustling pedestrian street Madero. Drop in to see the current show at quirky **Museo Del Estanquillo** or the grand **Palacio de Cultura Citibanamex,** both free, and note the many historic buildings along the avenue, including the **Casa de los Azulejos.** If you're interested in Mexican textiles, it's also worth a detour south on Isabel la Católica to visit **Remigio** at the **Shops at Downtown,** a shopping center housed in a beautiful 18th-century palace.

Once you reach the Eje Central, head one block north from Madero to Tacuba to see the opulent central post office, known as the **Palacio Postal,** and the equally opulent **Museo Nacional de Arte,** both fine examples of early 20th-century architecture in Mexico City.

### EVENING

Dusk is the perfect time to visit one of the Centro's traditional cantinas. Start at **Bar La Ópera,** a glamorous old-fashioned cantina on Cinco de Mayo that first opened in 1876. From there, it's a quick walk to charming **Tío Pepe,** which is even older than La Opera, and, like many long-running cantinas, a reliably relaxed place for a drink.

the Zócalo

# Best People-Watching

### MORNINGS AT CAFÉ JEKEMIR

There's a mix of seniors, students, and neighborhood locals sipping espressos at this long-running café in the Centro, located on the pedestrian street Regina (page 215).

### SATURDAY MORNING AT THE TIANGUIS CULTURAL DEL CHOPO

You'll find a pierced and tattooed crowd at this unique Saturday-morning punk-rock market, originally founded as an informal album exchange for music lovers (page 139).

### SATURDAY NIGHT IN THE ROMA NORTE

Stroll along Álvaro Obregón, the Roma's central avenue, on a Saturday night, when crowds often spill from the barroom into the street (page 193).

### SUNDAYS ON PASEO DE LA REFORMA

People from every age group, neighborhood, and walk of life come together on Sunday for the Paseo Dominical or the Ciclotón to pedal, skate, or stroll along the grand Paseo de la Reforma, which is closed to automobile traffic 8am-2pm (page 137).

### ANY HOUR, ANY DAY AT THE BASÍLICA DE SANTA MARÍA DE GUADALUPE

At the shrine to the Virgen de Guadalupe, mass is held every hour 6am-8pm daily, drawing mobs of worshippers from across Mexico and Latin America, many arriving in traditional dress, as part of a bicycle tour, or on their knees (page 248).

Paseo de la Reforma

paddleboaters on the lake in the Bosque de Chapultepec

## Day 2
## Chapultepec and the Condesa

**Metro:** *Chapultepec, followed by Sevilla*

### MORNING

Set aside the morning to tour the **Museo Nacional de Antropología,** a vast and absorbing museum dedicated to pre-Columbian and modern-day cultures in Mexico. You won't have time to see the whole museum, so start your visit in the spectacular rooms dedicated to the Mexica people of Tenochtitlan. Back outside, take an hour or two to explore a bit of the surrounding **Bosque de Chapultepec** on foot, strolling past the multidisciplinary cultural center **Casa del Lago Juan José Arreola,** the boats on the pretty lake beside it, and the striking modern facade of the **Museo de Arte Moderno.** Stop into the museum if the show interests you, or continue your walk past the **Castillo de Chapultepec,** which sits on a rocky outcropping overlooking the park and the Paseo de la Reforma.

Museo Nacional de Antropología

## AFTERNOON

Just below the Castillo de Chapultepec are the main gates to the park. From here, take a taxi or jump on the Metro one stop from Chapultepec to Sevilla, then walk into the Roma Norte for a late lunch at **Contramar,** a stylish seafood restaurant near the Glorieta de la Cibeles that has become a Mexico City classic over the past 25 years;

entrance to Museo Frida Kahlo

accordingly, reservations are advised or a wait is guaranteed.

## EVENING

After lunch, spend a few leisurely hours watching dogs romp and children play in **Parque México.** Stroll along Avenida Amsterdam, snapping photos of the Condesa's distinctive art deco architecture and enjoying the people-watching in the many neighborhood cafés. Wrap up the day with supper and a cocktail at Roma favorite **Páramo.**

## Day 3
### Coyoacán
**Metro:** *Viveros*
### MORNING

If you arrive in Coyoacán via the Metro stop Viveros, you can admire old country mansions and towering trees while walking into the heart of the neighborhood via Avenida Francisco Sosa. Peek into the rust-colored Moorish-inspired hacienda that is home to the **Fonoteca Nacional,** an interesting sound archive and gallery space. Down the road, take a breather in charming **Plaza Santa Catarina,** a quiet, cobbled square popular with locals and their dogs. Once you arrive in the center of town, spend some time people-watching in **Jardín Hidalgo** and **Jardín Centenario,** the two old-fashioned public plazas at the center of the neighborhood.

Grab a mocha at Coyoacán classic **Café El Jarocho,** then wander through the **Mercado Coyoacán,** where you can snack on a tostada or two (the market is famous for them) to tide you over till lunch. From there, it's a few blocks to the **Museo Frida Kahlo,** a moving museum dedicated to the life and legacy of its namesake artist.

## AFTERNOON

Walk back to the Jardín Centenario for a late lunch on the patio at **Los Danzantes,** and accompany your meal with a shot of their eponymous

the Palacio de Bellas Artes

mezcal. If you want to extend the evening, drop in for a craft beer (or another mezcal) at the convivial **Centenario 107,** just a few blocks away.

## Day 4
### Alameda Central
**Metro:** *Bellas Artes, Metrobús: Juárez or Bellas Artes*

**MORNING**
Start your fourth day in the Centro Histórico with breakfast at the impressive **Sanborns de los Azulejos,** an iconic diner-like restaurant located within one of the city's most dazzling colonial-era palaces. From there, cross Madero to visit the observation deck at the **Torre Latinoamericana.** The literally breathtaking 360-degree vistas will give you a true sense of the city's scale and a bird's-eye view of the Centro Histórico.

Back at ground level, cross the Eje Central to take a turn around the museum in the **Palacio de Bellas Artes,** one of the city's flagship cultural institutions, where the gorgeous art deco interiors are as opulent as its elaborate marble facade. It's worth the admission fee to ascend to the top floors of the building, where there are interesting murals by Diego Rivera, David Alfaro Siqueiros, and Rufino Tamayo, as well as art galleries that often feature excellent contemporary exhibits.

**AFTERNOON**
It takes about 15 minutes to walk east past the always-bustling **Alameda Central** and south through the San Juan neighborhood to **Paradero**

**Conocido,** a colorful Mexican bistro on a bustling commercial street. After lunch, cross the street Balderas to **La Ciudadela Centro Artesanal,** a sprawling open-air craft market that features an incredibly wide range of traditional handcraft and souvenirs. After a turn around the market you may be ready to rest your feet, but photo buffs won't want to miss the excellent **Centro de la Imagen,** a public gallery dedicated to artistic photography; it's just a block from the artisan market.

### EVENING
Hop the Metrobús from Balderas to Jardín Pushkin to spend the evening in the Roma neighborhood, Mexico City's most famous nightlife destination. There are galleries, shopping, cafés, bars, and a dizzying number of restaurants on and around the street Álvaro Obregón, but keep it simple with a classic Mexico City dinner: **tacos.** There is no shortage of outstanding taco spots in the Roma; meat palace **Orinoco** and 100 percent vegan **Gracias Madre Taquería Vegana** are both standouts.

## With More Time
### Day 5: Teotihuacán
**Metro:** *Line 6 to Terminal Autobuses del Norte, then a local bus to Teotihuacán*

Have a hearty breakfast in or near your hotel, slather on some sunscreen, and pack a big bottle of water before making your way to the Terminal Autobuses del Norte, the first stop in your journey to the ruins at **Teotihuacán.** Mexico's most famous and most visited archaeological site is just 30 km (19 mi) outside the city, and buses depart the terminal for the pyramids several times each hour.

Though little is known about its people, Teotihuacán was once the most powerful city-state in Mesoamerica, evidenced by its massive temples and visionary city planning: Today, you can get a glimpse into that mysterious past by walking along Teotihuacán's grand central avenue, the Calzada de los Muertos, to admire the twin pyramids that once stood at the city center, the Pirámide del Sol (Pyramid of the Sun) and the Pirámide de la Luna (Pyramid of the Moon).

# Mexico City with Kids

Mexico City is large, loud, and relentlessly urban, yet it's a remarkably agreeable place to visit with family. Here, children are treated with respect and kindness, graciously welcomed at most restaurants and hotels, and usually granted free or reduced admission to museums and other cultural institutions. The capital's rich history and diverse local culture make it a truly magical and eye-opening place to visit—at any age.

## Thursday
### Centro Histórico
**MORNING**

The Centro Histórico is a magical neighborhood, filled with old palaces, bustling with visitors, and buzzing with years of history. Start with breakfast in the historic dining room at **Café de Tacuba,** then walk to the **Zócalo,** where you'll often find brightly dressed concheros (also called "Aztec dancers") performing a rhythmic dance to the beat of a drum.

Located in the former headquarters of the federal Department of

Education, the **Museo Vivo del Muralismo** features Diego Rivera's most extensive mural series, covering three stories of open courtyard. Planned to be educational, these murals provide an engaging look into Mexican history and culture—as well as Rivera's communist political views.

## AFTERNOON

Have lunch at **Balcón del Zócalo,** a rooftop Mexican restaurant in the Zócalo Central hotel, which has gorgeous views of the cathedral and plaza. Next, walk down Cinco de Mayo to the **Dulcería de Celaya,** one of the oldest and most charming sweetshops in the city. It's particularly festive during Día de Muertos and Christmastime.

Cross the Eje Central to the Alameda, peeking into the amazing art deco lobby at the **Palacio de Bellas Artes.** Finally, let the kids stretch their legs along the paved paths in the **Alameda Central,** Mexico City's oldest urban park. From there, you can check out the **Laboratorio de Arte Alameda,** which often hosts experimental or interactive art exhibits, or walk south down the Eje Central for hot chocolate and churros at the original branch of famed **Churrería El Moro.**

traditional dancers in the Zócalo

trajineras at the dock in Xochimilco

## Friday
### Xochimilco

Set aside the day to boat along the canals in **Xochimilco,** a small remnant of the vast system of waterways that once ribboned the Valley of Mexico. You can take the light rail from Metro Tasqueña all the way to Xochimilco, and then a taxi to the docks; if you wait till midmorning, lighter traffic can make a taxi or Uber an easier and faster option.

Enlist the kids to help pick out a trajinera, one of the colorful flat-bottomed boats typical to Xochimilco, and plan to spend a few hours exploring the canals. Departing from any of the docks, the main tourist corridors are often jammed with boaters (and mariachi musicians paddling by in canoes, waiting to be commissioned for a tune), creating a convivial atmosphere. If you'd also like to visit the traditional "floating gardens," or chinampas, where people still live and grow food, ask the boat's driver to take you farther into the canals for the tour ecológico (ecological tour), outside the main tourist zone.

## Saturday
### Coyoacán
**MORNING**

There is an old-fashioned feeling in central **Coyoacán,** a popular weekend destination for both visitors and Mexico City locals. Arrive in the morning, taking a lap around the famous coyote fountain in **Jardín Centenario,** then wander through Jardín Hidalgo as it begins to fill up with vendors selling balloons, toys, and raspados (shaved ice). From the plaza, it's only a few blocks to the neighborhood's atmospheric market, **Mercado Coyoacán,** where there are artisanal crafts, textiles, and baskets for sale in addition to food and snacks. You can stop for a mocha and a doughnut at Coyoacán institution **Café El Jarocho** on the way.

the coyote fountain in Jardín Centenario by the Mexican sculptor Gabriel Ponzanelli

Go early to buy your tickets for a midday performance at **La Titería** (there's a garden and a small library where kids can play while you wait for the show to begin), a wonderful marionette theater in the center of historic Coyoacán. There are usually two performances daily on Saturday-Sunday, appropriate for kids of almost any age (though plays are in Spanish, they are both visually entertaining and include lots of music and dancing). After the show, get a low-key lunch at **La Barraca Valenciana,** where kids can have a ham-and-cheese torta (sandwich) while parents sip a glass of Spanish wine or a craft beer.

### AFTERNOON
After lunch, visit the **Museo Nacional de Culturas Populares,** a small museum that showcases work by traditional Mexican artisans. The exhibits, which change frequently and are often dedicated to themes like corn or textiles, are educational, but also visually engaging and colorful. During holidays, like Día de Muertos, the museum hosts artisanal markets or musical performances in their outdoor patio. Wrap up the day with a coffee and a snack at the garden restaurant at **La Mano Jardín**.

## Sunday
### Paseo de la Reforma and Chapultepec
#### MORNING
Closed to automobile traffic every Sunday till 2pm, the **Paseo de la Reforma** fills with cyclists, in-line skaters, pedestrians, and dog walkers. Get an early start on the day to ride a bike (or simply stroll) along Reforma, checking out the many famous monuments, like the **Ángel de la Independencia,** as you make your way north. A good place for lunch is the family-friendly restaurant **El Pialadero de Guadalajara,** just a few short blocks from the Paseo de la Reforma and the main gates to the **Bosque de Chapultepec.**

The Primera Sección (First Section) of Chapultepec is always thronged

toys for sale at Mercado Coyoacán

with families on Sunday, when museums are free and the footpaths are filled with vendors selling balloons, bubbles, rubber balls, tacos, fresh fruit, and other treats. Enjoy a stroll amid this madcap mass of humanity, then walk over the new footbridges or hop in an Uber to visit the Segunda Sección (Second Section) of the park. Save the **Papalote** children's museum for a weekday (it's often packed on the weekends) and instead visit the newly remodeled **Museo de Historia Natural,** with beautifully designed exhibits on Mexico's flora, fauna, geology, and more.

## AFTERNOON

From the natural history museum, it's a short and pleasant walk past artificial lakes and through freshly restored gardens to **Aztlán,** Chapultepec's small amusement park. The main attraction is the massive Ferris wheel, **Aztlán 360,** which opened in March 2024 and stands 85 m (279 ft) high.

Try to get a little rest in during the afternoon because Sunday is **family night at the Arena México,** where the whole family will delight in the showmanship and athleticism of a live lucha libre match.

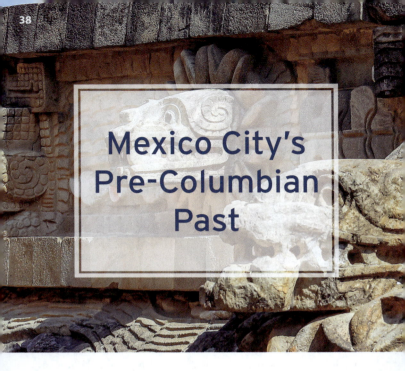

# Mexico City's Pre-Columbian Past

Mexico City's streets tell the story of its past, with institutions, architecture, and landmarks that are testament to 600-plus years of culture and change.

## Day 1
### Centro Histórico
#### MORNING

After the Spanish conquest of Tenochtitlan, Spanish settlers destroyed the Mexica capital, building a European-style settlement atop the ruins—and, in many cases, using the stones from fallen Mexica temples to construct their own churches and palaces. Five hundred years later, Mexico's **pre-Columbian heritage** is embedded throughout the Centro Histórico—in its layout, in its place-names, and, quite literally, in its architecture.

In the 1970s, the ruins of the **Templo Mayor,** a twin temple-pyramid at the heart of Tenochtitlan, were unearthed after more than four centuries under the city. After an extensive excavation that demolished a number of colonial-era buildings beside the Catedral Metropolitana, the archaeological site was opened to the public, alongside the fascinating **Museo**

**del Templo Mayor,** which contains dozens of pre-Columbian artifacts recovered from the site.

Although they haven't received permission to continue demolitions, archaeologists surmise that even more ruins lie beneath the 17th-century palaces on the street República de Guatemala, as evidenced recently at the **Centro Cultural de España,** a contemporary cultural center overseen by the Spanish government. In a planned expansion of the space, below-ground construction unearthed Mexica ruins, believed to have been part of a calmécac, a school for young Mexica nobles. The ruins are on display in the on-site **Museo del Sitio,** in the basement, a lovely complement to the center's avant-garde program of music and art events.

During the pre-Columbian era and throughout most of the last four centuries, canals linked central Mexico City to the farming communities in the southern Valley of Mexico, with a major waterway terminating in what is today the old Merced commercial district. Today's **Mercado de la Merced** remains one of the largest and most important markets in the city. You can walk to the Merced from the Zócalo (be aware that theft is not uncommon in this area), or take the Metro just one stop, from Pino Suárez to La Merced, on Line 1. Before boarding, take note of the **Templo Ehécatl-Quetzalcóatl** inside the Metro station; this unusual round Mexica pyramid was uncovered by transit workers during

Templo Mayor

# Best Murals

### CENTRO HISTÓRICO

The city's most famous mural is Diego Rivera's series *Epic of the Mexican People in Their Struggle for Freedom and Independence* in the north patio and staircase of the **Palacio Nacional** (page 68). A few blocks north, the headquarters of the **Secretaría de Educación Pública** reopened as the **Museo Vivo del Muralismo** (page 60) in 2024; numerous artists painted murals here, but the centerpiece is the astonishingly extensive murals by Diego Rivera, which cover three stories of two adjoining patios. At the **Antiguo Colegio de San Ildefonso** (page 61), find interesting early murals by Rivera, David Alfaro Siqueiros, Fermín Revueltas Sánchez, and Jean Charlot, among others, in addition to extensive works by José Clemente Orozco in the main patio.

### ALAMEDA CENTRAL

See monumental works by some of Mexico's modern art masters at the **Palacio de Bellas Artes** (page 94), including David Alfaro Siqueiros's *Nueva Democracia* (New Democracy), commemorating the Revolution of 1910. Cross the Alameda to see one of Rivera's most entertaining works in the **Museo Mural Diego Rivera** (page 104).

### POLANCO

There are several murals by Siqueiros inside the **Sala de Arte Público David Alfaro Siqueiros** (page 164), a nonprofit gallery that occupies the artist's former home. Different artists periodically repaint the building's facade.

### INSURGENTES SUR

The three-dimensional mural covering the arts space **Poliforum Siqueiros** (page 208) astonishes in its proportions, colors, and ambition. Inside, Siqueiros's *La Marcha de la Humanidad* covers the walls and ceiling of an entire room; it's currently being restored and is closed to the public.

### CIUDAD UNIVERSITARIA

Juan O'Gorman designed the giant volcanic-stone mosaic that covers the facade of the **Biblioteca Central** (page 250). Next door, a famous work by Siqueiros adorns the **Rectoría.**

---

**Above:** Museo Vivo del Muralismo

construction of the subway line. Plans for the station were altered to accommodate the temple; today, in a delightful mix of old and new, the pyramid is on display in an open-air plaza within the station.

**AFTERNOON**
Take your time wandering through the towering stacks of fruits and vegetables, home supplies, and crafts for sale at the Mercado de la Merced, making your way down the circuitous aisles to neighboring **Mercado Sonora,** known for its herbal remedies, witchcraft supplies, and live animals. Finish up the day with a late lunch at the chili pepper-centric Merced-inspired restaurant **Roldán 37,** located on a surprisingly quiet pedestrian street in the old Merced commercial district.

# Day 2
## Chapultepec
**MORNING**
The **Museo Nacional de Antropología** is a must for any visitor to the city, but those with an interest in pre-Columbian cultures could easily spend a full day in this spectacular museum. Set aside time for the rooms dedicated to the cultures of the Valley of Mexico, which include, among other treasures, the famous Piedra del Sol, a basalt monolith carved with Mexica calendar glyphs (an adaptation of the calendar round used throughout Mesoamerica). It's also worth touring the 2nd-floor ethnographic exhibits, which cover the dress, customs, language, and culture of Mexico's diverse cultures and ethnic groups.

**AFTERNOON**
The museum's greater home, the **Bosque de Chapultepec,** is itself a site of great historic importance: Its springs provided freshwater to the city of Tenochtitlan and later the capital of New Spain, via an aqueduct that ran along what is today the Avenida Chapultepec. Though little is left, you can visit the site of the springs where the Mexica emperors came to bathe, today known as the **Baños de Moctezuma.** Just beside it, amateur anthropologists will enjoy spotting the pre-Columbian reliefs carved onto the walls of the Cerro de Chapultepec. Although there are no ruins on the top of Cerro de Chapultepec, it is interesting to tour the Castillo de Chapultepec and look down on the greenery.

# Day 3
## Tlatelolco and San Juan
**MORNING**
During the 15th and 16th centuries, Tlatelolco was inhabited by Nahuatl-speaking people, allied with but separate from the people of Tenochtitlan.

When the Spanish launched their final attack on the Mexica during the summer of 1521, the remaining residents of Tenochtitlan fled to Tlatelolco, where they were eventually overcome. Today, the ruins of Tlatelolco are located in the **Plaza de las Tres Culturas,** in the Tlatelolco neighborhood. The interesting site contains the foundations of what were once towering religious and ceremonial buildings, including the Tlatelolco's Templo Mayor, which is adjoined by Ex-Convento de Santiago Tlatelolco, originally constructed with the stones of the destroyed city in the early 16th century.

Take the Metrobús on the Paseo de la Reforma from Glorieta Cuitláhuac to Hidalgo or have an Uber or a radio taxi pick you up at the ruins site, as it's a bit too far (and a bit too rough) to walk from Tlatelolco back to the Centro.

## AFTERNOON

Now head to the one-of-a-kind **Mercado San Juan** for a plate of imported cheese and charcuterie from one of the market's remarkably fancy deli counters, or continue with the pre-Columbian theme by seeking out mole, maguey worms, iguana meat, chapulines (grasshoppers), and chocolate. If you want to fill up further, **Tacos Domingo** is just a couple of blocks from the market.

ruins of Tlatelolco

Teotihuacán's main avenue, the Calzada de los Muertos

Next, set aside a few hours to learn more about Mexico's traditional cultures at the wonderful **Museo de Arte Popular,** just a few blocks from the market. The museum's exquisite collection of handicrafts from across the country includes some pre-Columbian art, which helps illuminate the aesthetic roots of today's artisanal traditions.

## Day 4
### Civilizations in the Valley of Mexico
**MORNING**

One of the finest ruin sites in the country, the city of **Teotihuacán** is a must-see for anyone interested in anthropology and pre-Columbian civilizations. If you've visited Teotihuacán in the past, take a trip to the smaller and lesser-known settlement of **Cuicuilco,** located in the south of the city, near the Line 1 Metrobús stop at Villa Olímpica. Flourishing just before the rise Teotihuacán, the city of Cuicuilco was largely destroyed in a lava flow from a nearby volcano, but its remains include an interesting circular pyramid.

**AFTERNOON**

From Cuicuilco, it's a quick Metrobús ride to the main campus of the Universidad Nacional Autónoma de México (UNAM), where the many architectural and artistic treasures include the **Biblioteca Central,** adorned with a lava-stone mural by Juan O'Gorman. Alternatively, head just a bit farther south to **Tlalpan,** a more off-the-beaten-path neighborhood that maintains a quiet, distinctly nontouristy feeling.

# A Day of Design

Mexico City is aesthetically vibrant and unique. The capital remains in the vanguard in art, design, and architecture, making it a top destination for many art- and design-centric travelers.

## Morning

Make a reservation for a morning tour at the **Casa Luis Barragán,** near Tacubaya. The former home of the famed architect—widely considered one of the most influential voices in modern Mexican design—was mostly left as it was when Barragán lived there, showcasing not only his talent as an architect but his pensive, minimalist personal style. Note the saturated colors and use of light, two of Barragán's signatures.

Just across the street, a large unmarked turquoise building is home to **Labor,** one of the more interesting contemporary galleries in the city. The gallery represents a range of international artists, including Mexican sensation Pedro Reyes.

## Afternoon

It's a short walk from the Casa Luis Barragán across Avenida Parque Lira and into the San Miguel Chapultepec neighborhood. This attractive

the daytime kitchen at Ticuchi

residential community, wedged between the historic neighborhood of Tacubaya and the Bosque de Chapultepec, is the location of some of the city's most renowned contemporary art galleries, giving the otherwise sleepy area a hint of the upscale.

Join the gallery crowd for a light lunch at chic Mexican-Indian restaurant **Mari Gold,** then visit **Kurimanzutto,** one of the city's preeminent art spaces, co-owned by artists Mónica Manzutto, José Kuri, and Gabriel Orozco. There are many more interesting modern and contemporary art galleries in the neighborhood, including long-running **Galería de Arte Mexicano,** which represents many important national artists, from Olga Costa to Francisco Toledo, and **La Laboratoire.**

You can take the Metro from Constituyentes to Auditorio in Polanco (it's just one stop), but it's easier to hop in an Uber for the short ride across Bosque de Chapultepec. Polanco's toniest avenue, Presidente Masaryk, is lined with designer shops from many of the world's celebrated labels (Dolce & Gabbana, Gucci), but it's much more fun to browse the Mexican-owned boutiques in the neighborhood, like famous silver shop **Tane** or wonderful boutique **Lago.**

## Evening

If all that window-shopping works up an appetite, drop in for drinks and supper at **Ticuchi,** where famed chef Enrique Olvera highlights artisanal Mexican spirits along with beautifully plated handmade maize-based small plates. Top off the evening with a tour of the fantastic mid-century **Camino Real Polanco México,** staying for a drink in one of the in-house bars or cafés.

# Saturday Shopping in the Roma

Saturday is a good time to stroll around the Roma, visiting small shops, browsing markets, and soaking up the atmosphere in this popular neighborhood.

## Morning

There's often a wait for Saturday brunch at the wildly (and deservedly) popular **Panadería Rosetta,** where you can enjoy some quality people-watching from a sidewalk table while enjoying avocado toast, a latte, and a perfect chocolate croissant. From there, walk a few blocks east to the **Mercado de Cuauhtémoc,** a weekly vintage market held in the Jardín Dr. Ignacio Chávez, on the border of the Roma and the Doctores neighborhood. Though not as well-known as the antiquities markets in La Lagunilla and the Plaza del Ángel, this weekly flea has some top-notch vendors and, often, excellent finds for sharp-eyed shoppers.

After the market, take your treasures out for a coffee at unpretentious but excellent café **Cardinal,** on Córdoba. After that, walk along the Roma's main corridor, Álvaro Obregón, which is filled with creaky old bookshops, hip cocktail bars, and 19th-century mansions. Stop inside the art gallery and bookshop at multidisciplinary cultural center **Casa Lamm.**

Next, walk south along Orizaba, wandering past the shaded fountains in the **Plaza Luis Cabrera,** then turning east on Campeche on your way to **Huerto Roma Verde.** This lovely urban garden and active ecological organization hosts a weekend market where lots of vegetarian and locally produced snacks are on sale. Often, these markets have special themes, like the annual edible-insect tasting or their flagship Festival de Maiz, el Frijol, y Amaranto (Corn, Bean, and Amaranth Festival), in addition to the garden's frequent workshops, yoga classes, and speakers.

## Afternoon

Do like the local crowd and set aside a few hours for lunch—though first you'll face the near-impossible task of deciding where to eat. If you don't have reservations for **Máximo Bistrot Local** or **Fogones,** line up for a table at **Mi Compa Chava,** an excellent, über-popular, always-bustling Sinaloan-style seafood restaurant.

After lunch, wander along the shady streets Colima and Orizaba, stopping in at funky skate shops and boutiques, or seeing what's on show at **Galería OMR** or gallery and design shop **Chic by Accident.** Top off the afternoon at **Salon Rosetta,** a tiny yet gorgeous 2nd-floor bar above the Italian restaurant Rosetta, or at the craft cocktail haven **Licorería Limantour.** Order some bar snacks and linger, or head down Álvaro Obregón to **Pizza Félix** for cocktails, kale salad, and Neapolitan-style pizza.

restaurant in the Roma Norte neighborhood

# Where to Eat

Mexico City's food culture spans classes, neighborhoods, and milieus. **Chilangos** are serious eaters, profoundly omnivorous, and discriminating even when snacking on the street. As a result, you will find good things to eat in every neighborhood and at every price point. From casual to elegant, here are the types of establishments you'll find in the capital.

## PUESTOS AND TAQUERÍAS

Quick bites at street stands and in neighborhood markets are ubiquitous and, by many accounts, among the best bites in the city. Tacos are a mainstay of the local diet, but you'll also see hundreds of other snacks for sale, including tamales, fresh fruit, seafood cocktails, smoked plantains, deep-fried quesadillas, corn on the cob, and corn flatbread-based snacks like **tlacoyos.** At some popular street stands, you can see a full pig being carved for **carnitas** as commuters rush past to the Metro. If you see a crowd around a **puesto,** it's a good bet that the food will be tasty.

A step up from balancing your plate in one hand and taco in the other, **taquerías** are simple sit-down eateries, sometimes with a bar and stools only, that serve tacos and other snacks, while a **tortería** is the same but for **tortas.** The Roma, Condesa, and Narvarte neighborhoods are good places to try some of the best taquerías in the city, like **Los Parados** (page 188), **Orinoco** (page 185), **El Vilsito** (page 212), **Tacos**

fresh fruits and vegetables at a local market

Los Condes (page 212), and, for veggies, **Gracias Madre Taquería Vegana** (page 184).

## FONDAS, COMEDORES, AND CANTINAS

You can have an inexpensive sit-down meal in the city's many **fondas** or **comedores,** small independent restaurants that usually serve breakfast, **almuerzo** (early lunch), and **comida** (the midday meal). At many of these places, the main offering is an inexpensive afternoon **comida corrida,** a 3-4-course meal that often includes a drink, soup, and entrée. A wait for a table around 2pm is often an indication that you've found a good **fonda.**

Also casual, **cantinas** are bars that serve food in addition to drinks. Many offer free **botanas** (snacks) when you order drinks. Some cantinas have become so popular for eating that they are more like restaurants than bars.

## RESTAURANTES

There's a very wide diversity of restaurants worth visiting in Mexico City, from an incredibly casual old-timey spot like **Café El Popular** (page 72) to a hot new neighborhood destination drawing hipsters and foodies, such as the superlative **Máximo Bistrot Local** (page 191), or an ultra-elegant fine-dining restaurant. **Pujol** in Polanco (page 152) is the most famous spot in this category.

# Centro Histórico  Map 1

Getting Around ........ 51
Centro Histórico Walk .. 54
Sights ............... 59
Restaurants ........... 71
Nightlife .............. 77
Arts and Culture ....... 79
Festivals and Events.... 82
Recreation ............ 83
Shops ................ 83

The Centro Histórico is the heart and soul of Mexico City, a fascinating mix of grand colonial-era architecture, quirky old-fashioned charm, and relentless urban energy. The oldest district in the capital, it was built in the 16th century atop the ruins of the island city of Tenochtitlan, following the Spanish defeat of the native Mexica people. Today, the blocks surrounding the Zócalo are dense with baroque palaces and churches, fascinating museums, and some of the best traditional restaurants in the city, as well as eye-opening pre-Columbian archaeological sites that were long buried beneath the modern city, including the Mexica's holiest site, the Templo Mayor.

# Highlights

✪ **Museo Vivo del Muralismo:** More than 3,000 m (9,843 ft) of murals cover the interior walls of this museum dedicated to muralism (page 60).

✪ **Torre Latinoamericana:** There are literally breathtaking views of the city in every direction from the observation deck atop this iconic 1950s skyscraper (page 62).

✪ **Zona Arqueológica and Museo del Templo Mayor:** The remains of the largest temple-pyramid in the pre-Columbian city of Tenochtitlan were buried belowground for centuries; today they are a fascinating archaeological site and museum (page 66).

✪ **Palacio Nacional:** The highlight of visiting this historic palace (and seat of the executive branch of government) is Diego Rivera's mural series, a moving retelling of the history of Mexico (page 68).

✪ **Mercado de la Merced:** With dried chilies, fried grasshoppers, and blue-corn quesadillas, Mexican culinary culture is on colorful display at this expansive traditional food market—an excellent place to shop as well as eat (page 70).

# Getting Around

- Metro lines: 1, 2, and 8
- Metro stops: Zócalo, Allende, Pino Suárez, Isabel la Católica, Merced
- Metrobús lines: 4
- Metrobús stops: Eje Central, El Salvador, Isabel la Católica, Museo de la Ciudad, Circunvalación

**Previous:** crowds outside the Catedral Metropolitana; **Above:** Torre Latinoamericana; Templo Mayor.

# MAP 1

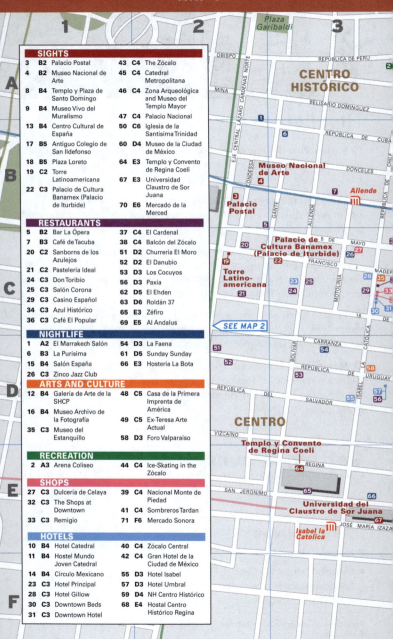

## SIGHTS
- 3 B2 Palacio Postal
- 4 B2 Museo Nacional de Arte
- 8 B4 Templo y Plaza de Santo Domingo
- 9 B4 Museo Vivo del Muralismo
- 13 B4 Centro Cultural de España
- 17 B5 Antiguo Colegio de San Ildefonso
- 18 B5 Plaza Loreto
- 19 C2 Torre Latinoamericana
- 22 C3 Palacio de Cultura Banamex (Palacio de Iturbide)
- 43 C4 The Zócalo
- 45 C4 Catedral Metropolitana
- 46 C4 Zona Arqueológica and Museo del Templo Mayor
- 47 C4 Palacio Nacional
- 50 C6 Iglesia de la Santísima Trinidad
- 60 D4 Museo de la Ciudad de México
- 64 E3 Templo y Convento de Regina Coeli
- 67 E3 Universidad Claustro de Sor Juana
- 70 E6 Mercado de la Merced

## RESTAURANTS
- 5 B2 Bar La Ópera
- 7 B3 Café de Tacuba
- 20 C2 Sanborns de los Azulejos
- 21 C2 Pastelería Ideal
- 24 C3 Don Toribio
- 25 C3 Salón Corona
- 29 C3 Casino Español
- 34 C3 Azul Histórico
- 36 C3 Café El Popular
- 37 C4 El Cardenal
- 38 C4 Balcón del Zócalo
- 51 D2 Churrería El Moro
- 52 D2 El Danubio
- 53 D3 Los Cocuyos
- 56 D3 Paxia
- 62 D5 El Ehden
- 63 D6 Roldán 37
- 65 E3 Zéfiro
- 69 E5 Al Andalus

## NIGHTLIFE
- 1 A2 El Marrakech Salón
- 6 B3 La Purísima
- 15 B4 Salón España
- 26 C3 Zinco Jazz Club
- 54 D3 La Faena
- 61 D5 Sunday Sunday
- 66 E3 Hostería La Bota

## ARTS AND CULTURE
- 12 B4 Galería de Arte de la SHCP
- 16 B4 Museo Archivo de la Fotografía
- 35 C3 Museo del Estanquillo
- 48 C5 Casa de la Primera Imprenta de América
- 49 C5 Ex-Teresa Arte Actual
- 58 D3 Foro Valparaíso

## RECREATION
- 2 A3 Arena Coliseo
- 44 C4 Ice-Skating in the Zócalo

## SHOPS
- 27 C3 Dulcería de Celaya
- 32 C3 The Shops at Downtown
- 33 C3 Remigio
- 39 C4 Nacional Monte de Piedad
- 41 C4 Sombreros Tardan
- 71 F6 Mercado Sonora

## HOTELS
- 10 B4 Hotel Catedral
- 11 B4 Hostel Mundo Joven Catedral
- 14 B4 Círculo Mexicano
- 23 C3 Hotel Principal
- 28 C3 Hotel Gillow
- 30 C3 Downtown Beds
- 31 C3 Downtown Hotel
- 40 C4 Zócalo Central
- 42 C4 Gran Hotel de la Ciudad de México
- 55 D3 Hotel Isabel
- 57 D3 Hotel Umbral
- 59 D4 NH Centro Histórico
- 68 E4 Hostal Centro Histórico Regina

# Centro Histórico

53

# Centro Histórico Walk

**TOTAL DISTANCE:** 2 km (1.2 mi)
**TOTAL WALKING TIME:** 2 hours

Walking is the best way to explore any neighborhood in Mexico City, but particularly the Centro Histórico. From the Zócalo, you can set out in any direction to find yourself surrounded by colonial-era palaces, stone chapels, old public squares, and bustling pedestrian corridors. The Centro's most spectacular streets run west from the Zócalo to the Alameda Central, amply demonstrating why Mexico City has been known for centuries as "the City of Palaces."

**1** Start your tour in the **Zócalo,** appreciating the history and splendor of this expansive public square. On the west end is the **Portal de Mercaderes.** Traders have sold goods in this historic arcade since the colonial era; today, the only notable establishment is legacy hat shop Sombreros Tardan.

*Head west along bustling pedestrian street Madero, which is lined with*

The historic street Madero is closed to automobile traffic and perfect for strolling.

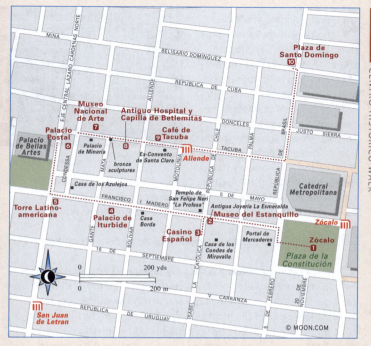

*historic palaces—many incongruously occupied by fast-fashion retailers and convenience stores.*

**2** On the corner of Isabel la Católica, the marvelous Antigua Joyería La Esmeralda was originally built for an upscale jeweler. Designed in the French style popular in 19th-century Mexico, the top floors are home to the lovely **Museo del Estanquillo**. Spend a little time at this free museum and take a few minutes to visit the rooftop terrace and café, with beautiful bird's-eye views of the streets below.

*Take a half-block detour south on Isabel la Católica.*

**3** Arrive at the **Casino Español,** a neoclassical palace constructed by Emilio González del Campo in the early 20th century. Take the elevator to the 2nd floor to admire the building's opulent interiors; better yet, come back later for a meal at the old Spanish restaurant of the same name. Across the street, the baroque **Casa de los Condes de Miravalle** is one of the oldest palaces in the Centro.

*Walk north to get back on Madero.*

**4** Along Madero you'll pass the **Templo de San Felipe Neri "La Profesa,"** a historic church that maintains a reserve of colonial-era religious artwork, and **Casa Borda,** a massive 18th-century palace that spans more than half a city block with its volcanic-stone facade ringed by iron balconies. One block west on Madero, the 18th-century **Palacio de Iturbide** (today the Palacio de Cultura Citibanamex) features ornate sandstone details and giant carved-wood doors—if they are open, stop in to see the soaring interior courtyard; admission is free.

Casa de los Azulejos

*Continue walking west to the intersection of the Eje Central and Madero.*

**5** **Torre Latinoamericana** is the only skyscraper downtown, affording unparalleled unobstructed views from the 44th-floor observation deck—worth the time and vertigo to visit. Across the street, admire one of the most stunning buildings in the Centro: the blue-and-white-tiled **Casa de los Azulejos.** Although this palace has played many important roles throughout its history, it has been a Sanborns restaurant since 1917—a wonderful place for breakfast.

*Turn right (north) on the Eje Central.*

**6** You'll see the gorgeous **Palacio de Bellas Artes** (earmark it for a future visit) on the opposite side of the street as you walk north toward the **Palacio Postal,** the city's main post office, two blocks north of the Torre Latinoamericana. It's one of the most spectacular examples of civic architecture in the city.

*Turn right and walk east along Tacuba.*

**7** On the first block, you'll pass the **Palacio de Minería,** now home to UNAM's engineering college, built between 1797 and 1813 by Spanish architect Manuel Tolsá. Check out the gigantic meteorites in the building's foyer; each were recovered from somewhere in Mexico. Tolsá's statue of Spanish king Carlos IV is located in front of the **Museo Nacional de Arte,** an interesting museum and architectural masterpiece, just across the street from the college.

Mexico City's main post office

*Continue along Tacuba.*

**8** On the corner of Filomena Mata, Jesús Fructuoso Contreras's **bronze sculptures** of emperors Itzcóatl, Nezahualcóyotl, and Totoquihuatzin celebrate the alliance between the city-states of Tenochtitlan, Texcoco, and Tlacopan in 1430. To the right (south) on this block, the **Antiguo Hospital y Capilla de Betlemitas** was, until 1820, a refuge for the poor and infirm, run by an order of nuns. The remains were beautifully restored in the 1990s and today house an interactive museum focused on economics.

*Continue along Tacuba.*

a bronze statue of Itzcóatl, third emperor of the Mexica people

**9** The **Ex-Convento de Santa Clara**, on the next corner, was built in 1661 and adjoins the bustling Allende Metro stop. Like many of the Centro's churches, it was once part of a larger convent and religious complex that was destroyed during the 19th-century Reformation. Across the street, restaurant **Café de Tacuba** is a mainstay in the Centro, in business here for more than 100

Plaza de Santo Domingo

years. Drop in for a hot chocolate and a tamal; the setting—with its old oil paintings, tiled walls, and soaring ceilings—is classic.

*Continue on Tacuba. (Alternatively, walk east along Donceles, one block north of Tacuba. Here, you'll find a cluster of old-school used booksellers who carry everything from encyclopedia sets and out-of-print paperbacks to dusty maps.)*

**10** When you get to the street República de Brasil (about 3-4 blocks east), swing left (north) and go two blocks to finish your walk at the **Plaza de Santo Domingo,** an important colonial-era square and the site of the Inquisition in Mexico. At the east end of the plaza, the archways known as the Portales de los Evangelistas are filled with kiosks attended by professional typists, printers, and scribes.

# Sights

## Palacio Postal

On the site of what was once the Franciscan hospital, Mexico City's central post office is one of the most distinctive architectural landmarks in the city, designed by Italian architect Adamo Boari (who also oversaw the Palacio de Bellas Artes across the street) and Mexican engineer Gonzalo Gorita. Constructed in 1902, the palace was built with a mix of sandstone and chiluca, a very light, almost translucent stone, and it is covered with fine detail, including iron dragon light fixtures and elaborate stone carving around the windows and the top-floor arches. It's hard to believe this gorgeous palace was built for public use—but even today, it is a fully functioning post office, where you can buy stamps or mail a postcard home.

**MAP 1:** *Tacuba 1; tel. 55/5510-2999; www.palaciopostal.gob.mx; 8am-7:30pm Mon.-Fri., 8am-4pm Sat., 10am-2pm Sun.; free; Metro: Bellas Artes*

## Museo Nacional de Arte

The Mexican National Art Museum holds the most extensive collection of Mexican artwork in the country, with thousands of pieces from the very early colonial era to the mid-20th century. A tour of the museum chronicles the changing attitudes toward religion, government, and education over the course of many centuries, providing an engaging look at Mexican social history through works of art. Particularly interesting are the 19th-century rooms, which show the emergence of a Mexican national character in the wake of the country's independence.

Completed in 1910, the building itself is a masterpiece of modernist architecture, designed by Italian architect Silvio Contri. The lavish interior unites architectural styles from classical to Gothic and is replete with curved marble staircases, gilded moldings, and elaborate iron lamps. In front, there is a bronze statue of King Carlos IV, one of the best-known works by Spanish architect Manuel Tolsá.

**MAP 1:** *Tacuba 8; tel. 55/8647-5430, ext. 5050 and 5066; www.munal.com.mx; 11am-5:30pm Tues.-Sun.; US$4 adults, free students, teachers, seniors, and people with disabilities, free Sun.; Metro: Bellas Artes or Allende*

Palacio Postal

### Templo y Plaza de Santo Domingo

Surrounded by churches and palaces, the Plaza de Santo Domingo was the second most important public square in colonial Mexico City after the Zócalo. On the north end, the Templo de Santo Domingo was constructed in 1530 as part of a Dominican convent, which included a hospital, libraries, and a cloister, largely destroyed during the 19th-century Reformation. Opposite the square, the 1730s-era Palacio de la Inquisición was home to the dreaded Inquisition in Mexico, an extension of its Spanish counterpart.

the Museo Nacional de Arte

Look for the dozens of professional scribes beneath the plaza's western archways. They have been producing typed documents for paying clients since the mid-19th century and can help compose anything from a résumé to a love note at their small kiosks, in addition to producing official forms, contracts, wedding invitations, business cards, and other printed materials.

**MAP 1:** *Brasil at Belisario Domínguez; tel. 55/5563-0479; Templo de Santo Domingo hours vary; free; Metro: Zócalo*

### ✪ Museo Vivo del Muralismo

Secretary of public education José Vasconcelos was the mastermind behind the famed public mural project of early 20th-century Mexico, which employed some of the country's most famous artists. During Vasconcelos's tenure, the offices of the Secretaría de Educación Pública (Secretary of Public Education), or SEP, moved into two adjoining colonial-era buildings on the Plaza de Santo Domingo. Here, Vasconcelos commissioned Diego Rivera to paint some of the city's most ambitious murals in two interior patios. Created between 1923 and 1928, the murals address themes in Mexican history, culture, and politics, and cover over 100 panels along the walls—even filling the stairwells and elevator vestibules.

While the murals have long been open to the public within the SEP's headquarters, in 2024 the building officially reopened as the Museo Vivo del Muralismo, a wonderful museum that celebrates the history of muralism in Mexico. Rivera's work is the centerpiece of the space, but there are also murals by Jean Charlot, Manuel Felguérez, and Amado de la Cueva, among other 20th-century masters, on view.

**MAP 1:** *República de Argentina 28; tel. 55/3601-7599; 9am-6pm Mon.-Sun.; free; Metro: Zócalo*

### Centro Cultural de España

Run by the Spanish government, this unique gallery, cultural center, and anthropology museum is housed in a 17th-century baroque palace behind the Metropolitan Cathedral. Throughout the year, the center presents exhibitions of contemporary work by Mexican and Spanish artists, often featuring experimental proposals and installations, in addition to hosting workshops, readings, and performances on-site. There's a design shop on the 1st floor, as well as a lovely terrace bar and café, with charming views of the back of the cathedral.

During an expansion of the space in 2006, construction workers encountered remains from the city of Tenochtitlan beneath the building's foundation. Archaeological study suggests these structures housed a calmécac, a Mexica school, from the 15th and 16th centuries. After the discovery, the CCE opened the **Museo del Sitio,** an interesting small museum in the basement of the building, which showcases both the ruins and artifacts recovered from the site.

**MAP 1:** *República de Guatemala 18; tel. 55/5521-1925; http://ccemx.org; 11am-9pm Tues.-Sat., 10am-4pm Sun.; free; Metro: Zócalo*

### Antiguo Colegio de San Ildefonso

The Antiguo Colegio de San Ildefonso was originally constructed as a Jesuit school in 1588, but this beautiful Spanish colonial building has served various function in its 400-plus-year history. In the 19th century, under President Benito Juárez, it was home to the Escuela Nacional Preparatoria, a prestigious public secondary school. Famously, artist Frida Kahlo was among the first class of 35 female students to enter the Escuela Nacional Preparatoria in 1922; it was there that she first met her future husband Diego Rivera, who was painting a mural on its walls.

Rivera was one of the many young artists whom Secretary of Public Education José Vasconcelos hired to paint the walls of the school; it was the beginning of the mural project that would become emblematic of early 20th-century Mexican art. Diego Rivera, José Clemente Orozco, David Alfaro Siqueiros, Fermín Revueltas Sánchez, Ramón Alva de la Canal, Fernando Leal, and Jean Charlot all painted sections of the interior. Among the building's most important works, Orozco's murals cover three stories in the main patio.

In 1992, San Ildefonso became a museum and cultural center. In addition to the murals, it hosts rotating art exhibits, usually showcasing contemporary work from Mexico and around the world, as well as special events and concerts.

**MAP 1:** *Justo Sierra 16; tel. 55/3602-0034, ext. 1028; www.sanildefonso.org.mx; 11am-6pm Wed.-Sun.; US$3, US$1 students and teachers, free under age 12, seniors, and people with disabilities; Metro: Zócalo*

### Plaza Loreto

A few blocks from the Zócalo, this modest public square is centered on a circular fountain designed by Manuel Tolsá in the 18th century. It is flanked by two historic churches, the **Iglesia de Nuestra Señora de Loreto** (San Antonio Tomatlán and Jesús Maria Loreto; tel. 55/5702-7850; 10am-5pm daily) and the smaller **Templo de Santa Teresa La Nueva** (Loreto 15; tel. 55/5702-3204; 10am-5pm daily). Perhaps the most striking aspect of the former is the dramatic angle at which its heavy baroque facade is sinking into the soft topsoil, creating something of a funhouse effect as you enter.

Facing the plaza to the south, the **Sinagoga Histórica Justo Sierra** (Justo Sierra 71; tel. 55/5522-4828; http://sinagogajustosierra.com; 11am-5pm Sun.-Fri.) was the first synagogue in Mexico City, and today it is open to the public as a cultural center and museum. Visitors will notice the building doesn't resemble a typical synagogue: The founders, many of whom came from anti-Semitic environments in Europe, built their temple behind a colonial-era facade, intentionally keeping their religious activities out of the public eye.

**MAP 1:** *Bounded by Calle Loreto, Justo Sierra, and San Ildefonso; free; Metro: Zócalo*

### ✪ Torre Latinoamericana

The iconic Torre Latinoamericana was the capital's tallest building at its inauguration in 1956. Though it long ago lost that distinction, the Latinoamericana is still one of the few skyscrapers downtown, giving its top floors one of the most privileged vantage points in the city. On the 44th floor of the building, an open-air observation deck affords stunning, panoramic views of the city. On clear days, the volcanoes Iztaccíhuatl and Popocatépetl may even be visible to the southeast. If you're feeling a little vertigo, take heart: The tower was specially designed to withstand Mexico City's seismic instability and soft topsoil, with a flexible structure that sways with ground movement. Indeed, the Torre Latinoamericana survived the 1957, 1985, and 2017 earthquakes. If you'd like to extend your visit, tickets to the observation deck include access to the Nivel 40 Skybar and Miralto restaurant on the 40th and 41st floors, which are no longer open to the public.

The Torre Latinoamericana, a city landmark, was built in the 1950s.

Palacio de Iturbide, now the Palacio de Cultura Citibanamex

**MAP 1:** *Eje Central Lázaro Cárdenas 2; tel. 55/5518-7423; https://torrelatinoamericana.com.mx; 9am-10pm daily; US$12 adults, US$8 children; Metro: Bellas Artes*

### Palacio de Cultura Citibanamex (Palacio de Iturbide)

A massive baroque mansion with elaborate sandstone carvings around the windows and doorframes, the Antiguo Palacio de Iturbide was constructed between 1779 and 1785 for the family of the count of San Mateo de Valparaíso. However, the palace is best known as the home of Emperor Agustín de Iturbide, who lived there briefly during his short reign during the tumultuous post-independence era.

Banamex purchased the palace in 1964, and after a long renovation project, it became the home of the Fomento Cultural Banamex, a foundation dedicated to the promotion and exhibition of Mexican art and handcrafts; it was officially inaugurated as the Palacio de Cultura Banamex in 2004 (changed to Citibanamex after the bank's merger with Citibank). Today, the foundation hosts high-quality exhibitions of painting, folk art, and crafts in the palace's impressive courtyard; recent shows have included a review of silver design throughout Mexico's history, colonial painting, and a selection from the grand masters of popular art in Ibero-America.

**MAP 1:** *Madero 17; tel. 55/1226-0247; www.fomentoculturalbanamex.org; 11am-7pm daily during exhibitions; free; Metro: Allende*

### The Zócalo

The Zócalo, also known as the Plaza de la Constitución, has been

## The City Beneath the City

This pre-Columbian temple is now part of a busy metro station.

When Hernán Cortés and his army arrived in the Valley of Mexico in 1519, they were dazzled by what they found: Tenochtitlan, an expansive, clean, and orderly city, larger than any in 16th-century Spain. Located on a small island in the middle of a wide and shallow lake, Tenochtitlan was linked to the mainland by causeways, and canoes transported goods to the large outdoor markets in the city center, which was replete with brightly painted temples, pyramids, and palaces.

Despite their admiration for the city, the Spanish laid siege to and destroyed Tenochtitlan during the conquest. Atop the vanquished city, they built a European-style capital to rule New Spain, often using the stones from the fallen Mexica temples for their own churches and palaces.

In the 20th century, a renewed interest in Mexico's pre-Columbian past sparked more extensive archaeological investigation of the Centro

a public square since the founding of Tenochtitlan in 1325. Adjoining the city's holiest site, the Templo Mayor, the plaza was a place of ritual and celebration during the 14th and 15th centuries, in addition to being an important market. The Mexica rulers' palaces lined the plaza, and causeways leading off the island radiated out from its four sides.

After the fall of Tenochtitlan, the Zócalo became the center of the Spanish city of Mexico, and it was known as the Plaza Mayor throughout the colonial era. It remained the center of government and religious activity: The cathedral borders the plaza to the north and the government palaces run along the east and south sides. Today, the empty

Histórico. Today, through accidental discovery and intentional excavation, the great city of Tenochtitlan continues to reveal itself to us. Here are some of the places that have emerged.

- In the 1960s, the Metro was under construction when transport workers tunneled into the remains of a pre-Columbian pyramid. Undeterred, the transportation authority built a station around the pyramid. Today, the structure is viewed by millions of commuters at the **Pino Suárez Metro Station** (Jose María Izazaga and Pino Suárez; 6am-midnight daily) every year.

- The **Zona Arqueológica and Museo del Templo Mayor** (page 66) contains the remains of the biggest and most sacred temple in Tenochtitlan, which was remarkably preserved beneath the city for over 450 years.

- The former home to the viceroy who oversaw the Spanish colonies, and today the seat of the executive branch of the government, the **Palacio Nacional** (page 68) was built directly atop Mexica emperor Moctezuma's former residence. Modern-day excavation has revealed the foundations of Moctezuma's home, visible beneath various glass-topped windows in the palace floor.

- During an expansion of the colonial-era mansion in which it's housed, the **Centro Cultural de España** (page 61) discovered the remains of a 15th-century calmécac, a Mexica school, now part of a small basement museum within this contemporary art and cultural space.

- The **Museo de la Secretaría de Hacienda y Crédito Público** (Moneda 4; tel. 55/3688-1248 or 55/3688-1710; www.shcp.gob.mx; 10am-5pm Tues.-Sun.; free) is an art museum run by the country's tax authority, but it was once the palace of the archbishop of New Spain. During the building's 1980s retrofit, construction workers discovered the foundations of the former Templo de Tezcatlipoca, along with artifacts and sculptures, which can be viewed in the museum's west wing.

square is often occupied with special events, like craft markets, concerts, political protests, and, every December, a massive holiday market.

**MAP 1:** *Plaza de la Constitución, bordered by Madero, Moneda, 16 de Septiembre, Corregidora, 5 de Febrero, República de Brasil, and Pino Suárez; free; Metro: Zócalo*

### Catedral Metropolitana

Dominating the Zócalo to the north, the Metropolitan Cathedral is a mortar-and-stone representation of the central role of the Catholic Church in Mexico's past and present. A modest church was built on this site in 1524 and named a cathedral in 1534. Shortly thereafter, New Spain's governors

Catedral Metropolitana

commissioned the construction of a bigger, grander church. The first stone was laid in 1553, but the cathedral wasn't completed for 240 years. Over the centuries, different architects left their mark on the cathedral, which mixes Renaissance, baroque, and neoclassical styles.

Within the cathedral's two bell towers, 25 multiton bells are still rung by hand. During the September 19, 2017, earthquake, a cross known as La Esperanza, which topped the eastern tower, toppled and fell to the ground. Tours of the bell towers have since been suspended indefinitely. Inside the cathedral, you can see the impressive golden baroque altars and tour the interior of the choir with its two enormous pipe organs (US$1). If you'd like to hear these impressive instruments play, there are concerts at 9am daily (free).

**MAP 1:** *Plaza de la Constitución, between Monte de Piedad and Pino Suárez; tel. 55/4165-4052; https://catedralmetropolitana.mx; 8am-6pm daily; free; Metro: Zócalo*

### TOP EXPERIENCE

### ✪ Zona Arqueológica and Museo del Templo Mayor

A massive temple-pyramid in the heart of the city of Tenochtitlan, the Templo Mayor was the locus of religious and political life for the Mexica people, who, in the 16th century, dominated Mesoamerica from their capital city in the Valley of Mexico. First built around 1325, the structure was enlarged by successive Mexica rulers, eventually reaching around 60 m (200 ft) high. Dual staircases led up its face to two crowning temples, one dedicated to Huitzilopochtli, the god of war and the sun, and the other to Tlaloc, the god of rain and agriculture.

After the Spanish conquest of Tenochtitlan, the Templo Mayor was razed and its stones were used to construct Spanish palaces and churches for a new European-style city, which would become the capital of New Spain and Mexico City today. The pyramid's exact location was eventually forgotten, though archaeologists long suspected it lay beneath or near the cathedral. On February 21, 1978, electric company workers digging near the cathedral uncovered an eight-ton monolith adorned with carvings of the moon goddess Coyolxauhqui. The discovery prompted a major excavation. After demolishing four city blocks, archaeologists uncovered the base of the Templo Mayor, along with a multitude of artifacts.

Excavation at the site is ongoing. In 2018, the space was expanded to reveal the partial remains of a round temple dedicated to the god Ehécatl. In 2022, the viewing area was further expanded to include a "subterranean museum" with a larger view of the temple as well as a partial staircase from a ball court and remains from early colonial-era structures.

The archaeological site is accompanied by a fascinating museum, which holds an extensive collection of pre-Columbian pieces, the majority recovered during the Templo Mayor's major excavation, including the Coyolxauhqui stone. Among other magnificent artifacts, the museum contains a 4-m-long (13-ft) carved monolith dedicated

Templo Mayor

to the goddess Tlaltecuhtli, discovered in 2006.

**MAP 1:** *Seminario 8; tel. 55/4040-5600, ext. 412930; www.templomayor.inah.gob.mx; 9am-5pm Tues.-Sun.; US$6; Metro: Zócalo*

## ⭐ Palacio Nacional

The deep-red facade of the Palacio Nacional stretches grandly across the eastern edge of the Zócalo. The site was originally the home of Mexica emperor Moctezuma; after the fall of Tenochtitlan, a palace was constructed on this site for Hernán Cortés. Reconstructed several times over its history, it later became the official home for Spanish viceroys governing the colonies. After independence, the palace became the seat of government, and the bell from the church in Dolores Hidalgo, Guanajuato, was hung over the presidential balcony. It was this very bell that war hero Miguel Hidalgo rang while issuing his famous battle cry, or grito, which heralded the start of the War of Independence from Spain. Today, it is the seat of the government and the home of the Mexican president.

For visitors, the highlight of the Palacio Nacional is the spectacular murals painted by Diego Rivera in the north plaza and stairwell. A masterwork of composition and color, Rivera executed this chronicle of the history of Mexico between 1929 and 1951. The panel titled *The Great City of Tenochtitlan* provides a detailed rendering of the Mexica city, viewed from the market in Tlatelolco. It is also worth seeking out several "archaeological windows" in the ground floor of the palace that reveal the foundations of Moctezuma's palace, which was buried until recently beneath the modern-day structure.

**MAP 1:** *Plaza de la Constitución, between Moneda and Corregidora; tel. 55/3688-1602; 10am-5pm Tues.-Sun.; free; Metro: Zócalo*

## Iglesia de la Santísima Trinidad

A baroque masterpiece tucked away on a scruffy pedestrian backstreet a couple of blocks east of the Zócalo, La Santísima has an elaborate churrigueresque facade that depicts saints, angels, and apostles in stunning relief. Though a smaller hermitage was built here in the 16th century, the current building dates from the 18th century. Since then, the church has sunk almost 3 m (10 ft) into the spongy soil below (it was built atop a former lakebed) and has undergone various restoration projects as a result.

**MAP 1:** *Emiliano Zapata 60, at Santísima; hours vary; free; Metro: Zócalo*

## Museo de la Ciudad de México

Three blocks south of the Zócalo, a colonial-era mansion is today the city museum. Historians surmise that one of the conquistadores built a home on this site shortly after the conquest: The building's famous cornerstone is a large carved serpent head, likely taken

Palacio Nacional

from the Templo Mayor after the building's destruction and placed at the corner as a sign of Spanish domination.

The building's current baroque facade was constructed by the Conde de Calimaya in the late 18th century. Inside, there is a small chapel dedicated to the Virgen de Guadalupe with three colonial-era religious paintings, as well as galleries exhibiting the museum's permanent collections of paintings and sketches of the city and rotating exhibits of contemporary work.
**MAP 1:** *Pino Suárez 30; tel. 55/8957-2933; 10am-5:30pm Tues.-Sun.; US$2, free Wed.; Metro: Pino Suárez*

Templo de Regina Coeli

### Templo y Convento de Regina Coeli

Once part of a larger Conceptionist convent founded in 1573, the massive Templo de Regina Coeli dominates the eastern end of the pedestrian street Regina. It was remodeled along with many of the convent's buildings in the mid-17th century, including several of its baroque altars, though most of the original pieces are missing or have been destroyed. It is still a Catholic parish, holding regular mass, and is often open to the public in the morning. It's worth stopping in when the doors are open to see the soaring nave and altar.
**MAP 1:** *Regina 3; tel. 55/5709-2640; hours vary, generally 10am-1:30pm and 4pm-6pm Tues.-Fri., 10am-4pm Sat.; free; Metro: Isabel la Católica*

### Universidad del Claustro de Sor Juana

During the late 17th century, beloved Mexican poet Sor Juana Inés de la Cruz wrote much of her remarkable, passionate verse from within the confines of her small room in the Convento de San Jerónimo in central Mexico City, a nunnery that was originally founded in 1585. By the middle of the 19th century, when it was closed by the Reform Laws, the convent had at least 200 permanent residents.

Today, the remains of the convent are beautifully restored and occupied by a small private university with an arts and cultural focus, called the Universidad del Claustro de Sor Juana. Register at the front desk to visit the ex-convent's main courtyard, around which the nuns' former cells are arranged. There is also a small contemporary art gallery, open to the public, in what was once a bathing area for the nuns, as well as occasional evening concerts in the college's auditorium, which contains a collection of antique instruments.

**MAP 1:** *Izazaga 92; tel. 55/5709-4066 or 55/5709-4126; www.ucsj.edu.mx; 10am-4pm Mon.-Fri., 10am-3pm Sat.; free; Metro: Isabel la Católica*

chilies for sale at Mercado de la Merced

### ✪ Mercado de la Merced

One of the largest retail markets in Mexico, the Mercado de la Merced is the centerpiece of a bustling commercial district known as the Antiguo Barrio de la Merced, which covers several city blocks on the eastern edge of the Centro. Trade has taken place here since the days of Tenochtitlan, when a canal transported goods from the agricultural communities of Xochimilco and Chalco to Moctezuma's palaces in what is now the Zócalo. Incredibly, some of these canals continued to flow into the Merced district as late as 1917, connecting the Centro Histórico with outlying townships. A public market building was built on the former grounds of the Merced convent in the 1860s, though the current market building was constructed in 1957.

Wandering through the Merced is a feast for the senses and a bonanza for curious foodies. In the main market, you'll find stacks of banana leaves, baskets towering with dried chilies, bags of black huitlacoche (corn fungus), and bins of traditional Mexican herbs and spices. Farther inside, stalls sell kitchen supplies, woven baskets, piñatas, and handicrafts, while aromatic food stands offer everything from quick quesadillas to a full meal at rock-bottom prices. Adjoining the Merced is the interesting **Mercado Sonora,** which sells home goods, herbal medicines, live animals, and products for spells and witchcraft. Today's market is generally safe, but stay aware of your belongings and take care walking the streets nearby.

**MAP 1:** *Circunvalación, between General Anaya and Adolfo Gurrión, Col. Merced Balbuena; generally 6am-6pm daily; Metro: La Merced*

# Restaurants

## PRICE KEY
$ Entrées less than US$10
$$ Entrées US$10-20
$$$ Entrées more than US$20

## MEXICAN

### Café de Tacuba $

Occupying two floors of a 17th-century mansion, this old-fashioned family restaurant has long been a keynote establishment in the Centro Histórico. The fun of eating here is enjoying the Old Mexico atmosphere in the dining room, with its tall wood-beamed ceilings, pretty frescoes, and old oil paintings. Fittingly, the kitchen serves a range of homey traditional dishes, like chicken in pipián (a sauce of ground pumpkin seeds and spices), enchiladas, and sopes (round corn cakes topped with beans and cheese). It's also a fine spot for a pan de dulce and hot chocolate in the evenings.
**MAP 1:** *Tacuba 28; tel. 55/5521-2048; www.cafedetacuba.com.mx; 8am-11pm daily; Metro: Allende*

### Sanborns de los Azulejos $

Owned by billionaire Carlos Slim, Sanborns has hundreds of locations across the city, all serving the same menu of traditional Mexican dishes. It's not uncommon to see one Sanborns directly across the street from the one you're sitting in. The restaurant's ubiquity has made it an institution in the capital, and if there's one Sanborns you should visit, it's the Casa de los Azulejos. Occupying a spectacular 16th-century palace adorned with hand-painted tiles, the dining room is perpetually packed with locals lingering over coffee.
**MAP 1:** *Av. Madero 4; tel. 55/5512-1331; www.sanborns.com.mx; 7am-1am Mon.-Sat., 7am-midnight Sun.; Metro: Bellas Artes or Allende*

### Azul Histórico $$

Chef Ricardo Muñoz Zurita's Azul Histórico is set in the tree-shaded courtyard of a colonial-era palace, which it shares with the Downtown Hotel and the Shops at Downtown. Its charming yet relaxed atmosphere is well suited to both a leisurely Sunday lunch and a fancy Saturday dinner, and also goes perfectly with the restaurant's appealing menu of creatively rendered Mexican

Café de Tacuba

dishes. With heavy influence from Veracruz, Campeche, and other southern states, the menu includes dishes like ceviche verde and hibiscus-stuffed tacos, in addition to monthly specials that showcase more unusual dishes from across the republic.
**MAP 1:** *Isabel la Católica 30; tel. 55/5510-1316; www.azul.rest; 9am-11pm daily; Metro: Zócalo*

### Café El Popular $

Chinese-owned cafés were ubiquitous in Mexico City during the early 20th century. These popular cafés originally served Chinese food and bread, but over the years their menus evolved to become more Mexican than international. Among the few survivors in this unique genre, old-fashioned Café El Popular has two locations on Cinco de Mayo—the more charming of which is the smaller spot to the east. It's a perfect place for a traditional Mexican breakfast accompanied by a café con leche, served in a glass tumbler at your table.
**MAP 1:** *Cinco de Mayo 50 and 52; tel. 55/5518-6081; 24 hours daily; Metro: Allende*

### Balcón del Zócalo $$

For many first-time visitors to Mexico City, lunching at one of the many restaurants overlooking the Zócalo is a must. While most of these touristy establishments offer lackadaisical service and overpriced steak, Balcón del Zócalo, on the top floor of the Zócalo Central hotel, offers a surprisingly nice menu of well-prepared Mexican food, a lovely plant-filled dining room, and, most importantly, a gorgeous view, overlooking the eastern wing of the cathedral.
**MAP 1:** *Av. Cinco de Mayo 61; tel. 55/5130-5130; www.balcondelzocalo.com; 10am-10pm daily; Metro: Zócalo*

### Don Toribio $

Located in an old-fashioned 3rd-floor dining room with balconies opening onto the bustling streets below, this popular breakfast-and-lunch spot has a classic Mexico City ambience. The inexpensive lunch menu, which includes soup of the day, an entrée, and a drink, is a big draw for the local crowd—come 2pm, the restaurants' tables are reliably filled with diners. You'll find a branch on the ground floor of the building, but it's worth huffing up three flights of stairs (or hopping in the elevator) to eat in the beautiful main dining room.
**MAP 1:** *Simón Bolívar 31; tel. 55/5510-9198; 8:30am-6pm daily; Metro: Allende*

### ✪ El Cardenal $$

This classic spot serves traditional Mexican dishes from across the republic, in addition to seasonal specials like chinicuiles, red maguey worms (Aug.-Oct.), and Valencia-style salt cod, a traditional Christmas dish, in December. With baskets of fresh breads and pitchers of hot chocolate, breakfast is a popular meal here, though you'll find many

## Sanborns: A Shopping and Dining Institution

Billionaire Carlos Slim's department store and restaurant chain **Sanborns** (www.sanborns.com.mx) is an institution in Mexico City, notable for its ubiquity. The restaurants all have a similar diner-like atmosphere, which is appropriate to their reasonably priced, pleasantly familiar, yet somewhat characterless menu of Mexican standards. In addition to the dining room, all locations have a separate bar, many of which feature live music in the evenings and drinks accompanied by the chain's signature salted peanuts. The most famous location, and the one most worth visiting, is located in the courtyard of the gorgeous 16th-century palace Casa de los Azulejos on the Madero in the Centro Histórico.

Sanborns dining room

At all of the department store's locations, you'll find a good selection of electronics, cameras and camera equipment, home goods, bath and beauty products, candy, and books, as well as a well-stocked newsstand. There are also pharmacies in every location, with over-the-counter and prescription medications. In addition, there are Inbursa ATMs inside all Sanborns branches, which charge a low commission and have good exchange rates (and are often a safe and private place to take out cash).

---

interesting options, from moles to Oaxacan-style chiles rellenos, on the lovely lunch and dinner menu. The original location on Palma occupies a multistory French-style mansion, but there are several other branches in the city, including in the Hilton Mexico City Reforma (Juárez 70, Centro; tel. 55/5518-6632) and in San Ángel (Av. de la Paz 32, San Ángel; tel. 55/5616-5187).

**MAP 1:** *Palma 23; tel. 55/5521-8815; www.elcardenal.com.mx; 8am-6:30pm Mon.-Sat., 9am-6:30pm Sun.; Metro: Zócalo*

### Paxia $$

Located on the plant-filled rooftop of the Umbral Hotel, this restaurant by well-known Mexico City restaurateur Daniel Ovadía brings creativity, care, and a touch of playfulness to every meal, from the beautifully plated dishes, like octopus with nopal, to the order of fresh salsa prepared with mortar and pestle at your table. Striking views, delicious cocktails, and gracious service make dining here a memorable experience—a good choice for a date night in the Centro Histórico.

**MAP 1:** *Venustiano Carranza 69; tel. 55/2289-6295; https://danielovadia.com/paxia; 1pm-11:30pm Tues.-Sat., 1pm-7pm Sun.; Metro: Zócalo*

### Roldán 37 $$

Deep within the Merced commercial district, a pedestrian street leads to an old two-story home where chef Rómulo Mendoza's family once stored green chili peppers that were sold at city markets. Today, that home has been transformed into a lovely traditional restaurant, where Mendoza and his team serve food "from the Merced." The specialty is chiles rellenos, served in a variety of styles, including Mexico's national dish, chiles en nogada, during the summer and fall season.

**MAP 1:** *Roldán 37; tel. 55/5542-1951; noon-7pm Mon.-Thurs., noon-9pm Fri.-Sat.; Metro: Pino Suárez or Merced*

### Zéfiro $$

The culinary school at the Universidad del Claustro de Sor Juana operates one of the best-known chef training programs in the country, with a course of instruction that focuses entirely on Mexican ingredients and preparations. At Zéfiro, the school's elegant student-run restaurant, you can taste the work of the Claustro's burgeoning chefs, who design the menu and helm the kitchen. A specialty of the house is pork shank served with manchamanteles, a highly seasoned and vibrant type of mole (the translation of its name means "tablecloth stainer").

**MAP 1:** *San Jerónimo 24; tel. 55/5130-3385; www.ucsj.edu.mx/zefiro; 1pm-5pm Tues.-Fri., 1pm-6pm Sat.; Metro: Isabel la Católica*

## CANTINAS

### ✪ Bar La Ópera $$

This historic cantina has been in operation since 1895, and the old-fashioned interior is filled with French-inspired carved-wood panels, glittering mirrors, and globe lamps. Waiters in vests and bow ties attend to the evening crowd of locals and tourists, who come hoping to locate the bullet hole that Pancho Villa allegedly shot into the cantina's tin ceiling. Atmosphere trumps the food here, but Mexican snacks, like chorizo, guacamole, and queso fundido (a pot of melted cheese), are nicely done.

**MAP 1:** *Av. Cinco de Mayo 10; tel. 55/5512-8959; www.barlaopera.com; 1pm-11:20pm Mon.-Sat., 1pm-6pm Sun.; Metro: Bellas Artes or Allende*

### Salón Corona $

This convivial family-owned cantina opened in 1928 and has since expanded to several locations beyond the original spot on Bolívar. It's a friendly, bustling place with good eats and cold drinks, perfect for watching a Sunday afternoon soccer game or passing an evening with beer and bar snacks, like beef tacos in mole verde (green mole) and tortas al pastor (chili-rubbed pork sandwiches). If the tables at the original location on Bolívar are full, there are branches on the pedestrian streets Gante (Gante 1; tel. 55/5512-2024; 11am-11pm Sun.-Thurs., 11am-2am Fri.-Sat.) and Madero (Madero 1; tel. 55/5510-3156; 1pm-9:45pm Sun.-Wed., 1pm-10:45pm Thurs., 11am-midnight Fri.-Sat.).

**MAP 1:** *Bolívar 24; tel. 55/5512-9007; www.saloncorona.com.mx; 11am-11pm Sun.-Thurs., 11am-2am Fri.-Sat.; Metro: Allende*

## TACOS, TORTAS, AND SNACKS

### Los Cocuyos $

When celebrity chef and adventurous eater Anthony Bourdain came to Mexico City for his television show *No Reservations,* his hosts quickly escorted him to this long-running street stand, where the specialty is beef tacos with a "nose to tail" approach. Despite its Hollywood connections, don't expect any glamour at this sidewalk joint. Call out your order over the vats of sizzling meats, then prepare to dine standing on the sidewalk.

**MAP 1:** *Bolívar 56; no phone; 10am-5am daily; Metro: San Juan de Letrán*

## SEAFOOD

### El Danubio $$

El Danubio is long heralded as the top seafood restaurant in the Centro, and the pride of that moniker emanates throughout the dining room, which is decorated with autographs of the famous people who have eaten here. In business since 1936, El Danubio is old-fashioned yet delicious, with a strong Spanish influence in the cuisine. House specialties like the sopa verde (green seafood soup) and langostinos (grilled crawfish) go equally well with a glass of rioja or a shot of tequila.

**MAP 1:** *Uruguay 3; tel. 55/5512-0912; www.danubio.com; 1pm-7pm Mon.-Fri., 1pm-7:30pm Sat.-Sun.; Metro: San Juan de Letrán*

## MIDDLE EASTERN

### El Ehden $

On the 2nd floor of a large mansion, tucked between the many textile merchants of Venustiano Carranza, this off-the-beaten-track Lebanese restaurant is a clean and simple spot popular with locals for its quality and price. Stacks of warm pita accompany dishes like grilled lamb, jocoque (Middle Eastern-style strained yogurt), stuffed grape leaves, and other regional specialties.

**MAP 1:** *Venustiano Carranza 148, 2nd Fl.; tel. 55/5542-2320; noon-6pm daily; Metro: Zócalo or Pino Suárez*

### Al Andalus $

There was a large influx of Lebanese immigrants to Mexico in the early 20th century, and as a result, you'll find some fine Middle Eastern cuisine in the capital. Among the best, Al Andalus, tucked into the heart of what was once a predominantly immigrant district, is in a renovated two-story colonial house, with professional, efficient service and a menu of excellent Middle Eastern specialties, like shawarma, hummus, and kepa

bola (a mix of wheat, ground lamb, and onion).
**MAP 1:** *Mesones 171; tel. 55/5522-2528; 10am-6pm daily; Metro: Pino Suárez*

## SPANISH

### Casino Español $$

Worth a visit for the old-world ambience alone, the Casino Español is an old-fashioned Spanish restaurant housed in a gorgeous early 20th-century mansion, with soaring ceilings, massive chandeliers, and stained-glass windows creating an opulent backdrop to the menu of delicious, traditional dishes like paella and lechón (suckling pig). There is a less formal café downstairs, popular for lunch with locals, but if you want the full experience, head to the more serious dining room upstairs, order a glass of rioja, and make an afternoon of it.
**MAP 1:** *Isabel la Católica 31; tel. 55/5521-8894; www.cassatt.mx; 8am-6pm daily; Metro: Allende*

## COFFEE AND SWEETS

### Pastelería Ideal $

Opened in 1927, Pastelería Ideal is a traditional Mexican bakery specializing in pan de dulce: lightly sweetened rolls, pastries, buns, and empanadas that are meant to be accompanied by coffee or hot chocolate. Here, as in most old-fashioned bakeries in Mexico, you grab a tray and a set of tongs, select the bread and pastries you want from the shelves, then bring it all to

Casino Español is an old-fashioned Spanish restaurant.

the register, where they'll tally up the cost and bag it.
**MAP 1:** *16 de Septiembre 18; tel. 55/5130-2970; http://pasteleriaideal.com.mx; 6am-8pm daily; Metro: San Juan de Letrán*

### Churrería El Moro $

Hidden within the chaos of the Eje Central, this old-time café specializes in a classic sugar fix: churros and hot chocolate, a combination made in heaven for a rainy afternoon. Peer into the kitchen to see how churros are swirled by hand into crunchy rounds. The simple 1935-vintage atmosphere makes the experience all the sweeter: blue-and-white tiles on the walls, wood-beamed ceilings, and Formica tables provide a quintessentially Mexican backdrop for a favorite Mexican treat. In recent years, the churrería has expanded to several other locations, including a lovely branch in front of Parque

México (Av. Michoacán 27) in the Condesa and another on the corner of Frontera and Álvaro Obregón in the Roma (Frontera 122).

**MAP 1:** *Eje Central 42; tel. 55/5512-0896; http://elmoro.mx; 7am-11pm Sun.-Thurs., 7am-midnight Fri.-Sat.; Metro: San Juan de Letrán*

# Nightlife

## CANTINAS
### Salón España
This old-fashioned cantina is known for its extensive selection of tequila, with more than 190 bottles on offer, from well-known to rare. Opened by Spanish refugees in 1925, it is a traditional spot, and—as in most old-school Mexico City cantinas—the daily menu of snacks (or botanas) is included with your drink order (2-drink minimum).

**MAP 1:** *Luis González Obregón 25; tel. 55/5704-0014; 11am-midnight Mon.-Sat., 11am-7pm Sun.; no cover; Metro: Zócalo*

### La Faena
Set in a lovely colonial-era building, this no-frills cantina pays homage to bullfighting: Here, ornate old matador costumes fill glass display cases around the barroom, while the old tile floors and dusty chandeliers make an oddly elegant contrast to the decidedly unpretentious plastic chairs and cantina tables that fill the space. Clientele is a varied local crowd, but don't be surprised to see a hipster or two in the mix. Cash only.

**MAP 1:** *Venustiano Carranza 49B; tel. 55/5510-4417; noon-6pm Mon., noon-8pm Tues.-Thurs., noon-11:30pm Sat., noon-6pm Sun.; no cover; Metro: San Juan de Letrán*

## LIVE MUSIC
### Zinco Jazz Club
This cosmopolitan jazz club is known for bringing some of the best performers to the capital, from international jazz trios to homegrown brass bands. The cozy venue has a classic cabaret atmosphere, with black walls, flickering candles, and a red curtain swaying behind the stage. If you're headed to Zinco, look for the basement door in the art deco Edificio Banco de México, on the corner of Motolinia and Cinco de Mayo.

**MAP 1:** *Motolinia 20; tel. 55/1131-7760; http://zincojazz.com; 9pm-2am Wed.-Sat.; showtimes vary; tickets US$10-30; Metro: Bellas Artes*

### Hostería La Bota
A lively, student-friendly watering hole, Hostería La Bota is a mainstay among the small crop of bars and mezcalerías on the pedestrian streets Regina and San Jerónimo. Come here for poetry readings, live music and dance, and book presentations, or just to enjoy a very cold beer in a low-key environment.

Hostería La Bota

With its worn wooden tables covered in notes and scribbles and a barroom filled floor-to-ceiling with posters, the atmosphere is funky-cool.
**MAP 1:** *San Jerónimo 40; tel. 55/5709-9016; 1pm-11pm daily; no cover; Metro: Isabel la Católica*

## NIGHTCLUBS
### Sunday Sunday
This ultra-popular Sunday-night dance party is held on a top-floor terrace of a high-rise just off the Zócalo. Expect big crowds and high-quality DJs who keep the weekend vibes rolling into Monday morning. Come early if you want to enjoy the views from the rooftop in daylight. Crowds get bigger and bigger as the night progresses.
**MAP 1:** *Tabaqueros 16; no phone; tickets https://ra.co; generally 3pm-2am Sun.; US$20; Metro: Zócalo*

## LGBTQ+
### El Marrakech Salón
This upbeat, ultra-fun, straight-friendly bar is hopping in the evenings, when an eclectic crowd convenes for DJs, people-watching, and kitschy entertainment. Things heat up around 11pm when strippers or drag shows start, and the dance floor rocks till closing. The friendly attitude and youthful crowd have made this gay bar one of the most popular spots on the lively strip of dance halls and cantinas on República de Cuba. If you're having a ball, cross the street to **La Purísima** (República de Cuba 17; tel. 55/9136-9378; 7pm-3am Thurs.-Sat.), a clubbier spot that nonetheless retains the same friendly atmosphere as its neighbor.
**MAP 1:** *República de Cuba 18; no phone; 6pm-2am Thurs.-Sat.; no cover; Metro: Bellas Artes*

# Arts and Culture

## GALLERIES

### Galería de Arte de la SHCP

The Mexican government allows working visual artists to pay a portion of their annual taxes with works of art. As a result, the Secretariat of Finance and Public Credit has amassed a rather diverse collection of work from across the republic. You can see a selection of that massive reserve at the free SHCP gallery, which is on the ground floor of a neoclassical 19th-century mansion, just behind the cathedral. Exhibits change frequently and include varied but generally high-quality painting and sculpture.

**MAP 1:** *Guatemala 8; tel. 55/3688-1718; 10am-5pm daily; free; Metro: Zócalo*

## MUSEUMS

### Museo Archivo de la Fotografía

This small museum and photo archive exhibits contemporary photographic work, as well as selections from its permanent collection of photographs of 19th- and 20th-century Mexico City. These images showcase the rapid and often miraculous transformations that took place in the capital during the previous decades, and are the highlight of visiting the galleries,

Museo del Estanquillo

located in the 16th-century Casa de las Ajaracas, the final structure on the street República de Guatemala beside the Templo Mayor. The buildings beside it were demolished in 1994 to continue excavation of the Templo Mayor archaeological site.

**MAP 1:** *República de Guatemala 34; tel. 55/2616-7057; 10am-5pm Tues.-Sun.; free; Metro: Zócalo*

### Museo del Estanquillo

This unique museum features the artwork and photography collected by Carlos Monsiváis, a political activist, journalist, and prolific chronicler of life in Mexico City, who remains highly influential in the capital even after his 2010 death. The museum organizes rotating thematic shows dedicated to Mexican art and culture. There are also permanent exhibits showcasing the writer's personal collection of sketches, photos, advertisements, comics, and photos. On the topfloor, Kato Café (10:30am-5:30pm Wed.-Mon.) is worth a visit for its stunning bird's-eye views of the surrounding blocks.

**MAP 1:** *Isabel la Católica 26; tel. 55/5521-3052, ext. 101; www.museodelestanquillo.cdmx.gob.mx; 10am-2pm and 3pm-6pm Sun.-Mon. and Wed.-Thurs.; free; Metro: Allende*

### Casa de la Primera Imprenta de América

Nestled amid the grand palaces of Moneda, this little building was likely constructed in the early colonial era and gained national importance when it became the home of New Spain's first printing press. Today it is a cultural center, operated by the Universidad Autónoma Metropolitana, showcasing ongoing exhibits related to books, typography, art, and film. It also holds a replica of the original printing press, which was brought to Mexico from Italy in 1539.

**MAP 1:** *Licenciado Primo de Verdad 10; tel. 55/5522-1535; 10am-5pm Mon.-Fri., 10am-2pm Sat., evenings for special events and film screenings; free; Metro: Zócalo*

### Ex-Teresa Arte Actual

On the small side street Licenciado Verdad, a towering 17th-century baroque church has been transformed into a wholly unique gallery space dedicated to contemporary performance, video, installation, and sound art, such as a 2022 show by artist Bill Viola. Shows often have an experimental focus, which contrasts sharply with the atmosphere in the old church, originally constructed from 1678 to 1884. What was once the nave—with its wobbly sinking floors—has

Ex-Teresa Arte Actual

## Noche de Museos

The last Wednesday of every month, museums throughout the city stay open late, generally providing free or reduced-price admission to visitors after official closing time. Many museums go far beyond simply opening their doors to the public, planning concerts, speakers, or guided tours of the galleries after hours. Some wonderful institutions participate in the event throughout the city, but you'll cover the most ground in the area around the Alameda Central and the Centro Histórico, where a great number of museums participate, and many are within close walking distance of each other.

In recent years, there has been a Celtic music concert at the Casa de la Primera Imprenta de América, a screening of *Nosferatu* with live music at the Museo Franz Mayer, free guided tours of the Palacio de Bellas Artes, an open mike at the Colegio de San Idlefonso, a flamenco concert at the Palacio Postal, and a mime show at the Museo de El Carmen. During the pandemic lockdown, many museums began offering free cultural programs online, including film screenings and cultural talks, and many continue to do so. Follow Noche de Museos on Facebook to see some of the in-person and online offerings each month.

been cleared to create the exhibition space. The gallery sometimes doubles as a cinema in the evening.
**MAP 1:** *Licenciado Verdad 8; tel. 55/4122-8020; https://exteresa.inba.gob.mx; 11am-5pm Tues.-Sun.; free; Metro: Zócalo*

### Foro Valparaíso
Owned and overseen by Citibanamex's cultural foundation, the colonial-era Palacio de los Condes de San Mateo de Valparaíso has been beautifully restored and opened to the public as a spectacular 22-room museum that showcases the bank's collection of Mexican artwork. Most rooms are dedicated to colonial-era painting—with some fascinating large-scale works depicting Mexico City in the early colonial era—though the collection includes Rufino Tamayo, Frida Kahlo, and other famous modern artists. Admission is free.
**MAP 1:** *Venustiano Carranza 60; tel. 55/1226-4290 or 55/2262-6367; www.banamex.com/valparaiso; 10am-6pm Wed.-Sun.; free; Metro: Zócalo*

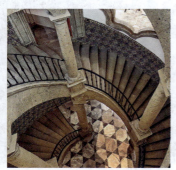

spiral staircase inside the Foro Valparaíso

# Festivals and Events

## SEPTEMBER
### Día de la Independencia
Mexico commemorates its 1810 independence from Spanish rule every year on September 16. In Mexico City, the president of the republic appears on the balcony in the Palacio Nacional at 11pm on the night of September 15, reenacting independence hero Miguel Hidalgo's cry for independence—also known as El Grito—to a crowd of thousands in the Zócalo below. There is a massive military parade through the Centro and along the Paseo de la Reforma the following day. In 2017 the parade featured the military's troupe of trained search-and-rescue dogs, who would become world famous just a few days later, in the aftermath of the earthquake on September 19, 2017, when they helped assist rescue efforts.

**Centro Histórico:** *Plaza de la Constitución; Sept. 15-16*

## DECEMBER
### Verbena Navideña
During the December holiday season, the Zócalo hosts a wide variety of cultural activities, including performances by the philharmonic orchestra, cumbia, games, food booths, and a holiday market. It's worth visiting the square

Día de la Independencia decorations in the Zócalo

in December to enjoy the beautiful illuminated decorations that are hung on the palaces.
**Centro Histórico:** *The Zócalo, Plaza de la Constitución, bordered by Madero, Moneda, 16 de Septiembre, Corregidora, 5 de Febrero, República de Brasil, and Pino Suárez; 11am-7pm daily mid-Dec.-mid Jan.; free; Metro: Zócalo*

# Recreation

## SPECTATOR SPORTS
### Lucha Libre
### Arena Coliseo

This popular wrestling arena is rougher around the edges than the larger and better-known Arena México, located to the north of the Plaza Santo Domingo—but it's an older and equally popular venue for Mexico City's most famous sport. The arena is often packed for the high-energy Saturday-night wrestling matches, and audience can get rowdy; on a first visit, it's best to choose seats farther from the ring to avoid flying bodies and chairs. Use caution coming and going from the stadium after dark.
**MAP 1:** *República de Perú 77; tel. 55/5588-0266; www.cmll.com; matches usually 7pm Sat.; US$4-20; Metro: Allende*

# Shops

## ANTIQUES AND COLLECTIBLES
### Nacional Monte de Piedad

First opened in 1775, this massive nonprofit pawnshop is one of the oldest financial institutions in the Americas. It was founded with the mission to support people in need by offering fixed low-interest loans in exchange for pawned household items, jewelry, and electronics. It's still not unusual to see sellers lined up outside the historic buildings with items they're wishing to exchange for a loan. Today, you'll mostly find jewelry, gemstones, watches, and smartphones for sale in the 2nd-floor shop, which is located in a colonial-era palace that was built atop the former palace of Mexica emperor Axayácatl and later the residence of Hernán Cortés.
**MAP 1:** *Monte de Piedad 7; tel. 55/2629-2790; www.montepiedad.com.mx; 8:30am-5pm Mon.-Fri., 9am-2pm Sat.; Metro: Zócalo*

## CLOTHING, SHOES, AND ACCESSORIES
### Remigio

Owned by one of Mexico's best-known textile merchants, Remigio Mestas, this wonderful shop sells

Nacional Monte de Piedad

fine handmade clothing and fabrics from the southern state of Oaxaca. Here, old painted chests and wooden shelves are piled with gorgeous hand-loomed textiles, meticulously embroidered blouses, colorful cotton huipiles (a traditional tunic from Oaxaca), and elegantly simple plant-dyed fabrics. The work here is high quality and original, with upscale prices to match.

**MAP 1:** *Isabel la Católica 30-7, 2nd Fl.; tel. 55/5512-4150; 11am-7pm Mon.-Sat., usually 2pm-7pm Sun.; Metro: Zócalo*

### Sombreros Tardan

This quality hat shop has been in business right on the Zócalo since 1847. Though it originally began as an import shop, it was later bought by the Tardan family, who developed their own line of felt and wool hats during the early 20th century. Even today, Tardan remains among the best hatmakers in Mexico. Come here to browse the nice selection of men's sombreros, which run from beanies to cotton caps to Panama hats.

**MAP 1:** *Plaza de la Constitutión 7; tel. 55/5512-3902; www.tardan.com.mx; 10am-7pm Mon.-Sat.; Metro: Zócalo*

## GOURMET FOOD AND IMPORTS

### Dulcería de Celaya

This old-fashioned sweet shop is a feast for the eyes as well as the taste buds: Its 19th-century interior is filled with gilded moldings, mirrored walls, and glimmering display cases packed with handmade candies. If you aren't familiar with Mexican sweets, this old shop is a great place to start, though it sets the bar high—it's been in business since 1874, so the recipes have been perfected. Try the excellent coconut-stuffed limes; crystallized fruit like figs, sweet potatoes, and acitrón (cactus); or lightly sweetened fluffy meringues.

Dulcería de Celaya

**MAP 1:** *Cinco de Mayo 39; tel. 55/5521-1787; https:// dulceriadecelaya.com; 10:30am-7:30pm daily; Metro: Allende*

## PUBLIC MARKETS
### Mercado Sonora
Just south of the Mercado de la Merced, the interesting Mercado Sonora sells traditional goods for home and kitchen and, most famously, supplies for healing and witchcraft. Some stands are dedicated to herbs and traditional remedies, while others sell esoteric items like amulets, candles, and colored stones. As is common in many markets in Mexico, animals are on sale in back, including dogs, cats, hamsters, snakes, rabbits, and birds, although authorities have taken measures to curb the once common sale of more exotic species, like owls and parrots.

**MAP 1:** *Av. Fray Servando Teresa de Mier 419; www.mercadosonora.com.mx; 8am-5pm daily; Metro: Merced*

## SHOPPING CENTERS
### The Shops at Downtown
Located within the same opulent colonial-era palace as the stylish Downtown Hotel, this small yet elegant shopping center is dedicated to Mexican-made products and Mexican-owned retail. With shops selling everything from chic clothing and specialty chocolate to high-end artisanal crafts and mezcal, this shopping center is a great place to browse for a gift—and its historic breezeways are wonderful for wandering on a warm afternoon.

**MAP 1:** *Isabel la Católica 30; tel. 55/5521-2098; http://theshops.mx; 11am-9pm daily, individual shop hours vary; Metro: Zócalo*

# Alameda Central

Map 2

Getting Around ........ 87
Sights ................. 90
Restaurants ........... 96
Nightlife .............. 101
Arts and Culture ...... 104
Recreation ............ 108
Shops ................. 109

On the western end of the Centro Histórico, the Alameda Central is the oldest park in Mexico City. Always bustling with activity, it is home to one of the most important arts institutions in the capital, the Palacio de Bellas Artes, and in the surrounding blocks, there are many fine colonial-era churches and excellent museums. The San Juan area, to the south, is a busy commercial district known for street food and a unique traditional market. To the north, the fascinating archaeological site in Tlatelolco is adjoined by a contemporary cultural center. Note that the western edge of the Juárez neighborhood, along the street Bucareli, is also included in this chapter.

# Highlights

✪ **Zona Arqueológica Tlatelolco:** The remains of the pre-Columbian market town of Tlatelolco, neighbor to the city of Tenochtitlan, are a today an interesting and surprisingly quiet urban archaeological site (page 90).

✪ **Palacio de Bellas Artes:** A stunning art deco interior and weekly performances by the famed Ballet Folklórico de Amalia Hernández are among the many reasons to visit this fine arts institution (page 94).

✪ **Museo de Arte Popular:** This vibrant museum showcases the inventiveness and range of Mexico's craft traditions, from the pre-Columbian era to the modern day (page 106).

✪ **Family Night at Arena México:** An all-ages crowd is welcome on Sunday night at the Arena México, the place to go for spectacularly entertaining lucha libre matches (page 108).

✪ **La Lagunilla:** The city's largest and most famous antiques market is a popular spot for browsing (with beer!) on Sunday morning (page 109).

# Getting Around

- Metro lines: 1, 2, 3
- Metro stops: Bellas Artes, Hidalgo, Balderas, Salto de Agua, San Juan de Letrán, Garibaldi, Tlatelolco
- Metrobús lines: 3, 4
- Metrobús stops: Hidalgo, Balderas, Plaza San Juan, Eje Central

---

**Previous:** Alameda Central; **Above:** Zona Arqueológica Tlatelolco; Palacio de Bellas Artes.

# MAP 2

# Sights

## Plaza de las Tres Culturas

Several blocks north of the Plaza Garibaldi, the Plaza de las Tres Culturas (Plaza of the Three Cultures) in Tlatelolco is surrounded by symbols of three distinct periods of Mexican history: the remains of the pre-Columbian city of Tlatelolco, the 16th-century Iglesia de Santiago Tlatelolco, and several modern buildings, including the tower housing the Secretaría de Relaciones Exteriores and a 1960s-era apartment complex designed by famous Mexican architect Mario Pani.

In the 16th century, Tlatelolco was a Mexica city-state, sister to the ruling city of Tenochtitlan. Here, after months of battle, Cortés and his men finally conquered the Mexica people and their leader Cuauhtémoc. The event is commemorated with a plaque in the middle of the Plaza de las Tres Culturas, with a famous inscription: "Heroically defended by Cuauhtémoc, Tlatelolco fell to the power of Hernán Cortés. It was neither a triumph nor a defeat. It was the painful birth of the mestizo nation that is the Mexico of today."

**MAP 2:** *Eje Central Lázaro Cárdenas and Ricardo Flores Magón; 24 hours daily; free; Metro: Tlatelolco*

## ✪ Zona Arqueológica Tlatelolco

A sister city-state to the Mexica capital of Tenochtitlan, Tlatelolco was founded in 1337 and became a major settlement in the Valley of Mexico, home to the largest and most important market in Mesoamerica. It was here that the Mexica leaders fled after withstanding months of siege by the Spanish forces in Tenochtitlan. On August 13, 1521, the Mexica people were at last defeated by Cortés and his forces on this site.

The Spanish forces destroyed most of the city of Tlatelolco and constructed a church atop the remains of the city—as in the Zócalo, the first church was likely built using rubble from the destroyed pyramids. The site was excavated in 1944 and again from 1960 to 1968, uncovering both pre-Columbian and colonial-era artifacts. Today, the surprisingly extensive and nicely maintained site reveals the foundations of religious and ceremonial buildings from the former city, including the Templo Mayor of Tlatelolco. The temple to Ehécatl-Quetzalcóatl is an interesting half-round, half-rectangular structure, where a late 1980s excavation recovered the remains of 41 people and more than 50 offerings. The smaller Templo Calendárico displays 13 glyphs from the Mesoamerican calendar carved into each of its four facades.

As part of your visit to the archaeological site, the fascinating **Museo Caja de Agua** (tel. 55/5583-0295; by appointment

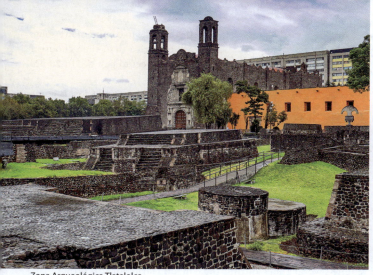
Zona Arqueológica Tlatelolco

only 9am-1pm Mon.-Fri.; free) showcases the remains of an early colonial-era water basin that was painted with murals that unite pre-Columbian and Spanish visual elements, including eagles, jaguars, and a cross with the monogram INRI. Visits are by appointment; it's recommended you call at least a week ahead to reserve a spot.

**MAP 2:** *Corner of Eje Central Lázaro Cárdenas and Ricardo Flores Magón; tel. 55/5583-0295; www.tlatelolco. inah.gob.mx; 8am-3pm daily; US$6; Metro: Tlatelolco, Metrobús: Glorieta Cuitláhuac*

### Centro Cultural Universitario Tlatelolco

Next to the Tlatelolco archaeological site in the Plaza de las Tres Culturas, this expansive cultural center is run by the Universidad Nacional Aútonoma de México (UNAM). The centerpiece of the museum is the **Memorial de 68,** which is dedicated to the legacy of October 2, 1968, the day on which several hundred student protesters were massacred in the Plaza de Tres Culturas by the Mexican military (guardias presidenciales) just before the start of the Mexico City Olympics. The museum also hosts a range of interesting temporary exhibits and art shows, many thematically related to Tlatelolco and its history, as well as a wide range of workshops and cultural events.

**MAP 2:** *Ricardo Flores Magón 1; tel. 55/5117-2818; https://tlatelolco.unam. mx; 11am-5pm Wed.-Thurs., 11am-6pm Fri.-Sun.; US$3; Metro: Garibaldi or Tlatelolco*

### Iglesia de Santiago Tlatelolco

Immediately following the Spanish conquest of Mexico, Cortés ordered the building of a church in Tlatelolco, the site of the last stand

Centro Cultural Universitario Tlatelolco

and fall of the Mexica people. Likely constructed using the stones of the Templo Mayor of Tlatelolco, which the Spanish razed, the church was rebuilt several times during the early years of the colonies. The current structure, made largely of the tezontle volcanic stone that was also used in the pyramids, dates from 1610. The adjoining convent and its pretty central garden are now overseen by the Secretaría de Relaciones Exteriores (SRE) and are also open to the public.

**MAP 2:** *Plaza de las Tres Culturas, Eje Central Lázaro Cárdenas and Ricardo Flores Magón; free; Metro: Tlatelolco, Metrobús: Glorieta Cuitláhuac*

### Plaza Garibaldi

In early 20th-century Mexico City, Plaza Garibaldi was a fashionable nightlife destination, filled with cabarets and glamorous nightclubs. It has since lost much of its madcap splendor, but it remains a vibrant part of the city, coming to life in the evenings as dozens of mariachi bands roam the square, playing tunes to the crowds of revelers. If you'd like to commission a song, ask the price first, then choose a tune. Expect to pay US$10-20 per song.

Many visitors and locals come to Garibaldi after a few tequilas to visit the many bars and pulquerías that ring the square, the most notable of which is **Salon Tenampa** (Plaza Garibaldi 12; tel. 55/5526-6176; https://salontenampa.com; 2pm-2am Sun.-Wed., 2pm-3am Thurs.-Sat.), the legendary mariachi bar that first opened in Garibaldi in 1925.

Although a 2012 renovation made Garibaldi safer, there is a history of crime in the area, and some bars along the plaza make a business of cheating tourists. Stick to the Tenampa or other recommended establishments, and never wander on the backstreets around Garibaldi after dark.

**MAP 2:** *Eje Central at República de Honduras; Metro: Garibaldi*

### Templo San Hipólito

This beautiful church, on the corner of Hidalgo and Zarco, is said to have been originally commissioned by the Spanish in

mariachi band in Plaza Garibaldi

remembrance of the Noche Triste, on June 30, 1520, when Hernán Cortés's forces fled the city of Tenochtitlan, resulting in major Spanish casualties. First erected in the 1550s, the church is located at what was once the start of the causeway that led to the mainland community of Tlacopan from the island of Tenochtitlan. In the following centuries, it marked the outer limits of the city. The church was repeatedly rebuilt over the centuries, with much of the building dating to the 1730s. Today, the church is dedicated to Jude the Apostle, and on the 28th of every month, a special mass is celebrated in the saint's honor.

**MAP 2:** *Zarco 12; tel. 55/5510-4796; 8am-9pm daily; free; Metro: Hidalgo*

### Alameda Central

Just west of Bellas Artes, the Alameda Central is the largest green space in the center of the city and the oldest public park in the Americas. Today, it is a tree-filled respite from the bustle of the Centro Histórico—despite being flanked by major avenues on all sides and serviced by two Metro stations and two Metrobús stops.

Inaugurated in the 16th century, the original Alameda was filled with poplars, or alamos, which give the park its name. Throughout the centuries, it evolved from an exclusive strolling park for the upper classes to a bustling family-oriented destination. The Alameda's popular spirit was celebrated by Diego Rivera in his famous work *Dream*

Alameda Central

of a Sunday Afternoon on the Alameda Central, located in the **Museo Mural Diego Rivera** on the west end of the park. The most prominent of the Alameda's many fountains and neoclassical statues is the **Hemiciclo de Benito Juárez,** a semicircle of eight marble columns facing Avenida Juárez on the south. Due to the monument's frequent defacement by political protesters, it is often blocked off from public access.

**MAP 2:** *Bordered by Juárez, Hidalgo, Eje Central, and Paseo de la Reforma; Metro: Bellas Artes or Hidalgo*

### TOP EXPERIENCE

### ✪ Palacio de Bellas Artes

The majestic Palacio de Bellas Artes (Palace of Fine Arts) is one of the city's finest buildings and a highly respected cultural institution that hosts live performances and art exhibitions overseen by the Instituto Nacional de Bellas Artes (National Institute of Fine Arts). Designed by Italian architect Adamo Boari, construction on the palace began in 1904 but halted when the Mexican Revolution began in 1910. Twenty years later, architect Federico Mariscal took over the project, completing the rooftop cupola and the building's interiors in art deco style. In the opulent main auditorium, a stunning Tiffany glass curtain was designed by Mexican artist Dr. Atl. You can enjoy this spectacular venue at the biweekly performances of the famed **Ballet Folklórico de México de Amalia Hernández** (https://balletfolkloricodemexico.com.mx; 8:30pm Wed., 9:30am and 6pm Sun.; tickets US$20-70), a contemporary dance troupe that interprets the traditional music and dance of Mexico, or simply drop in to take a guided tour of the space (1pm and 1:30pm Tues.-Fri.; no reservations; in Spanish; free).

On the 2nd and 3rd floors, the **Museo del Palacio de Bellas Artes** (tel. 55/8647-6500, ext. 2132; http://museopalaciodebellasartes.gob.mx; 10am-6pm Tues.-Sun.; US$4) hosts some of the city's best and highest-profile exhibitions, from a large-scale Frida Kahlo retrospective in 2007 to a survey of work by contemporary artist Damián Ortega in 2024. Admission includes access to the Palacio's many murals, which include David Alfaro Siqueiros's *Nueva Democracia* (New Democracy) on the 2nd level. On another wall, Diego Rivera's 1934 *El Hombre Contralor del Universo*

Palacio de Bellas Artes

Mexico City's small but atmospheric Chinatown

(known as *Man at the Crossroads* in English) was originally commissioned by Nelson Rockefeller; famously, the American business magnate canceled the project when Rivera included a likeness of Lenin in the piece. Guided tours of the murals (4pm Tues.-Fri.; in Spanish) are available. On the top floor, the **Museo Nacional de Arquitectura** exhibits building floor plans, photos, and other archived memorabilia related to Mexico City's historic buildings.

**MAP 2:** *Av. Juárez and Eje Central; tel. 55/8647-6500; www.palacio. bellasartes.gob.mx; 10am-6pm Tues.-Sun.; lobby free, museum and mezzanine level US$6; Metro: Bellas Artes*

### Barrio Chino

Established in the mid-20th century, Mexico City's tiny two-block Chinatown doesn't reflect the full influence of Chinese immigration to the city, which surged in the central districts the late 19th and early 20th centuries, and has been on the rise again since 2019. Even so, it is a fun and atmospheric street to stroll along, checking out the bevy of economical Chinese restaurants serving chop suey and street vendors selling Mexican-Chinese hybrid snacks, like steamed buns filled with Nutella or passion fruit. In 2008 a traditional Chinese-style archway was installed at the entrance to Chinatown, a collaborative project between the Chinese embassy and the administration in Mexico City.

**MAP 2:** *Dolores, between Independencia and Victoria; 24 hours daily; free; Metro: Bellas Artes or San Juan de Letrán, Metrobús: Juárez*

### Plaza de San Juan

In the bustling neighborhood four blocks south of the Alameda, this small plaza is closely associated with the El Buen Tono cigarette company, which once adjoined it. Founded by Frenchman Ernesto Pugibet in the late 19th century, El Buen Tono grew rapidly—eventually manufacturing 3.5 billion cigarettes per year—and the plant, employee housing, and warehouses overtook the neighborhood. Though much of the industrial complex has since been razed, there are vestiges of its presence: The adjoining artisan market, for example, was once part of the tobacco factory warehouses.

On the west side of the plaza, the pretty but often overlooked church of **Nuestra Señora de Guadalupe del Buen Tono** (once the site of the chapel of the old San Juan convent, established in the early colonial era) was constructed by Pugibet for

Plaza de San Juan

factory workers. It was designed by the well-known Mexican architect Miguel Ángel de Quevedo.

**MAP 2:** Buen Tono and Ayuntamiento; 24 hours daily; free; Metro: Salto de Agua or San Juan de Letrán

# Restaurants

## PRICE KEY

$       Entrées less than US$10
$$      Entrées US$10-20
$$$    Entrées more than US$20

## MEXICAN

### ✪ Café La Habana $

This spacious old-fashioned coffeehouse has long been frequented by journalists working at the periodicals headquartered nearby, in addition to being a favored spot for writers (including, formerly, Roberto Bolaño and Gabriel García Marquez!). Adding to the café's legend, the owners say that Che Guevara and Fidel Castro planned the Cuban Revolution here. Legend and literary pedigree aside, Café La Habana is an unpretentious place to enjoy a well-priced Mexican breakfast amid the rustling of newspapers and the whirl of ceiling fans, accompanied by one of the café's signature dark-roast drinks, which are prepared on an impressive hand-pulled espresso machine.

**MAP 2:** Morelos 62, Col. Juárez; tel. 55/5535-2620; 7am-midnight Mon.-Sat., 8am-midnight Sun.; Metro: Juárez, Metrobús: Juárez

### Paradero Conocido $$

This relaxed Mexican bistro brings a bit of contemporary panache to the bustling commercial district that surrounds it. You can take a seat at one of the wood-topped tables in the brightly colored dining room, or grab a stool at the bar overlooking the open kitchen, where a youthful team of chefs serve creative versions of traditional dishes, like mushroom ceviche, roast bone marrow, and enchiladas in a dried-chili sauce. Cheerful, well priced, and propitiously located, it is a great place for a light meal and coffee or drinks after a shopping trip to La Ciudadela or a visit to the Centro de la Imagen.

**MAP 2:** *Ayuntamiento 103; no phone; 10am-6pm Tues.-Thurs., 10am-7pm Fri.-Sat., 10am-5pm Sun.; Metro: Juárez, Metrobús: Juárez*

## TACOS, TORTAS, AND SNACKS

### Carnitas El Cherán $

This taquería built a loyal following at its original location in the massive Central de Abastos wholesale market in Iztapalapa. Now you can get a plate of their famed carnitas in the city center, at a location on Arcos de Belén. What distinguishes Cherán from other carnitas spots are the beloved tacos en trozo—a thick slice of panza (belly) or costilla (rib with the bone in) dropped right into a tortilla—though they also serve the classic carnitas lineup, spicy salsas, juice, and soft drinks. Service is quick and genial.

**MAP 2:** *Arcos de Belén 31; 7am-5pm daily; Metro: Salto de Agua; Metrobús: Balderas*

### El Cuadrilátero $

This popular neighborhood tortería was opened by former pro wrestler Super Astro, and the shop is decorated with lucha libre masks, posters, and other memorabilia from his career. The signature dish is La Gladiador, a 1.3-kg (3-lbs) torta stacked with egg, six kinds of meats, and cheese. Those who finish it in 15 minutes get the whole sandwich for free. Fortunately, any torta here will satisfy your appetite; try the pierna adobado (chili-rubbed pork), which is prepared in-house.

**MAP 2:** *Luis Moya 73; tel. 55/5510-2856; 8am-7pm Mon.-Fri., 8am-8pm Sat.; Metro: San Juan de Letrán*

### El Huequito $

Tacos al pastor are emblematic of the capital, and every taquería has

Carnitas El Cherán

# Street Snacks

Mexico City is well known for its tacos, tortas, and other garnachas (simple snacks). These quick bites are one of the most distinctive aspects of the capital's food scene. Here are some of the most ubiquitous.

## TLACOYOS

**What:** Torpedo-shaped corn cakes stuffed with beans, cheese, garbanzo paste, or chicharrón (pork rind), grilled and topped with nopal, cheese, onions, and salsa.

Elotes and esquites are sold on streets throughout the city.

**When:** Morning to midafternoon.
**Where:** At the Tuesday tianguis (open-air market) in the Condesa (page 217); outside markets like the **Mercado de Medellín** (page 203); at **El Parnita** (page 182) in the Roma; at **Siembra Taquería** (page 156) in Polanco.

## TORTAS

**What:** Sandwiches made on a telera (flat white roll), served with chiles en vinagre (pickled jalapeños). The telera is brushed with refried beans and piled with meat, lettuce, tomato, and avocado. Popular fillings include milanesa (breaded beef) and eggs with chorizo. Vegetarians can order tortas filled with avocado, cheese, eggs, or beans.
**When:** Breakfast, lunch, and dinner.
**Where:** Outside Metro stops; on street corners throughout the city; supersize at **El Cuadrilátero** (page 97); stuffed with chilaquiles at ultra-popular **La Esquina del Chilaquil** (page 185); made with Yucatec-style pulled pork at **Fonda 99.99** (page 212).

## PAMBAZOS

**What:** These popular sandwiches are made from a white roll (also called a pambazo) dipped in a mild guajillo chili sauce, stuffed with cooked potatoes and chorizo, and garnished with sour cream and lettuce.
**When:** All hours.
**Where:** At street stalls in tianguis throughout the city; as an appetizer at **Café de Tacuba** (page 71); meat-free at **Mictlan Antojitos Veganos** (page 211).

## PLÁTANOS MACHOS

**What:** Plátanos machos (plantains) and camotes (sweet potatoes) are

baked over mesquite coals, imparting a smoky flavor to these sweet, starchy treats. They are served with sweetened condensed milk and cinnamon.
**When:** Early evening.
**Where:** Vendors roam central neighborhoods at dusk; listen for their distinctive low-pitched whistle.

## TAMALES AND ATOLE

**What:** Tamales in hoja de maiz (corn husk) or hoja de plátano (banana leaf) are served at breakfast or dinner, often accompanied by atole, a warm, sweetened corn-based drink flavored with chocolate, rice, amaranth, or guava, or served natural and lightly sweetened.
**When:** Early mornings and dinnertime.
**Where: Tamales Madre** (page 124) in the Juárez; **Tamales Doña Emi** (page 185) in the Roma; at corner stands in the mornings; from bicycles and outside traditional Mexican bakeries at night; outside churches on Sunday mornings.

## TORTA DE TAMAL

**What:** A stick-to-your-ribs variation on the typical tamal for breakfast, this is a tamal in a corn husk, stuffed between a sliced bolillo (white-bread roll).
**When:** Early morning.
**Where:** Morning street-corner tamale vendors are the only place you'll find them.

## ELOTES AND ESQUITES

**What:** Elotes are boiled ears of corn served on a stick, slathered in mayonnaise and sprinkled with chili powder, salt, lime juice, and cheese. Esquites are corn kernels, sometimes cooked with the herb epazote, served in a small cup and then topped with mayonnaise, cheese, chili powder, and lime juice.
**When:** Nighttime.
**Where:** Public squares, parks, outside churches and convenience stores; at **Molino El Pujol** (page 183).

## QUESADILLAS

**What:** Hand-pressed corn tortillas stuffed with cheese and fillings, cooked on a griddle or deep-fried. Flor de calabaza (squash flower), hongos (mushrooms), and huitlacoche (corn fungus) are a few of the popular guisados (fillings) for quesadillas. In Mexico City quesadillas may only be filled with a guisado unless you specify that you'd like it con queso (with cheese).
**When:** Afternoon and evening.
**Where:** Parks and street corners; almost any restaurant.

its own secret recipe (and every local a favorite spot to get them). At El Huequito, which opened in 1959, you won't find the typical chili-rubbed pastor, but rather spit-roasted pork tacos that are doused in salsa and rolled into small tortillas. The original stand is still in operation, and you can order a plate of tacos to eat on the street. However, there's also sit-down service.

**MAP 2:** *Ayuntamiento 21; tel. 55/5510-3746; www.elhuequito.mx; 9am-9pm daily; Metro: San Juan de Letrán*

## CAFÉS

### Tacos Domingo $

Tacos al carbón (charcoal-grilled tacos) are the specialty of this taquería, which opened across the street from the tiny tree-filled Plaza Carlos Pacheco in 2024. Fresh off the grill, tacos are served in a soft flour or freshly made corn tortilla (your choice), and it's advisable to accompany them with an order of cebollas preparadas (grilled onions in a salty spicy sauce). The light-filled high-ceilinged space is more stylish than your typical taco joint, and it's a nice place to linger with a beer.

**MAP 2:** *Carlos Pacheco 5; WhatsApp tel. 56/3304-8998; 2pm-10pm Mon. and Wed.-Sat., 11am-7pm Sun.; Metro: Balderas, Metrobús: Balderas*

### Farmacía Internacional $

On the ground floor of a soaring multifamily apartment complex on the busy thoroughfare Bucareli, this all-day café has a cozy-cool ambience, with exposed brick walls and vintage tile floors. The appealing breakfast menu is short but hits all the right notes, with well-made dishes like avocado toast, vegetarian quiche, and soft-boiled eggs with asparagus. The coffee bar is excellent and there's craft beer and wine. You'll find a similarly excellent menu and atmosphere at the newer location in an art deco building in the Condesa (Nuevo Leon 120; tel. 55/1137-8445; 8:30am-6pm Sun.-Tues., 8:30am-11pm Wed.-Sat.).

**MAP 2:** *Bucareli 128-F; https://f-i.com.mx; 8:30am-8:30pm Mon.-Fri., 9am-5pm Sat.-Sun.; Metro: Cuauhtémoc or Balderas, Metrobús: Balderas*

## ASIAN

### Makan $$

A meal at Makan is an experience you'll want to share with friends—and not just because the menu is Singaporean-inspired dishes meant to be eaten family-style. Here, genial service and a jubilant atmosphere are perfect for a night out, complementing the vibrant menu of spicy noodle soups, chili-spiked vegetables, savory roast meats, and delicately seasoned whole fish. Cocktails and desserts are not an afterthought—both are outstanding.

**MAP 2:** *Emilio Dondé 68B; reservations WhatsApp tel. 55/4765-9626; 2pm-10pm Mon.-Sat., 1pm-7pm Sun.; Metro: Balderas, Metrobús: Balderas*

Mercado San Juan

## ITALIAN
### Supplì $

There's a simple sophistication to a meal at Supplì, a Roman-style trattoria built into a teeny-tiny corner dining room (with even smaller kitchen) on historic avenue Bucareli. The menu changes frequently, but the star of the show is always a lineup of homemade pasta dishes, which are accompanied by a short and sweet selection of excellent antipasti, salads, and specials. Come for a glass of rosé, an arugula salad, and a plate of handmade ravioli—and don't skip the tiramisu for dessert.

**MAP 2:** *Bucareli 69B; 2pm-10pm Tues.-Sat., 2pm-6pm Sun.; Metro: Balderas, Metrobús: Balderas*

## MARKETS
### Mercado San Juan $

The San Juan Market is best known for its high-quality and exotic fish, meats, produce, and cheeses, but it is also a great place to nosh. At the market's famous cheesemongers, you can order Spanish-style tapas, baguette sandwiches, or charcuterie and cheese plates; they'll even pour you a small glass of Spanish wine on the house. The most famous is **La Jersey** (Local 147), but most cheese shops offer the same lunch specials. The market is also a favored spot for seafood, freshly sourced from producers. Go to **Cabo San Juan** (Local 94; WhatsApp tel. 55/3655-6580; noon-5pm Wed.-Sun.) for delicious shrimp cocktail, fish tacos, or octopus tostadas.

**MAP 2:** *Ernesto Pugibet 21, between Luis Moya and Buen Tono; no phone; 7am-5pm daily; Metro: San Juan de Letrán*

# Nightlife

## CANTINAS
### ★ Tío Pepe

Located in the Centro's small and quirky Barrio Chino (Chinatown), Tío Pepe is a wonderful old cantina that maintains a worn but grand early 20th-century atmosphere with its polished dark-wood bar, turquoise walls, and gold molding along the ceilings. Come early in the evening to sip tequila at one of the cozy booths with red Formica-topped tables as a friendly relaxed crowd fills the space. Sometimes roving musicians will arrive, enlivening the atmosphere.

**MAP 2:** *Independencia 26; tel. 55/5521-9136; noon-10pm Mon.-Fri., noon-11pm Sat.; no cover; Metro: Bellas Artes*

## TEQUILA AND MEZCAL

### ✪ Bósforo

An unmarked bar a few blocks south of the Alameda Central, Bósforo's specialty is small-batch mezcal from Oaxaca and the greater republic. Bartenders can recommend a drink from the often-changing list, and shots are served with orange wedges and salt, as is traditional. Hidden behind metal doors but often crowded on the weekends, the bar has a great soundtrack and a pleasingly clandestine locals-in-the-know atmosphere.

**MAP 2:** *Luis Moya 31; tel. 55/5512-1991; 4pm-1:30am Wed., 4pm-2:30am Thurs.-Sat.; no cover; Metro: Bellas Artes*

## PULQUERÍAS

### ✪ Pulquería Las Duelistas

Las Duelistas is one of the oldest traditional pulquerías in Mexico City, but you'd never guess it from the predominantly young clientele, who bring a bit of punk-rock vibe to the joint. It's a friendly, convivial place, and the curados are delicious, made fresh daily and served ice-cold, in flavors like celery or guava. Like most traditional pulquerías, it opens early—and sometimes runs out of drinks before the 9pm closing.

**MAP 2:** *Aranda 28; tel. 55/1394-0958; 10am-9pm Mon.-Sat.; no cover; Metro: San Juan de Letrán*

## LIVE MUSIC AND DANCING

### Salón Los Angeles

This old-fashioned dance hall's proud motto is "Quién no conoce Los Angeles, no conoce México" (Who doesn't know Los Angeles, doesn't know Mexico). In operation for nearly 90 years, it is considered a mainstay in the capital's old-school dance scene. Top-quality live bands play son cubano, danzón, rumba, swing, and cumbia, among other tropical sounds, while well-dressed couples dance with purpose. The neighborhood is rough, so come and go by taxi or rideshare. It is only open Tuesday and Saturday.

**MAP 2:** *Lerdo 206, Col. Guerrero; tel. 55/5597-5181 or 55/5597-8847; http://salonlosangeles.mx; 5pm-10pm Tues. and Sat.; cover US$5-10; Metro: Garibaldi*

**TOP EXPERIENCE**

# Pulque: Ancient Drink with a New Life

A fizzy, lightly alcoholic, and nutritious drink called pulque is made from the sap of the maguey plant, native to Mesoamerica. It was considered sacred by the Mexica, who had strict rules regarding its consumption. After the Spanish conquest, pulque became more widely available, and by the 19th century there were pulquerías in every neighborhood of Mexico City. Pulque began to lose its loyal following as beer became more popular. Fortunately, this wonderful drink is experiencing a resurgence today.

pulque

With its viscous and fizzy texture, milky color, and notably sweet yet fermented flavor, pulque is an acquired taste for some. It can be drunk in its natural state, though it is more popular in curados, flavored with fruit pulp or nuts and sweetened with honey or cane sugar. Pulque must be kept cold and consumed within a few days of its production—and the fresher it is, the better it tastes.

Here are a few places, both new and historic, that serve pulque in Mexico City.

- **Pulquería Las Duelistas** is an excellent traditional pulquería, popular with a local crowd (page 102).

- In the Santa María la Ribera, **Pulquería La Joya** is one of the longest-running pulquerías in the city and an ultra-low-key spot for a mug of pulque (page 131). Also in the Santa María, the casual restaurant **Coyota** serves delicious natural pulque and other traditional fermented drinks on its creative bar menu (page 127).

- **El Hidalguense**, a country-style restaurant in the Roma, serves aguamiel (a nonalcoholic drink made from fresh maguey sap), ultra-fresh pulque, and a range of curados made with fresh fruit (page 183).

- **Corazón de Maguey** in Coyoacán specializes in mezcal, but it also serves pulque both natural and in flavored curados, as well as pre-Columbian snacks like fried grasshoppers (page 233).

# Arts and Culture

## MUSEUMS

### Museo del Tequila y El Mezcal

This small museum chronicling the history and culture of agave distillation in Mexico opened as a part of the Plaza Garibaldi's 2010 renovation. In addition to the permanent exhibit, which includes a site-appropriate display dedicated to mariachi music, the museum hosts special events and rotating exhibits related to spirits. Your tour of the museum ends on the roof deck, where guests can enjoy a view of Plaza Garibaldi over a small complimentary shot of tequila and mezcal. You can stay for another drink if you're enjoying the view of the plaza.

**MAP 2:** *Plaza Garibaldi; tel. 55/5529-1238; www.mutemgaribaldi.mx; museum 11am-10pm Sun.-Wed., 11am-midnight Thurs.-Sat.; terrace and cantina 1pm-10pm Sun.-Wed., 1pm-2:30am Thurs.-Sat.; US$4; Metro: Garibaldi*

### Museo Mural Diego Rivera

On a corner of the Alameda Central, this petite museum is dedicated to Diego Rivera's mural *Sueño de una Tarde Dominical en la Alameda Central* (Dream of a Sunday Afternoon in the Alameda

Museo del Tequila y El Mezcal

Central), which he originally created in the 1940s for architect Carlos Obregón Santacilia's Hotel del Prado, which collapsed in the 1985 earthquake. The marvelously composed park scene portrays many famous Mexican personalities, including Hernán Cortés, former presidents Porfirio Díaz and Antonio López de Santa Anna, printmaker José Guadalupe Posada, and artist Frida Kahlo.
**MAP 2:** *Corner of Balderas and Colón; tel. 55/1555-1900; https:// museomuraldiegorivera.inba.gob.mx; 10am-5pm Tues.-Sun.; US$2; Metro: Hidalgo, Metrobús: Hidalgo*

### Laboratorio de Arte Alameda

Mexico City's penchant for combining avant-garde ideas and old-fashioned spaces is beautifully manifested in the Laboratorio de Arte Alameda. Housed in the former convent of San Diego, right on the Alameda Central, this contemporary art museum's usually excellent exhibitions explore the relationship between art and technology. As such, there is often a heavy emphasis on video and electronic art, with many works conceived specifically for the space.
**MAP 2:** *Dr. Mora 7; no phone; https://artealameda.inba.gob.mx; 11am-5pm Tues.-Sun.; US$3, free for students, teachers, and seniors, free Sun.; Metro: Hidalgo, Metrobús: Hidalgo*

### Museo Kaluz

It's worth visiting this small museum to see the interior of the historic Hospedería de Santo Tómas de Villanueva, more recently known as the Hotel Cortés, which was constructed in the 17th century and long served as a hotel for visitors to the city. Note the beautiful baroque niche above the door, which dates from 1780. The museum, which opened in 2021, has a collection of Mexican art, historic and contemporary; some of the most interesting pieces depict Mexico City through history. The top-floor terrace has a quiet café and nice views of the Alameda Central.
**MAP 2:** *Hidalgo 85; tel. 55/2345-3168; https://museokaluz.org; 10am-6pm Wed.-Mon.; US$5, US$2 students, teachers, and seniors, free Wed.; Metro: Hidalgo, Metrobús: Hidalgo*

### Museo Franz Mayer

Explore the roots of Mexican artisanal and aesthetic traditions at this interesting design museum, which displays the impressive collection of German-born financier Franz Mayer, including furniture, religious artifacts, tapestries, and

the roof deck at Museo Kaluz

books dating from the 16th-19th centuries. In addition to Mayer's collection, the museum continues to make new acquisitions and hold ongoing shows dedicated to contemporary decorative arts. Located in the former San Juan de Dios monastery, the space itself is both historic and beautiful, and the popular patio café on the 1st floor is a wonderful spot to enjoy it with a cup of coffee.

**MAP 2:** *Av. Hidalgo 45; tel. 55/5518-2266; https://franzmayer.org.mx; 10am-5pm Tues.-Sun.; US$6, US$3 students, teachers, and seniors, free Tues.; Metro: Hidalgo or Bellas Artes, Metrobús: Hidalgo*

## Museo Nacional de la Estampa

Printmaking has an important place in Mexican art and popular culture, and the Museo Nacional de la Estampa, or MUNAE, celebrates that tradition with ongoing exhibitions of woodcut, lithography, engraving, and other printed works by Mexican artists. The museum's collection of more than 12,000 prints includes works by David Alfaro Siqueiros and Rufino Tamayo, as well as an extensive collection of work by celebrated Mexican satirist and printmaker José Guadalupe Posada.

**MAP 2:** *Hidalgo 39, Plaza de la Santa Veracruz; tel. 55/8647-5220; www.museonacionaldelaestampa.bellasartes.gob.mx; 10am-6pm Tues.-Sun.; US$3, free students and teachers, free Sun.; Metro: Bellas Artes, Metrobús: Hidalgo*

Museo Franz Mayer

## ✪ Museo de Arte Popular

The Museo de Arte Popular (MAP), in a five-story art deco building, is dedicated to the preservation and exhibition of Mexican folk art and craft. Unlike most craft museums, MAP isn't organized by region or chronology, but by theme, like "religion," "parties," and "daily life," with antique and contemporary pieces from a range of traditions exhibited together. Many of the pieces on display are highly original and rare, although the museum also makes space for beautiful everyday objects and simpler handicrafts. In the 5th-floor galleries, there is a wonderful 1947 mural by Mexican artist Miguel Covarrubias that was rescued from a nearby building and installed at the museum. On the 2nd floor, the museum hosts temporary exhibitions.

**MAP 2:** *Revillagigedo 11, entrance on Independencia; tel. 55/5510-2201; www.map.cdmx.gob.mx; 10am-6pm Tues.-Sun.; US$3; Metro: Juárez, Metrobús: Hidalgo*

## Museo Memoria y Tolerancia

This striking modern museum, designed to promote tolerance,

nonviolence, and human rights, has a permanent exhibition divided into two parts: Memory, which explores 20th-century genocides, starting with the Holocaust, and Tolerance, which explores diversity, dialogue, human rights, and related themes, both in Mexico and internationally. There is a kid-centric exhibit, designed to teach unity and tolerance to schoolchildren. Most interesting, however, are the museum's thematic exhibits, such as the artist-driven *LGBT+ allá del Arcoíris* in 2021 or the 2016 Yoko Ono show *Land of Hope*.

**MAP 2:** *Plaza Juárez s/n; tel. 55/5130-5555; www.myt.org.mx; 9am-6pm Tues.-Fri., 10am-7pm Sat.-Sun.; permanent collection US$8, temporary exhibits US$5, US$4 students, teachers, and seniors; Metro: Bellas Artes or Hidalgo, Metrobús: Bellas Artes or Hidalgo*

### Centro de la Imagen

Highly recommended for photographers and photography lovers, this breathtaking public photography gallery has extensive exhibition spaces, projection rooms, and a changing outdoor "photo mural." The center offers frequent workshops and special events, while ongoing exhibits focus on both contemporary work and the history of photography. It's worth visiting the space just to see the architectural creativity of the galleries, built inside a renovated 18th-century cigarette factory, and the exhibits are reliably high quality.

**MAP 2:** *Plaza de la Ciudadela 2; tel. 55/4155-0850; https://centrodelaimagen.cultura.gob.mx; 11am-6pm Wed.-Sun.; free; Metro: Balderas, Metrobús: Juárez*

## THEATER, CLASSICAL MUSIC, AND DANCE

### Palacio de Bellas Artes

The theater inside the Palacio de Bellas Artes is the building's opulent keystone, with box seats rising along the stage, murals on the walls, and a Tiffany glass curtain onstage. The performance schedule features international music and dance, but particularly noteworthy is the **Ballet Folklórico de México de Amalia Hernández,** which performs in the theater every Tuesday and Sunday and showcases traditional dances and music from across Mexico, performed in colorful costume.

**MAP 2:** *Eje Central and Av. Juárez; tel. 55/8647-6500, ext. 2152, 2153, or 2154; www.palacio.bellasartes.gob.mx, www.balletfolkloricodemexico.com.mx; showtimes vary; US$15-150; Metro: Bellas Artes*

Palacio de Bellas Artes

## Lucha Libre

Lucha libre, a theatrical, upbeat, and athletic style of wrestling, has been one of Mexico's most popular spectator sports since the early 20th century. Lucha libre bears some resemblance to professional wrestling in the United States, with dramatic choreographed performances, long-standing and contentious rivalries between wrestlers, and storylines driven by the divide between the "good guys" (known in Mexico as the tecnicos) and the "bad guys" (rudos). However, lucha libre matches are stylistically different from what you'd find in the WWE ring, incorporating fighters from lighter weight classes and a strong emphasis on acrobatics and aerial moves. The best wrestlers are superb athletes and charismatic showmen, drawing diverse fans and riling up the crowd with their performances.

lucha libre masks

### HEROES OF LUCHA

Although the sport emerged in Mexico at the beginning of the 20th century, its popularity reached an apex during the 1950s, when luchadores (wrestlers) became tremendously famous outside the ring. The most

# Recreation

## SPECTATOR SPORTS
### Lucha Libre

#### ✪ Arena México

The incredible showmanship and athleticism of Mexico's famed lucha libre matches are on display every week at Arena México, an upbeat and convivial professional wrestling ring, which has been in business for more than 50 years. Things can get a bit rowdy in the rows close to the ring—and it's par for the course for spectators to yell at the wrestlers. Sunday is family day, and the best choice for attending a match with kids, who also get a discount on ticket prices.

**MAP 2:** *Dr. La Vista 189, Col. Doctores; tel. 55/5588-0508; www.cmll.com; matches usually evening Tues. and Fri., afternoon Sun.; US$10-25; Metro: Cuauhtémoc*

notable name from that era, silver-masked El Santo (The Saint) remains the best-known Mexican wrestler to this day. El Santo and other big stars—like Blue Demon, Mil Máscaras, and, later, Blue Demon Jr. and El Santo's son (appropriately known as El Hijo de Santo)—are also beloved for their starring roles in a slew of hammy films from the 1950s and 1960s, wherein famous wrestlers duke it out with mummies, vampires, and other improbable villains.

### THE MASK

In the ring, many wrestlers have flamboyant alter egos, and they typically dress in flashy leggings and capes. Many don a signature face-covering mask, which conceals their true identity from the public. In important matches, opponents will often bet their masks in the duel; the loser must remove his mask at the end, the ultimate sacrifice for a luchador.

Today, wrestling masks are a popular souvenir; you can buy one from vendors outside the Arena México on the night of a match, or find them at markets, hip boutiques, and design shops, including **Blue Demon Jr. Galería** (page 110) and **La Ciudadela Centro Artesanal** (page 110).

### LUCHA TODAY

Like many of Mexico's inimitable traditions, lucha libre is experiencing a surge in popularity. New stars, like the wrestler Místico, attract huge crowds in Mexico, and the sport has gained an international following. In the United States, a popular children's cartoon, *Mucha Lucha,* stars Mexican wrestlers as protagonists. Mexican-style lucha libre is also very popular in Japan, and several Japanese luchadores have gained widespread popularity in Mexico.

# Shops

## ART, ANTIQUES, AND COLLECTIBLES

### ✪ La Lagunilla

The popular La Lagunilla flea market sets up along the Paseo de la Reforma every Sunday, spilling onto a few side streets heading east into the market neighborhood of Tepito. It's an interesting place to wander for an hour or two, browsing the piles of old books, silverware, luggage, curios, movie posters, vinyl records, antique furniture, art, tin toys, old photographs, vintage jewelry, and other unique items for sale. It's also a popular place for day drinking; as the supply of antiques has dwindled across Mexico, many vendors get by selling beer and micheladas to shoppers. Get there early for the best selection, and keep an eye on your belongings as you wander.

**MAP 2:** *Several blocks east of and along Paseo de la Reforma at Eje 1 Norte; 9am-5pm Sun.; Metro: Garibaldi*

### Blue Demon Jr. Galería

Lucha libre superstar Blue Demon Jr., son of the legendary wrestler Blue Demon, opened this gallery and souvenir shop across the street from the Plaza de la Ciudadela in 2022. Wrestling masks, plush toys, T-shirts, action figures, paintings, mugs, and myriad other souvenirs created in homage to Blue Demon Jr. are on sale, as well as Blue Demon Jr.'s own artwork. Blue Demon Jr. is sometimes in house on days when he doesn't have a fight, and he'll happily sign any merchandise you pick up—and even pose for a photo.

**MAP 2:** *Emilio Dondé 7; tel. 55/5444-1813; 10:30am-6:30pm daily; Metro: Balderas, Metrobús: Balderas*

## ARTS AND CRAFTS
### La Ciudadela Centro Artesanal

La Ciudadela is a sprawling open-air craft market where over 300 vendors sell handmade products from across the country. Prices here are incredibly reasonable, and the selection is extensive, covering many of Mexico's major craft traditions, from Tlaquepaque's colorful ceramics and Pueblan blue-and-white Talavera to wooden utensils, woven baskets, shawls, and musical instruments. Take your time browsing the selection as quality varies tremendously by vendor.

**MAP 2:** *Plaza de la Ciudadela 1 and 5; tel. 55/5510-1828; http://laciudadela.com.mx; 10am-8pm Tues.-Sat., 10am-4pm Sun.; Metro: Balderas; Metrobús: Balderas*

## PUBLIC MARKETS
### Mercado San Juan

The San Juan market is known for its exotic produce, unusual meats like crocodile and iguana, fresh fish, and abundance of gourmet and imported products. It's a great place to shop for food to take home, like mole sauce and vanilla beans, or to pick up something unusual, like starfruit or razor clams. It's small but densely packed, so wander around to see what's on offer; many vendors will offer you a taste of what they're selling.

**MAP 2:** *Ernesto Pugibet, between Luis Moya and Plaza de San Juan; 7am-5pm daily, vendor hours vary; Metro: San Juan de Letrán*

**TOP EXPERIENCE**

# Public Markets

Mercado San Juan

Often atmospheric and interesting, neighborhood markets are among the best places to shop for fruits and vegetables, dairy, meat, and tortillas. Many have a well-known specialty, like delicious seafood stands or a large selection of flowers and piñatas.

- If you only have time to visit one market, there is none more emblematic of the city than the immense and atmospheric **Mercado de la Merced** (page 70) on the edge of the Centro Histórico. Right next to the Merced, the **Mercado Sonora** (page 85) is best known for its offbeat, esoteric offerings, like medicinal herbs, healing candles, witchcraft products, and live animals.

- The **Mercado San Juan** (page 110) in the old San Juan neighborhood is known throughout the city for its unusual selection of meats and produce, like quail eggs, tropical fruits, alligator steaks, toasted grasshoppers, and other delicacies. It's also a great place for a snack.

- For traditional fruits, vegetables, tortillas, Mexican crafts, souvenirs, and lots of eateries serving seafood and tostadas, **Mercado Coyoacán** (page 235) in central Coyoacán is an atmospheric destination popular with both tourists and locals.

- For an on-the-ground perspective on Mexico City's food economy, head to the **Central de Abasto de la Ciudad de México** (page 261), a wholesale market that supplies 80 percent of the capital's edibles. There is nothing you won't find here, from potatoes to crabmeat, and the sheer size is astonishing.

# Paseo de la Reforma  Map 3

Getting Around........113
Paseo de la
   Reforma Walk........116
Sights.................120
Restaurants............124
Nightlife...............130
Arts and Culture.......132
Festivals and Events....134
Recreation.............135
Shops.................138

The Paseo de la Reforma is a monument-studded avenue lined with high-rise office buildings and luxury hotels. In the 19th century, as the Centro Histórico became more crowded, wealthy families began moving to new European-style neighborhoods that were cropping up around this grand avenue. Among these were the San Rafael, Tabacalera, and Santa María la Ribera neighborhoods to the north of Reforma and the Juárez to the south. Today auto shops, taco stands, and old coffee joints continue to operate alongside boutiques, contemporary art galleries, and museums. To the southwest of the San Rafael, the Cuauhtémoc neighborhood is a pretty residential area long inhabited by foreigners with business at the US Embassy.

# Highlights

✪ **La Alameda de Santa María:** In the heart of the Santa María la Ribera neighborhood, this public plaza has an impressive Moorish pavilion at its center and is adjoined by historic mansions (page 120).

✪ **Monumento a la Revolución Mexicana:** One of the city's stateliest monuments has art deco details and a rooftop observation deck (page 121).

✪ **Museo Universitario del Chopo:** Thought-provoking contemporary art exhibits, often with a focus on urban subcultures, are the focus of this alt museum and cultural center (page 134).

✪ **Paseo Dominical:** Thousands of cyclists, roller bladers, Zumba enthusiasts, and dog walkers flood the iconic Paseo de la Reforma on Sunday mornings, when the avenue is closed to motor traffic (page 137).

✪ **Juárez Shopping District:** The Juárez neighborhood now rivals the adjoining Roma as a dining, nightlife, and shopping destination, with lots of independent boutiques and galleries located in its 19th-century mansions (page 138).

# Getting Around

- Metro lines: 1, 2
- Metro stops: Insurgentes, Sevilla, Chapultepec, Cuauhtémoc, Revolución, San Cosme, Buenavista
- Metrobús lines: 1
- Metrobús stops: Insurgentes, Hamburgo, Reforma, Revolución, Buenavista

**Previous:** cycling the Paseo de la Reforma; **Above:** Museo Universitario del Chopo; Sundays on the Paseo de la Reforma.

113

# Paseo de la Reforma

# Paseo de la Reforma Walk

**TOTAL DISTANCE:** 3 km (1.8 mi)
**TOTAL WALKING TIME:** 45 minutes

The central stretch of the Paseo de la Reforma, which runs from the Centro Histórico through the Bosque de Chapultepec, is one of the city's main thoroughfares. A wide, old-fashioned avenue designed to resemble the grand boulevards of Europe, it was first commissioned by Hapsburg emperor Maximilian and completed by President Porfirio Díaz at the end of the 19th century. Fashionable neighborhoods cropped up quickly along Reforma, and the avenue remains one of the city's most exclusive addresses.

On Sunday, the avenue is closed to automobile traffic 8am-2pm, so it's a wonderful time to take a stroll or rent a bike for a leisurely exploration of Reforma's many monuments and public sculptures, from the Alameda Central to the main entrance of the Bosque de Chapultepec.

**1** Occupying the enviable address Paseo de la Reforma 1, the art deco **Edificio El Moro**—better known to many as La Lotería

statue of Diana Cazadora on the Paseo de la Reforma

Nacional, the home of the national lottery—was inaugurated in 1945. This elegant skyscraper, with its strip of windows running up the front facade, was once the tallest building in Mexico City. It suffered serious damage in the September 2017 earthquake, evident from the cracks in its facade, and is currently waiting for funds for its full restoration.

*Walk about 500 m (0.3 mi) west of La Lotería Nacional.*

**2** The statue of Christopher Columbus atop the **Monumento a Colón** was finally removed in 2020 by then-head of government Claudia Sheinbaum following decades of protest from political activists and the sculpture's frequent defacement. Today, the traffic circle honors Indigenous women with the replica of a pre-Columbian sculpture known as **La Joven de Amajac**.

*Walk another 500 m (0.3 mi) west.*

**3** **Monumento a Cuauhtémoc** stands at the intersection of Paseo de la Reforma and Insurgentes. Cuauhtémoc was the last leader of the city of Tenochtitlan, who led the Mexica people in their final stand against the Spanish invaders in 1521 in Tlatelolco, just a few kilometers from this spot.

*Continue on Paseo de la Reforma to the next traffic circle.*

Monumento a Cuauhtémoc

**4** The palm tree at the center of the traffic circle, just west of Insurgentes, grew sick and was removed, with great fanfare, in 2022, after over 100 years on the spot. It was replaced by an ahuehuete, a type of cypress native to Mexico and the country's national tree. Northwest of the tree, you'll see the futuristic **Bolsa Mexicana de Valores,** the home of the Mexican stock exchange, designed by architect Juan José Díaz Infante Núñez.

*Continue on Paseo de la Reforma, past the US Embassy.*

**5** At the next major intersection, one of the city's most iconic landmarks, the **Ángel de la Independencia,** was erected by President Porfirio Díaz as a tribute to Mexico's independence from Spain. It fell from the top of its pedestal and broke during the earthquake of 1957, but has survived all subsequent earthquakes from its post.

*Continue on Paseo de la Reforma to the westernmost traffic circle before Chapultepec.*

Ángel de la Independencia

**6** Admire the circular fountain topped by a statue of the Roman goddess **Diana Cazadora** (Diana the Huntress), constructed in 1942. Diana's nudity created such a scandal that the sculptor, Juan Francisco Olaguíbel, was forced to add bronze undergarments. The bronze clothing was removed in 1967, in anticipation of the Mexico City Olympics in 1968.

*Continue west on Paseo de la Reforma.*

Estela de la Luz and the Torre Mayor

**7** Just east of the main entrance to the Bosque de Chapultepec are four of the city's tallest skyscrapers—the **Torre Reforma,** the **Torre BBVA Bancomer,** the **Torre Mayor,** and **Chapultepec Uno,** which was completed in 2019 and is home to a new Ritz-Carlton hotel. On the opposite side of Reforma, just outside Chapultepec's main entrance, the **Estela de la Luz** (Pillar of Light) is a 104-m (341-ft) quartz-covered tower commemorating the 2010 bicentennial of Mexico's independence from Spain and the concurrent centennial of the Revolution of 1910. Its construction was mired in controversy, first by going massively over budget and later for overshooting its construction deadline by 15 months and missing the anniversary celebrations altogether. If you aren't worn out, continue your tour through the **Bosque de Chapultepec** (page 144).

# Sights

### Museo de Geología
UNAM's wonderful geology museum is housed in a historic mansion on the west side of the Alameda de Santa María. In the main galleries are massive woolly mammoth and dinosaur skeletons, while beautiful vintage glass cases hold the museum's collection of fossils, stones, minerals, and meteorites in adjoining rooms. The opulent building was originally commissioned by Porfirio Díaz in the 19th century, and some visitors are more interested in the space than its contents: The sweeping art nouveau wrought-iron staircase in the entryway is a highlight.

**MAP 3:** *Jaime Torres Bodet 176; tel. 55/5547-3948 or 55/5547-3900; www.geologia.unam.mx; 10am-5pm Tues.-Sun.; US$2; Metro: Buenavista, Metrobús: Buenavista*

### ✪ La Alameda de Santa María
The main attraction of this tranquil tree-filled park at the center of the Santa María la Ribera neighborhood is the gorgeous, brightly colored Moorish-style kiosk in the middle of the square, made entirely of iron. It was originally constructed for Mexico's pavilion at the World's Fair in 1886 and was moved to several locations around

Moorish kiosk in La Alameda de Santa María

Biblioteca Vasconcelos

computers, or attend free concerts in the library's auditorium. An on-site bookstore is run by Conaculta, the National Council for Culture and Arts.

**MAP 3:** *Eje 1 Norte (Mosqueta), at Aldama; tel. 55/9157-2800; https:// bibliotecavasconcelos.gob.mx; 8:30am-4:30pm daily; free; Metro: Buenavista, Metrobús: Buenavista*

Mexico City before settling in its current location in the Santa María.

**MAP 3:** *Between Dr. Atl and Salvador Díaz Mirón; 24 hours daily; free; Metro: Buenavista, Metrobús: Buenavista*

### Biblioteca Vasconcelos

This huge, architecturally stunning public library, designed by Mexican architects Alberto Kalach and Juan Palomar, opened next to the Buenavista train station in 2006. Its unique layout features "floating" bookshelves that surround a towering central atrium, filled with comfortable chairs and desks for reading. Hanging from the roof in the middle of the space is the famous "whale" sculpture, *Matrix Móvil,* by artist Gabriel Orozco.

Despite the overall beauty of the project, the library was mired in controversy for both its cost and unexpected construction issues after its opening. Even so, critics cannot diminish the original design of the building, which also serves as an informal public space where locals and families roam through the stacks, take advantage of the free internet-connected

### ✪ Monumento a la Revolución Mexicana

Mexico City's monument to the Revolution of 1910 wasn't originally designed as a war memorial: The towering dome was built during the first phase of construction on a luxurious, neoclassical congressional building, commissioned by President Porfirio Díaz in the early 20th century. When the Revolution of 1910 broke out, the project was abandoned.

In 1933, Carlos Obregón Santacilia took over the project. He completed the volcanic-stone facade and added art deco finishes to each of the four corners, working with sculptor Oliverio Martínez. Crypts in the monument's feet hold the remains of Revolution heroes Venustiano Carranza, Francisco I. Madero, Francisco "Pancho" Villa, Plutarco Elias Calles, and Lázaro Cárdenas.

Leading up to the 2010 centennial of the Revolution, the monument and surrounding plaza received a full renovation, which included the addition of a glass elevator that ascends from the ground floor to the monument's

the Monumento a la Revolución Mexicana

dome, where visitors can stroll beneath the vaulted roof and along outdoor balconies with a view of the city below, or have a drink at the rooftop café Emile, which operates while the monument is open to the public.

The basement-level **Museo Nacional de la Revolución** (tel. 55/5566-1902; 9am-5pm Mon.-Fri., 9am-7pm Sat.-Sun.) opened as a part of the renovation project. The permanent exhibit chronicles the major events and philosophies that drove different factions to action during the Revolution of 1910, as well as a few period artifacts, like Pancho Villa's riding saddle and vintage guns.

**MAP 3:** *Plaza de la República s/n, between Av. de la Republica and Gómez Farias; tel. 55/5546-0346; www.mrm.mx; noon-8pm Mon.-Thurs., noon-10pm Fri.-Sat., 10am-8pm Sun.; US$8; Metro: Revolución, Metrobús: Tabacalera, Caballito*

### Ángel de la Independencia

In the center of a busy traffic circle on the Paseo de la Reforma, the Ángel de la Independencia is a striking 36-m-high (118-ft) column topped with a gold-plated bronze angel. It was inaugurated by President Porfirio Díaz on September 16, 1910, to commemorate the country's centennial of independence from Spain. One of the city's most recognizable landmarks, it is the site of frequent political rallies and spontaneous street celebrations whenever Mexico's national soccer team pulls off a victory. And, like many Mexican monuments, it's had its share of drama: In 1957, the bronze angel toppled from its perch during a major earthquake.

When crossing Reforma to the

monument, use caution—there are no official crosswalks, and traffic flows from all four directions. Within the column's base, a small passageway contains three niches that store the remains of 12 heroes from the independence struggle.
**MAP 3:** *Paseo de la Reforma and Florencia; free; Metro: Insurgentes*

### Zona Rosa
Though its beautiful Porfiriato-era mansions were built in the 19th century, the Zona Rosa became a famous bohemian enclave in the mid-20th century, eventually becoming the most fashionable arts and nightlife district in the city. Once a must-see for any visitor, today it's less appealing, filled with fast-food restaurants, loud nightclubs, and currency exchange houses. That said, there are still some nice hotels and good eats in the area, and it is famous for its LGBTQ+-friendly attitude, with gay nightlife concentrated on the street Amberes.
**MAP 3:** *Bordered by the Paseo de la Reforma to the north, Av. Chapultepec to the south, Insurgentes to the east, and Florencia to the west*

Zona Rosa

# Goodbye, Columbus

The traffic circle that was dedicated to Columbus now honors Indigenous women.

Commissioned in the 19th century by short-lived Mexican monarch Emperor Maximiliano de Hapsburg, the Paseo de la Reforma is a wide tree-filled boulevard, originally designed to resemble the grand avenues of Europe. Today it is a well-known landmark and an important cross-city artery, running from the Lomas to Chapultepec to the shrine of the Virgen de Guadalupe at La Villa. Along its central section, the avenue is a bit of an open-air museum, dotted with tributes and statues to historic figures and events. Highly symbolic, these monuments are often sites of protest and gathering, particularly at the **Ángel de la Independencia,** where crowds gather to celebrate a victory in a soccer game or protest a rise in oil prices.

# Restaurants

## PRICE KEY

| | |
|---|---|
| $ | Entrées less than US$10 |
| $$ | Entrées US$10-20 |
| $$$ | Entrées more than US$20 |

## MEXICAN

### Tamales Madre $

Tamales, a staple of Mexican cuisine, are given star treatment at this tiny Juárez eatery. Made with heirloom corn and filled with locally sourced ingredients like cacao or plantain, they are delicate and delicious—and unlike most tamales, which are made with manteca de cerdo (lard), they are predominantly vegetarian. In addition to the namesake dish, there are

For many years, the **Monumento a Colón** was among the most prominent statues on the Paseo de la Reforma. Conservative president Antonio Escandón commissioned the statue, which showed Christopher Columbus surrounded by the figures of three Spanish friars who helped evangelize the western hemisphere. It stood at a prominent traffic circle near the hotel Fiesta Americana for close to 150 years.

For decades, activist groups protested the statue's placement and the legacy it glorifies. The monument was frequently defaced, and on several occasions protesters tried to topple the statue from its pedestal, although they were stopped by city police. Calls for the statue's removal intensified in the summer of 2020, when monuments, statues, and buildings in the United States and across the world were being renamed or removed as part of a massive social justice movement.

On October 10, 2020, just two days before the October 12 holiday that commemorates Columbus's landing in the Americas (celebrated in Mexico as Día de la Raza), the city government removed the statue of Columbus. It was initially announced that the figure had been removed for routine restoration; many months later, then chief of government Claudia Sheinbaum revealed that the statue would not be returned to the Paseo de la Reforma. In its place, the city would install a monument to honor Indigenous women, selecting the sculpture *Tlali* by well-known Mexican artist Pedro Reyes to top the pedestal.

In the days following the announcement, there was a public outcry regarding the selection of Reyes, a male artist who does not identify as Indigenous. In response, Sheinbaum shifted the selection process to the Comité de Monumentos y Obras Artísticas en el Espacio Público de la Ciudad de México (Committee for Monuments and Artistic Works in the Public Spaces of Mexico City), who later announced that the circle would display a replica of *La Joven de Amajac*, a pre-Columbian sculpture depicting a female goddess or ruler from the Huasteca region in Veracruz. The original is part of the collection at the Museo de Antropología in Chapultepec.

coffee drinks, hot chocolate, delicious atole (a sweetened corn-based drink), and beer.
**MAP 3:** *Calle Liverpool 44; tel. 55/3191-5331; https://tamalesmadre.com; 8am-6pm Tues.-Sun.; Metro: Cuauhtémoc, Metrobús: Hamburgo*

### El Pialadero de Guadalajara $
On the western edge of the Juárez neighborhood near Chapultepec, this always-bustling family-style restaurant serves food from the state of Jalisco, including an outstanding carne en su jugo (a beef stew typical to Guadalajara), birria (goat stew), and pozole, a hominy soup with spiced broth, served with oregano, diced onion, radishes, and cabbage. The service is lickety-split and the atmosphere is thoroughly Mexican, with framed portraits of horses on the walls, drinks served in big clay jugs,

and traditional wood-and-leather furniture.

**MAP 3:** *Hamburgo 332; tel. 55/5211-7708; www.elpialaderodeguadalajara.mx; 10am-9pm Mon.-Fri., 9am-9pm Sat.-Sun.; Metro: Chapultepec*

## Beatricita $

At the turn of the 20th century, a taco shop owned by Beatriz Muciño Reyes—nicknamed "La Beatricita"—was all the rage in the capital. The taquería proliferated throughout the city, and though most branches have since closed, the Beatricita in the Zona Rosa maintains the legacy. Now a small fonda, Beatricita caters to a local crowd with tasty, inexpensive breakfast and lunch, served with a basket of handmade tortillas, which come to the table so hot you can barely hold them.

view from the plant-filled sidewalk seating at Tamales Madre

**MAP 3:** *Londres 190D; tel. 55/5511-4213; 10am-5pm daily; Metro: Insurgentes*

El Pialadero de Guadalajara

### La Casa de Toño $

Inexpensive and centrally located, La Casa de Toño is a mainstay in the Zona Rosa and throughout the city, best known for its generously served pozole, a Mexican hominy soup garnished with onion, oregano, radishes, and lettuce—though you can also get a plate of enchiladas, flautas, tostadas, or guacamole at this super-casual spot. The restaurant is frequently packed, even in the off-hours, and a wait is guaranteed at weekend brunch.

**MAP 3:** *Londres 144; tel. 55/5386-1125; http://lacasadetono.com.mx; 24 hours daily; Metro: Insurgentes, Metrobús: Insurgentes*

### ✪ Coyota $$

Unconventional, creative, and ultra-casual Coyota, set beside a surprisingly tranquil urban park in the Santa Maria La Ribera, is ideal for a relaxed afternoon after sightseeing in the neighborhood. If you come with friends, it may be possible to sample everything on the petite menu, which changes monthly and is mostly plant-based, featuring dishes like cactus-mango ceviche and tamales in mole. Equally appealing is the bar, which offers traditional fermented drinks tepache (made from fermented pineapple) and a delicious natural pulque, and micheladas, margaritas, and craft beer. And don't miss dessert, especially if the luscious goat-cheese flan or dulce de frijol is on the menu.

**MAP 3:** *Jardín Mascarones 12, Local 9; no phone; 2pm-7pm Wed.-Thurs. and Sun., 2pm-10pm Fri.-Sat.; Metro: San Cosme, Metrobús: Reforma*

## CANTINAS

### ✪ Salón Ríos $

This lively bar and restaurant in the Cuauhtémoc neighborhood is contemporary in feeling, yet inspired by classic cantinas. The relaxed atmosphere, attentive service, boisterous crowd, and classic bar snacks (ceviche, duck tacos) make it a lovely Friday-evening destination—as the crowds attest. The centerpiece of the bustling salon is the handsome, huge, and well-stocked wood-and-mirror bar, where tattooed bartenders serve up an endless stream of drinks, all swiftly shuttled to waiting tables.

**MAP 3:** *Río Lerma 220, Cuauhtémoc; tel. 55/5207-5272; http://salonrios.mx; noon-2am Tues.-Sat., noon-midnight Sun.-Mon.; Metro: Chapultepec, Metrobús: El Ángel*

## TACOS, TORTAS, AND SNACKS

### Los Kuinitos $

At this long-running taquería in the Santa María la Ribera, tender carnitas (braised pork) are chopped on a wood block right before your eyes, scooped generously into warm tortillas, topped with cilantro and diced onion, and plated with a piece of fresh chicharrón (deep-fried pork skin). Los Kuinitos is also famous for its savory gorditas (round corn cakes) stuffed with chicharron prensado (spiced deep-fried pork skin).

Salón Ríos

**MAP 3:** *Sor Juana Inés de la Cruz 91-B; tel. 55/5547-6326; 9am-6pm daily; Metro: Buenavista, Metrobús: Buenavista*

## ASIAN

### Rokai and Rokai Ramen $$$

On a quiet street in the Cuauhtémoc neighborhood, the tiny bistro Rokai has earned a reputation for serving some of the best Japanese food in the city, including sushi that is superlatively fresh and delicious. Rokai Ramen, next door to the original izakaya, offers the same excellent sushi, but the focus is on the steaming bowls of ramen, filled with tender handmade noodles. Both restaurants, equally small, have an appealing Japanese-inspired minimalist design—and both are very popular. Reserve in advance or expect a wait on weekends.

**MAP 3:** *Río Ebro 87 and 89; WhatsApp tel. 56/3035-4220; www.edokobayashi.com; 1pm-11pm Mon.-Sat., 1pm-7pm Sun.; Metro: Insurgentes*

### Nadefo $

Once you walk through the doors of this spacious Korean spot, it's hard to believe you're still in Mexico City. Here, a predominantly Korean crowd gathers around big tables, each with a central grill, lingering late into the evening over boisterous conversation and bottles of soju. The thing to order here is cuts of raw meat (tongue, shrimp, and rib are all excellent), which you cook tableside and top with one of the many condiments brought out to you.

**MAP 3:** *Liverpool 183; tel. 55/5525-0351; 12:30pm-10:30pm daily; Metro: Sevilla*

# INTERNATIONAL

## Cicatriz Cafe $$

The menu is short and sweet at this Juárez bistro and cocktail bar, and the industrial-chic vibe inside goes well with the cool American-style fare on offer. Have ricotta toast or a chia bowl for breakfast, get a kale salad or tuna salad in the afternoon, or just drop in for a coffee or a cocktail. At night, it's as much a bar as restaurant, and worth visiting for the interesting, creative crowd.

**MAP 3:** *Dinamarca 44; no phone; www.cicatrizcafe.com; 9am-midnight daily; Metro: Insurgentes or Cuauhtémoc, Metrobús: Hamburgo*

## ★ Café Nin $

The perfectly made pastries, breads, and cakes from Panadería Rosetta deserve to be eaten on a pretty plate, in a gorgeous old home, and accompanied by a top-notch espresso drink. Achieving this particular breakfast-time nirvana is reason alone to visit Café Nin, the Juárez café run by Rosetta chef-owner Elena Reygadas. In addition to the breads, you can order from the full breakfast menu, which includes dishes like chilaquiles with burrata and a tomato-and-goat-cheese quiche; come in the afternoon for a sandwich or fresh-made gnocchi.

**MAP 3:** *Havre 73; tel. 55/9155-4805; www.cafenin.com.mx; 7am-9pm Mon.-Sat., 7:30am-6pm Sun.; Metro: Insurgentes, Metrobús: Hamburgo*

Cicatriz Cafe

## COFFEE AND SWEETS

### La Especial de Paris $

In operation since 1921, this tiny ice cream shop is easy to overlook along traffic-choked Insurgentes, but it is the surprising home of the best old-fashioned nieves in Mexico City. Every flavor here is crafted by hand using natural ingredients, and options run from old-fashioned choices like Veracruz vanilla bean to more unique choices like ginger, cardamom, and cacao. Sit at the bar, order a cone, and listen to the friendly ice cream scooper discuss the making of artisanal sweets.

**MAP 3:** *Insurgentes 117; tel. 55/9131-5937; noon-8:30pm daily; Metro: Revolución, Metrobús: Reforma*

### ✪ Chocolatería La Rifa $

At this small storefront and café, native Mexican chocolate, sourced from the states of Tabasco, Chiapas, and Oaxaca, is made into candies, bars, and, most notably, beverages, both hot and cold. When ordering, you can choose between a drink prepared sweet, bittersweet, or bitter, made with hot water (as is traditional in Mexico) or milk. La Rifa also serves coffee (some spiked with chocolate, naturally) and snacks, like tamales and sweet breads, to accompany your beverage.

**MAP 3:** *Dinamarca 47; tel. 55/9155-8551; 8:30am-9pm daily; Metro: Insurgentes, Metrobús: Hamburgo*

# Nightlife

## BARS AND LOUNGES

### Cananea

The wood-paneled walls, old-fashioned oil paintings, and stained-glass windows in this Juárez bar feel much more akin to 1924 than 2024, when this hot spot first opened its doors. But the anachronistic backdrop—complemented by an excellent selection of music and a supremely cool crowd—is part of what makes Cananea such a fun place for a cocktail. Even with a two-story barroom, there's a standing-room-only crowd on the weekend.

**MAP 3:** *Marsella 28; no phone; 4pm-2am Tues.-Sat.; Metro: Cuauhtémoc, Metrobús: Hamburgo*

### Fiebre de Malta

The expansion of pandemic-era sidewalk seating gave a needed improvement to the ambience at this small taproom, and the big selection of Mexican craft beer is the reason to put it on your list. Here, you'll find more than a dozen Mexican brews on tap—often including Mexico City breweries Falling Piano, Cyprez, and Morenos—and dozens more in bottles. Beer trumps food and cocktails, so this is a good place to come before or after dinner.

**MAP 3:** *Río Lerma 156, Cuauhtémoc; tel. 55/7589-8731; www.fiebredemalta.com; 1pm-midnight Mon.-Wed., 1pm-1am Thurs.-Sat., 1pm-11pm Sun.; Metro: Insurgentes*

### Fifty Mils

The upscale cocktail bar in the Four Seasons, widely reputed as serving some of the best drinks in the city, doesn't only attract the well-heeled travelers staying at this long-running luxury hotel. Amid the businesspeople and tourists, CDMX locals come to sip on chili-spiked mezcal cocktails or the bar's take on the margarita, with tequila, Aperol, and cardamom. The atmosphere matches the Four Seasons's luxe reputation, with plush couches and huge draped windows, though there is also more casual seating on the plant-filled outdoor patio.

**MAP 3:** *Four Seasons Hotel, Paseo de la Reforma 500; tel. 55/5230-1818 or 55/5230-1616; www.fiftymils.com; noon-midnight Tues.-Sat., 6pm-midnight Sun.; Metro: Chapultepec, Metrobús: Chapultepec*

## CANTINAS
### Salón Paris

This traditional cantina, located just off the central square in the Santa María neighborhood, has a notable claim to fame: Legendary ranchera singer and songwriter José Alfredo Jiménez once worked here, and it is said he made his performance debut in the cantina in the 1940s. It seems little has changed at Salón Paris since José Alfredo's days—except the slew of newspaper clippings about the singer's career that now adorn the cantina's walls. Like many neighborhood cantinas, it's a simple, straightforward place to relax with a beer or a tequila, filled with neighborhood locals and friendly waitstaff.

**MAP 3:** *Jaime Torres Bodet 151, Col. Santa María la Ribera; tel. 55/5547-3710; 12:30pm-10pm Mon.-Sat., 12:30pm-8pm Sun.; Metro: Buenavista, Metrobús: Buenavista*

## PULQUERÍAS
### Pulquería La Joya

When historic pulquería La Xochitl closed its doors in 2020, a pair of neighborhood locals continued its legacy by reopening the space as La Joya, changing the name and expanding the seating at this genial old spot. Here, top-quality pulque is served in a range of delicious curados (sweetened and flavored with fruit or nuts). With the wonderfully laid-back vibe typical to traditional pulquerías, it remains popular with locals in the Santa María la Ribera.

**MAP 3:** *Eligio Ancona 122, Santa María la Ribera; tel. 55/1186-9706; 11am-6pm Sun.-Mon., 11am-10pm Thurs.-Sat.; Metro: Buenavista, Metrobús: Buenavista*

## LIVE MUSIC
### Parker & Lenox

Hidden behind Parker—a stylish American-diner-style restaurant serving burgers and fries, among other classics—Lenox is a speakeasy jazz club with a cool old-timey design inspired by 1930s aesthetics. The period feel is furthered by nightly jazz performances, usually by high-quality local acts and some of the best in the city—and it all goes splendidly with a negroni or an old-fashioned from the bar menu. If you're going on the weekend, reserve a table in advance.

**MAP 3:** *Milan 14; tel. 55/5546-6979; https://parkerandlenox.com; 6pm-2am Tues.-Sun.; no cover-US$10; Metro: Cuauhtémoc, Metrobús: Reforma*

## LGBTQ+
### Sungay Brunch
Held once a month on Sunday, these huge daytime parties, which take place in different locations across the city, are a celebration of queer culture in CDMX. You can count on excellent live DJs and a friendly, upbeat crowd. Follow @sungaybrunch on Instagram to see upcoming events and venues, as well as a link for tickets. Parties sell out, so reserve in advance.

**MAP 3:** *Locations vary; usually 1pm-midnight; US$10-15*

# Arts and Culture

## CULTURAL CENTERS
### Centro Cultural Digital
Just outside the main gates to the Bosque de Chapultepec, the Centro Cultural Digital is a two-story subterranean cultural center dedicated to the intersection of technology, art, internet, video games, and new-media disciplines. Stop in and you might find a massive sound-and-light installation in the downstairs gallery, a workshop on curating online art exhibitions, or local teenagers participating in a weekend-long video game-programming competition.

**MAP 3:** *Paseo de la Reforma s/n at Lieja; tel. 55/1000-2637; www.centroculturadigital.mx; 11am-6pm Tues.-Sun.; free; Metro: Chapultepec*

## GALLERIES
### Acapulco 62
This contemporary art gallery occupies a gorgeous old mansion on the northeast corner of the Alameda of the Santa María la Ribera, with a street-level gallery and a 2nd-floor space with a balcony overlooking the street. A reliable place to see interesting work, the gallery represents a range of contemporary artists, most living and working in Mexico City. The back door of the gallery opens onto adjoining seafood restaurant El Revolcadero (Manuel Carpio 94; no phone; 1pm-10pm Tues.-Sat., 1pm-8pm Sun.) and opening events often spill over into the space.

**MAP 3:** *Dr. Atl 217; tel. 55/7822-0132; noon-8pm Tues.-Sun.; free; Metro: Buenavista, Metrobús: Buenavista*

### Casa Wabi

Designed by Mexican architect Alberto Kalach, this impressive multistory art gallery in the largely industrial Atlampa neighborhood (just north of the Santa María la Ribera) was founded by artist Bosco Sodi, who also runs nonprofit art spaces in Puerto Escondido and Tokyo. There are several spacious exhibition rooms that can accommodate large-scale works as well as striking views of the city center from the building's top floors.

**MAP 3:** *C. Sabino 336, Atlampa; https://casawabi.org; 10am-5pm Tues.-Sun.; free; Metro: Buenavista, Metrobús: Buenavista*

### Galería Hilario Galguera

Located in a restored mansion on a quiet street in the San Rafael neighborhood, this contemporary gallery garnered international press after hosting a major show by world-famous British artist Damien Hirst in 2006. In addition to this splashy exhibition, the gallery's excellence continues, with ongoing exhibitions of both Mexican and international artists, including Jannis Kounellis, James HD Brown, and Mauricio Limón. The gallery's front door is always closed, but they are welcoming to visitors; ring the doorbell to enter.

**MAP 3:** *Francisco Pimentel 3, Col. San Rafael; tel. 55/2121-6902; www.galeriahilariogalguera.com; 11am-5pm Mon.-Fri., 11am-2pm Sat.; free; Metro: San Cosme, Metrobús: Plaza de República*

## MUSEUMS

### Museo Nacional de San Carlos

Housed in the opulent former palace of the Marqués de Buenavista, the Museo Nacional de San Carlos holds an impressive collection of European artwork, ranging from the 14th to the early 20th centuries. The collection was originally established in the 18th century at the Academia San Carlos art school and later augmented with a sizable donation from the Mexican government. The design of the palace is attributed to celebrated 18th-century Valencian architect Manuel Tolsá.

**MAP 3:** *Av. Puente de Alvarado 50, Col. Tabacalera; tel. 55/8647-5800; www.mnsancarlos.com; 11am-6pm Tues.-Sun.; US$4; Metro: Revolución or Hidalgo, Metrobús: Plaza de la República*

### Museo Experimental El Eco

Another of the many valuable cultural institutions overseen by the Universidad Nacional Autónoma de México, this small avant-garde museum was originally founded by German-born Mexican artist Mathias Goeritz in the mid-20th century. The space aims to be both experimental and interdisciplinary, with several large galleries with towering ceilings, a "bar area" (which doesn't function as a bar, though it looks like one), and a patio, which includes a sculptural installation by Goeritz. The ongoing temporary exhibitions include installation, video, and sound art,

many of which are specifically commissioned for the space.
**MAP 3:** *Sullivan 43, Col. San Rafael; tel. 55/5535-5186; https://eleco.unam.mx; 11am-6pm Wed.-Sun.; free; Metro: Revolución, Metrobús: Reforma*

### ✪ Museo Universitario del Chopo

The Museo Universitario del Chopo occupies an impressive art nouveau structure that was built in Düsseldorf, Germany, and shipped to Mexico in the early 20th century. Later abandoned, the building was eventually declared a landmark, reopening as the Museo Universitario del Chopo in 1975. Featuring work by avant-garde artists, with themes addressing technology, gender identity, and other contemporary topics, the museum has a long connection to music and alternative subcultures. It helped to start the weekly album exchange that is today the famous Saturday music market **Tianguis Cultural del Chopo.**
**MAP 3:** *Dr. Enrique González Martínez 10, Col. Santa María la Ribera; tel. 55/5535-2288, ext. 100, or 55/5546-3471; www.chopo.unam.mx; 11:30am-6pm Tues.-Sun.; US$2, US$1 students, free Wed.; Metro: San Cosme, Metrobús: El Chopo*

Museo Universitario del Chopo

# Festivals and Events

## JUNE
### Marcha del Orgullo LGBTI CDMX (LGBTI Pride March)
The massively attended Marcha del Orgullo LGBTI CDMX, also known as the March del Orgullo Lésbico, Gay, Bisexual, Travesti, Transexual, Transgénero e Intersexual (LGBTTTI), takes places along the Paseo de la Reforma, usually on the same weekend as New York City's Pride festivities, in remembrance of the events at Stonewall Inn. The crowd, which usually numbers over 300,000, gets as glammed up as the marchers, and the party continues late in the evening and into the next day.
**Paseo de la Reforma:** *Ángel de la Independencia to the Zócalo; end of June*

Sundays on the Paseo de la Reforma

## OCTOBER
**Desfil de Alebrijes Monumentales**
Alebrijes, fantastical animal sculptures that are painted bright colors, are a handcraft typical to the state of Oaxaca. Every year, the Museo de Arte Popular near the Alameda Central hosts a parade of giant "alebrijes"—made with papier-mâché rather than the traditional carved wood—which process from the Zócalo to the Ángel de la Independencia, generally in the month of October. They remain on show along the Paseo de la Reforma for a month thereafter, making a visit to the famous avenue even more fun, especially with kids.
**Paseo de la Reforma:** *fall, usually Oct.*

## NOVEMBER
**Desfile Cívico Militar Revolución Mexicana**
In commemoration of the Revolution of 1910, there is a large-scale military parade that departs from the Zócalo and runs along the Paseo de la Reforma to Campo Marte every November (the official holiday is November 20). Traditional Mexican dance performances, tricolor fireworks, horsemanship, and period costumes are customary parts of the event, led by the Mexican armed forces.
**Paseo de la Reforma:** *on or around Nov. 20*

# Recreation

## PARKS
**Equal Bicigratis**
Nonprofit Equal Bicigratis offers free bike loans for those who'd like to pedal around the city. You'll need to leave a valid photo ID (like a passport) as a deposit, and the bike is yours for three hours. Many visitors take advantage of the service to join the thousands of cyclists on the Paseo de la Reforma on Sunday, but there are dozens of Bicigratis kiosks in the city, operating every day but Monday, including one in the Glorieta de la Cibeles in the Roma, another in Plaza Hidalgo in central Coyoacán, and several more along the Paseo de la Reforma, at the statue of Diana Cazadora, the Estela de la Luz, and the Ángel de la Independencia.
**MAP 3:** *Paseo de la Reforma near the Diana Cazadora; tel. 55/5574-6798; 10:30am-1pm and 1:30pm-6pm Tues.-Sat., 9:30am-3pm Sun.; free; Metro: Auditorio, Metrobús: Auditorio*

## Bike Mexico City

Not long ago, riding a bicycle in central Mexico City was a death-defying proposition, braved by only a few die-hard cyclists and those who had no more efficient means of getting around. Today, the city has cordoned off a network of bike lanes throughout the central neighborhoods and, most impressive, rolled out a massive (and still growing) urban bike-share program called **Ecobici** (tel. 55/5005-2424 or 800/326-2421; http://ecobici.cdmx.gob.mx). Now it's common to see riders of every stripe pedaling along the Paseo de la Reforma or through the Roma on their way to work, restaurants, or the movies.

Ecobici kiosk on the Paseo de la Reforma

Annual subscriptions to Ecobici cost less than US$30, though occasional users and visitors to the city can choose 1-, 3-, or 7-day passes. You can register within minutes via the phone app, which can also give you a real-time view of the bicycles available at each station and locate the station closest to you, or you can open an account online at https://ecobici.cdmx.gob.mx. If you don't have a smartphone or would like to pay cash, there is also an in-person kiosk (10:30am-7:30pm Mon.-Fri., 11am-3pm Sat.-Sun.) at Camellón de Reforma in front of Reforma 222.

Ecobici members can ride bicycles between stations for up to 45 minutes for no additional charge, and 90 minutes on Saturday-Sunday; if you keep your bike longer, you will incur a charge of about US$2.50 per hour. There are Ecobici stations throughout the Roma, Condesa, Centro Histórico, Juárez, Polanco, San Rafael, Del Valle, Nápoles, and Mixcoac neighborhoods, as well as along the Paseo de la Reforma.

# CYCLING

### Ciclotón

On the last Sunday of the month, the city closes several of its major thoroughfares to automobile traffic (in addition to the Paseo de la Reforma, closed every Sunday), allowing tens of thousands of cyclists to pedal uninhibited through the city's central districts. Hydration, medical, and bike-repair stations are set up throughout the designated route, which can run 19-45 km (12-28 mi). Check Ciclotón's official website for the most recent news and route updates.

**MAP 3:** *Ángel de la Independencia (Station 1); http://indeporte.cdmx.gob.mx; 8am-2pm last Sun. of the month; Metro: Sevilla*

Frontón México

### ⭐ Paseo Dominical Muévete en Bici

Through the city-sponsored environmental program Muévete en Bici, 8am-2pm the first three Sundays of every month, the iconic Paseo de la Reforma is closed to automobile traffic between the main entrance of the Bosque de Chapultepec and the Centro Histórico. The street is also closed the fourth Sunday of the month for Ciclotón. Thousands of people come to ride along this wide and beautiful avenue, or to take advantage of the space to jog, roller-skate, walk their dog, or even hula-hoop. There are often free Zumba classes at the Ángel de la Independencia, free bicycle lessons for children and adults near the statue of Diana Cazadora, and free bike-repair stations along the route. Check the program's Facebook page for information on road closures and events.

**MAP 3:** *Paseo de la Reforma, between Bosque de Chapultepec and the Alameda Central, and Avenida Juárez along the Alameda; www.semovi.cdmx.gob.mx; 8am-2pm Sun.; Metro: Chapultepec*

## SPECTATOR SPORTS
### Jai Alai
#### Frontón México

Frontón México, Mexico City's jai alai stadium, reopened in 2017 after almost 20 years of abandonment. The event heralded a significant comeback for the sport, similar to the Basque game pelota, which had disappeared from Mexico following its glamorous heyday in the mid-20th century. At Frontón México, a league of international pelotaris (jai alai players) have been recruited for a new generation of fans, and matches are fast-paced and fun to watch. In addition to jai alai, the beautiful art deco venue is used for music concerts and other special events.

**MAP 3:** *De la República 17; tel. 55/5128-3400; http://frontonmexico.com.mx; box office 10am-6pm Mon.-Sat., 10am-4pm Sun.; Metro: Hidalgo, Metrobús: Plaza de la República*

# Shops

## SHOPPING DISTRICTS

### ✪ Juárez Shopping District

When real estate became scarcer and more expensive in the adjacent Roma neighborhood, the Juárez became a hot spot for new restaurants, bars, and boutiques. Today, the district's 19th- and 20th-century mansions are filled with new concepts and flavors, making it a lovely place for a relaxed stroll, stopping into shops and cafés as you go. There are a number of independent boutiques in the neighborhood, many concentrated along the streets Marsella and Havre, with some notable shops including Carla Fernández, Fábrica Social, Utilitario Mexicano, Lorena Saravia, Simple by Trista, and Cihuah.

**MAP 3:** *Havre between Liverpool and Marsella, Marsella between Niza and Berlin; Metro: Cuauhtémoc, Metrobús: Hamburgo*

## ANTIQUES AND COLLECTIBLES

### Centro de Antigüedades Plaza del Ángel

This open-air plaza in the Zona Rosa is filled with atmospheric antiques shops. Here, you'll find furniture, paintings, art objects, silver, and decorative pieces from the 19th and mid-20th centuries, as well as a smattering of European and Asian pieces. On Saturday and Sunday, additional vendors sell jewelry, sculpture, old photographs, postcards, and other sundries in an outdoor market, where you can find everything from nicely preserved vintage to high-end antiques, laid out on rugs or on folding tables in the plaza.

**MAP 3:** *Londres 161 and Hamburgo 150; hours vary by shop 11am-7pm Mon.-Fri., 10am-4pm Sat., noon-5pm Sun., market 9am-4pm Sat.-Sun.; Metro: Insurgentes*

## CLOTHING, SHOES, AND ACCESSORIES

### Carla Fernández

Carla Fernández's eponymous line of men's and women's clothing is largely inspired by Mexico's traditional aesthetics. Working with artisanal communities, Fernández produces elegant contemporary dresses, blouses, pants, ponchos, and shawls that incorporate traditional details like elaborate embroidery and handmade textiles. There is another branch in the Roma Norte (Álvaro Obregón 200; tel. 55/5264-2226; 11am-7pm daily).

**MAP 3:** *Marsella 72; tel. 55/5511-0001; www.carlafernandez.com; 11am-7pm daily; Metro: Insurgentes, Metrobús: Hamburgo*

### Fábrica Social

The brightly colored clothing that swings on the racks at this small boutique unites social conscience and creativity. To create its unique apparel, this nonprofit group brings together contemporary designers and Indigenous artisans, who work together on the design and development of seasonal lines of womenswear that pair traditional techniques with a modern aesthetic. Though pricier than most traditional Mexican clothing, the styles are contemporary enough to suit more urban clients. In addition to their small Juárez storefront, there is a branch in the Condesa (Amsterdam 159; 11am-7pm daily).

**MAP 3:** *Dinamarca 66; tel. 55/5535-3431; www.fabricasocial.org; 11am-7pm daily; Metro: Cuauhtémoc, Metrobús: Hamburgo*

## MUSIC
### Tianguis Cultural del Chopo
Just north of the Buena Vista train station, this open-air street market was initially founded as a site of exchange for rare record collectors and music fans. Today, over 200 stands sell vinyl and CDs, band T-shirts, posters, and other punk- and music-related goods, with booths that specialize in thrash metal, rare or out-of-print titles, and bootlegs. Held on Saturday, it's always packed with a young crowd decked out in tattoos, piercings, and head-to-toe black.

**MAP 3:** *Along Aldama, at Eje 1 Norte, in Col. Buena Vista; 10am-4pm Sat.; Metro: Buenavista; Metrobús: El Chopo*

# Chapultepec and Polanco

Map 4

Getting Around . . . . . . . . 141
Chapultepec Walk
  (Primera Sección) . . . . 144
Sights . . . . . . . . . . . . . . . 148
Restaurants . . . . . . . . . . . 152
Nightlife . . . . . . . . . . . . . . 157
Arts and Culture . . . . . . . 158
Recreation . . . . . . . . . . . . 165
Shops . . . . . . . . . . . . . . . . 168

The Bosque de Chapultepec, a vast urban park, is filled with monuments, lakes, jogging paths, and wooded glens for picnicking. It is also the site of many of the capital's most important cultural institutions, including the spectacular Museo Nacional de Antropología, with its enormous collection of art and artifacts from Mexico's diverse pre-Columbian cultures. To the north of the park, across the Paseo de la Reforma, upscale Polanco is a destination for fine dining, upscale hotels, and quality shopping, while the San Miguel Chapultepec, to the park's south, is an attractive residential neighborhood and gallery district.

# Highlights

✪ **Museo Nacional de Antropología:** This extraordinary museum contains the country's largest collection art and artifacts from Mexico's diverse pre-Columbian cultures (page 148).

✪ **Casa Luis Barragán:** All the elements that made Luis Barragán of one of Mexico's most celebrated modernist architects are showcased in his home, today a museum and UNESCO World Heritage Site (page 151).

✪ **Complejo Cultural Los Pinos:** At this art and cultural center in the former presidential palace, there are often dance performances, culinary expos, live music, speakers, and other special events on the weekends (page 159).

✪ **Museo Jumex:** Admission is free at this prestigious and beautifully designed contemporary art museum, which showcases work by big-name international artists (page 161).

✪ **Bosque de Chapultepec: Primera Sección:** Historic sites, top-tier museums, and unusual landscape architecture are a few reasons to visit Mexico City's iconic urban park (page 166).

# Getting Around

- Metro lines: 1, 7
- Metro stops: Chapultepec, Juanacatlán, Constituyentes, Polanco, Auditorio
- Metrobús lines: 7, 18
- Metrobús stops: Chapultepec, Paseo de la Reforma

---

**Previous:** Monumento a Los Niños Héroes, Bosque de Chapultepec; **Above:** Museo Nacional de Antropología; boats on the lake in Bosque de Chapultepec.

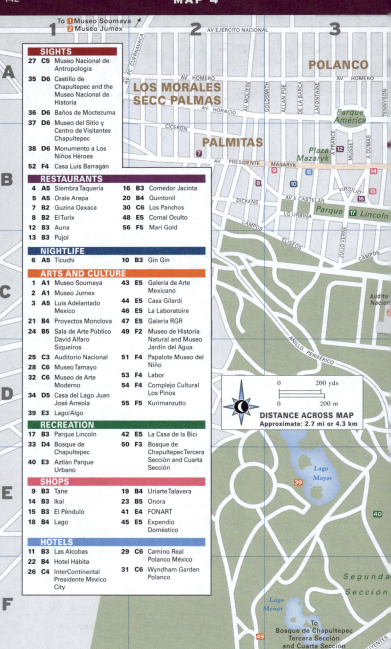

# Chapultepec and Polanco 143

# Chapultepec Walk (Primera Sección)

**TOTAL DISTANCE:** 3.75 km (2.3 mi)
**TOTAL WALKING TIME:** 1.5 hours

The Bosque de Chapultepec is a beloved and expansive urban park, as well as a place of great history and culture. On weekdays, it's the perfect place to escape the city's chaos; the park is surprisingly quiet and relaxing. On weekends, by contrast, it's a joyous jumble of humanity, as families from across the city come to relax, party, and play soccer amid the park's many meadows and wooded groves.

Chapultepec's remarkable landscape design includes dozens of fountains, gardens, and winding wooded footpaths, which make it a delight to explore. If you are inspired by what you find in the Primera Sección, consider visiting the Segunda Sección, a large swath of parkland filled with monuments and offbeat museums, including an unusual mural by Diego Rivera at the natural history museum, the colossal children's museum, and ALGO, a stunning art and cultural space

jacaranda trees in bloom in the Primera Sección of Chapultepec park

that adjoins the long-running restaurant Lago, just beside the park's largest lake.

**Tip:** If you want to cover more ground, consider renting a bicycle to tour the park (see Recreation for details). With wheels, you can easily visit every corner of the Primera Sección, including the carousel and the impressive Fuente a Nezahualcóyotl.

**1** Begin on the Paseo de la Reforma. Before you go inside the park, take a moment to visit the interesting **Centro Cultural Digital,** located just below the **Estela de la Luz,** a contemporary monument commemorating Mexico's 200 years of independence. Admission is free, and the center often hosts fun, eye-catching exhibits.

*Enter Chapultepec's regal main entrance marked by green wrought-iron gates and flanked by bronze lions.*

**2** Once you've entered the park, the first thing you'll see is the massive six-pillar **Monumento a Los Niños Héroes,** which commemorates the six young army cadets who jumped to their death rather than surrender to the US military during the 1847 American invasion of Chapultepec during the Mexican-American War.

*Continue along the footpath past the back of the Museo de Arte Moderno and its pretty sculpture garden onto the pedestrian street Colegio Militar.*

**3** Just ahead, one of the park's artificial lakes, the **Lago de Chapultepec,** is filled with ducks and paddleboaters. On a grassy meadow beside the lake, the **Casa del Lago Juan José Arreola** is one of the city's oldest cultural centers, with dozens of ongoing art and cultural events.

Casa del Lago Juan José Arreola

*As Colegio Militar loops back toward the entrance to the park (about 500 m/0.3 mi), look for the turnoff to the smaller footpath known as the Calzada del Rey, and head east.*

**4** Walking about 1 km (0.6 mi) along the wooded Calzada del Rey, you will pass the remains of **Baños de Moctezuma** to the south. One of the many spring-fed pools constructed by Mexica emperor Moctezuma, this historic site is now little more than a sad sunken pool encased in concrete—but the historic value is phenomenal.

*Continue along Calzada del Rey.*

**5** About 200 m (660 ft) farther ahead, you'll pass the **Tribuna Monumental,** a giant outdoor amphitheater. The **Audiorama,** in a quiet wooded grove just behind the amphitheater, is a quirky little corner of the park built in the 1970s. Here, speakers play a tasteful program of music, meant to be enjoyed on one of the many benches scattered throughout the space. Just beside the amphitheater is one of the oldest cypress trees in the park, known as **Ahuehuete El Saregento.** Though the tree is no longer living, its trunk shows it has stood here for more than 550 years, suggesting that it may have been among the many cypresses planted by the emperor of Texcoco, Nezahualcóyotl, in the 15th century.

Ahuehuete El Saregento

*Continue along Calzada del Rey.*

**6** In 1966, excavations revealed **pre-Columbian embellishments** carved into the stones, just below the castle on the Cerro de Chapultepec. Though only fragments of these works remain intact, it's fascinating to spot these historic pieces amid the natural landscape.

*Head up the Cerro de Chapultepec.*

**7** End your walking tour at the **Castillo de Chapultepec,** a fascinating museum that offers lovely views of the greenery below.

Castillo de Chapultepec

# Sights

TOP EXPERIENCE

### ⭐ Museo Nacional de Antropología

The National Anthropology Museum is an expansive, educational, and thought-provoking museum that provides an unparalleled look into the diverse cultures of pre-Columbian and modern-day Mexico. The massive two-story space is divided into 23 exhibition rooms and filled with an astounding array of artifacts from pre-Columbian cultures in Mexico, including the Olmecs of the Gulf Coast, Teotihuacán, the post-Teotihuacán Toltecs, the Zapotecs and people of Oaxaca, the Mexica, and the Maya. Some key pieces among the collection include the colossal Olmec heads carved from giant monoliths, the carved lintel from Yaxchilan in the Maya room, and the Toltecs' towering stone warriors.

The galleries dedicated to the Valley of Mexico are the centerpiece of the museum. Here, some of the collection's most stunning artifacts are on display, including a stone sculpture of the goddess Coatlicue (originally found in Mexico City's Zócalo), a richly carved sacrificial urn called the Piedra de Tizoc, and, the museum's most famous piece,

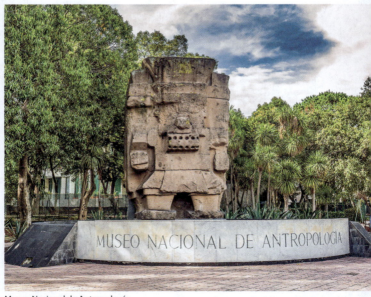

Museo Nacional de Antropología

the Piedra del Sol (also called the "Aztec calendar"), which illustrates the 20 signs and 13 numerals of the Mesoamerican calendar round. Start your tour of the museum here, then visit the rooms dedicated to the Toltecs and Teotihuacán, especially if you intend to visit the archaeological site.

The astounding array of pre-Columbian artifacts in the 1st-floor galleries should be the focus of your visit to the museum. However, if time allows, it's worth touring the less-visited 2nd floor, where ethnography exhibits are dedicated to the native cultures of Mexico today, including the Huichol, Cora, Purépecha, and Otomí. There are dioramas of typical dwellings and an excellent collection of textiles and crafts. An extensive wall text in Spanish and English gives depth to the exhibits.

**MAP 4:** *Paseo de la Reforma and Calzada Gandhi; tel. 55/4040-5300; www.mna.inah.gob.mx; 9am-6pm Tues.-Sun.; US$5; Metro: Chapultepec or Auditorio, Metrobús: Antropología*

### Castillo de Chapultepec and the Museo Nacional de Historia

Overlooking the Paseo de la Reforma from the Cerro de Chapultepec, this opulent castle and Mexican history museum was originally built as a country house for Spanish royalty under Viceroy Bernardo de Gálvez in the late 18th century. Later, the castle was taken over by the government, serving as a military college for several decades after the War of Independence. During the 1847 US Army invasion of Mexico City during the Mexican-American War, the castillo was the last bastion of defense. In an infamous moment in Mexican history, US forces overtook the castle, raising an American flag on its roof.

During the brief rule of Maximilian I in the 1860s, the emperor made the Castillo de Chapultepec his official residence, refurbishing it with grand salons, flowered terraces, and a rooftop garden. After Maximilian and Carlota were overthrown, the castle was converted to the Mexican presidential residence. Under President Porfirio Díaz, the castle's interior reached new heights of luxury. Progressive president Lázaro Cárdenas finally moved out in 1939, making the castle a public museum; it opened in 1944.

Today, the castle houses the **Museo Nacional de Historia,** with a permanent collection of paintings, documents, and artifacts documenting the changing eras in Mexican national history. Equally interesting are the many rooms preserved in period furnishings. The gardens are well-tended, and the views of the Paseo de la Reforma from the terraces are postcard-worthy.

**MAP 4:** *Primera Sección, Bosque de Chapultepec; tel. 55/5241-3100; www.mnh.inah.gob.mx; 10am-3pm Tues.-Sat.; US$6, free under age 13, seniors, teachers, and people with*

the Castillo de Chapultepec

disabilities; *Metro: Chapultepec, Metrobús: Chapultepec*

### Baños de Moctezuma

At the southern base of the Cerro de Chapultepec, behind the Niños Héroes monument, there are remains of one of the many spring-fed pools where Mexica emperors came to relax and bathe; the same site was later used by the Spanish as a retreat during the colonial era. Today, all that remains of the baths are empty concrete pools—not much to look at, but certainly of spectacular historic value. Nearby, on the rocks around the base of the Cerro de Chapultepec, there are pre-Columbian petroglyphs on the rock faces, rather weathered by the elements but exciting to spot amid the greenery.

**MAP 4:** *Primera Sección, Bosque de Chapultepec, south of the castle; Metro: Chapultepec or Constituyentes, Metrobús: Chapultepec or Gandhi*

### Museo del Sitio y Centro de Visitantes Chapultepec

The small but interesting visitor center in the Bosque de Chapultepec chronicles over 5,000 years of history of the park through illustrated texts and interactive exhibits. You'll also find a small gift shop and public restrooms inside the space. Just behind the Monumento a Los Niños Héroes at the main entrance to the park, this is a good place to get oriented before starting a bicycle or walking tour of Chapultepec.

**MAP 4:** *Calzada Mahatma Gandhi s/n; tel. 55/5925-4372; www.chapultepec.org.mx; 10am-5pm Tues.-Sun.; Metro: Chapultepec, Metrobús: Chapultepec*

## Monumento a Los Niños Héroes

At the foot of the Cerro de Chapultepec, this six-column monument commemorates the heroic defense of the Castillo de Chapultepec by six young soldiers against invading US troops during the Mexican-American War. On September 13, 1847, when it was clear the Americans would take the castle, six military cadets—Juan de la Barrera, Juan Escutia, Fernando Montes de Oca, Vicente Suárez, Francisco Marquéz, and Agustín Melgar—wrapped themselves in Mexican flags and jumped to their deaths from the castle ramparts rather than surrender. Their deaths are honored by six tall columns, each topped with a black eagle. The Americans ultimately prevailed and flew their flag over Mexico City.

**MAP 4:** *Primera Sección, Bosque de Chapultepec, east of the castle; free; Metro: Chapultepec*

## ✪ Casa Luis Barragán

Luis Barragán is one of Mexico's most celebrated modern architects and interior designers, known for integrating a clean modernist style with an innovative use of light, bright primary colors, local building materials, and subtle Mexican vernacular elements. Born in Guadalajara in 1902, he built several residences in his hometown before relocating to Mexico City, where his most famous work was completed.

Today, Barragán's former home and studio near Tacubaya, built in 1947 and 1948, is preserved as a museum. With its interesting use of natural light and intimate spaces, the building is representative of Barragán's work but also provides a rather touching look into the architect's life and personal aesthetic. Throughout the living quarters, Barragán's belongings, furniture, and art collection—which includes work by Miguel Covarrubias, Diego Rivera, and Henry Moore—are on display; you can even peek into the bathroom of the architect's monastic bedroom. In 1988, the home was named a national monument by the Mexican government, and in 2004, it was recognized as a UNESCO World Heritage Site.

The house, previously only accessible with a guided tour, is now open to the public for limited hours each week, though taking a guided tour is highly recommended for first-time visitors. Note that children under age 12 are not permitted. On your way out, the small bookshop at the entrance has a lovely selection of books on design and architecture.

**MAP 4:** *Av. General Francisco Ramírez 12-14, Tacubaya; tel. 55/5515-4908 or 55/5272-4945; www.casaluisbarragan.org; check website for hours Mon.-Tues. and Fri.; reservations required; US$30 adults, US$35 with guided tour, Mexican nationals and ages 12-21 US$20, students US$15; Metro: Constituyentes*

# Restaurants

## PRICE KEY
$ Entrées less than US$10
$$ Entrées US$10-20
$$$ Entrées more than US$20

## MEXICAN

### Guzina Oaxaca $$
Alejandro Ruíz, the founding chef behind the elegant restaurant Casa Oaxaca in the city of Oaxaca, and chef Carlos Galán bring a creative approach to one of Mexico's most famous cuisines at this lovely restaurant in Polanco. Try excellent renditions of typical Oaxacan plates, like tacos, stuffed duck, and mole coloradito (a complex sauce made with chilies, spices, and chocolate, native to Oaxaca), or the chef's signature mole negro, served with turkey, as is traditional, and accompanied by rice and plantains. Casual but attractive, the restaurant subtly recalls Oaxacan aesthetics with details like embroidered throw pillows on the dining room's benches.

**MAP 4:** *Presidente Masaryk 513, Col. Los Morales; tel. 55/5282-1820; www.guzinaoaxaca.com; 9am-11:30pm Mon.-Sat., 9am-6pm Sun.; Metro: Auditorio or Polanco, Metrobús: Auditorio*

### Comedor Jacinta $$
A refreshingly low-key option in Polanco's bustling restaurant and shopping district, this lovely restaurant is helmed by well-known fine-dining chef Edgar Núñez Magaña. The appealing menu caters to any mood, with options like nopal (prickly pear cactus) salad, crab-stuffed quesadillas, and bone marrow-topped sopes (round corn flatbreads). The setting, with potted cacti, handblown Mexican glassware, and a bar well-stocked with tequila and mezcal, complements the thoroughly Mexican menu.

**MAP 4:** *Virgilio 40; WhatsApp tel. 56/1984-8554; http://comedorjacinta.com; 1pm-11pm Mon.-Tues., 1pm-midnight Thurs.-Sat., 1:30pm-7pm Sun.; Metro: Polanco*

### ✪ Pujol $$$
No restaurant has had more influence on 21st-century Mexico City cuisine than the modernist Mexican fine-dining restaurant Pujol. Here, chef-founder Enrique Olvera made his name serving refined and innovative Mexican food, using traditional ingredients in contemporary presentations.

There is an appealing menu of diverse Mexican dishes at Comedor Jacinta.

The restaurant's signature tasting menu changes seasonally but always focuses on native ingredients, emphasizing the use of corn, vegetables, and seafood. There is also a more casual omakase-style tasting menu offered at the bar for groups of four or more. Pujol is located in a gorgeously designed modern building surrounded by lush gardens. In 2024, Pujol was one of only two restaurants awarded two stars by Michelin's first guide to Mexico.

**MAP 4:** *Tennyson 133; tel. 55/5545-4111; www.pujol.com.mx; 1:30pm-10pm Mon.-Sat.; Metro: Polanco*

### Quintonil $$$

Quintonil's focus is on modern food with native Mexican ingredients. Its name comes from the Nahuatl word for a type of quelites, wild greens consumed since the pre-Columbian era. There is a seasonal tasting menu, but you can also order appetizers and main courses à la carte, like a duck-stuffed tamal with corn cream or a mussel-topped tostada with mole. Along with Pujol, Quintonil was awarded two Michelin stars in 2024.

**MAP 4:** *Newton 55; tel. 55/5280-2680; www.quintonil.com; 1pm-midnight Mon.-Sat.; Metro: Polanco*

### Comal Oculto $

This tiny spot in the San Miguel Chapultepec is centered on the comal, the round Mexican griddle used to make tortillas and other corn flatbreads. The menu includes lots of antojitos (traditional Mexican snacks) like sopes (round corn flatbreads) and gorditas. A house specialty are the tacos with slow-cooked pork shoulder, though there are ample vegetarian options too. At this casual spot, patrons eat at a standing bar overlooking the open kitchen or a shared table off the sidewalk.

**MAP 4:** *General Gómez Pedraza 37; no phone; 10:15am-5pm Mon.-Sat.; Metro: Constituyentes*

## INTERNATIONAL

### Auna $$

If you'd like to dine with one of Mexico's celebrity chefs in a slightly more low-key environment, two-Michelin-starred chef Jorge Vallejo of Quintonil is one of the founders, along with chef Fernando Torres, of this fancy-casual lunch and dinner spot, which opened in 2023 in the heart of Polanco. With its blond wood tables in a plant-filled courtyard, the space and service are invitingly serene, if a bit stuffy. It's perfect for those who want to put down their shopping bags and work through a bottle of pét-nat, soft-shell crab in curry, and roast sweet potato amid a crowd of stylish locals.

**MAP 4:** *Anatole France 139; tel. 55/9237-5157; https://auna.com.mx; 1:30pm-11pm Mon.-Sat., 1:30pm-5pm Sun.; Metro: Polanco*

### Mari Gold $$

Mexican and Indian flavors can be surprisingly complementary, as chefs Norma Listman and Saqib Keval showcased at their first

## Pre-Columbian Foods

Today, Mexican chefs are using more indigenous Mesoamerican ingredients in their cooking, and foods that once seemed more adventurous—like insects and worms—have become almost commonplace in the city's top restaurants. Here are a few you'll find on menus in the capital.

### CHAPULINES

Grasshoppers, collected in the wild and then fried until crispy, are an excellent source of protein and deliciously salty. They add an acidic bite to guacamole and quesadillas.

a type of quelite that's eaten with the flowers and stems

**Find them:** In tacos at **Guzina Oaxaca** (page 152); mixed into melted cheese at **Corazón de Maguey** (page 233); in guacamole at **Las Tlayudas** (page 211) in the Narvarte neighborhood.

### QUELITES

Quelites refers to any wild indigenous greens, such as huauzontles (a bitter broccoli-esque vegetable) and pápalo (a perfumed citrusy herb that is popular in Puebla). In modern farming, many of these "weeds," which often grow naturally in the milpa, are eradicated by farmers, but as appreciation of the milpa and its many products grows, quelites have experienced a renewed popularity.

**Find them:** In salad at **Páramo** (page 194); with fish or meat at fine-dining restaurant **Quintonil** (page 153), which is named after a type

---

collaboration, Masala y Maíz, in the Juárez neighborhood (Marsella 72, Col Juárez; tel. 55/1313-8260; noon-6pm Wed.-Sun.). At this San Miguel Chapultepec hot spot, the chefs take up the concept again, with dishes like a delicate dosa topped with hoja santa. Natural wines are the highlight of the drink menu. The slender dining room, with tables lined up end to end, has an avant-garde feeling, which works well for the neighborhood's gallery crowd, who often show up at lunch hour.

**MAP 4:** *Protasio Tagle 66A; WhatsApp tel. 55/3726-2228; 9am-5:30pm Wed.-Sun.; Metro: Juanacatlán*

## TACOS, TORTAS, AND SNACKS

### El Turix $

El Turix does one thing, and it does it well: cochinita pibil, achiote-spiced pulled pork prepared in the Yucatec style. You can order it in soft tacos, in a torta (sandwich style), or on panuchos (thick, circular corn cakes

of quelite in the *Amaranthus* genus; at quesadilla stands throughout the city.

## HUITLACOCHE

The soft black fungus that grows naturally on corn is not only edible, it's delicious. With a mild mushroom-like flavor, huitlacoche is generally in season during the summer rains July-September. Huitlacoche has more nutritional properties—including essential amino acids—than the corn it grows on.

**Find it:** At produce stands in the **Mercado San Juan** (page 110); in ravioli at **Los Danzantes** (page 233); in tamales at **Tamales Doña Emi** (page 185).

## ESCAMOLES

Ant larvae, which have been consumed since the pre-Columbian era, are served fried in butter and seasoned with the herb epazote. Popular in Mexico City, escamoles are generally a pricey delicacy, as they are difficult to harvest and have a very short season (usually April-May).

**Find them:** During the spring at **El Cardenal** (page 72) and **Azul Histórico** (page 71) in the Centro Histórico; in the **Mercado San Juan** (page 110).

## CHINICUILES

A caterpillar commonly found in maguey and agave, chinicuiles are often fried and folded into a taco. Frying before serving gives the shells a crisp texture, complementing the caterpillars' pungent, savory flavor. They are usually in season during the fall.

**Find them:** At **El Cardenal** (page 72); as part of the annual April insect menu at **Los Danzantes** (page 233); at **La Casa de los Tacos** (page 234).

---

from the Yucatán). This singularly focused spot has garnered a loyal following, and at the hour of the afternoon comida, there is often a long line of expectant diners snaking out the door and around the block.

**MAP 4:** *Emilio Castelar 212; tel. 55/5280-6449; noon-10pm daily; Metro: Auditorio*

### Los Panchos $

In business since 1945, Los Panchos has been catering to a loyal local clientele for generations. The atmosphere here is a bit more upscale than what you'd find at most taquerías, with a full bar and table service. The food, however, is traditional, homey, and generously served. Best known for the carnitas (braised pork), the extensive menu includes plenty of other options, from a fresh guacamole to huge sopes (thick corn cakes) topped with beans and cheese.

**MAP 4:** *Tolstoi 9, Col. Anzures; tel. 55/5254-5430; www.lospanchos.mx; 9am-10pm daily; Metro: Chapultepec*

Orale Arepa in Polanco

### Siembra Taquería $$

What started out as a tortillería focused on the use of heirloom varieties of corn has grown into a modern taquería, with a taco menu that runs from classic (Ensenada-style shrimp) to unique (bone marrow with noodles). Tacos are upscale and generously served, with prices to match. They've also got corn-based snacks like tlacoyos and tamales on offer, as well as craft beer, kombucha, and desserts. A few doors down, in 2023 the same team opened a more formal sister restaurant, Siembra Comedor (Newton 300, Col. Polanco; 1:30pm-10pm Tues.-Sat., 9am-5pm Sun.), where heirloom corn and other native Mexican ingredients are the stars of the menu.

**MAP 4:** Newton 256; tel. 55/7875-0411; https://siempresiembra.com.mx; 9am-10pm Mon.-Sat., 9am-5pm Sun.; Metro: Polanco

## VENEZUELAN

### Orale Arepa $

Generously served Venezuelan arepas, cachapas (sweet corn pancakes), and patacones (plantain cakes) are made with quality ingredients and a lot of love at this casual Polanco eatery. While Venezuelan food uses many of the same building blocks (corn, beans, cheese) as Mexican cuisine, the flavors are very different, making for a satisfying contrast to Mexico City's predominant styles. There's a café-like feeling inside the casual blond-wood restaurant and plenty of sidewalk tables outside.

**MAP 4:** Schiller 330; tel. 55/9155-6133; 8am-9pm Mon.-Sat., 8am-7pm Sun.; Metro: Polanco, Metrobús: Auditorio

# Nightlife

## BARS AND LOUNGES

### ⭐ Ticuchi

All the details are attended to at this candlelit Polanco bar, owned by famed chef Enrique Olvera. The list of small-batch mezcal is among the most interesting in the city. The cocktails are unusual and delicious, incorporating artisanal spirits and local flavors. The service is elegant. The music is spot-on. And the kitchen is (as you'd expect) excellent, serving vegetable-forward, maize-centric small plates, perfect for a light dinner. There are occasionally live DJs, but on most nights, it's a relaxed, romantic place for a drink.

**MAP 4:** *Petrarca 254; tel. 55/2589-4363; https://ticuchi.mx; 6:30pm-11pm Mon.-Sat.; Metro: Polanco, Metrobús: Auditorio*

### Gin Gin

After opening one successful location in the Roma, this pre-Prohibition-style cocktail lounge found a second and more upscale home near Parque Lincoln in Polanco. As the name implies, the beautifully made cocktails are focused on gin, with the bar's signature drink featuring ginkgo, ginger, and other elixir-like ingredients. Come here for a pretty crowd and

Ticuchi

a pretty bar. It's best to reserve a table ahead.
**MAP 4:** *Pedro Calderón de la Barca 72; tel. 55/5214-8302; www.gingin. mx; 4pm-2am daily; Metro: Auditorio, Metrobús: Auditorio*

# Arts and Culture

## CINEMA
### Cineteca Nacional
The Cineteca Nacional, a long-running art movie house in Coyoacán, opened a much anticipated new branch in the fourth section of Chapultepec in late 2024. Located within a former military arms factory, which has been beautifully redesigned for the Cineteca, the complex includes eight cinemas as well as an amphitheater for outdoor screenings. And getting there really is half the fun! From the Constituyentes Metro stop, take the aerial gondola, or Cablebús, over the city to the Cineteca stop.
**MAP 4:** *Av. Vasco de Quiroga 1345, Campo Militar número 1-F, Panteón Santa Fe; www.cinetecanacional. net; showtimes vary; Metro: Constituyentes, then Cablebús Cineteca*

## CONCERT VENUES
### Auditorio Nacional
The city's preeminent concert hall, with a capacity of 10,000, the Auditorio Nacional has a varied lineup that runs from internationally famous singers like Marc Anthony and Elton John to popular cumbia groups like Los Ángeles Azules to classical music concerts by international orchestras. Next door, the smaller **Lunario** (tel. 55/9138-1350; www.lunario.com. mx) is a 1,000-seat venue, with programming running from jazz groups to funk. Tickets are available via Ticketmaster.
**MAP 4:** *Paseo de la Reforma 50; tel. 55/9138-1350; www.auditorio.com. mx; US$25-200; Metro: Auditorio, Metrobús: Auditorio*

## CULTURAL CENTERS
### Casa del Lago Juan José Arreola
Overseen by the Universidad Nacional Autónoma de México (UNAM), this multimedia cultural and educational center operates an ongoing program of cinema, visual arts exhibitions, concerts, theater, and poetry readings, in addition to offering workshops in disciplines as diverse as yoga, classical guitar, and chess. Housed in several

Auditorio Nacional

the former presidential mansion at Los Pinos, now a public arts and cultural center

turn-of-the-20th-century buildings next to the lake in Chapultepec park, the center was opened by writer Juan José Arreola in 1959, with a focus on promoting experimental artwork in a high-profile setting.

**MAP 4:** *Bosque de Chapultepec, Primera Sección s/n; tel. 55/5211-6086; www.casadellago.unam.mx; 11am-6pm Wed.-Sun.; free; Metro: Auditorio, Metrobús: Antropología*

### LAGO/ALGO

Among the most impressive art spaces in the city is ALGO, which shares a building with long-running restaurant Lago, in the Segunda Sección of Chapultepec. The striking modernist building was originally designed in the 1960s by architect Alfonso Ramírez Ponce and was carefully renovated in 2020-2021. Established Roma neighborhood gallery OMR oversees the excellent cultural end of the project, mounting varied and excellent contemporary shows in building's many unique spaces. Though the space is free to visit, reservations are required and can be made online.

**MAP 4:** *Bosque de Chapultepec, Pista El Sope s/n, 2a Sección; www.lago-algo.mx; 10am-7pm daily; free; Metro: Constituyentes*

### ✪ Complejo Cultural Los Pinos

When Andrés Manuel López Obrador took office in 2018, one of his first acts as president was to convert the opulent presidential mansion known as Los Pinos into a free multidisciplinary art and cultural center. AMLO moved into the old presidential residence in the Palacio Nacional, and Los Pinos was transformed into a beautiful public garden, exhibition space, and cultural hub, which continues to grow in size and scope.

Visitors to Los Pinos can stroll through the former presidential residences and gardens, view the art collection amassed by the presidency over the years, or attend one of the many special events, like plays, live music and dance performances, film screenings, and artisan markets, which take place on the weekend. A highlight of the complex is **Cencalli: La Casa del Maíz y la Cultura Alimentaria,** a museum that chronicles and celebrates the importance of maize in Mexican culture, from the pre-Columbian era through the present.

**MAP 4:** *Puerta 1, Primera Sección Chapultepec; tel. 55/4155-0200, ext. 2412; https://lospinos.cultura.gob.mx; 11am-6pm Tues.-Sat.; free; Metro: Constituyentes, Metrobús: Parque Lira*

# GALLERIES

## Proyectos Monclova

After establishing a strong reputation in contemporary art at its Colonia Roma gallery, Proyectos Monclova relocated to an airy multistory building in the heart of Polanco. Representing both Mexican and international artists, the gallery shows contemporary photography, sculpture, installation, and mixed-media pieces, and there are usually several reliably interesting exhibitions running in the gallery simultaneously.

**MAP 4:** *Lamartine 415; tel. 55/5525-9715; http://proyectosmonclova.com; 10am-6pm Mon.-Fri., 11am-4pm Sat.; free; Metro: Polanco*

## Galería de Arte Mexicano

Founded in 1935, the Galería de Arte Mexicano has a grand legacy, having once hosted shows by the 20th century's most famous names, including Diego Rivera, Frida Kahlo, José Clemente Orozco, Miguel Covarrubias, and Rufino Tamayo. In the residential San Miguel Chapultepec neighborhood, the gallery continues to focus on Mexico-based artists, representing well-known contemporary names, including Francisco Castro Leñero and Jan Hendrix. It's a beautiful space, and the exhibitions are high quality; ring the doorbell to visit.

**MAP 4:** *Gob. Rafael Rebollar 43, Col. San Miguel Chapultepec; tel. 52/5272-5529; www.galeriadeartemexicano.com; 10:30am-5pm Mon.-Thurs., 10:30am-2pm Fri.; free; Metro: Juanacatlán or Constituyentes*

## Kurimanzutto

Partners José Kuri, Mónica Manzutto, and Gabriel Orozco opened this spacious contemporary gallery in 2008. Orozco shows his work here, as do numerous other high-profile international and Mexican artists, including Allora y Calzadilla, Rirkrit Tiravanija, Abraham Cruzvillegas, Damián Ortega, and Akram Zaatari. Opening parties are well attended by a chic crowd, but the true attraction here is the excellent art. Drop by during the week and you're likely to have the gallery to yourself.

**MAP 4:** *Gob. Rafael Rebollar 94; tel. 55/5256-2408; www.kurimanzutto.com; 11am-6pm Tues.-Thurs., 11am-4pm Fri.-Sat.; free; Metro: Constituyentes or Juanacatlán*

## Labor

Located in an unmarked turquoise home just across the street from the Casa Luis Barragán, this tucked-away contemporary gallery represents an interesting roster of artists, including the excellent Mexican artists Pedro Reyes and Hector Zamora. Originally opened in 2010, it relocated to this quiet home in 2012, where a shaded garden adjoins the clean white gallery space. Ring the doorbell during business hours and you'll be buzzed in.

**MAP 4:** *Francisco Ramírez 5, Col. Daniel Garza; tel. 55/6304-8755; www.labor.org.mx; 11am-6pm Mon.-*

Museo Soumaya, designed by Fernando Romero

Thurs., 11am-3pm Fri.-Sat.; free; Metro: Constituyentes

### La Laboratoire
There are several floors of galleries and design shops within the "creative hub" **G.56** (https://g56.mx) in the San Miguel Chapultepec. Gallery La Laboratoire, on the 2nd floor, is a standout among them, showing an ongoing program of experimental and contemporary painting, photo, performance, sound art, and other disciplines. After visiting the gallery, stop in for a coffee at the G.56 café (9am-6pm Mon.-Fri., 9am-2pm Sat.) downstairs.

**MAP 4:** *General Antonio León 56; no phone; https://lelaboratoire.mx; 11am-2:30pm and 4:30pm-9pm Mon.-Fri., by appointment Sat.; Metro: Juanacatlán*

### RGR
Founded in Venezuela, this contemporary gallery has been based in Mexico City since 2018. Representing the work of famed Venezuelan artists Carlos Cruz-Diez and Jesús Rafael Soto, both of whom worked within the kinetic art and op-art movements, the gallery represents a range of contemporary abstract artists, many also focused on optical illusion, the interplay of color, and movement, making shows here dependably delightful.

**MAP 4:** *General Antonio León 48; tel. 55/8434-7759; www.rgrart.com; 10:30am-6:30pm Mon.-Thurs., 10:30am-4:30pm Fri., 11am-4:30pm Sat.; Metro: Juanacatlán*

## MUSEUMS
### Museo Soumaya
In the 1990s, Mexican multibillionaire Carlos Slim opened the Museo Soumaya as a place to house and exhibit his extensive art collection. Today the collection resides in a striking space designed by Slim's son-in-law Fernando Romero. The building's distinctive exterior, a glittery swoosh of asymmetrical metal, covers five stories of galleries exhibiting European and Mexican art from the Renaissance to the present day.

**MAP 4:** *Plaza Carso, Blv. Miguel de Cervantes Saavedra 303, Col. Ampliación Granada; tel. 55/1103-9800; www.soumaya.com.mx; 10:30am-6:30pm daily; free; Metro: Polanco or San Joaquín*

### ✪ Museo Jumex
Over the past two decades, the Fundación Jumex, owned by juice company heir Eugenio López Alonso, has assembled what is widely regarded as the most important collection of art in Latin America. In 2013, the foundation opened a

TOP EXPERIENCE

# An Art Lover's Guide to Mexico City

Mexico City has become one of the world's top destinations for contemporary art. There is a perceptible energy within the local art scene, with many distinctive institutions, gallerists, and artists at work here today.

## THE MUST-SEE INSTITUTIONS

Overseen by the renowned Fundación Jumex Arte Contemporáneo, **Museo Jumex** (page 161) has distinguished itself through a series of large-scale retrospectives of inter-

Museo Universitario Arte Contemporáneo

nationally celebrated artists like Urs Fischer, Ulises Carrión, and Andy Warhol. Tip: Admission is free, so get there early to beat the inevitable crowds.

**Museo Tamayo** (page 164) is known for its striking modern architecture and a lineup of thoughtful shows by contemporary artists like Ed Ruscha, Isamu Noguchi, Claudia Fernández, and others. Tip: Don't be misled by the name. Though the museum was founded by Oaxacan artist Rufino Tamayo and his wife, Olga, Tamayo's work is very rarely on show here.

Located on the Universidad Nacional Autónoma de México's main campus, **Museo Universitario Arte Contemporáneo** (page 257), or MUAC, is an outstanding contemporary museum that showcases work from Mexican and international artists, from British-Indian sculptor Anish Kapoor to Colombian painter Beatriz González. Tip: Check the schedule

contemporary art museum, designed by David Chipperfield, next to Carlos Slim's eye-catching Museo Soumaya in Plaza Carso. One of the most interesting contemporary art venues in the city, the museum distinguishes itself with a robust program of contemporary exhibits, including shows by internationally renowned artists, from Urs Fischer in 2022 to Damian Hirst in 2024. Free to visit, it's often crowded.

**MAP 4:** *Miguel de Cervantes Saavedra 303, Col. Ampliación Granada; tel. 55/5395-2615; www.fundacionjumex.org; 10am-5pm Tues.-Fri. and Sun., 10am-7pm Sat.; free; Metro: San Joaquín or Polanco*

### Museo de Arte Moderno

Inaugurated in 1964, Mexico City's largest modern art museum is housed in an industrial concrete building, with a central atrium

before trekking south to the university; sometimes the museum is closed to visitors while new shows are being installed.

## ALSO EXCELLENT

Though not strictly contemporary, the museum at the **Palacio de Bellas Artes** (page 94) has hosted excellent exhibits by Mexican artists such as Damián Ortega and Santiago Arau. On the opposite side of the Alameda, the **Laboratorio de Arte Alameda** (page 105) examines the intersection of art, science, and technology. Experimental exhibitions, often focused on subcultures, protest, and politics, are the focus at the **Museo Universitario del Chopo** (page 134) in the Santa María la Ribera.

There are dozens more contemporary art venues in Mexico City, with excellent shows held at institutions like the Museo de Arte Moderno, Museo Carrillo Gil, the Centro Cultural de España, LAGO/ALGO, Centro Cultural de Tlatelolco, and Museo Experimental El Eco, among others.

## MEXICO CITY ART WEEK

If you'd like to see the most in a short period time, visit during **Art Week Mexico,** held annually in February, when the well-established **Zsona MACO México** art fair is running, alongside newer proposals like **Salón Acme, Index Art Book Fair,** and **Material Art Fair.** For a week-plus, CDMX is all about art, with galleries and pop-up exhibits citywide.

## GALLERY DISTRICTS

There are excellent contemporary art galleries throughout the city's central neighborhoods, but you'll find the highest concentration in the San Miguel Chapultepec, where institutions like Kurimanzutto, Galería de Arte Mexicano, and RGR are based. There are also noteworthy galleries in the San Rafael, the Santa María la Ribera, the Juárez, Polanco, Tacubaya, Anahuac, and the Roma.

surrounded by the four main exhibition halls, three of which are dedicated to changing exhibits, while the fourth displays work from the permanent collection. The quality of the exhibits varies; however, the museum's permanent collection contains work by Diego Rivera, Leonora Carrington, and Remedios Varo, as well as Frida Kahlo's largest work, *Las Dos Fridas,* a twin self-portrait by the artist.

**MAP 4:** *Paseo de la Reforma and Gandhi; tel. 55/8647-5530; https://mam.inba.gob.mx; 10:15am-5:45pm daily; US$3, free students, teachers, and seniors, free Sun.; Metro: Chapultepec, Metrobús: Gandhi*

### Casa Gilardi

Luis Barragán's last project was this private home in the San Miguel Chapultepec neighborhood. Though it is still a home today (inhabited by one of the original owners), the first two floors are open to private tours (US$20) by appointment. If you've already visited Barragán's own house and studio nearby, Casa Gilardi will show an evolution in the artist's late stage and the full development of his point of view. The mirrorlike indoor pool, which stretches beside the dining room and almost seems to glow, is a highlight of the space. Reservations can be made via the website or by emailing casagilardi@gmail.com.

**MAP 4:** *General Antonio León 82; tel. 55/5271-3575; https://casagilardi.mx; tours by appointment; Metro: Constituyentes*

### Sala de Arte Público David Alfaro Siqueiros

Celebrated 20th-century muralist David Alfaro Siqueiros dedicated his life to creating public art, and this small but wonderful museum honors his legacy by displaying works by Siqueiros himself, in addition to hosting fine exhibitions of contemporary art. In keeping with the theme, the museum's facade is constantly repainted via the museum's Proyecto Fachada (Facade Project), exploring themes in politics and social justice that were close to Siqueiros's heart.

**MAP 4:** *Tres Picos 29, Polanco; tel. 55/8647-5340; https://saps-latallera.org; 10am-5pm Tues.-Sun.; US$2, free students, teachers, seniors, and under age 12, free Sun.; Metro: Auditorio*

Museo Tamayo café

### Museo Tamayo

Originally founded by Oaxacan artist Rufino Tamayo, this excellent contemporary art museum opened in 1981. Located on the Paseo de la Reforma in Chapultepec, it hosts high-quality temporary exhibitions by both Mexican and international artists. (Contrary to what some visitors expect, Tamayo's work is shown only infrequently, as part of special exhibits.) It's worth visiting for the beautiful modern space alone, designed by architects Abraham Zabludovsky and Teodoro González de León. There are expanded gallery spaces in the eastern wing, as well as a very attractive (and delicious) café and a design-centric gift shop on the premises.

**MAP 4:** *Paseo de la Reforma 51; tel. 55/4122-8200; www.museotamayo.org; 10am-6pm Tues.-Sun.; US$5, free under age 12, students, and teachers, free Sun.; Metro: Chapultepec*

### Museo de Historia Natural and Museo Jardín del Agua

Mexico City's natural history museum, housed in a series of unusual domed galleries built in the 1960s, remains open while undergoing a multiyear, multifaceted renovation. Chronicling Mexico's environment, geology, flora and fauna, and prehistoric past, the newly updated exhibit halls are well laid out, engaging, and colorful—an educational treat for the whole family. Note that exhibit text is in Spanish. After visiting the museum, stroll through the surrounding Museo Jardín del Agua, a large swath of Chapultepec park that has been designated as a living "museum" dedicated to the city's relationship with water. The highlight is the Cárcamo de Dolores, a collaboration between architect Ricardo Rivas and artist Diego Rivera, originally designed as part of the city's public water system in the 1950s. Tickets to the natural history museum include entry to Rivera's gorgeous mural *El Agua, Origen de la Vida en la Tierra* (Water, the Origin of Life on Earth), which covers the inside of a former municipal water tank.

**MAP 4:** *Av. de los Compositores s/n, Segunda Sección, Bosque de Chapultepec; tel. 55/5515-0739, ext. 112 and 113; 10am-5pm Tues.-Sun.; US$2 includes admission to Rivera mural, US$1 children and teachers, free seniors; Metro: Chapultepec*

### Papalote Museo del Niño

Mexico City's wonderful children's museum's playful exhibits range in themes from science and the human body to the natural world, engaging children with hands-on activities like blowing soap bubbles, shopping at a miniature supermarket, or climbing into a giant replica of a rain forest canopy. Note that audiovisual materials throughout the museum, including movies, are in Spanish. The museum has limited capacity (there can be a wait to get in), though it is still hugely crowded on the weekend.

**MAP 4:** *Av. Constituyentes 268, Segunda Sección, Bosque de Chapultepec; tel. 55/5237-1781; www.papalote.org.mx; generally 9am-6pm Mon.-Thurs., 10am-7pm Fri.-Sun.; US$10, free under age 2; Metro: Constituyentes*

# Recreation

## PARKS
### Parque Lincoln

In the heart of Polanco, this pretty, family-friendly park is a nice place for a stroll on a Sunday afternoon. There is a huge playground on the park's eastern edge, invariably packed on the weekend, as well as a small aviary (US$0.50) filled with noisy parrots, cockatiels, parakeets, and one splendid peacock. On the weekend there are motorized toy boats for rent on the park's mirror-like ponds (US$5 for 15 minutes). In addition to the permanent sculpture collection in the park, it is also a venue for art and design projects, notably a large shipping-container showroom set up during the annual Design Week Mexico.

**MAP 4:** *Bounded by Edgar Allan Poe, Luis G. Urbana, Emilio Castelar, and Aristóteles; 24 hours daily; free; Metro: Auditorio*

## ✪ Bosque de Chapultepec: Primera Sección and Segunda Sección

Covering nearly 700 ha (1,730 acres), the Bosque de Chapultepec not only provides respite for weekenders but helps control the climate and air quality in the water-starved, pavement-covered Valley of Mexico. With its natural springs and verdant vegetation, the area around the Cerro de Chapultepec was once a retreat for Mexica emperors and, later, colonial-era aristocrats; there are ruins of pre-Columbian baths in the park. Today, the tree-lined pathways of the Primera Sección (First Section) are home to some of the city's most important museums and cultural sights, as well as being a popular place for jogging, dog-walking, in-line skating, picnicking, and paddleboating on the Lago Menor or Lago Mayor ($5-8/hour). Generally quiet on weekdays, it's thronged with families and vendors on Saturday and Sunday.

A bit quieter than the more centrally located Primera Sección, the Segunda Sección (Second Section) of Chapultepec also has some beautiful green spaces and cultural institutions, like contemporary art space LAGO/ALGO and the wonderful children's museum. Since early 2023, the first and second sections of the park are connected by a series of footbridges, designed by artist Gabriel Orozco, making the second section of the park much more accessible to visitors on foot.

**MAP 4:** *Bounded by Paseo de la Reforma, Pedro A. de los Santos, Calzada de las Lomas, and Av. Constituyentes; Primera Sección 5am-4:30pm Tues.-Sun., other sections 24 hours daily; free; Metro: Chapultepec, Auditorio, Constituyentes*

## Bosque de Chapultepec: Tercera Sección and Cuarta Sección

The more rugged and lesser known Tercera Sección of Chapultepec is located to the west of the Segunda Sección and is filled with denser forest, hilly terrain, and walking paths. There are fewer monuments, attractions, and facilities in this section of the park, and it is far less visited than the first and second sections—though that is likely to change. In 2019, the government announced a plan to restore all three existing sections of Chapultepec, including new lighting, restored fountains, and expanded pedestrian paths, as well as to add new attractions and easier access to the third section.

In addition to the restoration project, the city government considerably expanded the park's size. In development since 2019, the new Cuarta Sección (Fourth Section) of Chapultepec opened to the public in the fall of 2024 on land that was previously occupied by the Secretary of National Defense. All 88 ha (217 acres) of the military camp, including its historic buildings, were donated to the city government. Among the most exciting programs in the Cuarta Sección is a massive new branch of the Cineteca Nacional, a government-supported art movie house, in a former gunpowder factory.

**MAP 4:** *Bordered to the south by Avenida Constituyentes; 24 hours daily; free; Metro: Constituyentes*

### Aztlán Parque Urbano

Chapultepec's long-running amusement park received a new name and some updated attractions when it reopened in 2021 as Aztlán Parque Urbano. There is a petite yet varied selection of rides inside the park, from an old-fashioned carousel to a 50-m (164-ft) free fall tower. For visitors, the main attraction is the giant Ferris wheel, Aztlán 360 ($7pp per ride), which opened in 2024 and affords incredible views of the surrounding city from its 85-m (279-ft) apex.

**MAP 4:** *Av. de los Compositores s/n, Bosque de Chapultepec Sección II; www.aztlanparqueurbano.com; noon-8pm Tues.-Sun.; park entry free, US$2-7 per ride; Metro: Constituyentes*

## CYCLING

### La Casa de la Bici Chapultepec

Incredibly, this tiny bicycle rental kiosk has been in operation since

paddleboats at Lago Menor

1921. If you are coming from the western entrances to the park near the San Miguel Chapultepec neighborhood, it's the closest place to rent a bike—and, unlike Igual Bicigratis, they have children's bikes as well. The limited fleet of bikes is squeaky and battered, but they're all you need to cruise through the park.

**MAP 4:** *Av. Parque Lira s/n; WhatsApp tel. 55/3559-7987; 10am-7pm Tues.-Sun.; US$4 per hour; Metro: Chapultepec or Constituyentes*

# Shops

## POLANCO SHOPPING DISTRICT

Polanco's tony main avenue, **Presidente Masaryk,** is lined with upscale European and American fashion houses like Fendi, Louis Vuitton, and DKNY; newer design and jewelry shops; and posh sidewalk cafés and restaurants. Come here to pick up some designer clothes and luxury items or to enjoy a bit of high-end window-shopping.

**MAP 4:** *Presidente Masaryk, between Newton and Moliere; Metro: Polanco*

## ARTS AND CRAFTS
### Uriarte Talavera

In the early colonies, Spanish settlers introduced Talavera-style tin-enameled glazing to Mexico's skilled Indigenous potters. The technique flourished, with artisans incorporating dazzling pigments and expressive painting styles to the process. Blue-and-white hand-painted Talavera ceramics became a hallmark of the state of Puebla, and Uriarte—established in 1824—is the country's oldest and most revered producer. Come to the Polanco store to browse the handmade and hand-painted flatware, mugs, tea sets, vases, and more.

**MAP 4:** *Galileo 67A; tel. 55/5280-0635; www.uriartetalavera.com.mx; 11am-7pm Wed.-Fri., 10am-7pm Sat.-Sun.; Metro: Polanco*

### Onora

Everything at Onora is handmade in Mexico by skilled traditional artisans working in tandem with a contemporary designer. The distinctive Mexican aesthetic and techniques are easily recognizable to anyone familiar with Mexican handcraft—you'll find everything from lacquered trays to tequila glasses—yet the pieces are also elegant and original, with designs unlike those found in most artisan markets or shops. It's a lovely place to pick up a set of mezcal glasses or a handwoven tablecloth to take home.

**MAP 4:** *Lope de Vega 330; tel. 55/5203-0938; http://onoracasa.com; 11am-7pm Mon.-Sat., 11am-5pm Sun.; Metro: Polanco*

Onora

### Expendio Doméstico

It's surprising how many covetable items are stocked into this tiny storefront in the San Miguel Chapultepec, a branch of a home goods and kitchen store that first opened in the upscale Lomas de Chapultepec neighborhood. Specializing in traditional Mexican products, the shop stocks many beautiful and duly useful everyday items, from metal lime juicers to hand-painted tequila glasses to burnished clay pitchers.

**MAP 4:** *General Cano 42; tel. 56/1995-4959; https:// expendiodomestico.mx; 11am-2:30pm and 3:30pm-7pm Mon.-Fri., 11am-4pm Sat.-Sun.; Metro: Juanacatlán*

### FONART

The Fondo Nacional para el Fomento de las Artesanías (FONART), a government department dedicated to supporting traditional artisans, runs several shops in the city, including a well-stocked branch on the Paseo de la Reforma (Av. Paseo de la Reforma 116; tel. 55/5546-7163; 11am-7pm Mon.-Fri., 11am-5pm Sat.-Sun.). At this newer branch in the Complejo Cultural Los Pinos, there is a beautiful selection of traditional Mexican furnishings, Talavera ceramic work, textiles and handmade clothing, dolls, toys, papier-mâché, burnished clay urns and flatware, and much more, representing artisans from across the republic. Prices are generally low for the quality of the work.

**MAP 4:** *Complejo Cultural Los Pinos., Av. Parque Lira s/n, Bosque de Chapultepec I Sección; no phone; 11am-7pm Tues.-Sun.; Metro: Constituyentes*

## BOUTIQUES

### Ikal

Ikal's urban-chic Polanco boutique represents a diverse array of independent Mexican designers, with clothes, jewelry, shoes, footwear, and beauty and home goods in a range of prices and aesthetics, from punk rock to rustic. Spend some time here and you're certain to find something that interests you, whether it's an embroidered blouse by Amor y Rosas, a pair of sunglasses by Camino, or a leather clutch by Tulum-based brand Gaela.

**MAP 4:** *President Masaryk 340; WhatsApp tel. 55/7922-9928; https://ikalstore.com; 10am-8pm daily; Metro: Polanco, Metrobús: Auditorio*

### Lago

This beautifully curated independent boutique stands out among the spate of international designers and luxury car shops that line Polanco's snazzy central avenue Presidente Masaryk. Showcasing clothes, jewelry, accessories, and home goods by emerging and established Latin American designers, you'll find labels like Juun, Belisa Pulido, and Carla Fernández among the racks. From embroidered blouses to contemporary silver jewelry, the pieces here are high quality and unique. In 2024 the boutique opened a smaller second location in the Juárez neighborhood (Havre 84; no phone; 10am-7pm daily).

**MAP 4:** *Presidente Masaryk 310;*

Lago boutique

*tel. 55/7261-9343; https://lagolatam. com; 9am-8pm Mon.-Sat., 10am-7pm Sun.; Metro: Polanco, Metrobús: Auditorio*

## BOOKS
### El Péndulo

This high-quality bookstore first opened in the Condesa (Nuevo León 115; tel. 55/5286-9493; 8am-11pm Mon.-Fri., 9am-11pm Sat.-Sun.), but it has since expanded across the city, with shops in the Zona Rosa (Hamburgo 126; tel. 55/5208-2327; 8am-11pm Mon.-Fri., 9am-11pm Sat.-Sun.) and the Roma (Álvaro Obregón 86; tel. 55/5574-7034; 8am-11pm Mon.-Wed., 8am-midnight Thurs.-Fri., 9am-midnight Sat., 9am-11pm Sun.) as well as this one in Polanco. Branches share a cozy decor with an earthy color scheme as well as an in-house coffee shop called the **Cafebrería.** Though predominantly stocking Spanish-language titles, the Polanco branch has a nice English fiction selection, mixing both classics and contemporary novels.

**MAP 4:** *Alejandro Dumas; tel. 55/5280-4111; https://pendulo.com; 8am-11pm Mon.-Sat., 9am-10pm Sun.; Metro: Polanco*

Tane

## JEWELRY
### Tane

Tane is one of the oldest and finest silver shops in Mexico, producing both jewelry and silver accessories for the home. Designs are generally elegant and highly contemporary, and the collections include some one-of-a-kind pieces and artist-designed series. Prices are high-end, but the workmanship is beautiful. There are additional locations in San Ángel (San Ángel Inn, Altavista 147, no. 7; tel. 55/5550-5632) and in the Four Seasons Hotel (Paseo de la Reforma 500; tel. 55/5203-2624).

**MAP 4:** *Presidente Mazaryk 430; tel. 55/5282-6200; https://mx.tane.com; 10am-7pm Mon.-Fri., 11am-7pm Sat.; Metro: Polanco*

# Roma and Condesa  Map 5

Getting Around ........ 173
Roma and
  Condesa Walk........ 176
Sights ................. 180
Restaurants............ 181
Nightlife ............... 193
Arts and Culture ....... 198
Recreation............. 200
Shops ................. 200

Through most of the 20th century, these adjacent residential neighborhoods were home to writers, journalists, artists, and many middle-class families. The Roma and Condesa became popular with the city's expatriate community during the early 2000s; today, the areas are ground zero for Mexico City's celebrated dining and nightlife scene. The tree-shaded Avenida Amsterdam and lush Parque México are emblematic of the Condesa, where the art deco and modern buildings make a pleasant backdrop for the neighborhood's boutique hotels and stylish eateries. In the youth-oriented Roma, many of the late 19th-century mansions are now home to galleries, restaurants, and popular cocktail bars.

# Highlights

✪ **Parque México:** At the center of the Condesa neighborhood, this beautiful oval-shaped park is notable for its unique landscape architecture and lush vegetation (page 181).

✪ **Museo del Juguete Antiguo:** This quirky museum in the Colonia Doctores features a madcap collection of vintage toys—and, unlike most museums in CDMX, it's open on Monday (page 198).

✪ **Huerto Roma Verde:** There are frequent eco-fairs, organic markets, public workshops, and performances at this active urban garden and social project in the southern Roma (page 200).

✪ **Roma Shopping District:** The wide range of locally owned boutiques and specialty shops in the Roma neighborhood are a reflection of the city's creative culture (page 200).

# Getting Around

- Metro lines: 1, 3, 9
- Metro stops: Insurgentes, Sevilla, Hospital General, Niños Héroes, Chilpancingo, Patriotismo
- Metrobús lines: 1
- Metrobús stops: Insurgentes, Álvaro Obregón, Sonora, Campeche

---

**Previous:** tree-shaded Avenida Amsterdam; **Above:** the fountain in Parque Mexico; Avenida Álvaro Obregón in the Roma Norte neighborhood.

# MAP 5

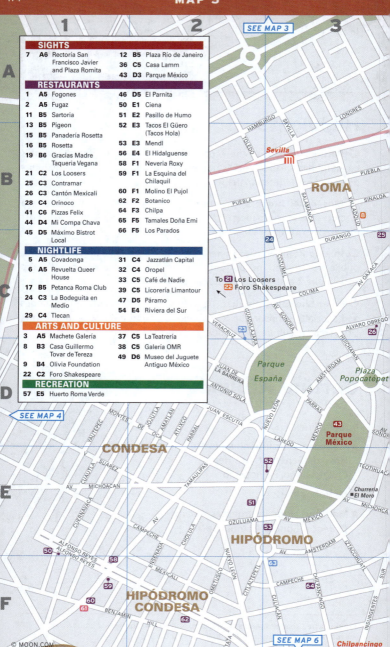

### SIGHTS
| # | Grid | Name |
|---|---|---|
| 7 | A6 | Rectoría San Francisco Javier and Plaza Romita |
| 12 | B5 | Plaza Río de Janeiro |
| 36 | C5 | Casa Lamm |
| 43 | D3 | Parque México |

### RESTAURANTS
| # | Grid | Name |
|---|---|---|
| 1 | A5 | Fogones |
| 2 | A5 | Fugaz |
| 11 | B5 | Sartoria |
| 13 | B5 | Pigeon |
| 15 | B5 | Panadería Rosetta |
| 16 | B5 | Rosetta |
| 19 | B6 | Gracias Madre Taqueria Vegana |
| 21 | C2 | Los Loosers |
| 25 | C3 | Contramar |
| 26 | C3 | Cantón Mexicali |
| 28 | C4 | Orinoco |
| 41 | C6 | Pizzas Felix |
| 44 | D4 | Mi Compa Chava |
| 45 | D5 | Máximo Bistrot Local |
| 46 | D5 | El Parnita |
| 50 | E1 | Ciena |
| 51 | E2 | Pasillo de Humo |
| 52 | E3 | Tacos El Güero (Tacos Hola) |
| 53 | E3 | Mendl |
| 56 | E4 | El Hidalguense |
| 58 | F1 | Neveria Roxy |
| 59 | F1 | La Esquina del Chilaquil |
| 60 | F1 | Molino El Pujol |
| 62 | F2 | Botanico |
| 64 | F3 | Chilpa |
| 65 | F5 | Tamales Doña Emi |
| 66 | F5 | Los Parados |

### NIGHTLIFE
| # | Grid | Name |
|---|---|---|
| 5 | A5 | Covadonga |
| 6 | A5 | Revuelta Queer House |
| 17 | B5 | Petanca Roma Club |
| 24 | C3 | La Bodeguita en Medio |
| 29 | C4 | Tlecan |
| 31 | C4 | Jazzatlán Capital |
| 32 | C4 | Oropel |
| 33 | C5 | Café de Nadie |
| 39 | C5 | Licorería Limantour |
| 47 | D5 | Páramo |
| 54 | E4 | Riviera del Sur |

### ARTS AND CULTURE
| # | Grid | Name |
|---|---|---|
| 3 | A5 | Machete Galería |
| 8 | B3 | Casa Guillermo Tovar de Tereza |
| 9 | B4 | Olivia Foundation |
| 22 | C2 | Foro Shakespeare |
| 37 | C5 | La Teatrería |
| 38 | C5 | Galería OMR |
| 49 | D6 | Museo del Juguete Antiguo México |

### RECREATION
| # | Grid | Name |
|---|---|---|
| 57 | E5 | Huerto Roma Verde |

# Roma and Condesa

175

### SHOPS
| | | | | |
|---|---|---|---|---|
| 4 | A5 | Casa Bosques | 30 C4 | Delirio |
| 10 | B5 | Chic by Accident | 35 C5 | Álvaro Obregón |
| 14 | B5 | La Canasta | 42 C6 | Laguna |
| 18 | B5 | 180° Shop | 55 E4 | Mercado de Medellín |
| 20 | B6 | Mercado de Cuauhtémoc | 61 F1 | Librería Rosario Castellanos |
| 27 | C4 | Happening Store | | |

### HOTELS
| | | | | |
|---|---|---|---|---|
| 23 | C2 | Condesa DF | 48 D5 | Ignacia Guest House |
| 34 | C5 | Casa Nima | 63 F3 | RedTree House |
| 40 | C6 | Hotel Stanza | | |

# Roma and Condesa Walk

**TOTAL DISTANCE:** 2.2 km (1.3 mi)
**TOTAL WALKING TIME:** 1.5 hours

In a stroll through the attractive, walkable Roma and Condesa neighborhoods, you'll pass many eye-catching old mansions, pretty green parks, and popular public plazas. Though food and nightlife are their most famous attractions, these neighborhoods are also known for their beautiful early 20th-century architecture and unique urban design, which includes ample green spaces. If you want to see some of the key spots, here's where to start.

## The Roma

Largely constructed during the opulent Porfiriato era at the end of the 19th century, the northern blocks of the Colonia Roma are filled with impressive mansions, some beautifully preserved, others abandoned since the 1985 earthquake. The greatest concentration of historic architecture is along Avenida Álvaro Obregón and Calle Colima, as well as around the Plaza Río de Janeiro. Some of the

a grand traffic circle in the Roma

neighborhood's wildly original buildings are good examples of 19th-century eclecticism, which incorporates elements from different eras, including art nouveau, art deco, and neocolonial styles.

**1** Start your day in the pleasant **Plaza Río de Janeiro,** a favored gathering spot for dog walkers and Roma families. With an unusual peaked roof, the **Edificio Río de Janeiro** apartment building—known locally as La Casa de las Brujas (Witches' House)—is on the east side of the park. It was constructed by British architect Regis A. Pigeon in 1908, and it was among the first buildings erected in the plaza. Architect Francisco Serrano added its deco facade in the 1930s.

*Walk south along Orizaba to Álvaro Obregón, the Roma's central avenue and the hub of its happening dining and nightlife scene.*

**2** On the northeast corner of Orizaba and Álvaro Obregón, **Casa Lamm** is a beautifully restored mansion, now home to a cultural center, restaurant, and gallery, with restored interiors and gardens open to the public (the entrance is half a block east on Álvaro Obregón). Just across the street, on another corner of Álvaro Obregón and Orizaba, **Edificio Balmori** (Orizaba 101) is a palace-like building with a sandstone facade and elegant French windows, originally constructed as residence apartments. The slightly sunken 1st floor is now filled with street-level boutiques.

Casa Lamm

*Continue south.*

**3** Arrive at **Plaza Luis Cabrera,** at Guanajuato and Orizaba. Stroll around the large fountain at the center of the plaza, which is ringed by restaurants and beautiful old buildings. From the plaza, head west along Guanajuato, toward the Condesa.

*Cross a few large and noisy avenues—first Monterrey, then Avenida Insurgentes, then Avenida Yucatán—to reach the tree-lined street Popocatépetl, to the southwest, which will take you into the quiet heart of the Condesa.*

## The Condesa

The Condesa was mainly built in the 1920s, on land that was part of a hacienda owned by the Condesa de Miravalle, the neighborhood's eponymous condesa, or countess. In an unusual move, the Condesa's developers incorporated a former horse racing track into their street plan, creating the oval-shaped Avenida Amsterdam, which runs in a circle around likewise oval-shaped Parque México. Today, Amsterdam is one of the most beautiful streets in the city, ringed with art deco and modern architecture, filled with trees, and popular with joggers and dog walkers.

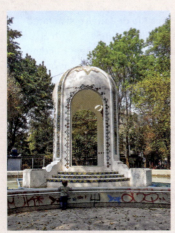
art deco fountain in the Plaza Popocatépetl

**4** Walk west on Popocatépetl; one block later you'll be standing at the intersection of Avenida Amsterdam. Continue southwest on Popocatépetl to arrive at shady **Plaza Popocatépetl,**

private residences designed by architect Luis Barragán on Avenida México in the Condesa

just a block south of Avenida Amsterdam. From the plaza, walk south along Avenida México, passing one of the most famous buildings in the neighborhood: the **Edificio Basurto** (Avenida México 187). It is a 1940s gem of art deco design, with a unique horseshoe-shaped lobby. It was badly damaged in the September 2017 earthquake, but remained standing after extensive renovation. Just across the street from the Basurto, the **Edificio Tehuacán** is another jewel of Mexican art deco. Today it's the **Hippodrome Hotel.**

*Cross Avenida Sonora to the park.*

**5** Enter **Parque México,** a jewel of landscape architecture filled with cypresses and palm trees. Wander the footpaths past art deco fountains, the large duck pond, and the unique outdoor theater, Foro Lindbergh, known locally El Redondel. On the east side of the park, stop at the **Edificio San Martín** (Av. México 167), built in 1931 by celebrated architect Luis Barragán, who also constructed homes at **Avenida México 141** and **143.** Both are private homes and not open to the public, but their exteriors display the beginnings of Barragán's style.

Finish up your afternoon with a hot chocolate and a churro at the Condesa branch of the CDMX classic Churrería El Moro (Michoacán 27), overlooking Parque México. If you'd like to explore more of the neighborhood, it's an easy walk to the Condesa's many restaurants and nightspots, many of them concentrated just west of the park, near the intersection of Michoacán and Tamaulipas.

Parque México

# Sights

### Rectoría San Francisco Javier and Plaza Romita

Long before the 19th-century development of the Roma neighborhood, the land was a part of the small pre-Columbian settlement of Aztacalco. There, in 1530, Spanish settlers built a small chapel named Santa María de la Natividad to serve the community. Many centuries later, that chapel was the center of a subdistrict of the Roma neighborhood known as La Romita. Though the greater Roma was wealthy, La Romita became famous for its crime, thieves, and poverty. Luis Buñuel filmed part of his famous movie *Los Olvidados*, about destitute children in Mexico, in La Romita. Today, it is a pretty tree-filled plaza, adjoined by the Rectoría San Francisco Javier, which is believed to stand in the original 16th-century chapel's place.

**MAP 5:** *Plaza Romita; 24 hours daily; free; Metro: Niños Héroes*

Parque México

### Plaza Río de Janeiro

A nice place to start a stroll around the Roma neighborhood is the Plaza Río de Janeiro. Surrounded by old mansions and apartment buildings, this low-key park rings a central fountain, with a rather incongruous replica of Michelangelo's *David* statue in the center. On the east side of the square, **La Casa de las Brujas** (Witches' House), as the Edificio Río de Janeiro is popularly known, is a redbrick castle, built in 1908, with notable art deco accents.

**MAP 5:** *Durango and Orizaba; Metro: Insurgentes*

### Casa Lamm

An opulent Colonia Roma mansion, Casa Lamm was originally built by architect Lewis Lamm in 1911. Today, it's home to a small art school (which offers workshops as well as undergraduate and graduate programs), a light-filled contemporary art gallery, and chic fusion restaurant **Nueve Nueve** (tel. 55/5525-9795; www.nuevenueve.com.mx; 1:30pm-midnight Mon.-Sat., 1:30pm-7pm Sun.). In the basement, the well-stocked **Biblioteca de Arte** has a large selection of contemporary and modern art books.

**MAP 5:** *Álvaro Obregón 99; tel. 55/5525-1332; www.casalamm.com.mx, www.casalamm.com.mx; cultural center 1:30pm-10pm Mon., 1:30pm-11pm Tues., 1:30pm-midnight Wed.-Sat., 1:30pm-7pm Sun.; free; Metro: Insurgentes*

## ⊙ Parque México

One of the prettiest urban respites in Mexico City, the Parque México is a big reason why the Condesa has become one of the nicest neighborhoods in the city. Much beloved by locals, the large oval-shaped park, encircled by the tree-lined Avenida México, was built in the center of what was once a horse track. Officially named Parque San Martín (though no one ever calls it that), Parque México provides a wonderful, surprisingly peaceful respite from the noise and traffic of the city, filled with footpaths, towering trees, and lush gardens. In addition to being a relaxing neighborhood spot, Parque México is known for its art deco landscape architecture. Wander past its ponds and unusual fountains, and stop to admire the graffiti-covered outdoor auditorium **Foro Lindbergh,** where kids often ride bikes or kick soccer balls after school. During the week, Condesa locals come here to jog, walk their dogs, host Scout meetings, or read; on the weekends, families come to stroll and play.

From Parque México, walk one block in any direction to Avenida Amsterdam, an oval-shaped avenue with a tree-filled pedestrian median, lined by many architecturally interesting buildings. From Amsterdam, follow Michoacán four blocks west, across Nuevo León and Tamaulipas; you'll find yourself in the middle of the Condesa restaurant and café zone. Or, swing north on Nuevo León to visit **Parque España,** a smaller but equally pretty park just a few blocks from Parque México.

**MAP 5:** *Av. México, between Av. Sonora and Av. Michoacán; Metro: Chilpancingo, Metrobús: Sonora*

# Restaurants

## PRICE KEY
$     Entrées less than US$10
$$    Entrées US$10-20
$$$   Entrées more than US$20

## MEXICAN

### ⊙ Los Loosers $$

Los Loosers began as a delivery service (with meals pedaled to your door on one-speed bicycles) and built a loyal following with its famous mushroom burger. The nonmobile version, on a shady street in the Condesa, retains a bit of the original project's rebellious spirit—and you can still order the burgers, though the menu includes both Mexican and Asian-inspired dishes. Creative flavors and techniques stand out in dishes like tacos al pastor made with grilled mushrooms and the bean-stuffed tetela (triangle-shaped corn flatbread) wrapped in hoja santa and topped with almond-milk cheese.

**MAP 5:** *Sinaloa 236; no phone; www.losloosers.mx; 2pm-9pm Tues.-Sat.,*

## 20th-Century Architectural Masterpieces

Mexico City's unique cityscape has been shaped by a long tradition of creative architecture, from the baroque masterpieces of the colonial era to the showy design of its newest museums. During the first half of the 20th century, many important architects left their mark on the growing city, creating some of its most iconic sights.

- **Art Deco Icon:** Among the most famous of the many art deco buildings in the Condesa, the **Edificio Basurto** (Av. México 187) was built from 1942 to 1945 by Francisco J. Serrano (1900-1982). At 14 floors, it was one of the city's tallest buildings at the time of its construction.

- **First Functionalist:** An architect, university professor, and artist, Juan O'Gorman (1905-1982) was one of the first functionalist architects in Latin America. He designed Frida Kahlo and Diego Rivera's former residences in San Ángel, today the **Museo Casa Estudio Diego Rivera** (page 255); famously, the home was divided into two separate parts (one for each of them), linked by a footbridge.

- **Mexican Modernism:** Blending European modernist and Mexican vernacular elements, the architect Luis Barragán (1902-1988)'s signature use of color, light, and spaces is on display at his home and studio, **Casa Luis Barragán** (page 151), now a museum and UNESCO World Heritage Site.

- **Family-Style Functionalism:** Mario Pani (1911-1983) was a pioneer in designing and constructing affordable multifamiliares (multifamily apartment buildings) throughout the city, none more iconic than the **Conjunto Urbano Nonoalco Tlatelolco** (Av. Ricardo Flores Magón

---

noon-8pm Sun.; Metro: Chapultepec, Metrobús: Chapultepec

### El Parnita $

Whether you come at lunch for a relaxed meal with friends and family, or join the lively crowds late in the evening for drinks and snacks, El Parnita is a solidly delicious, reliably fun, and pleasantly low-key place to eat. With a menu dedicated to antojitos, or snacks, you can mix and match to create a meal from the selection of items like shrimp tacos, ceviche-topped tostados, or tlacoyos (corn cakes) filled with cheese. And, of course, top everything with the restaurant's excellent trio of fresh salsas.

**MAP 5:** Yucatán 84; tel. 55/5264-7551; http://elparnita.com; 9am-10pm Tues.-Sun.; Metro: Insurgentes or Chilpancingo, Metrobús: Sonora

and Insurgentes Norte), a 101-tower housing project in the Tlatelolco neighborhood that included schools, shops, and hospitals.

- **Modern Masterpieces:** A tour of the modernist architectural work by Pedro Ramírez Vázquez's (1919-2013) is in many ways a tour of Mexico City's most famous sites. His iconic work includes the breathtaking **Museo Nacional de Antropología** (page 148), with its soaring central canopy and fountain; the modern shrine at the **Basílica de Santa María de Guadalupe** (page 248); and the mammoth stadium **Estadio Azteca** (page 261).

- **Magnificent Museums:** Architect Teodoro González de León (1926-2016) had an eye for cultural spaces, and his masterpieces include the **Museo Tamayo** (page 164) and the **Auditorio Nacional** (page 158), both designed with longtime collaborator Abraham Zabludovsky (1924-2003), and the stunning **Museo Universitario Arte Contemporáneo** (page 257), the contemporary art museum on UNAM's central campus.

- **World-Class Collaboration:** Designed by more than 60 architects, artists, landscape designers, and engineers, the central campus of the **Universidad Autónoma de México** has been recognized as "one of the most significant icons of modernity in Latin America" by the United Nations; a highlight is the lava-rock mosaics on the UNAM's iconic **Biblioteca Central** (page 250), designed by Juan O'Gorman.

- **Vibrant Minimalism:** Built in 1968, the colorful **Hotel Camino Real** in Polanco is emblematic of the era, employing both minimalist modern design and vibrant colors. It was designed by prolific architect Ricardo Legorreta (1930-2011), who also designed the master plan for the **Centro Nacional de los Artes** (page 239), among other architectural jewels.

## ✪ El Hidalguense $

All the food at this casual weekend-only restaurant comes directly from the owner's ranch in the state of Hidalgo. It is best known for the barbacoa (slow-cooked lamb), which is prepared to melt-in-your-mouth perfection, but everything on the menu is fresh and delicious, from the simple nopal (prickly pear) salad to the frijoles aztecas (refried beans mixed with spices and scrambled egg), the wild-mushroom mixiotes (roasted in a maguey leaf), and the wonderfully fresh pulque, which is served natural and in a variety of fresh fruit curados.

**MAP 5:** *Campeche 155; tel. 55/5564-0538; 7am-6pm Fri.-Sun.; Metro: Centro Médico, Metrobús: Campeche*

## Molino El Pujol $

Famed chef Enrique Olvera has dedicated his career to traditional

Mexican cooking, and this simple but superlative tortillería is an outgrowth of that work. The cornerstone of the project are tortillas, made in house with heirloom corn and sold by the dozen, along with other kitchen items, like honey and salsas. There is also a lovely menu of traditional Mexican breakfasts and snacks, served at the small indoor bar and sidewalk tables. Try the seasonal tamales, esquites (heirloom corn kernels topped with mayonnaise, chilies, and cheese), or conchas (sugar-topped sweet rolls).

**MAP 5:** *Benjamín Hill 146; tel. 55/5271-3515; 8am-6pm daily; Metro: Chilpancingo or Patriotismo, Metrobús: Campeche*

### Chilpa $

This relaxed sidewalk café draws the brunch crowd with its irresistible "build your own chilaquiles" option. Depending on what you're craving, you might order chilaquiles in spicy habanero salsa with a fried egg and avocado on top, or go for bean-sauce-topped baked tortillas with chicken and goat cheese—and the options go on from there. Accompany your meal with a coffee or a fresh fruit smoothie and you might not need to eat till dinner.

**MAP 5:** *Chilpancingo 35; tel. 55/5264-4976; https://chilpa.mx; 8am-6pm Mon.-Fri., 9am-5pm Sat.-Sun.; Metro: Chilpancingo, Metrobús: Chilpancingo*

### ✪ Fogones $$

Part of an ambitious culinary heritage project, Fogones isn't a typical restaurant but an exploration of Mexico's regional cuisines. At both the Roma and the original branch in Coyoacán (Escocia 58, Parque San Andrés, Coyoacán), a traditional female chef is invited to Mexico City to design a multicourse set-price menu, highlighting lesser-known dishes from across the republic—think grasshopper tamales from Tlaxcala or pork in plum sauce from Guerrero. Food is served to the whole dining room simultaneously (there are two seatings daily), usually accompanied by commentary from the chef. Don't mind the rather characterless atmosphere: Here, food takes center stage.

**MAP 5:** *Av. Chapultepec 266; WhatsApp tel. 44/9193-8210; www.fogonesmx.com; reservations required; seatings 1pm and 3pm Fri., 10am, 1pm, and 3pm Sat.-Sun.; Metro: Insurgentes, Metrobús: Insurgentes*

## TACOS, TORTAS, AND SNACKS

### Gracias Madre Taquería Vegana $

The plant-based tacos at this small and super-popular taco shop are remarkably similar to their traditional counterparts. The pastor is crisp and earthy; the arrachera has a nice beef-like chew; and the taco de chicharrón en salsa verde has a texture that is a dead ringer for the real thing—and perhaps even more delicious than many versions that include real pig skin.

**MAP 5:** *Tabasco 97; www.graciasmadretaqueriavegana.com; 9am-11pm Mon.-Sat., 9am-10:30pm*

Gracias Madre Taquería Vegana

known for its tasty and economical tacos de guisado. You choose your fillings from the daily offerings—like potato with chorizo, shredded chicken, or spinach—which are stuffed into a double tortilla and topped with beans, cheese, or guacamole on request. If you come during the midmorning rush, don't be deterred—just join the crowd and be patient. The efficient taqueros will make sure everyone gets served.

**MAP 5:** *Amsterdam 135; tel. 56/1866-8923; 10:30am-around 4pm Mon.-Sat.; Metro: Chilpancingo*

Sun.; *Metro: Insurgentes, Metrobús: Álvaro Obregón or Jardín Pushkin*

### Orinoco $

"TACOS" shout the signs in the window of Orinoco, a new-school taquería that has accrued an avid loyal following for its delicious renditions of the capital's favorite dish, including a beloved chicharrón taco and tacos al pastor. At the Roma location, you can sit inside the ultra-casual white-tiled dining room and see the tacos being made or grab a sidewalk table along Avenida Álvaro Obregon. It's always bustling and open late.

**MAP 5:** *Álvaro Obregon 100; tel. 55/5514-6917; https:// taqueriaorinoco.com; 1pm-3:30am Sun.-Wed., 1pm-4am Thurs., 1pm-5am Fri.-Sat.; Metro: Insurgentes, Metrobús: Álvaro Obregon*

### Tacos El Güero (Tacos Hola) $

This hole-in-the-wall spot is a neighborhood institution, widely

### La Esquina del Chilaquil $

There are often dozens of hungry patrons waiting in line at this friendly Condesa food stand, where the specialty is a stick-to-your-ribs concoction: A telera (white roll) is stuffed with chilaquiles (fried tortillas, bathed in red or green salsa—your choice), and then stuffed some more with breaded chicken breast or pulled pork. Take your heavy-duty sandwich to a nearby park bench for an efficient, cheap, and delicious meal.

**MAP 5:** *Alfonso Reyes and Tamaulipas; no phone; 8am-1pm daily; Metro: Chilpancingo, Metrobús: Chilpancingo*

### Tamales Doña Emi $$

Tamales at this Roma institution often run out within hours of their opening, and for good reason: They are among the best you'll find in the city, served steaming hot, rich in flavor, and filled with top-notch

TOP EXPERIENCE

# Tacos: Mexico City's Main Dish

From ultra-cheap to gourmet, simple to elaborate, vegan to viscera-stuffed, tacos are a surprisingly wide-ranging dish. Here are just a few of the many types of tacos you can find in the capital.

## AL PASTOR

Tacos al pastor are a specialty of the capital and one of its most ubiquitous dishes. Spit-roasted pork, usually marinated in a bright red chili-and-achiote rub, is topped with a slice of pineapple, cilantro, lime, white onion,

Tacos al pastor are a capital favorite.

and red or green salsa. This is a late-night snack; most taquerías specializing in pastor don't open till evening and are busiest after 10pm or 11pm.

**Where to get it: El Vilsito** (page 212), **Orinoco** (page 185), **Los Parados** (page 188), **El Huequito** (page 97), **Tacos Los Condes** (page 212), or **Hostal de los Quesos** (page 213), among many others.

## BARBACOA

This early- to midmorning snack is lamb wrapped in maguey leaves and slow-cooked in a pit, topped with diced white onion, cilantro, lime juice, and spicy salsa. It's often accompanied by consomé de barbacoa, a rich lamb-broth soup with garbanzo beans, believed to be a hangover cure.

**Where to get it: El Hidalguense** (page 183); **Arroyo** (page 254); on the corner of Durango and Cozumel in the Roma Norte (Sat.-Sun. mornings only).

## CARNITAS

Slow-cooked braised pork, traditionally prepared in a huge copper or stainless-steel pot, carnitas are eaten in the morning or early afternoon. Carnitas are also popular stuffed into gorditas, round corn flatbreads toasted on a griddle.

Most or all of the pig is used in carnitas: Maciza is the shoulder. Costilla (rib), panza (belly), and chamorro (leg) are popular choices. Adventurous eaters can try buche (stomach), trompa (snout), tripa (tripe), or more unusual parts like nana (uterus). Or get them surtida, a mix of meats.

**Where to get it: Rincón Tarasco** (page 213), **Carnitas El Cherán** (page 97), and **Los Kuinitos** (page 127); street stands across the city.

## TACOS ÁRABES

The historic precursor to tacos al pastor, tacos árabes are filled with spit-roasted pork and served in a soft pita-like flour tortilla, often with chipotle salsa and jocoque (Middle Eastern-style strained yogurt).

**Where to get it:** Traditional at **Tacos Manolo** (page 212); northern style at **Tacos Domingo** (page 100); at **Tacos Beyrut** (page 293) in the city of Puebla, where tacos árabes were invented.

## TACOS DE GUISADO

These tacos are stuffed with guisos (stews), like roasted chile poblano, picadillo (seasoned ground beef), and papa con chorizo (potato with sausage). These are often good for vegans and vegetarians, as rajas (strips of chili), Swiss chard, and chile poblano are classic guisos. Some taquerías offer guacamole, rice, black beans, or hard-boiled egg in your taco in addition to the guiso.

Enjoy in early and midmorning. At popular spots, they will start to run out by early afternoon.

**Where to get it:** **Tacos El Güero** (page 185) or **Beatricita** (page 126); at street stands near the corner of Álvaro Obregón and Insurgentes.

## CHORIZO, LONGANIZA, MORONGA, AND CECINA

You'll find a wide range of Mexican sausages, from red to green, sweet to spicy, and usually made of pork. Longaniza is a long red sausage. Moronga (or morcilla) is blood sausage. Cecina is salt-cured beef, also called tasajo when prepared in the Oaxacan style.

**Where to get it:** Try longaniza at **Los Cocuyos** (page 75) or **Tacos Los Condes** (page 212). Get cecina or chorizo at **Tacos Chupacabras** (page 234).

## COCHINITA PIBIL

Try achiote-seasoned shredded pork, typical to the state of Yucatán, topped with habanero salsa and pickled red onions.

**Where to get it:** **El Turix** (page 154) in Polanco; at Yucatec restaurants like **Fonda 99.99** (page 212) in the Del Valle.

## TACOS DE CANASTA

Also called tacos al vapor (steamed tacos), these small tacos are stuffed with simple fillings—chicharrón, beans, and potato are typical options—and warmed in oil, then stored and served in giant baskets, where the steam keeps them warm.

**Where to get it:** From baskets in Chapultepec; at tiny stands in the Centro Histórico.

ingredients, from classics like pork with salsa verde to more unusual combinations like huitlacoche with goat cheese. Though most customers take their tamales to go, there are a few outdoor tables and some barstools for eating.

**MAP 5:** *Jalapa 278; WhatsApp tel. 55/4535-0103; 8am-noon or until sold out Mon.-Fri., 8:30am-noon Sat.-Sun.; Metro: Centro Médico*

### Los Parados $

The name of this famous taquería means roughly "the stand-ups," and indeed you must be prepared to eat while standing, perhaps jostled within a crowd of people, when visiting this long-running taco joint. There are a wide variety of delicious tacos here (and top-notch salsas to top them), including nopal (prickly pear) with cheese, chorizo, and Mexico City staple pastor.

**MAP 5:** *Monterrey 333; tel. 55/8596-0191; 12:30pm-3am Mon.-Thurs., 12:30pm-5am Fri.-Sat., 12:30pm-1am Sun.; Metro: Chilpancingo or Centro Médico, Metrobús: Chilpancingo*

## SEAFOOD
### Contramar $$

An ultra-popular lunch spot in the Roma Norte, Contramar is widely cited as the city's top spot for seafood, as the constant crowds attest. Ceviches, tacos de camarón, fried fish, and the beloved tostadas de atún (tuna tostadas) are reliably fresh and deliciously prepared and go as well with a glass of white wine as a cold cerveza. The bright, airy dining room is always alive with loud, happy, well-heeled diners.

**MAP 5:** *Durango 200; tel. 55/5514-9217 or 55/5514-3169; www.contramar.com.mx; noon-8pm Mon.-Fri., 11am-8pm Sat.-Sun.; Metro: Sevilla, Metrobús: Durango*

### ✪ Mi Compa Chava $$

There's always a joyous bustle in the dining room at this superlative Mexican-style seafood spot. As waitstaff rush trays of iced oysters to waiting tables, diners tuck into seafood cocktails or snap Instagram-worthy pictures of the beautifully plated tuna-topped tostadas. Micheladas, craft beer, mezcal, and surprisingly excellent coffee and desserts complete the experience. Reservations are not available on weekends, and the wait for a table can be two hours or more, but once you're seated, order a bucket full of iced beer and make your way through the menu.

**MAP 5:** *Zacatecas 172; reservations Tues.-Fri. via WhatsApp tel. 55/7838-5054; noon-8pm Tues.-Sun.; Metro: Insurgentes, Metrobús: Álvaro Obregón*

## ASIAN
### Cantón Mexicali $$

In the 19th century, an influx of Chinese immigrants from California to Northern Mexico led to a surge in Chinese-style cuisine in the city of Mexicali—the inspiration for the kitchen and aesthetic behind this Roma hot spot. Here, you'll find creative and straight-up delicious versions of well-known

Chinese-American dishes like wontons, chop suey, chow mein, kung pao chicken, and deep-fried sweet-and-sour fish, matched by a nostalgic old-school atmosphere. Excellent cocktails, an upbeat ambience, and jovial service make dining here a delight.

**MAP 5:** *Av. Álvaro Obregón 264; tel. 55/1701-1479; www.cantonmexicali.com; 1pm-1am daily; Metro: Insurgentes, Metrobús: Álvaro Obregón*

## ITALIAN
### Sartoria $$

Everything is handmade, from the pasta to the limoncello, at Sartoria, an Italian restaurant from chef Marco Carboni. The use of fresh locally sourced ingredients is showcased in colorful salads, tender house-made pastas, and seasonal risottos, which are prepared with care and plated with panache. While the food is Italian, native Mexican ingredients make an appearance in dishes like quelite-stuffed raviolis. The dining room, with its arched roof and wood tables, has a subdued elegance, lovely for a date night.

**MAP 5:** *Orizaba 42; tel. 55/7265-3616; https://sartoria.mx; 1pm-midnight Mon.-Sat., 1pm-11pm Sun.; Metro: Insurgentes, Metrobús: Insurgentes*

### Rosetta $$$

Star chef Elena Reygadas serves consistently creative, fresh, and lovingly prepared Italian food in an elegantly restored Roma mansion. Start the meal with an appetizer, like roasted bone marrow, then follow up with one of the delicious pastas or entrées, which always include interesting options that emphasize local produce, such as beet risotto or gnocchi with huitlacoche and vegetables. Even if you aren't eating at the restaurant, you can have a drink at romantic **Salon Rosetta,** right above the restaurant, which serves interesting craft cocktails and bar snacks.

**MAP 5:** *Colima 166; tel. 55/5533-7804; http://rosetta.com.mx; 1pm-5:30pm and 6:30pm-11pm Mon.-Sat.; Metro: Insurgentes, Metrobús: Álvaro Obregón*

### Pizza Félix $

Chewy Neapolitan-style pizzas, served hot from the oven and topped with ingredients like house-made ricotta and shiitake mushrooms, are the main attraction of a meal at Félix, but the menu is rounded out with top-notch starters like kale Caesar and cucumber-chili salad as well as a bar menu that includes craft cocktails, local beer, mezcal, and wine. It's an upbeat spot at any time of day and open late enough for a post-bar nosh before bedtime.

**MAP 5:** *Álvaro Obregón 64; http://pizzafelix.mx; 1pm-11:45pm Sun.-Wed., 1:30pm-1:30am Thurs.-Fri., noon-1:30am Sat.; Metro: Insurgentes, Metrobús: Álvaro Obregón or Jardín Pushkin*

# Eating in the Off-Hours

New York has claimed the reputation as "the city that never sleeps," but Mexico's capital has its own round-the-clock culture. For many CDMX residents, late nights aren't an anomaly but a way of life, and there's never an hour of the day when you won't find great eats and a good time here. Here's where to go.

### IF YOUR ONE-YEAR-OLD GOT YOU UP AT 5AM

Take advantage of the early rising to have breakfast at traditional **Fonda Margarita** (page 211), a super-casual and beloved breakfast-only restaurant where a line starts to form before the 6:30am opening.

### IF YOUR FAMILY WANTS A TREAT AFTER THE SHOW AT BELLAS ARTES

Go out for a creamy hot chocolate and a sugar-topped churro at **Churrería El Moro** (page 76), a lovely old-fashioned sandwich and churro shop that's open till 1am on the weekend.

### IF YOU NEED A 3AM PICK-ME-UP

Old-time **Café El Popular** (page 72) in the Centro Histórico will set you up with spicy enchiladas, tamales, and a glass tumbler filled with their signature café con leche, at any hour of the day or night.

### IF YOU CAN'T DECIDE BETWEEN SLEEP AND TACOS

In the Roma, you can hit **Orinoco** (page 185) or **Los Parados** (page 188), both open till 5am on the weekend. In the Centro, **Los Cocuyos** (page 75) is open all night.

### IF THE COCKTAIL BARS HAVE ALL CLOSED IN THE ROMA

Join other revelers for a late-night taco run at the corner of **Insurgentes and Álvaro Obregón,** where popular tacos stands are open all night long.

### IF YOU'RE MASSIVELY JET-LAGGED AND ALREADY MISS PARIS

Join other stylish jet-setters for a 3am meal at **Au Pied de Cochon** (Campos Elíseos 218; 55/5327-7756; https://aupieddecochon.com.mx), a fancy French restaurant in the InterContinental Presidente Mexico City. It is, remarkably, open 24 hours daily.

# INTERNATIONAL
## Pigeon $$

The famous art nouveau Edificio Río de Janeiro, also known as La Casa de las Brujas, has found a stylish match in bar and restaurant Pigeon, which occupies the ground floor of the building. Dishes like roasted sweet potato, house-made gnocchi with ricotta, or grilled chicken are great for sharing or eating solo, and the cocktails are delicious. Amiable service, an upbeat crowd, and views of the tree-filled plaza across the street make it a perfect spot for a late dinner.

**MAP 5:** *Río de Janeiro 56; 1:30pm-midnight Tues.-Wed., 1:30pm-2am Thurs.-Sat., 1:30pm-8pm Sun.; Metro: Insurgentes, Metrobús: Durango*

## Máximo Bistrot Local $$$

The market-to-table ethos is fundamental to the menu at Máximo Bistrot Local. Depending on what's in season, lunch offerings could include octopus ceviche, grilled quail, or steamed red snapper. Since its 2011 opening, Máximo has helped put the Roma Norte on the map as a dining destination, and reservations here are still a must—even after the restaurant moved to a larger space in 2020. Fans of the chef can also try his casual breakfast-and-lunch spot **Lalo** (Zacatecas 173; tel. 55/5564-3388; http://eat-lalo.com; 8am-5pm daily), also in the Roma Norte.

**MAP 5:** *Álvaro Obregón 65; tel. 55/5264-4291; www.maximobistrot.com.mx; 1pm-11pm Mon.-Sat.; Metro:*

Pigeon

Cuauhtémoc, Metrobús: Jardín Pushkin or Álvaro Obregón

### Botánico $$$

A lush tree-filled patio is the oasis-like setting for this upscale Condesa restaurant, which draws a mix of well-heeled locals and visitors for the unique ambience and delicious kitchen. The palate here is distinctive and draws heavily on the use of fresh herbs and produce, from a deeply scented kale salad with sage dressing to pork belly with orange and pico de gallo—though you'll also find classic choices like a burger on the constantly changing menu. If you'd just like to enjoy the atmosphere, make a reservation for the beautiful in-house bar, which stays open past the restaurant's closing.

**MAP 5:** *Alfonso Reyes 217; WhatsApp tel. 55/2913-9791; restaurant 1pm-11pm Tues.-Sun., bar 6pm-1:30am Tues.-Sun.; Metro: Chilpancingo, Metrobús: Álvaro Obregón*

### Ciena $$

Ciena is the type of place where you'll want to order a glass of champagne with breakfast. Here, the atmosphere, the service, the clientele, and the menu reflect the upscale but unfussy chic of the Condesa neighborhood today. Try short-rib chilaquiles and homemade scones in the morning; come for a supper of pillowy raviolis and onion soup—and don't skip a drink from the excellent bar menu.

**MAP 5:** *Alfonso Reyes 101; no phone; https://ciena.mx; 8am-11pm Mon.-Fri., 8am-midnight Sat., 9am-6pm Sun.; Metro: Patriotismo, Metrobús: Campeche*

### Fugaz $$

This perfect little restaurant in the Roma Norte has an unpretentious vibe and cool Roma crowd, but the reason to come is the appealing menu of Mexican-Mediterranean small plates, which lean heavily on vegetables and seafood. The menu changes constantly, but may include dishes like cured trout with melon, tuna ceviche with herbs and peanuts, or cucumber-chili salad. There's a short bar menu with mezcal cocktails and Carta Blanca beer: everything you need for a leisurely afternoon meal.

**MAP 5:** *Orizaba 3B; no phone; 2pm-10pm Thurs.-Sat., 2pm-6pm Sun.; Metro: Insurgentes, Metrobús: Insurgentes*

### Mendl $$

Just about everything recommends brunch at Mendl: an appealing menu inspired by traditional Jewish delis, a gorgeous space just a block from Parque México, and delicious espresso drinks (it's run by the team behind beloved Mexico City café Quentin). The only downside is there is often a considerable wait for a table. If you don't get there before the crowds, order a cup of coffee and a croissant from the to-go window and enjoy the sidewalk scenery while you wait.

**MAP 5:** *Citlatépetl 9; tel. 55/9347-9944; https://mendl.mx; 8am-6pm* daily; Metro: Chilpancingo, Metrobús: Campeche

## COFFEE AND SWEETS

### Neveria Roxy $

This wonderful vintage ice cream parlor has been in business since the 1940s, serving generations of Condesa families who keep the place in business with their enthusiastic patronage. Here, there is both ice cream and traditional Mexican nieve (similar to sorbet or sherbet, generally with a lower dairy content than most ice creams). Everything is made in-house, with flavors ranging from familiar, like pistachio and lemon, to more unusual, like maracuyá (passion fruit) and tamarind. There's a second equally charming branch (Av. Fernando Montes de Oca 89; tel. 55/5286-1258, 11am-8:30pm daily).

**MAP 5:** *Tamaulipas 161; tel. 55/5256-1854; http://neveriaroxy.com.mx; 11am-8pm daily; Metro: Patriotismo*

### Panadería Rosetta $

There are near-constant crowds at this superlative bakery, which has earned its reputation for excellence with a daily assortment of breads, pastries, cookies, and sweets, ranging from cacao-and-ricotta Danish to loaves of chestnut bread to the lightly sweet pan de pulque. Once a hole-in-the-wall shop, the bakery has expanded into a larger space, including sidewalk tables for those who want to eat breakfast here—though you should still expect a considerable wait for weekend brunch, when you can accompany your bread with perfectly made espresso drinks or a slice of quiche.

**MAP 5:** *Colima 179; tel. 55/5207-2976; 7am-9pm Mon.-Tues., 7am-10pm Wed.-Sat., 7:30am-9:30pm Sun.; Metro: Insurgentes, Metrobús: Álvaro Obregón*

# Nightlife

## BARS AND LOUNGES

### Café de Nadie

An invariably stylish crowd, expertly made cocktails by invariably stylish bartenders, and live DJs spinning vinyl make this small bar a destination for locals and visitors to the capital. Located at the southern entrance to El Parián market, it manages to be both ultra-cool and laid-back, like the city surrounding it. It's an ace spot to spend the evening—if you can get a table. There's usually a wait and no reservations are accepted.

**MAP 5:** *Chihuahua 135; no phone; www.cafedenadie.mx; 4pm-11pm Mon., 2pm-2am Tues.-Thurs., noon-2am Fri., 10am-2am Sat., 10am-11pm Sun.; Metro: Insurgentes, Metrobús: Álvaro Obregón*

Licorería Limantour cocktail bar

### ✪ Licorería Limantour

Right on Álvaro Obregón, the Roma's main drag, this buzzing two-story bar has been a mainstay in the CDMX nightlife scene since its opening in 2011. In addition to the lively atmosphere, the bar distinguishes itself with a lineup of ultra-creative cocktails, carefully made with local herbs, fresh produce, and interesting mixers. Grab a seat at the bar before it fills up—which it always does on the weekends—to chat with the friendly bartenders. Despite the top-shelf drinks and constant crowds, it's an unpretentious and welcoming spot.

**MAP 5:** *Álvaro Obregón 106; tel. 55/5264-4122; https://limantour.tv; 6pm-midnight Sun.-Wed., 6pm-2am Thurs.-Sat.; no cover; Metro: Insurgentes, Metrobús: Álvaro Obregón*

### ✪ Páramo

There's a convivial house party-like ambience at this often packed 2nd-floor bar and eatery, located just above restaurant El Parnita and owned by the same family. The top-notch food and drinks are a big part of the appeal: Snacks like fried fish tacos and guacamole go perfectly with the selection of craft beer, Mexican wine, and mezcal on offer. But it's the fun crowd and ace atmosphere that's the real draw here, whether you're seated in the plant-filled barroom or one of the cozy smaller salons. Things get going early here and don't wrap till closing.

**MAP 5:** *Yucatán 84; tel. 55/5941-5125, reservations WhatsApp tel. 55/7349-0436; 3pm-1:30am daily; no cover; Metro: Insurgentes, Metrobús: Álvaro Obregón*

### Oropel

This sidewalk bar specializes in vermouth, natural wines, and a low-key vibe that's 100 percent Mexico City. The low prices and excellent products have made it a local favorite, great for a weeknight drink. No matter what day you drop in, it's best to come with an attitude that's as relaxed as the place itself: There's no host, no reservations, no printed menu, and often a wait for a table, even on a Monday.

**MAP 5:** *Chihuahua 182; no phone; 5pm-midnight Mon.-Sat., 4pm-10pm Sun.; Metro: Insurgentes, Metrobús: Álvaro Obregón*

## CANTINAS
### Covadonga

This spacious cantina near the Plaza Río de Janeiro was once a quiet neighborhood watering hole where people gathered to play dominoes and sip tequila served from the fine old bar. In the past decade, however, it has also become popular with a hip Roma crew. Now, the seniors are joined by a bevy of artists and scenesters converging for drinks and Spanish food. It's a fun place for an evening out, uniting the old and new Roma.

**MAP 5:** *Puebla 121; tel. 55/5533-2922; 1pm-2am Mon.-Sat., 1pm-7pm Sun.; no cover; Metro: Insurgentes*

### Riviera del Sur

This wonderful cantina in the southern Roma has an airy dining room decorated with wood paneling and filled with game tables, in the traditional CDMX style. There is sometimes live music in the afternoons and dominoes to play at your table. It's worth dining here too; the kitchen makes lovely Yucatec-inspired food, including sopa de lima (lemon soup), panuchos (corn cakes topped with pulled pork), and vaporcitos (tamales in banana leaf).

**MAP 5:** *Chiapas 174-B; tel. 55/5264-1552; 1pm-midnight Sun.-Wed., 1pm-2am Thurs.-Sat.; Metro: Centro Médico, Metrobús: Michoacán*

## TEQUILA AND MEZCAL
### Tlecan

One thing that distinguishes Tlecan from the many hot spots in the Roma neighborhood is the genuinely attentive and genial service. Bartenders and waitstaff are eager to talk about the small but beautifully curated list of mezcal, Mexican spirits, and mixed drinks on the menu, which includes more unusual offerings like tecuino, a fermented maize drink, and bacanora, a distilled spirit from Sonora. It's a dark, tiny spot that gets packed with patrons late in the evening, but the buzzy atmosphere is part of the fun.

**MAP 5:** *Álvaro Obregón 228; no phone; https://tlecan.com; 6pm-2am daily; no cover*

## LGBTQ+
### Revuelta Queer House

On an open-air rooftop terrace in the Roma Norte, this relaxed bar is an ideal place for an evening drink

## TOP EXPERIENCE

## Cantina Culture

Sometimes historic, invariably low-key, and usually inexpensive, cantinas are quintessential places to eat and drink in Mexico City. Some cantinas fill up at night while others are more like restaurants, popular for a leisurely afternoon meal. Most traditional cantinas offer free snacks, called botanas, with your drinks, which can range from a plate of peanuts to a 3-4-course meal. In fact, there are traditional cantinas with food that rivals the best eateries in the city. Here are a few noteworthy cantinas to check out.

La Bipo

- **For Romantics: Bar La Ópera** is a classic cantina that operates more like a restaurant, with a large menu of traditional Mexican food. It's historic, beautiful, and ideal for a shot of tequila accompanied by a sangrita chaser (page 74).

- **For Hipsters: Covadonga** is a classic cantina, popular with both the old-timers who come here for dominoes and drinks and a youthful Roma crowd (page 195).

- **For Karaoke:** Not your typical cantina, **La Bipo** in Coyoacán hosts DJs, live bands, and karaoke nights, with no cover charge (page 236).

- **For Mariachi: La Coyoacana** in Coyoacán is a friendly cantina where musicians often wander through the crowds on the weekends (page 236).

- **For Families: La Valenciana** is a pretty neighborhood cantina that draws Narvarte locals for food and drinks (page 216).

- **For Traditionalists: Tío Pepe,** on the atmospheric edge of Chinatown, is one of the city's oldest cantinas (page 101).

- **For Friday Night: Salón Ríos** is a modern take on a classic cantina (page 127).

amid an upbeat ambience and unpretentious crowd. Beyond the bar, Revuelta Queer House is designed as a queer gathering place and cultural center, and it often hosts special events like live music, DJs, and film screenings (which sometimes include a cover charge). The art gallery downstairs hosts rotating contemporary exhibitions with LGBTQ+ themes.

**MAP 5:** *Puebla 94; www.revueltaqh. com; 4pm-midnight Wed.-Sun.; Metro: Insurgentes, Metrobús: Insurgentes*

## LIVE MUSIC
### La Bodeguita en Medio

A nod to the famous Havana bar of the same name, this Cuban spot has an upbeat atmosphere every night of the week, with party-happy patrons sipping the Bodeguita's signature mojitos, nibbling on rice, beans, and fried plantains, and shouting over the live band. Inside the multilevel dimly lit space, the walls are scribbled with notes and photographs. For those who want to practice their groove, there are salsa classes at least once a week.

**MAP 5:** *Cozumel 37; tel. 55/5553-0246; http://labodeguitadelmedio. com.mx; 1:30pm-2am Tues.-Sat., 1:30pm-midnight Mon.-Sun.; no cover; Metro: Sevilla*

### Jazzatlan Capital

There's a bohemian feeling at this cozy Roma jazz club and cocktail bar, which features high-quality live music six nights a week. Though it's a relaxed environment, the bar can get quite crowded on the weekends, when there are bands playing both in the upstairs "club" and the downstairs "salon." Reservations are required for shows upstairs, and there is often a wait to get in (and standing room only) downstairs. It's worth the hassle and the advance planning, as the music and ambience are excellent.

**MAP 5:** *Guanajuato 239; WhatsApp tel. 55/1390-1631; www.jazzatlan. club/capital; 6pm-2am Tues.-Sun., club shows generally 10pm; no cover-US$20; Metro: Insurgentes, Metrobús: Álvaro Obregón*

## BILLIARDS AND GAMES
### Petanca Roma Club

The French garden game pétanque has a small but enthusiastic following in Mexico City, and this relaxed bar and gathering place has become a favorite with locals who love to play. There are four pétanque courts at this surprisingly spacious joint, which are available first-come, first-served and free of charge. If the courts are full, which is often the case in the evenings, it's just as fun to order some bar snacks, a craft beer, or a glass of wine on tap (a rarity in the capital) and watch the games.

**MAP 5:** *Colima 124A; tel. 55/6586-0544; 5pm-midnight Tues.-Thurs., 1pm-midnight Fri.-Sat., 1pm-6pm Sun.; no cover; Metro: Insurgentes, Metrobús: Jardín Pushkin*

# Arts and Culture

## GALLERIES

### Galería OMR

OMR has maintained a strong reputation for contemporary art in Mexico City since its founding in 1983. Preceding many of the popular galleries in the Roma, OMR has in many ways set the tone for the neighborhood, supporting emerging artists and avant-garde propositions. In 2016, it moved from its longtime space beside the Plaza Río de Janeiro to the Sala Margolin, which was, for 60 years, a wonderful bookstore and record shop that specialized in classical music—an attractive environment for the top-quality art on show.

**MAP 5:** *Córdoba 100; tel. 55/5511-1179 or 55/5207-1080; https://omr.art; 10am-6pm Tues.-Fri., 10am-4pm Sat.; free; Metro: Insurgentes, Metrobús: Parque Pushkin*

### Olivia Foundation

A classic 19th-century Roma townhouse was strikingly renovated to create this multistory private gallery, which opened in 2024. Owned by a team of Mexico City art collectors, the gallery exhibits work from their collection, which includes artists like Cecily Brown, Ruth Asawa, and Joan Mitchell. There are plans to expand their cultural programming. Reservations to visit are preferred, but they also allow drop-ins.

**MAP 5:** *Tonalá 46; no phone; https://oliviafoundation.mx; by appointment 11am-6pm Wed.-Sun.; Metro: Cuauhtémoc, Metrobús: Durango*

## MUSEUMS

### ✪ Museo del Juguete Antiguo

Avid toy collector Roberto Shimizu and his son, Roberto Jr., have united a huge collection of over 40,000 dolls, model cars and trucks, stuffed animals, wrestling figurines, and other curiosities in this unconventional and utterly delightful museum, which also functions as a cultural center and a laboratory for graffiti art and urban muralism. It's a short hop from the Roma into the more rough-around-the-edges Colonia Doctores to visit this unusual space—which, unlike many cultural institutions in the capital, is open on Monday.

**MAP 5:** *Dr. Olvera 15, Col. Doctores; tel. 55/5588-2100; 9am-5pm Mon.-Fri., 9am-4pm Sat., 10am-4pm Sun.; US$3, Metro: Obrera*

Museo del Objeto del Objeto in the Roma

### Museo del Objeto del Objeto (MODO)

This small museum, housed in a lovely beaux arts mansion, focuses on the history of design and communications in Mexico City. Every few months the museum inaugurates a new exhibit dedicated to a theme like lucha libre or the history of the Roma neighborhood. Stories are often told via everyday objects, like matchbooks, enameled tin boxes, toys, watches, and posters, many of which are part of the museum's collection of over 100,000 design pieces.

**MAP 5:** *Colima 145; tel. 55/5533-9637; www.elmodo.mx; 10am-6pm Tues.-Sun.; US$3, US$1.50 students, teachers, and Roma neighborhood residents, free under age 12; Metro: Insurgentes, Metrobús: Álvaro Obregón or Parque Pushkin*

### Casa Guillermo Tovar de Tereza

Early 20th-century writer and historian Guillermo Tovar de Tereza was a chronicler of Mexico City and a collector of art. His former home, a Porfiriato-era mansion in the Roma Norte, is now owned by Mexican billionaire Carlos Slim's Museo Soumaya. Free to enter and filled with Tovar de Tereza's collection of art, it's a petite but engaging spot that offers a nice glimpse into the life and interests of a preeminent Mexican intellectual.

**MAP 5:** *Valladolid 52; tel. 55/1103-9800; www.museosoumaya.org; 10:30am-6:30pm daily; free; Metro: Insurgentes, Metrobús: Insurgentes*

## THEATER, CLASSICAL MUSIC, AND DANCE

### Foro Shakespeare

Originally founded as a bookshop specializing in theater, the Foro Shakespeare eventually grew to include several performance spaces. Today, it's a nonprofit arts organization with a reputation for launching the careers of playwrights and actors. The 200-seat main venue puts on a range of musicals, comedies, and dramas (in Spanish), while you might find monologues or stand-up comedy in the smaller performance spaces.

**MAP 5:** *Zamora 7; WhatsApp tel. 55/7948-5597; www.foroshakespeare.com; generally matinees 1pm, evening performances 7pm-10:30pm; US$8-25; Metro: Chapultepec*

### La Teatrería

See both well-known names and new talent in acting, direction, and playwriting at this active theater company, located in the heart of the Roma. For a small theater, the number of shows La Teatrería produces is impressive, with new plays constantly opening, many by Mexican playwrights. There are sometimes theater performances for families.

**MAP 5:** *Tabasco 152; tel. 55/5207-3234; www.lateatreria.com; box office 2pm-7pm Mon.-Fri., 11am-2pm and 4pm-7pm Sat.-Sun., showtimes vary; tickets US$15-20; Metro: Insurgentes, Metrobús: Álvaro Obregón*

# Recreation

## COMMUNITY CENTERS

### ⭐ Huerto Roma Verde

This wonderful ecological organization in the Roma has multiple facets. It maintains a large urban garden and chicken coop; hosts workshops in urban farming, composting, sustainable architecture, and other green topics; and oversees an ongoing program of ecology- and food-related events on the weekend, with themes ranging from edible insects to Mexican wines. If you stop by on the weekend, you can wander around the garden or have vegan snacks and craft beer on tap at one of the many shaded picnic tables.

Huerto Roma Verde

**MAP 5:** *Jalapa 234; tel. 55/5564-2210; http://huertoromaverde.org; 10am-7pm daily; Metro: Centro Médico, Metrobús: Campeche*

# Shops

## ⭐ ROMA SHOPPING DISTRICT

**Álvaro Obregón** has long been the heart of the Roma, and as the neighborhood becomes trendier, cute boutiques and galleries have cropped up alongside the avenue's old bookshops and ice cream parlors. More recently, the parallel street **Colima** has become a hub of popular fashion design and concept shops, as has Córdoba, where you'll find everything from super-funky vintage clothing stores to a Doc Martens shop.

**MAP 5:** *Colima between Insurgentes and Av. Cuauhtémoc, and Álvaro Obregón between Insurgentes and Av. Cuauhtémoc; Metro: Insurgentes*

## ANTIQUES AND COLLECTIBLES

### Mercado de Cuauhtémoc

One of the funkiest vintage markets in the city is the weekly Mercado de Cuauhtémoc, in the Jardín Dr. Ignacio Chávez. Though the market also sets up on Sunday, you'll find the best vendors and largest selection on Saturday morning. Intrepid buyers with a good eye will stumble upon some real gems here, like mid-century furniture, eyeglasses from the 1950s and 1960s, unusual vinyl records, desk lamps, vintage toy trains, and discontinued Lego sets.

**MAP 5:** *Jardín Dr. Ignacio Chávez, Av. Cuauhtémoc and Dr. Liceaga, Roma; 9am-3pm Sat.; Metro: Niños Héroes*

## BOOKS
### Casa Bosques
It's pleasant to browse in this pretty 2nd-floor bookshop, which has a range of well-selected titles in art, architecture, theory, and design as well as independent magazines and artists books, in both English and Spanish. The decor reflects the owners' interest in aesthetics, with pleasing white-painted floors, unusual wood bookshelves, and lots of natural light. The doors to the building are closed, even when the bookstore is open; ring the doorbell and the staff will buzz you in.

**MAP 5:** *Córdoba 25; tel. 55/6378-2976; https://casabosques.net; 11am-7pm daily; Metro: Insurgentes, Metrobús: Insurgentes*

### Librería Rosario Castellanos
Run by the Fonda de Cultura y Económica (FCE), this bookshop has one of the best selections of Spanish-language titles in the city, including literature, culture, history, and sociology books published by the FCE. Located in the art deco Cine Lido building in the **Centro Cultural Bella Época,** the light-filled space has high ceilings decorated with glass panels by artist Jan Hendrix. There are comfy chairs throughout the stacks, a carpeted kids section, and an in-house coffee shop.

**MAP 5:** *Tamaulipas 202; tel. 55/5276-7110; www.fondodeculturaeconomica.com; 9am-10pm Mon.-Sat., 10am-8pm Sun.; Metro: Patriotismo*

## CLOTHING, SHOES, AND ACCESSORIES
### 180° Shop
Among the most well-stocked and charming of the Roma's many cool boutiques, 180° Shop sells a fun collection of urban wear and accessories, like graphic tees, tennis shoes, skateboards, handbags, and design books and city guides, in addition to their proprietary line of hoodies, miniskirts, ball caps, T-shirts, and other hipster essentials. They also carry a small line of children's clothes, including hand-embroidered shirts and adorable silk screen tees.

**MAP 5:** *Colima 180; WhatsApp tel. 55/7394-4772; www.180grados.mx; 10am-7:30pm Mon.-Sat., 10:30am-6pm Sun.; Metro: Insurgentes*

### Happening Store
This well-stocked design-centric home, clothing, and gift shop has a cool Roma vibe but a friendly and unpretentious attitude. It's a great place to pick up something that will remind you of CDMX, like graphic tees, leather handbags, color-block swimsuits, journals, and colorful kids toys, among other cool home accents, clothes, and accessories, all

designed in Mexico. The selection changes frequently, so it's worth a repeat visit.

**MAP 5:** *Tabasco 210; tel. 55/5919-1254; 11am-7pm daily; Metro: Insurgentes, Metrobús: Durango*

## DESIGN, ART, AND GIFT SHOPS
### Chic by Accident

This eye-catching design shop and gallery specializes in unique mid-century Mexican furniture and home accessories in addition to showing a selection of artwork by contemporary artists. Occupying the 2nd floor and rooftop terrace of an old Roma mansion, the space is gorgeous—don't miss the terrace, where there are more pieces on view and a lovely in-the-treetops feeling. Appointments are preferred, but if you drop by, buzz from the street to be let in.

**MAP 5:** *Orizaba 28; tel. 55/3376-0412; www.chicbyaccident.com; 10am-7pm Mon.-Fri., 10am-6pm Sat.; Metro: Insurgentes, Metrobús: Insurgentes*

### La Canasta

Artes de Mexico is a small press that publishes a high-quality collectible magazine series covering Mexican traditions, culture, and people. At its headquarters in the Roma neighborhood, the press operates a lovely gift shop, where you can find a nice selection of handcrafts from across the country, including wool textiles and embroidered blouses, traditional

La Canasta

Mexican toys, handwoven baskets, and alebrijes (hand-painted wood animals from Oaxaca), in addition to a large selection of their magazine titles. It's a good spot to find a last-minute, thoroughly Mexican gift for a friend.

**MAP 5:** *Córdoba 69; tel. 55/5525-5905; www.artesdemexico.com; 11am-7pm Wed.-Sun.; Metro: Insurgentes, Metrobús: Álvaro Obregón or Parque Pushkin*

## GOURMET FOOD AND IMPORTS
### Delirio

This popular bistro and deli sells a range of gourmet products, many with a Mexican heritage. You can pick up olive oil from Baja California, a bottle of wine from Casa Madero in Coahuila, or guava jam and dried-chili salsa from chef Monica Patiño's label. If browsing makes you hungry, order a fresh salad, a slice of quiche, and a cup of coffee at one of the sidewalk tables. There is another Patiño-owned café and deli, **Abarrotes** (Abarrotes Delirio, Colima 114;

tel. 55/5264-1468), also in the Roma Norte, with a smaller selection of her products on sale.

**MAP 5:** *Monterrey 116; tel. 55/5584-0870; www.delirio.mx; 8am-10pm Mon.-Sat., 9am-7pm Sun.; Metro: Insurgentes, Metrobús: Álvaro Obregón*

## PUBLIC MARKETS
### Mercado de Medellín

This neighborhood market in the Roma Sur is spacious and well-lit, with dozens of produce stands piled high with fresh fruits and vegetables, cheese, and fresh tortillas on sale. Mercado de Medellín is known for its excellent seafood sold in bulk as well as for the vendors selling goods from the Yucatán peninsula, like habanero salsas and pickled onions.

**MAP 5:** *Medellín 234; 8am-5pm daily; Metro: Chilpancingo, Metrobús: Campeche*

## SHOPPING CENTERS
### Laguna

A collaborative art, shopping, business, and culinary space located in a renovated 1920s textile factory, Laguna is a surprising oasis of calm in the decidedly urban Colonia Doctores. You must check in with the security guard at the door, then you are free to wander around the space, which houses art gallery Llano and longtime Mexican kitchenware company Anfora (note that not all spaces are open to the public). It's also nice to simply hang out with a margarita pizza and a craft beer from Bar Mini (10am-5pm Mon.-Fri.) in the sunny plant-filled patio. In addition, the space hosts artists in residence and offers creative workshops to the community.

**MAP 5:** *Doctor Lucio 181, Col. Doctores; https://lagunamexico.com; 9am-7pm Mon.-Sat.; Metro: Niños Heroes or Cuauhtémoc, Metrobús: Parque Pushkin*

# Insurgentes Sur-Narvarte

Map 6

| | |
|---|---|
| Getting Around | 205 |
| Sights | 208 |
| Restaurants | 210 |
| Nightlife | 215 |
| Recreation | 218 |

Traveling south from the city center, Avenida Insurgentes is flanked on both sides by sprawling residential neighborhoods. Filled with family-friendly parks, tree-lined streets, and plenty of low-key eateries, these neighborhoods are becoming increasingly popular with visitors to the city, though they maintain a lovely local ambience. Just south of the Condesa, the bustling Escandón has a bit of stylish spillover, but remains a low-key, local-centric area, filled with taquerias, traditional panaderías, coffee shops, and mechanics. Farther south, the Nápoles, on the west side of Insurgentes, is a quiet but centrally located residential area. On the east side of Insurgentes, the tree-filled Narvarte is known for its many taco stands

# Highlights

✪ **Poliforum Siqueiros:** Undisputably one-of-a-kind, this eye-catching cultural center was designed by mid-20th-century artist and political activist David Alfaro Siqueiros (page 208).

✪ **Parque Hundido:** A local crowd and a family-friendly atmosphere recommend this green park along the southern stretch of Insurgentes (page 209).

✪ **Tianguis de los Jueves:** You'll find loads of local produce, hungry crowds, and street snacks galore at this expansive outdoor market, held weekly on Thursday (page 217).

✪ **Fútbol:** Catch a live fútbol match at Estadio Ciudad de los Deportes, home to several pro soccer teams (page 218).

# Getting Around

- Metro lines: 3
- Metro stops: Etiopía, Eugenia, División del Norte
- Metrobús lines: 1
- Metrobús stops: Poliforum, Nápoles, Del Valle, Ciudad de los Deportes, Parque Hundido, Félix Cuevas, Río Churubusco, Teatro Insurgentes

---

**Previous:** Obrero Mundial street in the Narvarte neighborhood; **Above:** Parque Hundido; Poliforum Siqueiros.

1
2
3
A
B
C
D
E
F
SEE MAP 5
SEE MAP 8
AVENIDA PROGRESO
CALLE JOSÉ MARTÍ
CALLE MINERÍA
VIADUCTO PRESIDENTE MIGUEL ALEMÁN
AVENIDA REVOLUCIÓN
CALLE PUENTE DE LA MORENA
CALLE CHICAGO
CALLE DAKOTA
AVENIDA INSURGENTES SUR
CALLE COYOACÁN
XOLA
CALLE PEDRO ROMERO DE TERREROS
AVENIDA DIVISIÓN DEL NORTE
COLONIA NAPOLES
Poliforum Siqueiros
CALLE TORRES ADALID
CALLE LUZ SAVIÑON
CALLE AMORES
GABRIEL MANCERA
San Pedro de los Pinos
CALLE 9
CALLE TEXAS
CALLE OKLAHOMA
CALLE LOUISIANA
CALLE ALABAMA
CALLE PATRICIO SANZ
CALLE ADOLFO PRIETO
Jardín Esparza Oteo
CALLE PENNSYLVANIA
CALLE NEBRASKA
CALLE CONCEPCIÓN BEISTEGUI
CALLE 17
AVENIDA COLONIA DEL VALLE
CALLE GEORGIA
CALLE WISCONSIN
CALLE NUEVA YORK
CALLE KANSAS
AVENIDA EUGENIA
AVENIDA DIVISIÓN DEL
AVENIDA SAN ANTONIO
San Antonio
CALLE TINTORETO
CALLE SAN BORJA
ÁNGEL URRAZA
AVENIDA COYOACÁN
CALLE AMORES
GABRIEL MANCERA
AVENIDA PATRIOTISMO
CALLE AUGUSTO RODIN
AVENIDA PORFIRIO DÍAZ
CALLE MATÍAS ROMERO
Parque Hundido
Jardín del Arte Tlacoquemécatl
CALLE TLACOQUEMÉCATL
CALLE PILARES
Parque Arboledas
CALLE JOSÉ ENRIQUE PESTALOZZI
CALLE JUAN FRANCISCO MILLET
Mixcoac
Parque San Lorenzo
CALLE SAN FRANCISCO
CALLE PATRICIO SANZ
CALLE MORAS
CALLE ADOLFO PRIETO
CALLE DOCTOR ROBERTO GAYOL
CALLE MIGUEL LAURENT
CALLE NICOLÁS SAN JUAN
CALLE JUAN SÁNCHEZ AZCONA
CALLE HERIBERTO FRÍAS
AVENIDA UNIVERSIDAD
CALLE ANAXÁGORAS
EXTREMADURA
MANZANAS
CALLE FRESAS
Insurgentes Sur
FÉLIX CUEVAS
SAN LORENZO
Hospital 20 de Noviembre
Zapata
CUAUHTÉMOC
AVENIDA
CALLE OSO
CALLE PARROQUIA
CALLE SAN FRANCISCO
AVENIDA COYOACÁN
PORTALES NORTE
CALLE FÉLIX PARRA
CALLE PLATEROS
JOSÉ MARÍA RICO
CALLE RODRÍGUEZ SARO
Teatro de los Insurgentes
0 500 yds
0 500 m
DISTANCE ACROSS MAP
Approximate: 3.5 mi or 5.6 km

and outdoor markets, while the expansive and largely residential Colonia del Valle's many mid-20th-century apartment buildings are complemented by ample greenery. While there are some notable sights, these neighborhoods are best explored with the intention of experiencing everyday life in the capital.

# Sights

### ✪ Poliforum Siqueiros

On Insurgentes Sur, in the shadow of the 50-story World Trade Center de México, this eye-catching arts complex is covered with huge three-dimensional murals created by artist David Alfaro Siqueiros. Commissioned by ex-revolutionary Manuel Suárez, the mural was originally intended for a building in Cuernavaca, but the project was relocated to its present site in 1965, opening in 1977. Inside, in the 2nd-floor Foro Universal, Siqueiros created a massive, marvelous, three-dimensional mural titled *La Marcha de la Humanidad* (The March of Humanity), a tribute to the people who fought to better society. The building is currently undergoing extensive renovations with the plan to create an adjoining public plaza and cultural center, during which time there is no public access to the interior and some of exterior is also, unfortunately, out of view.

**MAP 6:** *Insurgentes Sur 701, Col. Nápoles; tel. 55/5536-4520; www.polyforumsiqueiros.com; US$2 Foro Universal, gallery free; Metro: San Pedro de los Pinos or Eugenia, Metrobús: Poliforum*

### Centro SCOP

The headquarters of the Secretariat of Communications and Transportation, or Centro SCOP, was a functionalist office building covered in a breathtaking 20,000 sq m (215,278 sq ft) of sculptures and volcanic-stone mosaics, created by 20th-century Mexican artists Juan O'Gorman, Jose Chavez Morado, and Arturo Estrada, among others. A landmark of mid-century architecture in Mexico City, it was conceived as part of integración plástica, a movement to unite art and architecture in public spaces.

The top floors of Centro SCOP collapsed during the 1985 earthquake in Mexico City, and though the building was retrofitted, it was damaged again, this time irreparably, in the earthquake of 2017. The SCT announced that the building would be demolished, and after much public debate, the department began removing the murals from the edifice. In 2023, the murals were removed and the demolition of the buildings began, with plans to reopen the site as the Parque del Muralismo. At press time, there was no date for

Centro SCOP

reopening, but some of the murals are still visible from the street.
**MAP 6:** *Eje Central Lázaro Cárdenas and Xola; no phone; free*

### ✪ Parque Hundido

On weekends, this big urban park is a popular destination for local families, who come to buy ice cream, visit the playground, and take a ride on the small motorized "train" that weaves through the park. On weekdays, it's much quieter, and a nice spot to take a stroll along the park's pretty footpaths, which are adjoined by about 50 reproductions of pre-Hispanic sculptures, including a large Olmec head. Across Insurgentes from Parque Hundido in the Colonia del Valle is the smaller Parque San Lorenzo (at the intersection of San Lorenzo and Fresas), which surrounds the Capilla de San Lorenzo Mártir, a small but beautiful 16th-century chapel.
**MAP 6:** *Av. Insurgentes Sur between Porfirio Díaz and Millet; 24 hours daily; free; Metro: Mixcoac, Metrobús: Parque Hundido*

### Teatro de los Insurgentes

This prestigious theater on the southern stretch of Avenida Insurgentes, built in 1953, has a striking round facade decorated with a colorful mural by Diego Rivera titled *La Historia del Teatro* (The History of Theater), which includes the portraits of many Mexican actors, including the beloved film star and friend of Rivera's, Cantinflas. The theater generally puts on major dramatic productions by Mexican playwrights, many starring big-name actors; tickets are available through Ticketmaster.
**MAP 6:** *Av. Insurgentes Sur 1587; tel. 55/5598-6894; shows usually Thurs.-Sun.; US$20-60; Metro: Barranca del Muerto, Metrobús: Teatro de los Insurgentes*

# Restaurants

**PRICE KEY**
$ Entrées less than US$10
$$ Entrées US$10-20
$$$ Entrées more than US$20

## MEXICAN

### La Secina $

In a bustling corner of the Colonia Narvarte, La Secina is a super-lowkey spot to unwind with drinks and generously served plates of antojitos (snacks) in the evening, when it's busy with neighborhood locals. The menu leans heavily on the namesake cecina (salt-cured beef), which the restaurant sources from Yecapixtla, Morelos, where some of the country's best cecina is produced. Try it in tacos, in Oaxacan-style tlayudas, or on sopes (round corn breads), or order some of the other delicious Mexican dishes on offer, like a plate of grilled cactus with panela cheese.

**MAP 6:** *Obrero Mundial 305; tel. 55/6730-2462; www.lasecina.com; 1pm-11pm Mon.-Wed., 1pm-2am Thurs.-Sat., 1pm-7pm Sun.; Metro: Etiopía, Metrobús: Obrero Mundial*

### Montejo $$

The old-style Mexico City atmosphere recommends this long-running cantina in the southern Condesa, with a menu that focuses

Montejo

on food from the state of Yucatán. Panuchos (round corn cakes topped with pulled pork), sopa de lima (citrus soup), or a fresh ceviche go well with a shot of tequila and top-notch people-watching. Service is old-fashioned and efficient, but there's no rush to leave your table. Note that the downstairs cantina is adults-only; families are welcome in the pretty upstairs dining room.

**MAP 6:** *Benjamín Franklin 261; tel. 55/5516-5851; 1pm-midnight Mon.-Sat.; Metro: Chilpancingo, Metrobús: Chilpancingo*

### Las Tlayudas $

If the no-frills dining room at Las Tlayudas doesn't initially strike you as promising, sit tight until the food comes. At this small, unpretentious, and surprisingly delicious Oaxacan restaurant, you'll find nicely rendered regional dishes like spicy salsa de queso (Oaxacan cheese in tomato salsa) and crisp, savory tlayudas (giant corn tortillas stuffed with beans, cheese, and, optionally, meat). There's a very nice selection of craft beer and legitimately tasty Oaxacan hot chocolate to accompany your meal.

**MAP 6:** *Luz Saviñon 1161, Narvarte Poniente; tel. 55/6379-2496; www.lastlayudas.com.mx; 10am-6pm Sun.-Mon., 10am-10pm Tues.-Thurs., 9am-11pm Fri.-Sat.; Metro: Etiopía*

### ✪ Mictlan Antojitos Veganos $

An itsy-bitsy vegan eatery, Mictlan serves first-rate plant-based versions of classic Mexican fare, like mushroom-stuffed gorditas made with top-quality heirloom corn and savory meat-free pambazos (a traditional chorizo-and-potato sandwich). Popular with neighborhood locals, there's often a wait in the afternoon, when the economically priced comida corrida (three-course lunch) is served. Complete your meal with a glass of their ultra-fresh pulque or kombucha.

**MAP 6:** *Luz Saviñon 1354, Narvarte Poniente; tel. 55/4036-2821; https://mictlanantojitosveganos.com; 2pm-8pm Mon., 2pm-10pm Wed.-Sun.; Metro: Eugenia, Metrobús: Luz Saviñon*

### ✪ Fonda Margarita $

Even if you get there as dawn is breaking, you might still have to wait for a seat at this super-popular, ultra-casual breakfast spot, touted by many as the best traditional fonda in the city. As soon as you walk in, you'll see a row of clay pots filled with different Mexican dishes, gentling bubbling over an open charcoal fire. They sometimes run out of certain guisos (dishes) by midmorning, but you can't go wrong with anything on the menu, which changes daily and includes classics like chicharrón (fried pork rind) in salsa verde and scrambled eggs with beans.

**MAP 6:** *Adolfo Prieto 1354; tel. 55/5559-6358; 6:30am-noon Tues.-Sun.; Metro: Insurgentes Sur, Metrobús: Parque Hundido*

### Fonda 99.99 $

Popular with Del Valle locals, this delicious and economical lunch spot specializes in food from the Yucatán peninsula, like puerco al pibil (pulled pork spiced with achiote seeds), sopa de lima (citrus soup), papadzules (egg-filled tortillas covered in a green pumpkin-seed sauce), and tacos stuffed with cazón (dogfish) or crab, all accompanied by fiery habanero salsa. During the daily lunch rush, servers in buttoned-up guayaberas rush trays to the flocks of diners chattering at the vintage Formica tables.
**MAP 6:** *Moras 348; tel. 55/5559-8762; 1pm-7pm Tues.-Sat., 1pm-6pm Sun.; Metro: Insurgentes Sur, Metrobús: Parque Hundido*

## TACOS, TORTAS, AND SNACKS

### Tacos Los Condes $

At this bright and friendly neighborhood taquería, you can order a plate of perfectly seasoned pastor, suadero, or a much-beloved tripa (tripe), but you'll also find gorditas (round corn flatbreads) and quesadillas (both deep-fried and al comal) on the menu—with options for fillings like huitlacoche or poblano chilies that even vegetarians will love. Located on a tree-filled street corner, Los Condes has plenty of sidewalk seating, and the service is genial.
**MAP 6:** *Pedro Romero de Terreros 14; tel. 55/8661-0506; 9am-midnight Mon.-Wed., 9am-1am Thurs.-Sat.; Metro: Etiopía, Metrobús: La Piedad*

### Tacos Manolo $

In the late afternoon, hours before the crowds descend, two huge spits of meat (trompos) begin sizzling outside Tacos Manolo in preparation for the evening rush. One is bright red achiote-rubbed pastor, while the other is herb-flecked pork for tacos árabes. Both of these classic tacos are deliciously rendered at this no-frills traditional taco shop, and you can accompany them with an agua fresca or a Mexican beer.
**MAP 6:** *Luz Saviñon 1305, Narvarte Poniente; tel. 55/7095-8071; 2pm-midnight Sun.-Thurs., 2pm-2:30am Fri.-Sat.; Metro: Etiopía, Metrobús: Dr. Vertiz or Luz Saviñon*

### ✪ El Vilsito $

The Narvarte neighborhood is well known for its many excellent taquerías, and El Vilsito is widely regarded as offering one of the best (if not the very best) pastor tacos in the city, to which the nightly crowds attest. (And crowds are only

Tacos Los Condes

Tacos Manolo

getting bigger now that the taquería was given a nod from Michelin as one of its Bib Gourmand winners in 2024.) In a classic Mexico City twist, this evening-only joint is a mechanic shop by day, so head there after the sun's gone down for a quintessential Mexico City experience.

**MAP 6:** *Av. Universidad 248, Col. Narvarte; tel. 55/5682-7213; 8pm-3am Mon.-Thurs., 8pm-5am Fri.-Sat., 4pm-midnight Sun.; Metro: Eugenia, Metrobús: Dr. Vertiz or Luz Saviñon*

### Hostal de los Quesos $

This taco palace in the southern Del Valle neighborhood has been in business since the 1970s and serves such a wide range of tacos that it can be hard to limit your order. Among the options on offer are nopalitos (prickly pear), rib eye, chuleta (pork chop), liver and onions, chorizo, chicken, and legitimately delicious pastor as well as pozole (hominy soup), tortas, chicharron de queso (crispy griddled cheese), tortilla soup, frijoles charros (stewed beans), and much more.

**MAP 6:** *Pilares 205; tel. 55/5559-9651; www.hostaldelosquesos.com.mx; 8:30am-1am Mon.-Thurs., 8:30am-2am Fri.-Sat., 8:30am-midnight Sun.; Metro: División del Norte, Metrobús: Parque Hundido*

### Rincón Tarasco $

Some of the best carnitas (slow-cooked braised pork) in the city can be had at this low-key restaurant in the Escandón neighborhood, just a short walk south of the Condesa. Order the soft maciza (shoulder), the excellent rib (served bone-in), or rich panza (belly)—or, if you're feeling more adventurous, try parts like nana (uterus) or buche (stomach), which aren't listed on the menu but available to those who ask. Tacos are generously served in a perfect handmade corn tortilla.

**MAP 6:** *Comercio 131, Escandón II Sección; tel. 55/5516-7802; 9:30am-4pm Wed.-Sun.; Metro: Patriotismo*

## SEAFOOD

### ✪ Mi Gusto Es $$

In the tree-filled Narvarte neighborhood, this ultra-popular Sinaloa-style seafood restaurant brings you as close to the beach as you can get in Mexico City, with flavorful marlin-stuffed chilies or incredibly fresh and spicy aguachile verde. There's often a wait at lunchtime, especially on the weekends, but you can sip a beer on the sidewalk in the meantime (there are coolers by the host station). Though they have other locations across the city, the Narvarte original remains the most fun.

## Outstanding Cafés

Mexico is a coffee-producing country, with high-quality beans cultivated in Veracruz, Oaxaca, Chiapas, and Guerrero. In the capital, a spate of creative third-wave coffee shops are using native coffee for world-class beverages. Here are a few outstanding coffee shops to visit across the city's central neighborhoods.

Mexican latte

The baristas at **Camino a Comala** (Miguel E. Schultz 7, Col. San Rafael; tel. 55/5592-0313; 8am-10pm Mon.-Sat., 9am-9pm Sun.) prepare drinks with remarkable perfectionism. It's a nice spot to order a flat white or a pour-over after walking around the San Rafael or Santa María la Ribera neighborhoods.

At **Cardinal** (Córdoba 132, Col. Roma; tel. 55/6721-8874; 8am-9pm Mon.-Sat., 9am-8pm Sun.), coffee beans are carefully selected and then matched with one of the café's many brewing methods, among them Aeropress, siphon, drip, Chemex, and, of course, espresso. The staff can tell you about the flavor and provenance of the beans they are currently brewing.

Serious coffee drinkers frequently point out the excellence of itsy-bitsy **Café Avellaneda** (Higuera 40, La Concepción, Coyoacán; tel. 55/6553-3441; 8am-9pm daily), in downtown Coyoacán, where house-roasted

---

**MAP 6:** *Diagonal San Antonio 1709-C, Narvarte Poniente; tel. 55/5235-3217; https://migustoes.com.mx; noon-7:30pm Mon.-Thurs., noon-8pm Fri.-Sun.; Metro: Etiopía, Metrobús: Dr. Vertiz*

## SWEETS

### Chiandoni $

In the heart of the Colonia Nápoles, this old-fashioned ice cream shop is worth visiting for the authentic mid-century ambience, with a Formica-topped bar with turquoise barstools and a blue-and-white checkered floor. The ice cream is likewise old-fashioned, with classic flavors like vanilla, chocolate, and lemon served in small metal bowls at your table, in addition to a menu of nostalgic sundaes, like banana splits.

**Map 6:** *Pennsylvania 225, Nápoles; tel. 55/7592-0839; 11am-9pm daily; Metro: San Antonio, Metrobús: Colonia del Valle*

beans are transformed into a range of hot and cold beverages, including some unusual offerings, like a cold-brew-based "oatmeal punch."

**Buna** (Doctor Lucio 181, Doctores; https://buna.mx; 9am-7pm Mon.-Sat.) roasts their line of carefully sourced Mexican coffee beans at a plant in the art-and-shopping center Laguna, in the Colonia Doctores. If you drop by during open hours, you can taste those fresh roasts in pour-overs, espressos, and even coffee cocktails.

**Alma Negra** (Av. Universidad 420, Col. Narvarte; tel. 55/4162-5899; https://almanegra.cafe; 7:30am-9pm daily) takes sourcing seriously, selling beans from producers across Mexico, including lesser known regions like Nayarit and Michoacán, in addition to beans from Africa, Asia, and South America. They always feature one international and one Mexican coffee in their eye-catching Narvarte shop.

If you make your way to Tlalpan, seek out **El Desastre Libros y Café** (Francisco I. Madero 15, Tlalpan; no phone; 9am-9pm Mon.-Sat., 9am-6pm Sun.), for an eclectic bookshop and excellent coffees, brewed with organic beans from Coatepec, Veracruz.

**Café Jekemir** (Regina 7; tel. 55/5709-7086; https://cafejekemir.com; 8am-9pm Mon.-Sat.; Metro: Isabel la Católica), which traces its roots back to the 1930s, occupies a spacious spot on the pedestrian street Regina. No espresso martinis here, but you will find a loyal clientele of neighborhood locals, students, and newspaper-reading intellectuals who come for the espresso drinks made from 100 percent Mexican beans.

In a pinch for caffeine? Skip the international brands for Mexican-owned coffee chains **Cielito Querido, Café Punta Del Cielo,** and **Tierra Garat,** which feature Mexican coffee at their branches throughout the city.

# Nightlife

## BARS

### ✪ Kaito

This hip cocktail bar is tucked into a cozy barroom above Japanese restaurant Deigo in the quiet Del Valle neighborhood. Here, the woman-run bar team creates creative and often playful Japanese-inspired cocktails, like the Godzilla, which includes wasabi syrup and lemongrass, and is served with a side of wasabi peas. On weeknights, it's a popular dinner spot with neighborhood locals, but the quality has made it a destination for cocktail connoisseurs citywide. Make reservations for the nights when guest bartenders or DJs are in the house.

**MAP 6:** *Enrique Pestalozzi 1238, Del Valle; tel. 55/9133-1476; 1pm-6:30pm Mon., noon-12:30am Tues.-Sat., noon-10:30pm Sun.; Metro: División del Norte, Metrobús: División del Norte*

# Tianguis: Outdoor Markets

fruit for sale at a street market in the Narvarte

Mesoamerican civilizations as far back as the early Olmecs on the Gulf Coast established open-air marketplaces for trade and commerce. After the Spanish conquest, many important pre-Columbian markets continued to operate throughout the region, including the giant market square in what is today the Zócalo.

In addition to neighborhood markets (see Public Markets, page 111), most colonias also have an outdoor market that sets up once a week on a closed street or sidewalk. Some are simple affairs, with 10-15 stands; others are massive 100-plus-vendor markets, where you can buy all your kitchen basics and find some of the city's best street snacks. Often referred to as mercados sobre ruedas (markets on wheels), or tianguis (from the Nahuatl word for an open-air market), they are wonderful places to shop, munch, and get a sense of a neighborhood.

Most mercados sobre ruedas run from about 9am or 10am to 6pm, though they tend to wind down after the comida, around 4pm. Here is a

# CANTINAS

### La Valenciana

For a long lunch or a leisurely evening with a group of friends, this pretty tile-covered cantina is a great place for hours of easygoing fun. The place has a relaxed local-watering-hole vibe, catering to neighborhood families on the weekends. The specialty here is the molcajete, a stone bowl filled with a stew-like mix of meats, nopales (cactus), onion, and other savories. Even if you don't order anything off the menu, the kitchen will send out snacks to accompany your drinks, as is traditional in a cantina.

**MAP 6:** *Av. Universidad 48, Col.*

small selection of the dozens of outdoor markets that set up across the city's central neighborhoods every day.

### PACHUCA AND JUAN DE LA BARRERA, CONDESA

This bustling market takes over Calle Pachuca in the northwest Condesa every **Tuesday.** Shop for handmade tortillas, fresh fruit, herbs, vegetables, and mushrooms, or simply chow down on tacos, flautas, handmade quesadillas, and huaraches.

### TIANGUIS DEL ORO, GLORIETA DE LA CIBELES, AND CALLE DE ORO, ROMA

This open-air market, which sets up along Calle de Oro in the Roma on **Wednesday, Saturday,** and **Sunday,** has many food stalls, but particularly notable is the Argentine grill **Parrilladas Bariloche,** which serves excellent South American-style steaks to the market crowd.

### MERCADO EL 100, PLAZA DEL LANZADOR, ROMA

Everything at this Sunday market is produced from within 160 km (100 mi) of Mexico City, including fresh fruits and vegetables, local honey, jams, Mexican coffee, and other gourmet goods. Note that this market closes around 2pm-3pm.

### ✪ TIANGUIS DE LOS JUEVES, CAROLINA AND HOLBEIN, NOCHEBUENA

A massive open-air market fills the streets between the Plaza de Toros and the Estadio Azul in the Noche Buena neighborhood every **Thursday.** With hundreds of vendors, it's a labyrinth of delicious aromas, tropical colors, and human traffic jams. Come for the gorditas, tacos, nieves, and the excellent food shopping.

### OBRERO MUNDIAL, COLONIA DEL VALLE

On **Sunday,** a beautiful neighborhood market stretches along the street of Casa del Obrero Mundial from Monterrey to Amores. There are vendors selling tortillas, fruit, vegetables, and herbs as well as flowers, plants, and clothing. Notable are the plethora of excellent food stalls with their loyal clientele.

*Narvarte Oriente; tel. 55/3330-7505; noon-midnight Mon.-Fri., noon-2am Sat.,1pm-8pm Sun.; Metro: Xola, Metrobús: Xola*

## LIVE MUSIC

### Jazzorca

An underground jazz club owned by virtuoso saxophonist Germán Bringas, Jazzorca puts on highly experimental jazz shows every Saturday night, featuring both Mexican and international artists—most often with Bringas himself on sax. An intimate and no-frills venue with a limited bar and coffee menu, as well as limited seating, this place is for avant garde jazz lovers. Check

Jazzorca's Facebook page to see what's coming up.
**MAP 6:** *Municipio Libre 37A, Col. Portales; tel. 55/5539-3082; shows 9pm Sat.; cover US$8; Metro: Portales*

# Recreation

## SPECTATOR SPORTS

### ★ Estadio Ciudad de los Deportes

This attractive midsize stadium was long the home of soccer club Cruz Azul—in fact, it was referred to as "Estadio Azul" for years. As Mexico prepares to host the 2026 World Cup alongside the United States and Canada, the city's stadiums have been alternately undergoing renovation, leading to a bit of a shuffle in soccer teams. At press time, Cruz Azul, as well as rivals Las Águilas de América and Atlante, were all based here. Whoever is playing, the small size and central location make this a good choice for a fútbol match while visiting Mexico City.

**MAP 6:** *Indiana 255, Ciudad de los Deportes; tel. 55/5801-9679; hours vary; most games US$5-15; Metro: San Antonio, Metrobús: Ciudad de los Deportes*

soccer stadium and the Monumental Plaza in the Ciudad de los Deportes

**Monumental Plaza de Toros México**

After years of activism in opposition to bullfighting in Mexico, a sport that retained a small but passionate following in the capital, a federal judge permanently suspended all activities at the Monumental Plaza de Toros México in June 2022. Citing the cruel treatment of bulls used in the fights, the judge called the decision "a benefit to the whole society." Located right next to the soccer stadium in the Ciudad de los Deportes, the 42,000-seat stadium, previously the largest bullfighting ring in the world, is now a venue for concerts and other events.

**MAP 6:** *Augusto Rodin 41, Ciudad de los Deportes; showtimes vary; Metro: San Antonio, Metrobús: Ciudad de los Deportes*

# Coyoacán

Map 7

| | |
|---|---|
| Getting Around | 221 |
| Coyoacán Walk | 224 |
| Sights | 228 |
| Restaurants | 232 |
| Nightlife | 235 |
| Arts and Culture | 238 |
| Recreation | 243 |
| Shops | 243 |

Once part of a colonial-era settlement far outside the city limits, Coyoacán's quiet plazas and cobblestone streets are today a pleasant oasis within the capital, retaining a charming small-town feeling. Lined with restaurants and shops, the twin squares at the center of Coyoacán, Jardín Centenario and Jardín Hidalgo, are often bustling with students, tourists, and local families on weekends. For visitors, Coyoacán is best known as the home of Mexican painter Frida Kahlo; her childhood home, now Museo Frida Kahlo, is today a moving museum that chronicles her life and work.

## Highlights

✪ **Museo Casa Leon Trotsky:** Engaging and a touch macabre, the former Coyoacán home of Leon Trotsky has been largely preserved as it was on the night the famous Russian revolutionary was assassinated in his study (page 228).

✪ **Museo Frida Kahlo:** Fans of Frida Kahlo will get a deeper look at her life and work at this moving museum, located in the artist's childhood home (page 228).

✪ **Jardín Hidalgo:** When strolling around Coyoacán's lovely central plaza, it's easy to imagine the neighborhood as the quaint colonial-era settlement it once was (page 230).

✪ **Cineteca Nacional:** From classic film series to avant-garde festival selections, an impressive variety of films are screened daily at this long-running public cinema (page 238).

✪ **Viveros de Coyoacán:** Spend a peaceful morning walking along the shaded pathways in this large tree-filled park, which first opened in the 1930s (page 243).

## Getting Around

- Metro lines: 3
- Metro stops: Coyoacán, Viveros, Miguel Ángel de Quevedo, Copilco, Universidad
- Metrobús lines: 1
- Metrobús stops: La Bombilla, Dr. Gálvez, Ciudad Universitaria

**Previous:** colorful colonial buildings and cobblestone streets in Coyoacán;
**Above:** Museo Frida Kahlo courtyard wall; Jardín Hidalgo.

221

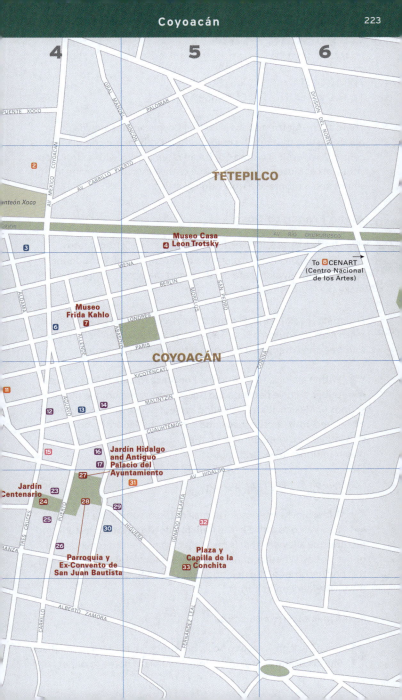

# Coyoacán Walk

**TOTAL DISTANCE:** 4.5 km (2.8 mi)
**TOTAL WALKING TIME:** 2.5 hours

There are no Metro stations in central Coyoacán, nor any major avenues passing through the neighborhood's charming colonial-era centro. As a result, a visit to Coyoacán often begins with a stroll. End your walk at Museo Frida Kahlo, one of the city's most moving art museums and a tribute to a truly original artist.

## Along Francisco Sosa

**1** At a brisk pace, it takes 15-20 minutes to walk from **Metro Viveros,** on Line 3, to central Coyoacán, though considering how many lovely sights are dotted along the way, it's unlikely you'll make the journey so quickly.

*Departing the station, walk south along Avenida Universidad until you reach Avenida Francisco Sosa. Swing a left, and slow your gait: This historic tree-lined avenue leads right into the heart of Coyoacán.*

**2** Within a block, you'll find the **Fonoteca Nacional,** an unusual public archive dedicated to documenting the unique music and sounds of Mexico. It's a fascinating project housed in Casa Alvarado, a brick-red 18th-century hacienda with strong Moorish and Andalusian influences. Wander through the lush gardens, where speakers play traditional music and sounds.

*Continue on Avenida Francisco Sosa.*

**3** A few blocks later, make a small detour south along the street Tata Vasco to arrive in the **Callejón del Aguacate,** a historic and picturesque alleyway that is the subject of numerous legends and ghost stories. Whether or not the alley is haunted, it is worth seeing this pretty corner of the neighborhood, marked by a small altar to the Virgin Mary on its corner.

*Return to Avenida Francisco Sosa.*

**4** Once back on Francisco Sosa, backtrack a half block to the **Plaza Santa Catarina,** a serene colonial-era plaza home to paper flags

Iglesia de Santa Catarina

fluttering between leafy trees and the picturesque Iglesia de Santa Catarina, built in the 18th century.

*Cross Avenida Francisco Sosa.*

**5** Just across the street, the **Casa de Cultura Jesús Reyes Heroles** (Francisco Sosa 202) is a multipurpose cultural center, set in another lovely hacienda; join locals relaxing in the pretty coffee shop in back.

*Continue east along Avenida Francisco Sosa.*

## Jardín Hidalgo and the Plaza de la Conchita

**6** Continue along Francisco Sosa until you arrive at **Jardín Centenario,** in the center of Coyoacán. As you arrive, you'll pass through two colonial-era archways that were once part of the massive Dominican convent that dominated central Coyoacán. Wander through the square, or settle in for a drink at **Los Danzantes,** one of the many bars and restaurants that adjoin the plaza.

*Head east to Jardín Hidalgo.*

**7** Just east, the **Jardín Hidalgo** is Coyoacán's central square, over which the historic Parroquia de San Juan Bautista presides. The first parish church was built here in 1528, atop a native school (the ruins of which still lie below the cloister), although the current edifice was constructed several decades later.

*Exit the jardín from behind the church and onto the small street Higuera, heading southeast. Continue down Higuera until you reach the end.*

**8** At the very end of Higuera, take note of the dark-red **Casa de la Malinche,** widely believed to be the house Cortés shared with his lover and interpreter Malintzin, better known as La Malinche. According to other legends, it is the house where Cortés's first wife, Catalina Suárez Marcayda, died, possibly at his hand. Though historians entirely discredit these stories, the site is now a city landmark.

*Cross Higuera to the plaza.*

**9** The quiet **Plaza y Capilla de la Conchita** is the setting for one of the earliest colonial-era chapels in Mexico. This fragile old church recently went through a complete renovation; admire its ornate (but still weathered) facade. According to archaeological evidence, this plaza may have been a central ceremonial space for pre-Columbian cultures in Coyoacán. Walk through the plaza to the **Jardín Frida Kahlo,** a pretty public garden dedicated to the famous Coyoacán painter.

### To Museo Frida Kahlo

**10** Walk along the quaint and cobbled Fernández Leal, filled with the towering trees and country houses emblematic of residential Coyoacán. Stop at the cultural center and bookstore **Centro Cultural Elena Garro** for a coffee or to thumb through a book.

*Follow Hidalgo west.*

**11** Heading back toward the center of town via Hidalgo, you'll pass coffee shops and taco stands, as well as the **Museo Nacional de Culturas Populares,** a craft museum, where a large ceramic árbol de la vida (tree of life) sits in the central courtyard.

*Turn right and continue along Allende, one of the neighborhood's main avenues.*

**12** A block farther, you'll likely notice a bit of bustle at the perennially popular seafood spot Jardín del Pulpo right on the corner of the **Mercado Coyoacán,** the neighborhood's municipal market. Wander amid flower vendors or stop to try one of Coyoacán's famous tostadas.

*Continue along Allende.*

**13** A few blocks farther, on the corner of Allende and Londres, Frida Kahlo's childhood home, now the **Museo Frida Kahlo,** is known as the "Casa Azul" or Blue House for its striking cobalt color.

# Sights

### ✪ Museo Casa Leon Trotsky

During the 20th century, Mexico's leftist government offered asylum to political exiles from many different countries, including anti-Fascist intellectuals from Spain and Cold War exiles from the United States. Following a power struggle with Josef Stalin, Russian Marxist revolutionary Leon Trotsky left the Soviet Union in 1929, eventually coming to Mexico with his wife, Natalia, in 1937, at the invitation of Frida Kahlo and Diego Rivera.

Leon Trotsky's former home, now a museum

In 1940, a Spanish Stalinist named Ramón Mercader gained Trotsky's confidence, then fatally wounded him with an ice axe while Trotsky was in his study. Today, Trotsky's final home in Mexico City has been converted into an interesting museum that chronicles the rise of communism, Trotsky's life, and politics in Mexico and throughout the world, as well as exhibiting dozens of wonderful photographs of Trotsky and his Natalia with Mexican politicians, artists, and intellectuals. Many of the rooms in the home have been left entirely untouched since the day he died, giving a glimpse of the Bolshevik revolutionary's documents, personal effects, and furnishings.

**MAP 7:** *Río Churubusco 410, Col. Del Carmen; tel. 55/5554-0687; http://museocasadeleontrotsky.blogspot.com; 10am-5pm Tues.-Sun.; US$2; Metro: Coyoacán*

### TOP EXPERIENCE

### ✪ Museo Frida Kahlo

Frida Kahlo produced a small body of work during her lifetime, yet her paintings are so unique and powerful that she is now one of the most recognizable names in modern art. The Museo Frida Kahlo is located in the house where Kahlo grew up, lived with her husband, artist Diego Rivera, and died. Known as the Casa Azul for its cobalt color, this wonderful museum is both an art gallery and a re-creation of the home when Kahlo and Rivera lived there. It's an absolute must for Kahlo fans.

The ground-floor galleries exhibit some of Kahlo's work—including a lovely portrait she painted of her father, Guillermo—as well as some of her modern art collection. Perhaps the most moving rooms are upstairs, where visitors can see Kahlo's studio, with her wheelchair at the easel, as well as the bed where Kahlo spent so much time after a tragic trolley accident in her teenage years left her permanently disabled. Kahlo was a collector of traditional Mexican clothing and jewelry, which became a huge part of her public persona, as well as a key element in her artistic work. Many of her outfits are displayed throughout the museum.

The museum's collection became more robust after a remarkable discovery within its own walls. In 2002, the home's bathrooms were unsealed, revealing a treasure of clothing, documents, toys, books, and other artifacts from the artists' lives. The collection was so extensive that the museum acquired the adjoining Porfiriato-era house to exhibit them. Note: Advance tickets are required and can be purchased via the museum's website.

**MAP 7:** *Londres 247; tel. 55/5554-5999; www.museofridakahlo.mx; 10am-6pm Tues. and Thurs.-Sun., 11am-6pm Wed.; US$18; Metro: Coyoacán*

### Plaza Santa Catarina

A few blocks west of Jardín Centenario along Avenida Francisco Sosa is a lovely cobblestone square, fronted by the bright yellow **Capilla de Santa Catarina** and surrounded by restored colonial-era houses. On one side is the **Casa de Cultura Jesús Reyes Heroles** (Francisco Sosa 202; tel. 55/5658-7826; 8am-6pm daily), which often holds cultural events

Museo Frida Kahlo

and art exhibits. Stop in to admire the rambling old hacienda, or enjoy the lush gardens in back, where there is also an attractive coffee shop with shaded tables. Back toward the center of Coyoacán, on Francisco Sosa, the **Instituto Italiano di Cultura** (Francisco Sosa 77; tel. 55/5554-0044; www.iicmessico.esteri.it) often hosts art exhibits and other special events.

**MAP 7:** *Francisco Sosa at Tata Vasco; Metro: Viveros*

### Jardín Centenario

If you arrive in Coyoacán via Avenida Francisco Sosa, you will find yourself first at the Jardín Centenario, a shady plaza that adjoins the Jardín Hidalgo, another large plaza, to the west. The square is accessed via a lovely arched entryway, built by hand in the 16th century; it was once a part of the cloister of the San Juan Bautista monastery and church. The centerpiece of the garden is a circular stone fountain featuring bronze sculptures of two coyotes, a reference to the neighborhood's Nahuatl name, "Place of Coyotes." The fountain has become a symbol of Coyoacán. Both sides of the plaza are lined with restaurants and cafés, and there is often a friendly, upbeat vibe in the square, where students play guitars on park benches, intellectuals converse over coffees, and locals stroll along the stone paths with their dogs.

**MAP 7:** *Carrillo Puerto and Tres Cruces; Metro: Viveros*

coyote sculpture in Jardín Centenario

### ✪ Jardín Hidalgo and Antiguo Palacio del Ayuntamiento

Jardín Hidalgo is Coyoacán's lovely central plaza, bordered to the east by the impressive **Parroquia de San Juan Bautista,** one of the oldest churches in the city. Larger than the adjoining Jardín Centenario, this sun-drenched esplanade features an iron kiosk with a stained-glass cupola, constructed in France in the 19th century. Filled with benches and constantly patrolled by shaved-ice carts and toy vendors, this plaza is a popular place for a weekend stroll with the family.

Today, Coyoacán's main government offices are located in the **Antiguo Palacio del Ayuntamiento de Coyoacán** (Plaza Hidalgo 1), a rust-colored building constructed in 1755 and stretching across the entire north end of Jardín Hidalgo. Also known as the Casa de Cortés, the building stands on the site of what many historians believe to have been the administrative offices of Hernán Cortés, Marquis of the Valley of Oaxaca, in the 16th century.

**MAP 7:** *Bordered by Felipe Carrillo*

Plaza y Capilla de la Conchita

Puerto and Caballocalco; Metro: Viveros

### Parroquia y Ex-Convento de San Juan Bautista

One of the oldest Catholic churches in Mexico City, this huge baroque gem was originally built right after the conquest, in the mid-16th century, on land granted to the Franciscans by Hernán Cortés, and some elements of the original construction remain embedded in the building today. Like many churches of its era, it was once part of a much larger monastery complex at the center of Coyoacán, with buildings and gardens stretching all the way to the arches at the entrance to adjoining Jardín Centenario. The interior of the church was thoroughly and beautifully reconstructed, with the altars restored and recoated in gold leaf, and frescoes restored and added to the walls.

**MAP 7:** *Jardín Centenario 8; tel. 55/5554-0560; 8am-7:30pm daily; free; Metro: Viveros*

### Plaza y Capilla de la Conchita

The colonial-era street Higuera cuts diagonally southeast from the Jardín Hidalgo, terminating at the picturesque Plaza de la Conchita. The chapel here, one of the oldest in the city, was originally constructed in 1521 by order of Hernán Cortés, though the facade that stands today dates from the 18th century. By some accounts, it was the site of the very first Christian church in Mexico. Although officially known as **Capilla de la Purísima Concepción,** the chapel and surrounding garden are more commonly known by the affectionate nickname La Conchita (the Little Shell). According to archaeological evidence, this plaza may have been a central ceremonial space for pre-Columbian cultures in Coyoacán.

On one corner of the Plaza de la Conchita, the brick-red **Casa de la Malinche** is said to be the house Cortés shared with his lover and interpreter Malintzin, better known as La Malinche. The story is likely apocryphal: Historians say the house was constructed many centuries after Cortés and La Malinche lived in the Valley of Mexico.

**MAP 7:** *Fernández Leal and Vallarta; Metro: Viveros*

Merendero Las Lupitas

# Restaurants

## PRICE KEY
$ Entrées less than US$10
$$ Entrées US$10-20
$$$ Entrées more than US$20

## MEXICAN

### Casa del Pan Papalotl $

This long-running vegetarian and vegan café (which also has a branch in San Cristóbal de las Casas, Chiapas, and another in Cuicuilco, in southern Mexico City) serves house-baked breads and breakfast foods, baguette sandwiches, and other tasty vegetable-centric fare, with an emphasis on local, organic ingredients. The small dining room opens onto the street, where sidewalk tables are filled with hippie-esque diners. The perfect spot to pass a Sunday morning with a cup of tea and the paper, it often has a wait for weekend brunch.

**MAP 7:** *Av. México 25; tel. 55/3095-1767; www.casadelpan.com; 8am-10pm daily; Metro: Viveros*

### Merendero Las Lupitas $

A merendero is a traditional restaurant serving light suppers, and although old-time Merendero Las Lupitas is open in the daytime (it started serving breakfast and lunch in the 1980s), it's nice to go in the evening, when the pleasant atmosphere, on the tranquil Plaza Santa Catarina, makes it the perfect place to wrap up the day. The menu includes a notable selection of dishes from northern Mexico. Try the enchiladas potosinas (fried-cheese enchiladas) or the burritos stuffed with chilorio (slow-cooked pork in chili sauce).

**MAP 7:** *Jardín Santa Catarina 4; tel. 55/5554-3353; 8am-9:30pm Mon.-Thurs., 9am-11pm Fri.-Sat., 9am-8:30pm Sun.; Metro: Viveros*

### Corazón de Maguey $$

This colorful mezcalería and restaurant has a modern Mexican atmosphere and an ultra-fun menu of traditional food from across the republic, with a particularly strong emphasis on Oaxacan cuisine. On a leisurely afternoon in Coyoacán, this is a perfect place to order a flight of mezcal and a bunch of unusual bar snacks, like nopal salad, guacamole with fried grasshoppers, or chicken in mole negro.

**MAP 7:** *Plaza Jardín Centenario 9A; WhatsApp tel. 55/7406-8199; https://corazondemaguey.com; 12:30pm-11pm Mon., 9:30am-11pm Tues.-Thurs. and Sun., 9:30am-midnight Fri.-Sat., kitchen closes 1 hour earlier; Metro: Viveros*

### Los Danzantes $$$

An elegant yet relaxed restaurant with a big outdoor dining area in the Jardín Centenario, Los Danzantes serves contemporary Mexican dishes with a strong emphasis on local Mexican ingredients and a notable influence from the culinary traditions of Oaxaca and other southern states. The appealing menu includes a range of interesting and well-rendered dishes, like turkey in mole negro, seafood soup, and tostadas topped with refried beans and bone marrow. Los Danzantes is famous for its excellent line of Oaxacan mezcal, which, naturally, is served in-house.

**MAP 7:** *Jardín Centenario 12; tel. 55/4356-7185; http://losdanzantes.com;*

dining al fresco at Corazón de Maguey

12:30pm-11pm Mon.-Wed., 9am-11pm Thurs. and Sun., 9am-midnight Fri.-Sat.; Metro: Viveros

## TACOS, TORTAS, AND SNACKS

### Tacos Chupacabras $

One of the most famous taco stands in the city, this impressive street-side operation is a meat lover's dream, with busy taqueros rapidly plating orders for tacos filled with chorizo, bistec (beef), and cecina (salt-cured beef) as well as the signature taco "chupacabras," with its secret spices, to a swarm of customers. One thing that distinguishes Chupacabras from so many other taco stands is the variety of toppings—like potatoes, beans, and grilled prickly pear—lined up at the bar, which customers can pile onto their tacos.

**MAP 7:** Under the overpass at Lateral de Churubusco at Av. México; no phone; 9am-3am Tues.-Sat., 9am-midnight Sun.; Metro: Coyoacán

### La Barraca Valenciana $

There are Spanish-style tapas on the menu—including classics like tortilla española (egg-and-potato omelet) and patatas bravas (fried and spiced potatoes)—but the thing to get at this low-key eatery is a torta (Mexican-style sandwich), served on a soft white roll. Try the breaded eggplant or the calamari with chimichurri, which come served (as any good torta should) with a bowl of pickled chilies. Big plus: The restaurant's owner is a craft beer aficionado, so there's always a nice selection of Mexican microbrews in the fridge.

**MAP 7:** Av. Centenario 91-C; tel. 55/5658-1880; 1pm-8pm daily; Metro: Viveros

### La Casa de los Tacos $

For a quick bite in central Coyoacán, this small and lively taquería is conveniently located just down the street from Jardín Centenario. Here, you can get tacos filled with a range of ingredients, from "pre-Hispanic" choices like chinicuiles (a worm that lives in the root of the maguey cactus) to more standard fare like chorizo; however, the best bites might be those that come fresh off the comal (griddle) at the restaurant's entrance, like gorditas (thick round corn flatbreads). The accompanying salsas are varied and delicious.

**MAP 7:** Carrillo Puerto 16; tel. 55/5124-2444; https://casadelostacos.com; 8am-11pm daily; Metro: Viveros

## COFFEE AND SWEETS

### Café El Jarocho $

A neighborhood institution since 1953, the aromatic corner coffee stand Café El Jarocho is often jammed with neighborhood locals sipping inexpensive mochas and nibbling doughnuts. The only seating is the occasional milk crate outside or the iron benches along the sidewalk, where people gather for casual conversation throughout the week. There are several more branches of El Jarocho throughout

the city's south, all popular with locals.
**MAP 7:** *Calle Cuauhtémoc 134; tel. 55/5554-5418; 6am-11pm daily; Metro: Viveros*

### La Mano Jardín $
Bring a good book or good company to this restaurant, café, and cultural center on the historic cobblestone avenue Francisco Sosa. With its expansive garden dining area and tranquil vibe, it's a great place to spend an hour or two relaxing after a walking tour of downtown Coyoacán. To accompany your respite, there are nice Mexican breakfasts and coffee in the morning, and craft beer and snacks in the afternoon, including staples like tamales, esquites, and tacos made with heirloom corn. After you eat, take a moment to browse the shop, with its interesting collection of Mexican-made design books, clothing, accessories, and gifts.
**MAP 7:** *Francisco Sosa 363; no phone; www.culturalamano.com; 9:30am-8pm daily; Metro: Viveros*

## MARKETS
### Mercado Coyoacán $
A few blocks from Coyoacán's central plaza, this pretty covered market stocks fresh fruits, vegetables, and other kitchen staples, as well as flowers and handicrafts. It is particularly well-known for its marisquerías, seafood stands serving shrimp cocktails, ceviches, and fried fish. The most famous of these is **Jardín del Pulpo,** at the corner of Allende and Malintzin. Inside the market, there are also popular tostada stands, each offering cazuelas (clay pots) filled with an array of savory toppings.
**MAP 7:** *Malintzin and Ignacio Allende; no phone; hours vary by vendor 7am-5pm daily; Metro: Viveros*

# Nightlife

## BARS AND LOUNGES
### ⭐ Centenario 107
This amiable spot in the heart of Coyoacán is a low-key place for a beer (there's an excellent selection of craft options on tap), a cocktail, or a shot of mezcal at any time of day. The spacious downstairs bar, with its high ceilings and big booths, is adjoined by a small outdoor patio, and there is an additional space upstairs. Chill and family-friendly during the day, the place gets busy with Coyoacán locals in the evenings, when there is sometimes live jazz and other performances.
**MAP 7:** *Centenario 107; tel. 56/3647-2249, WhatsApp tel. 55/5332-1048; https://centenario107.mx; 9am-11pm Sun.-Mon., 9am-midnight Tues.-Wed., 9am-1am Fri.-Sat.; Metro: Viveros*

### Mezcalero

A spacious bar just behind the Parroquia de San Juan Bautista, Mezcalero is a nice place to have a drink on the sidewalk tables in the late afternoon—or, alternatively, to stay up late partying, buoyed by the exuberance of Coyoacán's youthful night scene. As the name hints, there is a nice selection of mezcal, as well as beer and cocktails. If all the tables are full, grab a seat at La Celestina, another youthful cocktail bar, next door.

**MAP 7:** *Caballocalco 14; tel. 55/5554-7027; 1pm-1am Sun.-Wed., 1pm-2am Thurs.-Sat.; no cover; Metro: Viveros*

## CANTINAS
### La Bipo

With a convivial local crowd and an atmosphere that blends new-school hip with quirky old-school kitsch, this casual nouveau cantina is a relaxed place to chat about parties or politics accompanied by an Indio on draft and a plate of fancy bar snacks, like fish tacos or hibiscus-filled quesadillas. Upstairs, there is an open-roof terrace where smokers converge, though the funky downstairs bar has more style. There's often DJs spinning music.

**MAP 7:** *Malintzin 155; tel. 55/5484-8230, WhatsApp tel. 55/1241-1142, 1pm-11pm Sun.-Tues., 1pm-midnight Wed., 1pm-2am Thurs.-Sat.; no cover; Metro: Viveros*

### La Coyoacana

Right in the heart of historic Coyoacán, this traditional cantina is a popular spot for families and day-trippers to have a few drinks and a bite to eat in the traditional dining room or on the pretty covered patio. On busy days, mariachi musicians mingle amid the diners and revelers. With its low cost, central location, and merry atmosphere, there is often a wait for a table on the weekend.

**MAP 7:** *Higuera 14; tel. 55/5658-5337; www.lacoyoacana.com; 1pm-midnight Mon.-Wed., 1pm-2am Thurs.-Sat., 1pm-9pm Sun.; no cover; Metro: Viveros*

## LIVE MUSIC
### El Vicio

A varied lineup can be found at this venue in Coyoacán, an incarnation of the long-running El Hábito, originally founded in 1954 by poet and essayist Salvador Novo. Often funny and irreverent shows include stand-up comedy, independent music, and monologues, and some performances benefit social organizations. As at many cabarets in Mexico City, you'll need proficient Spanish and some familiarity with Mexican politics and society to enjoy the show.

**MAP 7:** *Madrid 13; tel. 55/3753-3529; www.elvicio.com.mx; shows generally Wed.-Mon.; tickets US$15-25; Metro: Viveros*

# A Film Lover's Guide to Mexico City

Love to see movies? In Mexico City, you're not alone. In addition to international blockbusters at chains like Cinépolis and Cinemex, there are dozens of art movie houses around the city.

- In the Roma Sur, **Cine Tonalá** (Tonalá 261; tel. 55/5264-4101; www.cinetonala.com; US$4) is an art house cinema, multidisciplinary performance space, and underground nightspot with an admirable focus on independent director-driven films. The lineup changes weekly but usually includes 3-4 movies every day, with titles from across the world.

- The **Cineteca Nacional** is the movie house par excellence in Mexico City. In September 2024, a much-anticipated additional location of the Cineteca opened in the newly annexed Cuarta Sección of Chapultepec (page 238).

- **Cine Lido** (Tamaulipas 202; tel. 55/5276-7110; US$4), in the Condesa, was an early 20th-century movie house; years after it closed, the space was reimagined as a spacious bookshop and cultural center, Centro Cultural Bella Época, which operates a screening room and event spaces showing alternative and festival circuit movies.

- A funky alternative cinema, **La Casa del Cine** (República de Uruguay 52; tel. 55/5512-4243; http://lacasadelcine.mx; US$4) was founded with the mission to promote young Mexican filmmakers. It shows works from international film festivals, independent Mexican films, and bigger-budget movies that are a few years old, in addition to participating in film festivals in the city.

- Located in the Santa María la Ribera's **Museo Universitario del Chopo** (page 134), **Cinematógrafo del Chopo** (Dr. Enrique González Martínez 10; www.chopo.unam.mx; usually at noon, 5pm, and 7:30pm daily; US$2.50) shows independent, avant-garde, and classic films throughout the week in the museum's small on-site cinema, curated by the UNAM film program.

- In addition to the program at El Chopo, UNAM's film program, called the Filmoteca, includes frequent screenings at the **Sala Julio Bracho** (Centro Cultural Universitario; tel. 55/5622-7004; US$2.50) on the main university campus, as well as the annual **Festival Internacional de Cine UNAM** (www.ficunam.org), a juried film competition that screens dozens of contemporary independent films. Venues range from the university's cinemas to Cine Tonalá to outdoor plazas.

# Arts and Culture

## CINEMA

### ✪ Cineteca Nacional

Founded in 1974, the Cineteca Nacional is a movie lover's paradise, with a lineup of international, independent, and art house films, shown by the dozens each week. Here you can see everything from experimental Mexican short films to an Akira Kurosawa retrospective to new blockbuster releases. The Cineteca maintains a huge film archive and publishes its own line of books on film. In 2012, the Cineteca buildings were renovated and expanded, including the addition of a new outdoor cinema that shows movies alfresco. At press time, movie lovers were anxiously awaiting the debut of the Cineteca's new space in Chapultepec park (Av. Vasco de Quiroga 1345, Campo Militar no. 1-F, Panteón Santa Fe). **MAP 7:** *Av. México Coyoacán 389; tel. 55/4155-1200; www.cinetecanacional.net; 12:30pm-9pm Mon.-Fri., 11:30am-9pm Sat.-Sun.; US$4, US$3 students, under age 25, and seniors, US$3 Tues.-Wed.; Metro: Coyoacán*

## MUSEUMS

### Fonoteca Nacional

The Fonoteca Nacional is a rather unusual project: Through a mix of recordings and audiovisual

Fonoteca Nacional

material, this archive seeks to preserve the unique sounds of Mexico, from the brassy tones of a band playing outside a Metro station to the sizzle of meat frying at a taco stand. Housed in Casa Alvarado, an 18th-century hacienda, the Fonoteca exhibits work by artists and historians documenting sound and hosts ongoing musical performances—all gratis—as well as guided listening tours of the archive.

**MAP 7:** *Francisco Sosa 383; tel. 55/4155-0950; 10am-7pm Mon.-Fri., 9am-6pm Sat.; free; Metro: Viveros or Miguel Ángel de Quevedo*

### Museo Nacional de Culturas Populares

Dedicated to Mexico's diverse popular art and craft traditions, this museum is interesting from both an anthropological and aesthetic perspective. Overseen by the National Council for Culture and Arts, the museum doesn't have a permanent collection; instead, it organizes temporary exhibitions featuring work from specific regions or cultures, or around certain themes, like lunar metaphors or the milpa; it also occasionally exhibits work by Indigenous cultures from other parts of the world, in addition to hosting special events and performances on its back patio.

**MAP 7:** *Av. Hidalgo 289; tel. 55/4155-0920; https://mncp.cultura.gob.mx; 11am-6pm Tues.-Thurs., 11am-7pm Fri.-Sun.; US$1, free under age 12 and over age 60; Metro: Viveros*

# THEATER, CLASSICAL MUSIC, AND DANCE

### CENART (Centro Nacional de los Artes)

Not far from central Coyoacán, CENART is a government-run institution dedicated to the study and promotion of performing, visual, and applied arts, from dance and circus arts to painting and architecture. The massive 5-ha (12-acre) campus, designed by a host of famous architects like Enrique Norten and Ricardo Legorreta, is visually striking, and includes five art galleries, an art store, three theaters, a library, a bookshop, a small café, and even some landscaped green space. There are frequent musical and dance performances on the weekends, often presented by CENART students, from classical music and ballet to children's cinema.

**MAP 7:** *Río Churubusco 79, Colonia*

Museo Nacional de Culturas Populares patio

# Best Souvenirs

## FOR THE HOME COOK

Lightweight **dried chilies,** of which you'll find a grand variety in Mexico City's markets, are the cornerstone of many Mexican salsas, and they can also be dropped into a pot of cooking beans to add both kick and flavor. **Mole paste** can be mixed with chicken or vegetable broth (or just water) to create a dish from this distinctively Mexican sauce.

traditional Oaxacan textiles

Mole can be bought in paste or powder, though it is generally easier and quicker to prepare from a paste. Note that mole paste may be confiscated by security at the airport, since some pastes are considered liquids. Pack it securely in your checked luggage to avoid problems.

**Where to find it:** The **Mercado San Juan** (page 110) is a favorite shopping spot for many chefs, both amateur and professional. The **Mercado de la Merced** (page 70) has a dizzying array of dried chilies, moles, spices, and other packable goodies.

## FOR THE CAFFEINE LOVER

Mexico's southern states are major producers of high-quality **coffee beans** and **cacao.** Both beans have been consumed in Mexico for centuries, and you'll find hundreds of artisanal chocolatiers and small-batch coffee roasters in the city today. Hip third-wave coffee roasters have taken over in the capital, but you'll also find excellent coffee beans for sale at some of the city's oldest shops, many of which have Middle Eastern heritage.

**Where to find it:** Art bookshop **Casa Bosques** (page 201) carries a proprietary line of Mexican chocolate bars, some with unusual accents like wasabi and almond, rosemary, or cardamom. **Chocolatería La Rifa** (page 130) sells top-quality bars for eating and for hot chocolate, made with Mexican cacao. **Café Jekemir** (page 215) has been roasting coffee for almost a century, and **Café Avellaneda** (page 214) roasts its own line of premium Mexican coffee beans.

## FOR THE CREATIVE DECORATOR

From hand-loomed rugs to delicately embroidered blouses to warm wool ponchos, **traditional clothing** and **textiles** are produced in communities throughout Mexico. Some popular gifts are embroidered manta tunics and huipiles from Oaxaca, geometrically stitched Magdalena huipiles from Chiapas, and silk wraps or shawls from Tenancingo, Santa María del Río, and other regions.

Textiles made from hand-dyed, hand-loomed natural fibers are always the priciest, but the quality is superlative. Look for wool dyed in the traditional style with cochineal, a crimson-colored tint derived from insects.

**Where to find it:** For the highest-quality pieces, try **Remigio** (page 83) at The Shops at Downtown. **Onora** (page 168) in Polanco has an excellent selection of textiles and crafts. For a fun and contemporary twist on traditional Mexican clothing, try **Fábrica Social** (page 138) in the Juárez.

## FOR THE SOPHISTICATE

There is a long tradition of silver design in Mexico, dating back to the early colonial era. Some of the Mexico's most famous **silverwork** comes from the former mining town of Taxco, Guerrero, much inspired by early 20th-century designer William Spratling. Though it's not an ironclad guarantee, real silver will generally be stamped with 925, 920, MEX, or MEXICO.

**Where to find it:** **Tane** (page 171) could be considered the Tiffany & Co. of Mexico, with multiple lines of high-quality silverwork from top designers, most contemporary in style. You can also find vintage silver at antiques markets like the **Centro de Antigüedades Plaza del Ángel** (page 138).

## FOR THE ECLECTIC COLLECTOR

There are endless finds, from splendid to quirky, at Mexico City's varied **antiques** and vintage markets. At all of Mexico City's antiques markets, serious buyers arrive early to snag the best pieces. Prices are often negotiable for higher-priced items. Before buying anything, take a turn around the entire market; you might find two vendors have similar products at different prices or with different quality.

**Where to find it:** **La Lagunilla** (page 109), on Sunday morning, is the biggest and most popular antiques market in the capital. **Centro de Antigüedades Plaza del Ángel** (page 138) has many upscale items on sale. **Mercado de Cuauhtémoc** (page 200) is a low-key and accessible place with some interesting vendors, especially on Saturday.

## FOR THE COCKTAIL ENTHUSIAST

**Mezcal** and **tequila** have become immensely popular internationally, and are now exported throughout the world, but you'll still find the best selection of Mexican liquors in Mexico.

**Shopping tips:** For the drinks connoisseur, bring home a lesser-known spirit, like sotol, or a bottle of mezcal distilled with a scorpion inside (it lends the spirit a bright, acidic taste).

**Where to find it:** You can buy bottles of small batch mezcal at **Mis Mezcales** (Coahuila 138 Local 2; www.mismezcales.mx) or **La Clandestina** (Av. Álvaro Obregón 298; 55/5212-1871; https://laclandestina.mx), both in the Roma.

Centro Nacional de los Artes

Country Club; tel. 55/4155-0111; ticket office tel. 55/4155-0000; www.cenart.gob.mx; Metro: Viveros

### La Titería

This wonderful children's theater, which has a creative focus on puppetry and marionettes, presents colorful and joyous original shows every weekend. There's popcorn for sale on the patio outside, books and games for children to play with while they wait for the show to begin, and general good vibes from the staff and actors. Productions here are in Spanish, but children who don't speak the language may be able to follow along with the upbeat programming.

**MAP 7:** Vicente Guerrero 7; WhatsApp tel. 55/6964-9520; www.latiteria.mx; shows generally afternoon Sat.-Sun. and school holidays; US$10; Metro: Viveros

La Titería in Coyoacán patio

# Recreation

## PARKS

### ⭐ Viveros de Coyoacán

In 1901, architect and early environmentalist Miguel Ángel de Quevedo donated 1 ha (2.5 acres) of land to the city to create a public nursery. Officially inaugurated in 1907, it was the first open space dedicated to growing trees and plants for public use in the city. Today, it's a popular place for neighborhood locals out for a stroll, especially during the early morning and late afternoon. Open yoga and tai chi classes are often held in the park.

**MAP 7:** *Bounded by Universidad, Madrid, Melchor Ocampo, and Pérez Valenzuela; 6am-6pm daily; free; Metro: Viveros*

# Shops

## ARTS AND CRAFTS

### Bazar Reto

Bazar Reto, a huge antiques vendor in the Portales neighborhood (Fernando Montes de Oca 391; tel. 55/3241-7243), operates a small but charming shop in central Coyoacán. Here, you'll find a selection of treasures like old maps, vintage artwork, mid-20th-century lamps and furnishings, old wall clocks, violins, and other curiosities. Half of the shop is dedicated to vintage clothing and shoes, in both men's and women's styles.

**MAP 7:** *Centenario 25; tel. 55/4389-8422; 9am-6:30pm daily; Metro: Viveros*

## BOOKS

### Centro Cultural Elena Garro

Run by the Fondo de Cultura Económica, this multistory bookstore and cultural center is beautiful, with a towering glass facade that completely envelops the original early 20th-century mansion it's housed in, creating an atmosphere both modern and historic. The bookstore is well-stocked, with a good selection of literature and children's books, but note that most titles are in Spanish.

**MAP 7:** *Fernández Leal 43; tel. 55/3003-4091; www.educal.com.mx/elenagarro; 10am-9pm daily; Metro: Viveros*

# Greater Mexico City  Map 8

Getting Around ........ 245
Sights ................ 248
Restaurants ........... 253
Arts and Culture ....... 255
Festivals and Events.... 259
Recreation ............. 260
Shops ................. 261

It can take months to explore central Mexico City, but there is also a wide range of neighborhoods and experiences outside the most well-known districts, including many memorable museums, restaurants, archaeological sites, and markets—many located in the city's expansive residential neighborhoods to the south.

In the city's south, near Avenida Insurgentes, upscale San Ángel is a colonial-era neighborhood with an old-fashioned feeling and some excellent museums. Continue south along Insurgentes to the Ciudad Universitaria, the main campus for the Universidad Nacional Autónoma de México (UNAM), the largest and most prestigious university in Mexico. The

# Highlights

✪ **Basílica de Santa María de Guadalupe:** The famous shroud that bears the image of the Virgen de Guadalupe draws millions of visitors to this shrine in northern Mexico City, one of the world's most visited Catholic pilgrimage sites (page 248).

✪ **Biblioteca Central:** The mosaic-covered main library is the most iconic building on UNAM's central campus, a UNESCO World Heritage Site (page 250).

✪ **Canals at Xochimilco:** The lakes and waterways in southern Mexico City are a place of tremendous history, ecological significance, and raucous partying (page 252).

✪ **Museo Universitario Arte Contemporáneo:** This wonderful university-run museum hosts consistently high-caliber and thought-provoking contemporary art exhibits (page 257).

✪ **Bazaar Sábado:** Visit the colonial-era neighborhood of San Ángel on a Saturday, when the central plaza is filled with art and artisan vendors (page 263).

# Getting Around

**Northern Mexico City**
- Metro lines: 6 and 8; stops: La Villa and Deportivo, 18 de Marzo
- Metrobús lines: 7; stops: Garrido or De Los Misterios

**Southern Mexico City**
- Metro lines: 3; stops: M.A. Quevedo, Universidad
- Metrobús lines: 1; stops: La Bombilla, Dr. Galvez, Ciudad Universitaria, Centro Cultural Universitario, Perisur, Fuentes Brotantes

**Previous:** boats in the Xochimilco canal; **Above:** Biblioteca Central; the canals in Xochimilco.

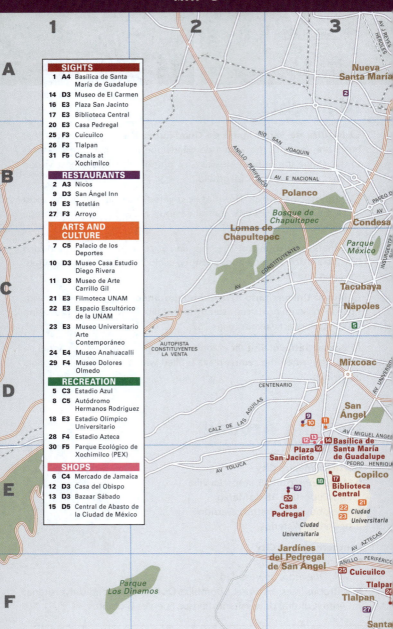

# Greater Mexico City

247

entire central campus was named a World Heritage Site for its modernist architecture, engineering, and landscape design, and it is home to a plethora of arts and cultural attractions, including one of the city's best contemporary art spaces, the Museo Universitario Arte Contemporáneo. Not far from the university, the affluent neighborhood of El Pedregal and, farther south, the colonial village Tlalpan are also worth visiting on a trip to the city. A highlight of the south is the historic neighborhood of Xochimilco, where you can take a flat-bottomed boat tour of the neighborhood's centuries-old canals and farmland. And there is always a colorful crowd at the Basílica de Santa María de Guadalupe, one of the world's most colorful and beloved Catholic pilgrimage sites, located in Mexico City's northern reaches.

## Sights

### NORTHERN MEXICO CITY

#### ★ Basílica de Santa María de Guadalupe

The second most-visited Catholic pilgrimage site in the world is the Basílica de Santa María de Guadalupe in northern Mexico City. It was here, on December 12, 1531, that Saint Juan Diego had a vision of a dark-skinned, Nahuatl-speaking Virgin Mary—known today as the Virgen de Guadalupe—whose image miraculously appeared imprinted on his cloak. Since the 16th century, numerous chapels have been built on the site and many remain standing. The modern basilica was designed by architect Pedro Ramírez Vásquez and opened in 1976. Here, you can get a closer look at Juan Diego's cloak, which hangs behind the altar, where a moving walkway below it helps prevent human traffic jams. It is particularly crowded on and around December 12, the anniversary of the date when the Virgin appeared to Juan Diego.

The basilica is located in northern Mexico City. If you plan to travel there via public transportation, you can take Metro Line 6 to La Villa or Line 8 to Deportivo 18 de Marzo, then walk 10-15 minutes to the Basilica. Metrobús Line 7, which runs along the Paseo de la Reforma, stops close to the basilica at the stations Garrido and De Los Misterios. Board in the direction of Indios Verdes or Campo Marte.

**MAP 8:** *Fray Juan de Zumarraga 2, Col. Villa Gustavo A. Madero; tel. 55/5118-0500; www.virgendeguadalupe.org.mx; 6am-9pm daily; free; Metro: La Villa, Metrobús: Garrido*

Basílica de Santa María de Guadalupe

# SOUTHERN MEXICO CITY
## San Ángel
### Museo de El Carmen

A former Carmelite convent, established in 1615, is a fitting backdrop to the collection of Mexican colonial art and furniture at this wonderful museum. Including oil paintings, sculpture, and religious pieces from the 17th-18th centuries, the large and interesting collection has been overseen by INAH, the National Institute of Anthropology and History, since the 1930s; the organization opened the museum here in 1955.

Once the religious and economic center of San Ángel, the convent housed an order of Carmelite nuns. While touring the museum, note the vestry (where priests' robes were hung) with its elaborate gold-leaf carvings, the old restroom and washbasins with Talavera-tile bowls, and the beautiful crypt downstairs, where naturally mummified bodies were discovered and are now on display in a somewhat macabre exhibit. Next door, the adjoining church, Iglesia de El Carmen, with its three beautiful tile-covered domes, was built in 1624.

**MAP 8:** *Av. Revolución 4; tel. 55/5616-2816; 10am-5pm Tues.-Sun.; US$3.50 adults, free students and teachers, free Sun.; Metro: Miguel Ángel de Quevedo or Barranca del Muerto, Metrobús: La Bombilla or Dr. Gálvez*

### Plaza San Jacinto

The fine cobblestone plaza at the heart of San Ángel is ringed by cafés and restaurants. Although it's just a couple of blocks from a sea of traffic on Insurgentes and Avenida Revolución, wandering around the relaxed plaza makes it easy to imagine San Ángel as a village far from Mexico City, as it once was. Up San Jacinto street, on the west side of the plaza, the **Iglesia de San Jacinto** was once part of a Dominican monastery built between 1564 and 1614. Notable are the principal retablo inside and the carved stone cruz atrial (atrium cross) standing in front of the church.

**MAP 8:** *Av. Madero at San Jacinto; Metro: Miguel Ángel de Quevedo, Metrobús: La Bombilla or Dr. Gálvez*

## UNAM and Pedregal
### ✪ Biblioteca Central

The Universidad Nacional Autónoma de México (UNAM), the country's oldest, largest, and most prestigious college, can trace its founding to the early colonial era. In its modern incarnation as the national university, it was inaugurated in 1910 and granted its unique status as autonomous from the government in 1923. UNAM's main campus, built from 1949 to 1952 by more than 60 architects, engineers, and artists, is a UNESCO World Heritage Site. There are many architectural gems within the central campus, known as the Ciudad Universitaria, though none more iconic than the Biblioteca Centra, or Central Library. All four sides of the library are covered in a dazzling mosaic made of colored volcanic stone. Designed by artist and architect Juan O'Gorman (a graduate of the university), the mural illustrates themes from Mexican history in four eras: pre-Hispanic, colonial, modern, and the present.

Just south of the library is the **Rectoría,** the campus's main administration building, whose south wall is covered with a three-dimensional mural by David Alfaro Siqueiros. Just below, **Museo Universitario de Ciencias y Artes CU** (Av. Insurgentes Sur 3000; tel. 55/5622-0206; 10am-7pm Mon.-Fri., 10am-6pm Sat.-Sun.) is a public museum that hosts free exhibits by predominantly Mexican artists. Across Insurgentes, the **Estadio Olímpico** is the home field for the Pumas soccer club, with a mosaic of the university's shield created in colored stones by Diego Rivera.

**MAP 8:** *Circuito Interior, Ciudad Universitaria; tel. 55/5622-1625; http://bibliotecacentral.unam.mx; 8:30am-9:30pm daily; free; Metro: Copilco, Metrobús: Ciudad Universitaria*

### Casa Pedregal

When famed architect Luis Barragán designed this expansive residential home in the Pedregal neighborhood in 1948, the area was entirely undeveloped. With this project, he set the tone for this sprawling upscale suburb, designing not just the house but its interiors, gardens, and furniture. Casa Pedregal, also known as Casa Prieto López, was sold in 2006; the new owners, who inhabit the property, meticulously restored the building to Barragán's original specifications. Generously, they open their home to the public via guided tours, which are given by the in-house historians. Reservations are required and can be made at visitas@casaspedregal.com.

**MAP 8:** *Av. de las Fuentes 180, Col. Jardines del Pedregal; no phone; visitas@casapedregal.com; https://casapedregal.com*

## Cuicuilco

In the south of the city, the pre-Columbian settlement of Cuicuilco is the oldest archaeological site in the Valley of Mexico, built during the Pre-Classic period of Mesoamerican history, and the first major ceremonial center in the region. First established around 800 BCE, the settlement was once home to an estimated 40,000 inhabitants, though it was abandoned after the volcano Xitle erupted around 250 CE and lava covered the site. Today, the most notable structure is the settlement's expansive and unusual conical pyramid, which was built 600-400 BCE and was once topped with a ceremonial altar.

The small on-site museum provides more information about Cuicuilco's inhabitants and displays some artifacts found at the site. Visitors can also walk along the footpaths in the small surrounding nature preserve. It's easiest to arrive via the Villa Olímpica Metrobús stop, but you can also take a bus marked Cuicuilco from the Universidad Metro station.

**MAP 8:** *South of the intersection of Insurgentes and Periférico Sur, Col.*

shaded walkways in Tlalpan

*Isidro Fabela; tel. 55/5606-9758; 9am-5pm daily; US$2.50; Metro: Universidad, Metrobús: Villa Olímpica*

## Tlalpan

Tlalpan is a lesser-known colonial-era settlement on the southern edge of the city, now part of the greater Mexico City urban area. Tlalpan's heart is the **Plaza de la Constitución,** a lovely public square with swaying trees and iron benches. On the east side of the plaza is the 17th-century **Parroquia de San Agustín de las Cuevas** (Francisco I. Madero 10), surrounded by well-kept gardens. Behind the municipal building, on the south side of the plaza, **Mercado de la Paz** is a large market good for a quick bite. Cross the street to have a drink at **La Jaliscience** (Plaza de la Constitución 6; 12:30pm-11:30pm Mon.-Sat.), a traditional cantina. Next, follow Moneda east to the **Capilla de las Capuchinas** (Miguel Hidalgo 43; tel. 55/5573-2395; call

the canals at Xochimilco

to arrange a tour 10am-noon Tues.-Sun.), designed by architect Luis Barragán.

Most visitors come by taxi, but the extension of the Metrobús has made it relatively easy, albeit time-consuming, to get to Tlalpan via public transport. From anywhere along Insurgentes, take a southbound Metrobús marked El Caminero past the university to the Fuentes Brotantes stop; the center of Tlalpan is a few blocks east.

**MAP 8:** *Between Insurgentes Sur and Calzada de Tlalpan, Calvario and Av. San Fernando; Metrobús: Fuentes Brotantes*

## Xochimilco

### ✪ Canals at Xochimilco

As early as the 13th century, people living in the community of Xochimilco began cultivating crops on chinampas, small patches of farmland built atop the shallow lakes and marshes that covered the Valley of Mexico. Eventually, a massive system of canals, dams, and chinampas blanketed the valley.

Though most of this unique agricultural system has since been destroyed, a network of canals and family-owned farms survives in the Xochimilco neighborhood, now a district in southern Mexico City. Visitors to Xochimilco can explore the main canals on colorful trajineras (flat-bottomed boats), which depart from the 10-plus public docks in the neighborhood. Saturday-Sunday is the most spirited time to visit, when the waterways are crammed with families and revelers, steering past mariachi musicians and marimbas floating by on canoes. To see a quieter side of the neighborhood, request the four-hour "ecological tour" to visit the lesser-known farmland

and residential areas along the waterways.

Food and alcohol are permitted on the boats, and many visitors pack elaborate meals to bring along. If you don't bring your own lunch, there are plenty of floating vendors offering handmade quesadillas, ears of corn, ice cream, beer, and other snacks.

To reach Xochimilco by public transportation, take Metro Line 2 to Tasqueña, then take the Tren Ligero (light rail) to Xochimilco. Several embarcaderos (docks) are close to the Tren Ligero station, along Calle Violeta, off Avenida Cuauhtémoc. (Embarcadero Nativitas is about a 30-minute walk.)

Alternatively, you can take a taxi or car service to any embarcadero in Xochimilco. There are many different docks, and you can access the canals from any one of them; Nuevo Nativitas and Zacapa are considered the best launch points for a traditional tour of the canals. (Ignore the many "tour guides" along the route who tell you a dock is closed in attempt to lead you elsewhere; this is rarely the case.) To see the quieter side of Xochimilco at the Zona Natural Protegida (the nature preserve), go to Cuemanco.

Parroquia de San Agustín de las Cuevas, Tlalpan

**MAP 8:** *Xochimilco; http:// xochimilco.gob.mx; boats 8am-8pm daily; US$22 per hour for a boat for up to 12 people; Tren Ligero: Xochimilco*

# Restaurants

## PRICE KEY

$     Entrées less than US$10
$$    Entrées US$10-20
$$$   Entrées more than US$20

## WESTERN MEXICO CITY

### ✪ Nicos $$

This traditional family-style fonda in Azcapotzalco was doing its own thing for many years, drawing dedicated locals with its excellent traditional food and homey atmosphere. Word got out, and Nicos is now one of the best-known restaurants in the city. Come here for a lovely, low-key Mexican breakfast, or make a reservation for comida (the midday meal) to try some of the restaurant's specialties, like the goat-cheese soup, organic chamorro (pork leg), or shrimp in chipotle. After, stroll around nearby Parque de la China and along Avenida Claveria.

**MAP 8:** *Av. Cuitláhuac 3102, Clavería; tel. 55/5396-7090; www.nicosmexico.mx; 8am-6pm Mon.-Wed., 8am-9pm Thurs.-Sat., 8am-5pm Sun.; Metro: Cuitláhuac*

# SOUTHERN MEXICO CITY
## San Ángel
### San Ángel Inn $$$

Built in the 17th century as a Carmelite monastery and later incorporated into a sprawling hacienda, the famed San Ángel Inn has more than three centuries of history behind it. Today, the historic building is still called San Ángel Inn, but it's a restaurant, not a hotel, serving traditional Mexican food in a truly old-fashioned atmosphere. The most famous items on the menu are undoubtedly the margaritas, served in little pitchers kept chilled in individual ice buckets.

**MAP 8:** *Diego Rivera 50; tel. 55/5616-1402; www.sanangelinn.com; 12:30pm-midnight Mon.-Sat., noon-10pm Sun.; Metro: Barranca del Muerto, Metrobús: La Bombilla*

## UNAM and Pedregal
### Tetetlán $$

The sunken dining room at Tetetlán is built right into volcanic stone bedrock, a striking backdrop to the restaurant's menu of pan-Mexican dishes, from tlayudas to ceviches. Occupying the former stables at Casa Pedregal (page 250), it's a lovely place to come after touring the house, with a welcoming atmosphere and service—often enlivened by live music or listening events (check their social media accounts for details). Note that the closest public transportation are the microbuses that run along Avenida San Jeronimo, which connect to Line 1 of the Metrobús at the station Dr. Galvez.

**MAP 8:** *Av. de las Fuentes 180, Col. Jardines del Pedregal; no phone; https://tetetlan.com; 7:30am-11:30pm Sun.-Wed., 7:30am-12:30am Thurs.-Sat.*

## Tlalpan
### Arroyo $$

Though a bit off the beaten path, this massive family-style restaurant in Tlalpan is hugely entertaining. Opened in the 1940s, the restaurant has an extensive menu of Mexican classics, from enchiladas to mole, though the best item is the flavorful barbacoa (lamb), slow-cooked in a brick pit on-site. There is a small playground for kids adjoining the two massive dining rooms, fluttering with paper flags, and, best of all, live music and dance shows take place throughout the afternoon on Saturday-Sunday.

**MAP 8:** *Insurgentes Sur 4003, Tlalpan Centro; tel. 55/5573-4344; 8am-8pm daily; Metrobús: Fuentes Brotantes*

# Arts and Culture

## CONCERT VENUES
### Southern Mexico City
**Palacio de los Deportes**
Major rock shows by international groups touring in Mexico, like The White Stripes, Bon Jovi, Lenny Kravitz, and others, are often held at the "Sports Palace." The indoor arena was originally built for the 1968 Olympics and has a capacity of close to 20,000. Major concerts are also sometimes held at the outdoor **Foro Sol** in the adjacent Autódromo Hermanos Rodríguez car racetrack.
**MAP 8:** *Av. Río Churubusco at Viaducto; no phone; https://palaciodelosdeportes.mx; hours and prices vary by event; Metro: Velódromo, Metrobús: Goma*

## MUSEUMS
### Southern Mexico City
**Museo Anahuacalli**
Diego Rivera was a prodigious collector of pre-Columbian art, and he constructed this pyramid-shaped museum to house his marvelous acquisitions. In addition to showcasing Rivera's varied art, artifacts, and sculpture from Mixteca, Mexica, Teotihuacán, and Veracruz cultures, among others, there are often contemporary exhibits in the space, as well as famously beautiful altars assembled in the courtyard for Día de Muertos.
**MAP 8:** *Calle de Museo 150, Col. San Pablo Tepetlapa; tel. 55/5617-4310; www.museoanahuacalli.org.*

Museo Anahuacalli

*mx; 10am-6pm Tues.-Sun.; US$6; Tren Ligero: Xotepingo*

### San Ángel
**Museo Casa Estudio Diego Rivera**
In 1931, artist Juan O'Gorman designed two small functionalist homes, joined by a footbridge, for Frida Kahlo and Diego Rivera. Kahlo lived there until 1941 and Rivera until his death in 1954. The homes were opened to the public as a museum in 1986. Rivera's studio has been preserved as it was during his lifetime, providing an intimate look into the artist's enchanting personal aesthetics; some of his pre-Columbian artifacts and Mexican handicrafts are also on display.
**MAP 8:** *Av. Diego Rivera at Altavista; tel. 55/8647-5470; www.estudiodiegorivera.bellasartes.*

# Xochimilco: Unique Urban Farmland

## PRE-COLUMBIAN ORIGINS

Around the 13th century, people living in the community of Xochimilco developed an ingenious farming system atop the broad lakes that covered the Valley of Mexico. Using tree limbs, reeds, and earth, the Xochimilcas created a network of "floating gardens," called chinampas. With abundant water and the fertile soil of the lakebed to feed them, the chinampas flourished.

When the Mexica established the island city of Tenochtitlan in the 14th century, they also built an extensive network of chinampas. By 1519, the chinampas covered almost all of Lake Xochimilco, supporting a population of at least 200,000 (and by some estimates up to 350,000) people in Tenochtitlan.

## COLONIAL-ERA DECLINE

During the colonial era, the lakes in the Valley of Mexico were slowly drained as the Spanish replaced the original system of dams and chinampas with plazas and avenues. Lake Xochimilco was channeled into canals that linked farmland to the center of capital.

With the creation of the huge drainage pipe in central Mexico City in the 1800s—designed to stop persistent flooding in the capital—the lakes dried up almost entirely. Around the same time, natural springs in Xochimilco were canalized to channel water to central Mexico City. As the wetlands disappeared, the chinampas were abandoned. Of the estimated

gob.mx; 10am-5pm Tues.-Sun.; US$2; Metro: Barranca del Muerto, Metrobús: La Bombilla

## UNAM
### Espacio Escultórico de la UNAM

A 1970s collaboration between artists including Federico Silva, Mathias Goeritz, Helen Escobedo, and Manuel Felguérez resulted in the national university's unique Espacio Escultórico, a monumental sculpture garden built within an open expanse of volcanic rock and scrubby brush. It is an iconic destination on the UNAM campus, drawing art and ecology into a unique dialogue. The keynote piece is a massive, circular concrete sculpture, often used for performances or student meetings. **MAP 8:** *Circuito Mario de la*

Espacio Escultórico de la UNAM

40,000 chinampas in Xochimilco at the beginning of the 18th century, only 15,000 remained when the 20th century began.

## 20TH-CENTURY TOURISM

In 1929, Xochimilco was officially incorporated into Mexico City. Around that time, the canals in Xochimilco became a popular tourist destination for locals, who visited the canals in colorful flat-bottomed boats called trajineras. Xochimilco earned the moniker "the Venice of Mexico." Tourism remains one of the major industries in Xochimilco, and visiting the canals on a busy weekend is a highlight of a trip to the capital.

## REFORESTATION AND THE FUTURE

In 1987, along with Mexico City's Centro Histórico, Xochimilco and its canals were designated a World Heritage Site by the United Nations, recognizing the area's vast historical and cultural value. In 1989, the Mexican government announced a plan to treat water supplies and promote conservation in Xochimilco. As part of that plan, the **Parque Ecológico de Xochimilco,** a 215-ha (531-acre) botanical and wildlife reserve, was opened and parts of the existing system of canals were protected.

Local nonprofits have also been working to revitalize the area. Agricultural and conservationist organization **Arca Tierra** (www.arcatierra.com) offers guided tours of the canals (US$45 pp), which include a meal with seasonal Xochimilco-grown ingredients; they also host charitable dinner parties in Xochimilco with a rotating roster of famous chefs. Another collective, **De La Chinampa** (www.delachinampa.mx), sells produce baskets, which come from a collective of farmers cultivating crops in Xochimilco in the traditional manner.

---

Cueva s/n, Ciudad Universitaria; tel. 55/5622-7003; www.cultura.unam.mx; 7am-4pm daily; free; Metro: Universidad, Metrobús: CCU

### Museo de Arte Carrillo Gil

One of the nicest art museums in the city, the Carrillo Gil is housed in a modern multistory stone building in San Ángel. The museum's permanent collection, originally donated by its namesake, includes works from modernist masters like Pablo Picasso and contemporary art stars like Gabriel Orozco. Even more interesting, the museum mounts ongoing large-scale exhibitions of artwork by current Mexican and international artists, for which opening parties are usually packed to the brim.

**MAP 8:** Av. Revolución 1608; tel. 55/8647-5450; https://museodeartecarrillogil.inba.gob.mx; 10am-6pm Tues.-Sun.; US$4, free Sun.; Metro: Barranca del Muerto, Metrobús: La Bombilla

### ✪ Museo Universitario Arte Contemporáneo (MUAC)

In the heart of the UNAM campus, this superb museum has

consistently been one of the best places to see contemporary art in Mexico City since it opened in 2008. Designed by Teodoro González de León, the building is architecturally stunning and well situated for viewing art, with large glass walls flooding gallery spaces with indirect natural light. Frequently rotating exhibitions feature work from internationally recognized artists from Mexico and abroad, including recent exhibitions by celebrated Colombian painter Beatriz González, Mexico City-based Belgian artist Francis Alÿs, and Mexican painter Manuel Felguérez.

**MAP 8:** *Insurgentes Sur 3000; tel. 55/5622-6972; www.muac.unam.mx; 10am-6pm Wed.-Sun.; US$2.50, free under age 12; Metro: Universidad, Metrobús: CCU*

## CINEMA
### Filmoteca UNAM

UNAM has a major film program, which includes film studies, restoration, and a huge film library. The Sala Julio Bracho, Sala José Revueltas, and Sala Carlos Monsiváis, the university's three main screening rooms, are located on the university campus in the southern part of the city. Each month has a thematic focus, from movies featuring Mexican luchadores (wrestlers) to James Dean. In addition, UNAM runs screening rooms at the **Museo Universitario del Chopo** and at the **Casa del Lago** in Chapultepec.

**MAP 8:** *Av. Insurgentes Sur 3000, Ciudad Universitaria in UNAM; no phone; https://filmoteca.unam.mx; hours vary; US$2, US$1 students; Metro: Universidad*

## THEATER, CLASSICAL MUSIC, AND DANCE
### Sala Nezahualcóyotl

In the heart of the university's cultural center, this picturesque and highly respected concert hall is the home of UNAM's philharmonic orchestra, and it also hosts national and international performers in jazz, chamber music, and other genres. Built in the mid-1970s, the theater was designed to resemble Amsterdam's Royal Concertgebouw theater, and there are excellent acoustics throughout the space. Balcony seats are often a bargain.

**MAP 8:** *Insurgentes Sur 3000; tel. 55/5622-7125; https://musica.unam.mx; hours vary; US$5-15, half price for students and teachers; Metro: Universidad, Metrobús: Ciudad Universitaria*

# Festivals and Events

## FEBRUARY
### Zsona MACO
Inaugurated in 2004, Mexico City's most prestigious contemporary art fair, Zsona MACO (México Arte Contemporáneo), is the keynote event of Mexico City Art Week in February. It's a high-quality and well-attended event, with a roster of exhibitors coming from both the surrounding city and overseas, including some well-known names from the United States and Europe. Held in the expansive Palacio de Cultura Banamex in the Lomas de Sotelo neighborhood, it is currently the biggest art fair in Latin America.

**Greater Mexico City:** *Centro Citibanamex, Av. Del Conscripto 311, Lomas de Sotelo, Hipódromo de las Américas; tel. 55/5280-6073; www.zsonamaco.com; early Feb.*

## APRIL
### Semana Santa
The week before Easter, or Holy Week, is one of the most important religious holidays of the year in Mexico. It is celebrated with enormous solemnity, tradition, and pageantry throughout the country, including in Mexico City—though many capitaleños also take advantage of the break in work or school to spend the week outside the city, at the beach, or in the country. During this time, traffic is subdued, museums are close to empty, and you'll rarely need a reservation at a restaurant—though you'll often find restaurant and bar owners close up shop for the week too.

The celebrations (and vacations) officially begin on Domingo de Ramos, or Palm Sunday, when handwoven palm crosses and other adornments are sold outside the city's churches. The following Friday, Viernes Santo (Good Friday) is the single most important day of the season. (In fact, it's more likely that a restaurant or a shop will close on Good Friday than on Easter Sunday.) In Iztapalapa, a working-class neighborhood in southeast Mexico City, a very solemn and dramatic Passion Play is performed, with literally thousands of participants and even more spectators.

**Greater Mexico City:** *Iztapalapa; Palm Sun. to Easter Sun.*

## DECEMBER
### Día de Nuestra Señora de Guadalupe
The feast day of the Virgin of Guadalupe, December 12, is one of the most important holidays across Mexico. On the days and weeks leading up to it, groups of pilgrims can be seen walking toward the Basílica de Santa María de Guadalupe in northern Mexico City, often setting off noisy fireworks as they go. Special masses are held throughout Mexico, and in Mexico City, the area around the basilica is packed with thousands

of pilgrims. In December 2023, the city government reported that more than 11 million people visited the basilica between December 9 and December 12.

**Greater Mexico City:** *Basílica de Santa María de Guadalupe, Plaza de las Américas 1, Col. Villa de Guadalupe; tel. 55/5118-0500; www.virgendeguadalupe.org.mx; Dec. 12*

# Recreation

## PARKS
### Southern Mexico City
#### Parque Ecológico de Xochimilco (PEX)

This recreational park was founded as part of the Ecological Rescue Plan for Xochimilco, an ambitious program of water reclamation, agricultural reactivation, and historical and archaeological studies to restore and revitalize the historic Xochimilco community. The 189-ha (467-acre) grounds consists of lakes, ciénegas (underground springs), canals, chinampas, and gardens. There are paddleboats for rent, lots of areas for picnicking, and a small train for children. The best way to get to the park, which is a couple of kilometers from downtown Xochimilco, is to take a taxi.

canal in Xochimilco

**MAP 8:** *Periférico Sur at Canal de Cuemanco, Xochimilco; tel. 55/5673-7653; 9am-5pm Tues.-Sun.; US$3 adults, US$1 over age 60, US$0.50 under age 12; Tren Ligero: Xochimilco station, then by taxi*

## SPECTATOR SPORTS
### Formula One
#### Autódromo Hermanos Rodríguez

Ricardo and Pedro Rodríguez were stars of Formula One racing in Mexico during the 1960s, and both of their lives were cut short in racing accidents. The brothers lend their name to this racecourse in eastern Mexico City, where 15 Grand Prix championships were held 1963-1970 and 1986-1992. In 2015, the Formula One Grand Prix returned to Mexico for the first time in more than two decades, as part of a five-year deal for continuing championships, with other car racing events throughout the year. If you're lucky, you may catch a race with Mexican sensation Checo Pérez.

**MAP 8:** *Av. Viaducto Río de la Piedad s/n, Iztacalco; tel. 55/5237-9920; https://ahr.mx; tickets via Ticketmaster; Metro: Ciudad Deportiva*

## Soccer
### Estadio Azteca
Mexico's largest stadium, Estadio Azteca is a major concert and event venue in addition to being the longtime home to popular soccer clubs América and Los Rayos de Necaxa, both owned by media conglomerate Televisa. Opened in 1966, it was designed by architects Pedro Ramírez Vázquez and Rafael Mijares Alcérreca, with a capacity to seat almost 100,000. Despite the size, the field feels surprisingly close, even in the cheaper seats, and the roar of the crowd can be exhilarating. Note that Estadio Azteca is undergoing renovations ahead of the 2026 FIFA World Cup and most soccer matches have been relocated to the Ciudad de los Deportes.
**MAP 8:** *Calzada de Tlalpan 3465, Col. Santa Úrsula; www.estadioazteca.com.mx; hours vary; most games US$5-15, tickets via Ticketmaster; Tren Ligero: Estadio Azteca*

### Estadio Olímpico Universitario
This attractive and unusually intimate soccer stadium is home to the Pumas, a professional soccer team that is frequently among the best teams in Liga MX (although it is owned by UNAM and located on the university campus, students rarely play on the team). If you're interested in seeing a pro team play, Estadio Olímpico is easily accessible, and games are rowdy and fun. The Pumas have a fiercely loyal following, and the porras (fan clubs) are known for their enthusiastic cheers at games.
**MAP 8:** *Insurgentes Sur, just south of Eje 10 Sur, Ciudad Universitaria; hours vary; most games US$5-15, tickets via Ticketmaster; Metro: Universidad, Metrobús: Ciudad Universitaria*

# Shops

## PUBLIC MARKETS
### Southern Mexico City
#### Mercado de Jamaica
Mexico City's largest flower market, the Mercado de Jamaica is a colorful, sweetly scented destination. You'll find stalls selling thousands of varieties of flowers as well as potted plants, fruit, and (naturally) food stalls for snacking. Fresh flowers are used abundantly in Mexico for decoration, altars, religious services, birthdays, and other special occasions. Visit in the days leading up to Día de Muertos to see tremendous shipments of cempasúchil (marigold), the flower of the dead.
**MAP 8:** *Guillermo Prieto 45, Venustiano Carranza; no phone; 8am-6pm Mon.-Fri., 7am-7pm Sat.-Sun., many vendors operate 24 hours daily; Metro: Jamaica*

#### Central de Abasto de la Ciudad de México
Covering 3 sq km (1.2 sq mi) in Iztapalapa, the Central de Abasto

## Mondays in Mexico City

As in many major cities, most of Mexico City's important cultural institutions and galleries (and even some restaurants) are closed on Monday. Here are a few options for a Monday in the capital.

### DAY TRIP TO TEOTIHUACÁN
Teotihuacán, one of the largest and most spectacular archaeological sites in Mexico, is just an hour outside Mexico City by car or bus (page 280).
**Hours:** 9am-5pm daily

### MUSEO SOUMAYA
This eye-catching museum is one of the few art spaces open on Mondays (page 161). In the Roma, the small but lovely **Casa Guillermo Tovar de Tereza,** overseen by Museo Soumaya, is also open daily (page 199).
**Hours:** 10:30am-6:30pm daily

### FOOD AND MARKET TOURS
Traditional markets like the Mercado de la Merced or the Mercado de Jamaica don't slow down on Mondays. Take your shopping bags to pick up some edibles or snack your way through a market with a tour guide like **Eat Like a Local Mexico** or **Eat Mexico** (page 21).
**Hours vary**

---

(Supply Center) is Mexico City's main wholesale market. It is the biggest food supplier in the country and the second-biggest point of commerce in Mexico, after the Mexican Stock Exchange. Around 30,000 tons of food are sold here daily, from banana leaves and sugarcane to dried chilies and grains. The 9-ha (22-acre) seafood section called La Nueva Viga displays a huge variety of fish from across the country. By its own estimates, the market receives 350,000 visitors annually and employs more than 70,000 people. Though it's not the most atmospheric shopping area in the city, the sheer quantity of products will interest curious travelers.

**MAP 8:** *Canal Churubusco and Canal Apatlaco, Iztapalapa; http://ficeda.com.mx; 24 hours daily; Metro: Aculco*

## ARTS AND CRAFTS
### San Ángel
#### Casa del Obispo
Set in a colonial-era mansion, the Casa del Obispo is one of the most impressive craft shops in the city—with prices to match. If you'd like to browse high-quality works of folk art and artesanía, you will

### CASA PEDREGAL

Guided tours of the Luis Barragán-designed home Casa Pedregal (page 250) are available on Monday, and you can make a day of it by having lunch afterward at adjoining restaurant **Tetetlán** (page 254).
**Hours:** By appointment only Mon.-Sat.

### XOCHIMILCO ECOLOGICAL TOUR

If you'd like to see a quieter side of Xochimilco, you'll have the canals virtually to yourself on a Monday morning. It's an ideal time to take a longer tour of the waterways, reaching the residential areas and farmland that most visitors never see (page 252).
**Hours:** Boats leave from any dock after 8am daily

### BASÍLICA DE SANTA MARÍA DE GUADALUPE

There are hourly masses and massive crowds every day of the week at this fascinating historic site and Catholic shrine in northern Mexico City (page 248).
**Hours:** 6am-9pm daily

### TURIBUS

You can get the lay of the land, see some of the city's most iconic sights, and take some stunning pictures on the Turibus, which runs double-decker bus tours of the capital every day of the year (page 21).
**Hours:** 9am-9pm daily

---

find many gorgeous pieces from across Mexico at this well-curated store, from ceramics from Mata Ortiz, Chihuahua, to splendid hand-painted wooden chests from Michoacán. The owner can give you background on any piece you're eyeing.
**MAP 8:** *Juárez 1, San Ángel; tel. 55/5616-9079; 10am-6pm Tues.-Fri. and Sun., 10am-7pm Sat.; Metro: Miguel Ángel de Quevedo, Metrobús: La Bombilla*

### ✪ Bazaar Sábado

Originally established in 1960, this lovely arts and crafts market is located in the courtyard of a 17th-century stone building and spills out into the Plaza San Jacinto. You'll find traditional artisanal work, including blown glass, jewelry, ceramics, traditional masks, paper flowers, and clothing as well as some contemporary designers selling their work. It's a popular Saturday destination for both residents and tourists, often bustling with browsers and filled with cheerful marimba music.
**MAP 8:** *Plaza San Jacinto; 10am-6pm Sat.; Metro: Barranca del Muerto or Miguel Ángel de Quevedo, Metrobús: La Bombilla*

# Where to Stay

Centro Histórico .......269
Paseo de la Reforma ...272
Chapultepec
  and Polanco .........273
Roma and Condesa ....275
Insurgentes
  Sur-Narvarte.........276
Coyoacán..............276

Mexico City offers a lot of variety when it comes to accommodations, from creaky backpackers' favorites to full-service luxury high-rises that are destinations in themselves. Though once a rarity, there are an increasing number of charming bed-and-breakfasts in residential neighborhoods, as well as some new boutique hotels with popular nightclubs and design-centric hostels that cater to the Instagram-loving budget traveler. For a destination of its size and importance, Mexico City is filled with friendly, attractive, and surprisingly affordable hotels.

The neighborhood you choose will be just as important in determining your experience as the place you stay. Many of the main attractions are located in the blocks

# Highlights

✪ **Best Midrange Hotel:** For a comfortable, reasonably priced space in the Centro Histórico, **Hotel Catedral** is the perfect choice (page 269).

✪ **Most Fashionable Palace:** The gorgeous **Downtown Hotel** occupies the top floors of a colonial-era palace in the Centro. Ultra-modern decor complements the historic architecture (page 269).

✪ **Most Socially Minded Space:** More than an inexpensive crash pad, **Casa de los Amigos** is a social justice organization, a house for refugees, and a gathering place for socially minded people (page 272).

✪ **Most Comfortable Landmark:** A jewel of mid-century modernist architecture, **Camino Real Polanco México** is one of the city's most interesting buildings. Consider a drink in the lobby bar, even if you're staying elsewhere (page 274).

✪ **Best Guesthouse:** Tucked inside an early 20th-century Roma mansion, **Casa Nima** is a luxurious and intimate guesthouse in the city's trendiest neighborhood (page 275).

✪ **Warmest Atmosphere:** In the heart of the Condesa, the **Red Tree House** is famous for its friendliness, creating a spirit of camaraderie among its guests, who gather in the gardens during happy hour (page 276).

surrounding the Zócalo, making the Centro Histórico and the area around the Alameda a good choice for first-time visitors. Given the capital's vast size, however, you're more likely to eat and go out in places near your hotel, which is one reason that travelers increasingly gravitate toward neighborhoods like the Roma and the Condesa. Polanco has always been a bastion of upscale luxury hotels, and it remains so to this day.

All hotels charge a 15 percent

**Previous:** the JW Marriott, the W., and the InterContinental Presidente overlook Chapultepec from Polanco; **Above:** Downtown Hotel; facade of charming four-room guesthouse Casa Nima in the Roma.

# Where to Stay If...

In such a large, sprawling city, what neighborhood you stay in is often as important as the accommodations you choose. Depending on how you plan to spend your time, some neighborhoods will be better suited to your trip than others.

## YOU ONLY HAVE A WEEKEND

Stay in the **Centro Histórico,** where the city's most important sights and cultural institutions are walking distance from your doorstep.

## YOU WANT TO GET AWAY FROM IT ALL (AND DON'T MIND PAYING FOR IT)

Book a room along the park in **Polanco,** where fresh air, gorgeous views, and fancy service take the edge off city living.

## YOU WANT TO PARTY

You won't be alone in the **Colonia Roma,** Mexico City's hippest neighborhood.

## YOU'RE TRAVELING ON A BUDGET

Look in the **Centro Histórico** or the **Tabacalera** neighborhood, where you'll find a higher concentration of hostels and budget hotels.

## YOU AREN'T REALLY A CITY PERSON

**Head south.** There aren't many hotels south of the Viaducto, but those who want a less urban environment will be happiest in the clean and sunny south.

## A MORNING JOG IS PART OF YOUR ROUTINE

Stay in **Polanco** and enjoy the proximity to the many trails snaking through the forested Bosque de Chapultepec.

## YOU WANT THE LOCAL EXPERIENCE

Book an Airbnb in the **Nápoles, Narvarte,** or **Del Valle** neighborhoods in Insurgentes Sur-Navarte, or one of the other beautiful residential neighborhoods south of the Viaducto.

---

IVA (value-added tax) and 2 percent city lodging tax. More expensive hotels may also tack on a 10 percent service charge, as well as additional costs for amenities like internet service. When booking, ask whether tax and service are included in quoted rates.

## CHOOSING WHERE TO STAY

### Centro Histórico

The Centro Histórico is the heart of it all: dense, noisy, and pulsing with energy. Staying in the Centro is an excellent choice for **first-time visitors.** Plus, some of the very best breakfast options—from Sanborns de los Azulejos to El Cardenal to Café El Popular—are downtown. There are many excellent accommodations in the Centro in every price category. Though you'll find some new upscale options, the area remains a **backpacker's paradise,** with tons of cheap hotels and hostels scattered throughout the district.

### Paseo de la Reforma

Mexico City's grand central avenue is known for its **luxury hotels,** anchored by the celebrated Four Seasons, just to the east of the Bosque de Chapultepec. Closer to the Centro, you'll find a few more inexpensive options along Reforma. The Tabacalera neighborhood, near the Monumento a la Revolución Mexicana, has long been a hub of **inexpensive hotels.** There are many more options for this area beyond those listed in this book, though some are rather shabby, so check your room before you check in.

### Zona Rosa and Cuauhtémoc

**Central, safe,** and **tourist-friendly,** the Zona Rosa has always been a popular place to stay, even if it isn't the city's most enchanting neighborhood. Here, you'll find hotels at a range of price points, a major public transportation hub at the Glorieta Insurgentes, and a **late-night party scene** that makes it safer to walk the streets after dark (though nightclubs can also be a noisy nuisance for guests with

WHERE TO STAY

Gran Hotel de la Ciudad de México

street-view rooms). Just northwest of the Zona Rosa, the area around the US Embassy is also a safe and central destination, with lodging options near main thoroughfares Insurgentes and the Paseo de la Reforma, as well as plenty of dining and nightlife options.

### Polanco

Affluent Polanco has some of the **most luxurious hotels** in the city, including the string of famous high-rises overlooking Bosque de Chapultepec from the street Campos Eliseos. Many of these establishments are favored by **international businesspeople,** though tourists also book in Polanco, particularly at the architecturally notable Camino Real or the party-centric W and Hábita.

### Roma and Condesa

The **hippest neighborhoods** in Mexico City have become increasingly popular places to stay. There are no high-rise and few chain hotels in these residential districts, but in keeping with the neighborhoods' chic, independent reputation, there are boutique properties and bed-and-breakfasts. There is also a smattering of lower-priced hotels, some with A-plus locations, and an abundance of charming Airbnb and vacation rentals in the area, some basic and others downright luxurious.

### Insurgentes Sur and Narvarte

You'll get a taste of local life in these quiet, clean, and largely residential neighborhoods. Though hotel options are limited, they are excellent places to look for a well-priced Airbnb or vacation rental.

### Coyoacán and Southern Mexico City

Mexico City's southern neighborhoods are **greener** and **more peaceful** than the city's urban heart. Yet with few businesses headquartered in the area and zoning restrictions making it more difficult to build, the south of the city has **very few hotel options.** Most travelers will end up staying in the city center and visiting Coyoacán and San Ángel during day trips. If the hotels down south are booked, try Airbnb or another short-term apartment rental service.

### Alternative Lodging Options

Mexico City has a robust presence on **Airbnb,** with a range of well-priced options throughout the city. You can also find bedrooms, rental apartments, and vacation homes on VRBO and online hotel booking sites. In many central neighborhoods, including the Roma, hotels can sometimes beat the prices of an apartment rental, so it's worth checking all your options before booking. In the neighborhoods south of the Viaducto—Coyoacán and San Ángel among them—Airbnb is a good option.

## PRICE KEY

| | |
|---|---|
| $ | Less than US$100 |
| $$ | US$100-200 |
| $$$ | More than US$200 |

# Centro Histórico                    Map 1

**Hostel Mundo Joven Catedral $**
Just a block from the Zócalo, this popular hostel has dozens of dorm-style rooms with wood floors, in-room lockers, and clean bunk beds. A handful of private rooms have views of the Catedral Metropolitana (though note that street-facing rooms also get more ambient noise than interiors). On the top floor is a picturesque terrace bar, where guests convene to swap travel tips and snap photos of the back of the cathedral. It is best to reserve ahead for dorm beds and necessary for private rooms, which book well in advance.
**MAP 1:** *República de Guatemala 4; tel. 55/5518-1726; https://mundojovenhostels.com; Metro: Zócalo*

### ✪ Hotel Catedral $
Located between the Zócalo and the Plaza Santo Domingo, Hotel Catedral is a great value, combining a wonderfully central location with comfortable modern guest rooms and genuinely affable service. The accommodating staff is always willing to call a taxi or give directions. It's popular with Mexican families, business travelers, and tourists, and there's always a pleasant buzz in the lobby. The same group owns the well-priced Hotel Gillow (Isabel la Católica 17; tel. 55/5518-1440; www.hotelgillow.com), also in the Centro Histórico.

**MAP 1:** *Donceles 95; tel. 55/5518-5232; www.hotelcatedral.com; Metro: Zócalo*

### Círculo Mexicano $$
This elegantly minimalist hotel in the heart of the Centro Histórico provides a peaceful respite from its bustling environs. Located in a restored 19th-century residential building that was once the home to photographer Manuel Álvarez Bravo, guest rooms are arranged around a light-filled central patio and have high ceilings, white walls, and king beds. Breakfast is served in a glass-walled room on the upstairs terrace, with intimate views of the cathedral.
**MAP 1:** *República de Guatemala 20; tel. 55/9689-0543; www.circulomexicano.com; Metro: Zócalo*

### ✪ Downtown Hotel $$
This small hotel in a stunning 17th-century palace makes wonderful use of its historic architecture through a simple yet elegant design that emphasizes the high ceilings and old stone walls of the original building. While there's no lobby, the hotel shares the palace with several restaurants and a lovely Mexican design-centric shopping center. The rooftop bar and swimming pool are enviably cool places to relax. On the ground-floor level, the hotel operates a stylish low-budget backpacker hostel called Downtown

Beds (tel. 55/5130-6855; www.downtownbeds.com).
**MAP 1:** *Isabel la Católica 30; tel. 55/5130-6830; www.downtownmexico.com; Metro: Zócalo or Isabel la Católica*

### Zócalo Central $$

On the northeast corner of the Zócalo, this contemporary hotel has a perfect location, with a bank of guest rooms looking directly over the Zócalo. Accommodations are clean and comfortable, with a conservative dark color scheme and marble baths, and the staff are accommodating and friendly. The same hotelier operates a similar property, **Histórico Central** (Bolívar 28; tel. 55/5130-5130), just a few blocks away, in a 300-plus-year-old building on Bolívar.
**MAP 1:** *Cinco de Mayo 61; tel. 55/5130-5130; www.centralhoteles.com; Metro: Zócalo*

### Gran Hotel de la Ciudad de México $$

Replete with tiered balconies and old steel-cage elevators, the art nouveau lobby at the Gran Hotel de la Ciudad is crowned by a vaulted Tiffany glass ceiling, made in Paris in 1908. Guest rooms, arranged around the central atrium, have an ultra-romantic vibe, with floral bedspreads and TVs hidden from view behind white-and-gold cabinets. Rooms overlooking the Zócalo are the most coveted; keep in mind that they can be noisy too.
**MAP 1:** *16 de Septiembre 82; tel. 55/1083-7700; https://granhoteldelaciudaddemexico.com.mx; Metro: Zócalo*

### Hotel Isabel $

This rambling five-story hotel has long been a favorite with budget travelers, offering ramshackle charm at a low nightly rate. The 74 guest rooms vary widely in character (ask to see another if you don't like the accommodations you were assigned), though all have a scruffy old-fashioned feeling, with creaky wood furniture and high ceilings. You can shave a bit off the nightly price if you are willing to stay in a room with shared bath.
**MAP 1:** *Isabel la Católica 63; tel. 55/5518-1213; www.hotel-isabel.com.mx; Metro: Isabel la Católica*

# Hotel Bars

Just because you aren't staying in a fancy hotel doesn't mean you can't enjoy some of its amenities. As in many big cosmopolitan cities, some of the capital's nicest bars are located in its upscale hotels. Here are a few of the best.

### THE ROOFTOP BAR AT THE DOWNTOWN HOTEL

While taking a break from a tour around the Centro (or waiting for a table at Azul Histórico downstairs), head up to the shaded rooftop bar in the **Downtown Hotel,** where you can drink a cold margarita while looking out over the Porfiriato-era facade of the Casino Español across the street.

### TERRACE BAR AT CÍRCULO MEXICANO

The rooftop terrace at **Círculo Mexicano** is relaxed and beautiful, with an intimate view of the bell towers and cupolas of the city cathedral. Rarely crowded, it's a great place for a respite while touring the Centro.

### TERRAZA CATEDRAL AT MUNDO JOVEN

The casual backpacker bar on the roof of the **Mundo Joven** caters to budget travelers, but the views and low-key vibe will appeal to any visitor.

### TERRAZA RESTAURANT AND BAR AT THE GRAN HOTEL DE LA CIUDAD DE MÉXICO

At the bar and restaurant in the **Gran Hotel de la Ciudad de México,** the attraction is the view of the Zócalo (and the chance to walk through the Gran Hotel's gorgeous lobby). It offers a full menu and a buffet brunch on the weekends, but you can come for drinks in the afternoon.

### LA TERRAZA AT CONDESA DF

It's no wonder the rooftop bar and Japanese fusion restaurant at the boutique **Condesa DF** is frequented by Condesa locals: The views of leafy treetops in Parque España make it the perfect place to unwind with a drink in the evening.

### FIFTY MILS AT THE FOUR SEASONS

The posh cocktail bar **Fifty Mils** (page 131) in the Four Seasons Hotel has become a city favorite for its creative cocktails and surprisingly fun crowd.

# Paseo de la Reforma — Map 3

### El Patio 77 $$
This small guesthouse is in a renovated mansion in a corner of the San Rafael neighborhood that is still largely off the beaten track for most tourists. Guest rooms are individually decorated yet consistently beautiful; color palettes are muted, and furnishings are a mix of antique and handcrafted. The suites are spacious, with light-filled baths and street-facing balconies; there are also several reasonably priced rooms with shared baths. The ecofriendly hotel collects rainwater, recycles gray water, and heats showers with solar power.
**MAP 3:** *Icazbalceta 77, Col. San Rafael; tel. 55/5592-8452; www.elpatio77.com; Metro: San Cosme*

### ✪ Casa de los Amigos $
A guesthouse and social justice organization, Casa de los Amigos offers basic dorm accommodations and private rooms with shared baths. As part of its mission, Casa de los Amigos houses and acclimates political refugees, so you may be sleeping next to someone who's come to Mexico from very far away (in addition to meeting the long-term volunteers, who live on-site). A shared kitchen serves as an informal gathering spot, while the peaceful upstairs library was once the studio of muralist José Clemente Orozco, the home's former owner.
**MAP 3:** *Ignacio Mariscal 132, Col. Tabacalera; tel. 55/3500-8139; www.casadelosamigos.org; Metro: Revolución, Metrobús: El Caballito*

### Casa Pani $$
Celebrated 20th-century architect Mario Pani lived in a quiet corner of the Cuauhtémoc neighborhood, and today his personal home has been converted into a stylish guesthouse that preserves and celebrates Pani's aesthetic principles, even in the parts of the hotel that have been remodeled and expanded. There are only six rooms, each nicely decorated in a style that is minimalist yet cozy. Despite the stylish atmosphere, the vibe is zero percent pretentious.
**MAP 3:** *Río Po 14; tel. 56/2717-9260; www.casapani.com; Metro: Insurgentes, Metrobús: El Ángel*

### Casa González $
Close to the US and British Embassies in the central Cuauhtémoc neighborhood, this friendly family-run guesthouse has 22 cheerful private bedrooms located in several buildings that share a plant-filled central courtyard. Bedrooms are reasonably priced, cute, and clean, and some have private patios. Just a couple of blocks from the Paseo de la Reforma, the hotel is perfectly central and an all-around good value.
**MAP 3:** *Río Sena 69; tel. 55/5514-3302; www.hotelcasagonzalez.com;*

*Metro: Insurgentes, Metrobús: Hamburgo*

### Four Seasons Hotel $$$

The stately Four Seasons, ideally located near the main entrance to Chapultepec, has long been known as the premier high-end choice in Mexico City. Even with the introduction of new properties like the St. Regis and the Ritz Carlton nearby, the Four Seasons hasn't lost its golden reputation for attentive service and luxury amenities. The eight-story hotel's guest rooms are elegant yet cozy, filled with armchairs, lamps, and writing desks; some have French doors opening onto the pretty central garden.

**MAP 3:** *Paseo de la Reforma 500; tel. 55/5230-1818; www.fourseasons.com/mexico; Metro: Sevilla, Metrobús: Chapultepec*

# Chapultepec and Polanco   Map 4

### Las Alcobas $$$

In the heart of Polanco, this boutique hotel has enough style to warrant its chic zip code, but its intimate size distinguishes it from nearby establishments. The 35 elegant guest rooms are warm and modern, with rosewood furniture and huge plate-glass windows allowing in ample natural light (but, fortunately, not much sound from the street below; the glass is double-paned). Details are taken seriously: Beds are dressed in Italian linens, flat-screens are equipped with home-theater sound systems, and marble baths have rain showers stocked with handmade soaps.

**MAP 4:** *Presidente Masaryk 390; tel. 55/3300-3900; www.lasalcobas.com; Metro: Polanco, Metrobús: Auditorio*

### Hotel Hábita $$$

Open since 2000, this boutique hotel is still one of the chicest places to stay in the city. Behind its frosted-glass facade, designed by Enrique Norten and Ten Arquitectos, the 36 guest rooms are elegantly minimalist, with classic modern furniture in dark neutral tones, long glass desks, and, in most, small terraces. It features a cool lobby restaurant and a glassed-in exercise room upstairs; the signature establishment, however, is the popular rooftop nightclub and bar.

**MAP 4:** *Av. Presidente Mazaryk 201; tel. 55/5282-3100; www.hotelhabita.com; Metro: Polanco, Metrobús: Auditorio*

### InterContinental Presidente Mexico City $$$

The InterContinental Presidente is the oldest of the grand park hotels, originally built in 1977, and later joined by the JW Marriott, the Hyatt Regency, and the W. Its multistory pyramid lobby, topped with an immense skylight, is impressive, though the 660 rooms are more modern and subdued. The hotel is known for its dining, with six restaurants and a bar, including Au Pied de Cochon, a French restaurant that is open 24 hours daily, and the Balmoral tea room, with English-style afternoon tea and snacks.

**MAP 4:** *Campos Eliseos 218; tel. 55/5327-7700; www.presidenteicmexico.com; Metro: Auditorio, Metrobús: Auditorio*

### ✪ Camino Real Polanco México $$$

One of the most original architectural concepts in Mexico City, famed architect Ricardo Legorreta's Camino Real is a marvel of mid-20th-century design, from its pink sculptural wall at the entryway to its royal-blue lobby lounge. On top of that, the Camino Real is a luxury establishment, known for its fine service and amenities (though, in some places, the facilities show their age). It has three swimming pools, rooftop tennis courts, and numerous in-house bars and eateries, including a branch of the world-famous restaurant Morimoto.

**MAP 4:** *Av. Mariano Escobedo 700, Col. Anzures; tel. 55/5263-8888 or 800/901-2300; www.caminoreal.*

the Camino Real Polanco México

*com; Metro: Chapultepec, Metrobús: Gandhi*

### Wyndham Garden Polanco $$

This hotel typically attracts business travelers, but the price and quality make it a good choice for any visitor to the city. Rooms are modern and functional, though a bit nondescript; on the higher floors, however, you'll have lovely views of the park. For those who like the Polanco neighborhood, it's a good alternative to the pricier hotels that dominate the skyline along the Bosque de Chapultepec.

**MAP 4:** *Tolstoi 22; tel. 55/5262-0844; www.wyndhampolanco.com; Metro: Chapultepec, Metrobús: Chapultepec*

# Roma and Condesa  Map 5

### Condesa DF $$$
Located in a fine triangular mansion overlooking the tree-filled Parque España, this design-centric boutique hotel is beloved by bloggers, neighborhood hipsters, and chic travelers who place equal value on comfort and aesthetics. Here, 24 modern guest rooms and 16 suites surround a central atrium with an in-house restaurant and lobby, stylishly decorated with globe lamps, an eclectic mix of tables and chairs, and an aqua-and-white color scheme.
**MAP 5:** *Av. Veracruz 102; tel. 55/5241-2600; Metro: Sevilla, Metrobús: Sonora*

### ✪ Casa Nima $$$
This perfect four-room guesthouse is housed in a gorgeous early 20th-century mansion, right in the heart of the Roma. Each of the rooms is warmly decorated, with king beds, blackout curtains, and French doors opening onto the home's central atrium or a street-view balcony. Guests can relax with a drink in the cozy living room or on the upstairs roof deck, which is filled with plants and flowers (there are honor bars in both). The warm, solicitous service and generous morning breakfast top off the experience.
**MAP 5:** *Colima 236; tel. 55/1171-8585; http://nimalocalhousehotel.com; Metro: Insurgentes, Metrobús: Álvaro Obregón*

### Hotel Stanza $
At the easternmost end of Álvaro Obregón, this nice midrange hotel isn't known for its contemporary design, but its well-priced guest rooms are comfortable and generally quiet, and the downstairs restaurant and bar is surprisingly pleasant, overlooking Jardín Pushkin. Though it's a step up in price from other budget hotels in the city, Stanza delivers an overall nicer environment and better service than many of its neighbors.
**MAP 5:** *Álvaro Obregón 13; tel. 55/5208-0052; http://stanzahotel.com; Metro: Niños Héroes or Insurgentes, Metrobús: Parque Pushkin*

### Ignacia Guest House $$$
There are a multitude of restaurants and bars along Jalapa and Chiapas, but once you step inside Ignacia Guest House, the noise and bustle are behind you. Located in a renovated 20th-century mansion, the hotel's four lovely color-themed rooms overlook an interior garden. Guests can use the main living room for reading or relaxing. The amiable staff will help you make plans around the city or set up Mexican cooking classes with the chefs next door, who design the hotel's signature breakfasts.
**MAP 5:** *Jalapa 208; tel. 55/2121-0966; http://ignacia.mx; Metro: Hospital General, Metrobús: Sonora*

### ✪ Red Tree House $$

A lovely bed-and-breakfast in the heart of the Condesa, Red Tree House occupies a converted family home, with comfy guest rooms opening onto the central garden. The genuinely friendly staff and relaxed atmosphere—which is plenty stylish but still cozy—seem to instill a sense of community among guests, who often gather in the common areas or enjoy a glass of wine together during complimentary afternoon happy hours. It's one of the most popular spots in the capital, so make reservations well ahead.

**MAP 5:** *Culiacan 6; tel. 55/5584-3829; http://theredtreehouse.com; Metro: Chilpancingo, Metrobús: Chilpancingo*

## Insurgentes Sur-Narvarte     Map 6

### El Diplomatico $

There are few nice places to stay in Mexico City's quieter southern neighborhoods. This glass-fronted hotel, on the southern stretch of Avenida Insurgentes, is an exception. Rooms are impeccably clean and spacious, all equipped with Wi-Fi, coffeemakers, air-conditioning, and cable TV. Though a bit off the beaten path for most visitors, it's close to San Ángel and Coyoacán, and a quick ride on the Insurgentes Metrobús if you want to head downtown.

**MAP 6:** *Av. Insurgentes Sur 1105, Col. Noche Buena; tel. 55/1948-7806 or 800/007-3845; www.eldiplomatico.com.mx; Metro: San Antonio or Insurgentes Sur, Metrobús: Parque Hundido*

## Coyoacán     Map 7

### Casa Jacinta $$

This neat, friendly, and well-located bed-and-breakfast occupies a pretty little house in residential Coyoacán. Cozy wood-floored guest rooms have French doors or windows that open onto the garden and patio and private baths with colorful tiles. A freshly prepared breakfast is included in the nightly price and served on the pretty back patio—a lovely way to begin a day in the south of the city.

**MAP 7:** *2da. Cerrada de Belisario Domínguez 22; tel. 55/7098-9384; www.casajacintamexico.com; Metro: Viveros*

### La Casita del Patio Verde $$

There are only three rooms in this itty-bitty bed-and-breakfast, located on a charming cobblestone street in residential Coyoacán. The largest room is in its own detached cottage, with two double beds and a fireplace. In the main house, there are two considerably smaller but lovely bedrooms on the 2nd floor. For those who want to experience life in this quiet neighborhood, La Casita is one of the few options—and fortunately, it's a lovely choice. **MAP 7:** *Callejón de la Escondida 41; tel. 55/4170-3523; http://la-casita-del-patio-verde.mexico-hotels-mx.com; Metro: Viveros*

# Day Trips

Choosing
   an Excursion ........ 279
Teotihuacán .......... 280
Puebla and Vicinity ..... 286

For most first-time visitors to Mexico City, a day trip to the pyramids at Teotihuacán is a must. Just an hour east of the city, Teotihuacán is the most visited archaeological site in Mexico, an awe-inspiring example of city planning in 5th-century Mesoamerica.

For culture, Puebla is one of the most rewarding destinations near the capital, just 90 minutes south (depending on traffic). Boasting a gorgeous Centro Histórico, Puebla is also known throughout Mexico for its inventive cuisine and its traditions in handicrafts, particularly Talavera pottery.

# Highlights

⭐ **Pirámide del Sol:** For its scale and beauty, the ancient city of Teotihuacán was named "place of gods" by the Nahuatl-speaking people in the Valley of Mexico. Walk through history in the plaza between the Pirámide de la Luna and the 75-m-high (246-ft) Pirámide del Sol, the most iconic structure in Teotihuacán (page 283).

⭐ **Puebla's Zócalo:** The heart of Puebla's gorgeous colonial downtown, the Zócalo is adjoined by the city's impressive cathedral and surrounded by sidewalk cafés, perfect for sipping a coffee while planning your walking tour of the city's Centro Histórico (page 289).

⭐ **Museo Amparo:** There is an excellent collection of pre-Columbian art along with interesting contemporary exhibits at Puebla's top-notch Museo Amparo (page 290).

# Choosing an Excursion

## Teotihuacán

- **Why visit?** Mexico's most visited archaeological site, Teotihuacán is one of the finest examples of pre-Columbian architecture and city planning in the country, crowned by two towering temple-pyramids.
- **Distance from Mexico City:** 1.5 hours by bus
- **Length of visit:** 2-4 hours

## Puebla

- **Why visit?** This bustling old-fashioned city has a splendid Centro Histórico, some of the best food in Mexico, and a long tradition of traditional craftwork.
- **Distance from Mexico City:** 1.5 hours by bus, depending on traffic
- **Length of visit:** 1-3 days

---

**Previous:** shopping for handcraft in Puebla; **Above:** ruins of Teotihuacán and the Pyramid of the Sun; Puebla's Zócalo.

# Day Trips

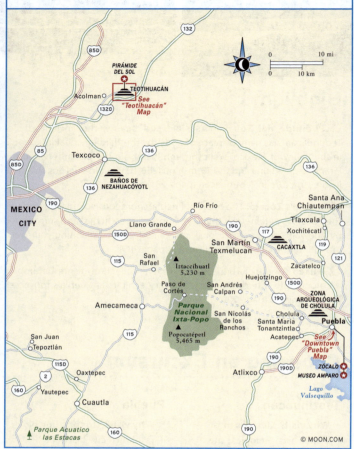

# Teotihuacán

**TOP EXPERIENCE**

Little is known about the people who built the ancient city of Teotihuacán in the northern Valley of Mexico. The name itself, which means "the place of gods" in Nahuatl, was given to the ancient city several centuries later. What the people of Teotihuacán called their city, what language they spoke, and what ethnic heritage they came from is unknown. One of the largest archaeological sites in the Americas, Teotihuacán is known today for its towering temple-pyramids as well as for its impressive city planning and architecture.

Though the area in the northern Valley of Mexico was inhabited long before Teotihuacán was settled, construction of the major buildings in Teotihuacán took place between 100 BCE and 250 CE. The population increased rapidly as the city-state grew powerful; by the 4th century, Teotihuacán's cultural hegemony was evident in cities throughout Mesoamerica. Anthropologists estimate that, at its height, Teotihuacán was home to as many as 150,000 people and covered over 20 sq km (8 sq mi), forming the largest city in the western hemisphere at the time. Under unknown circumstances, Teotihuacán began to decline in the 7th century CE, possibly under attack from nearby tribes; the city was largely abandoned, leaving only 30,000 residents through the Late Classic period. By 900, the city was almost entirely empty.

With its impressive architecture and proximity to Mexico City, it's not surprising that Teotihuacán is the most visited archaeological site in Mexico. It is particularly popular on the spring equinox, when thousands of people assemble at the ruins to absorb the special energy of the sun.

## SIGHTS

### Calzada de los Muertos (Avenue of the Dead)

Teotihuacán's principal artery, the Calzada de los Muertos, runs 2 km (1.2 mi) south to north between La Ciudadela and the Pyramid of the Moon. The avenue is impressive at its current scale, but archaeological evidence suggests it originally ran another 1 km (0.6 mi) farther south during Teotihuacán's height. It's flanked on either side by pyramid-shaped residences.

### La Ciudadela (The Citadel)

On the south end of the Avenue of the Dead, there is a large fortresslike enclosure, once located at the geographic center of the city. Archaeologists surmise that this area, called the Main Plaza, was where ritual performances took place. At the southeast end of the plaza is the impressive **Templo de Quetzalcóatl** (Temple of Quetzalcóatl or, as it is sometimes called, the Temple of the Feathered Serpent), which is decorated with elaborate stone carvings of serpents' heads protruding from the facade.

The remains of more than 200 men and women were found buried here. Evidence suggests they were Teotihuacano warriors, sacrificed during the construction of the pyramid.

### Museo del Sitio de la Cultura Teotihuacana

Just beside the Pirámide del Sol, the Museo del Sitio de la Cultura Teotihuacana (Site Museum; 9am-4:30pm daily; free with admission to archaeological site) contains a collection of artifacts excavated from the site (although

# Teotihuacán

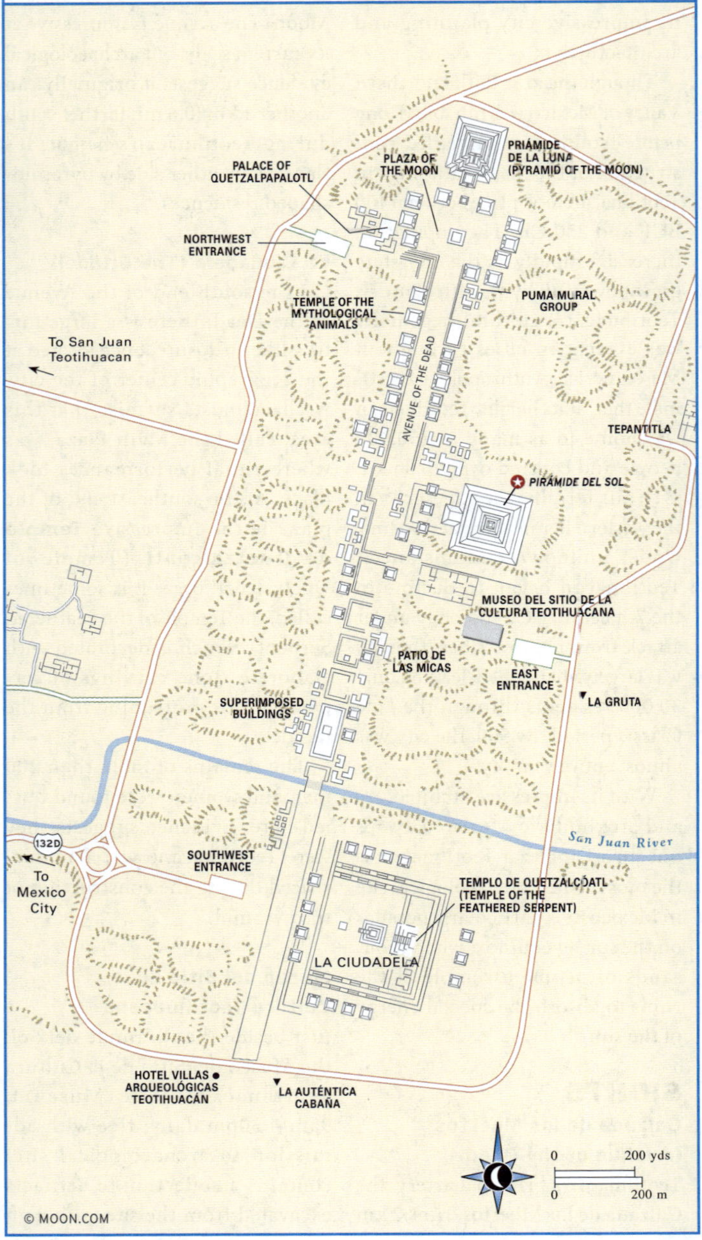

the best collection of art and artifacts from Teotihuacán is in the Museo Nacional de Antropología in Mexico City). The building also has a snack bar, a bookshop, and restrooms as well as a small but nicely tended botanical garden.

### ⭐ Pirámide del Sol (Pyramid of the Sun)

One of the most impressive pyramids in the world, the Pirámide del Sol measures just under 70 m (230 ft) in height. Until recently, it was possible to ascend to the top of the pyramid via a steep stone staircase, a challenging but rewarding climb that was undertaken by hundreds of people every day. At the beginning of the pandemic lockdown in 2020, access to the pyramid was closed and will remain closed indefinitely. Although it's disappointing for visitors, archaeologists and cultural advocates have long worried that the constant foot traffic was causing irrevocable damage to the pyramid. The deterioration of the staircase was evident, even to non-experts. Today, you can admire this impressive monument from below, as the ordinary citizens of Teotihuacán would have.

In 1971, a long stairway was discovered that ended in a four-chamber lava cave, 100 m (328 ft) long, under the pyramid. Archaeologists surmise that the cave was considered by the city's builders to be a sacred entryway to another world, which is why they

the Pirámide del Sol (Pyramid of the Sun) in Teotihuacán

chose the location to build their largest pyramid.

### Pirámide de la Luna (Pyramid of the Moon)

At the north end of the Calzada de los Muertos is the beautiful Pyramid of the Moon, centered on the Plaza of the Moon, which, along with the Main Plaza at the Ciudadela, was one of the principal ritual areas in the city. Built later than the other principal monuments in the city, the Pyramid of the Moon is 46 m (151 ft) high. When approaching the pyramid along the Avenida de los Muertos, note how the outline of the structure mirrors that of Cerro Gordo, the mountain behind it.

### Palace of Quetzalpapalotl

Just to the west of the Pirámide de la Luna, the impressive Palacio de Quetzalpapalotl is far more ornate than the other dwellings in the city and was likely the home of a ruler or priest of Teotihuacán. In the main patio, principally excavated in the 1960s, there are beautiful stone columns carved with bas-relief butterflies and birds in profile. The roof was partially reconstructed by anthropologists in a style thought to be consistent with Teotihuacán's original architecture.

Calzada de los Muertos from the Pyramid of the Moon

Just behind the palace, the **Patio of the Jaguars** is a small rectangular room that still retains its original red-tinted frescoes, depicting jaguars with conch shells in their mouths.

## RESTAURANTS

There are lots of casual places to eat near the archaeological site, catering to families and day-trippers, with the highest concentration of eateries on the east side of the pyramids, near parking lot 5. Of these, the most distinctive is undoubtedly **La Gruta** (tel. or WhatsApp 55/5191-9799; http://lagruta.mx; 8am-6pm daily; US$10). The menu covers Mexican basics, like sopa de tortilla (tortilla soup) and grilled meats, but the setting is the real

carved stone column in the Palace of Quetzalpapalotl

La Gruta

attraction: The restaurant is in an underground cave, lit by candles, just behind the Pirámide del Sol.

For something more low-key, there are dozens of ultra-casual family-style eateries on the road that circles the archaeological site, many offering similar menus of grilled meats, barbacoa (slow-cooked lamb), and antojitos (snacks) like quesadillas. One such spot, **La Auténtica Cabaña** (Circuito Pirámides 24; tel. 56/2740-8824; 8am-6pm daily; US$5), has an appealing menu of traditional Mexican cuisine and a decent touch with food, but it's the beautiful country setting that recommends this place. If it's a warm day, order a cold drink and sit on the restaurant's palapa-shaded (thatched palm roof) patio, from which you can see the pyramids of Teotihuacán.

## WHERE TO STAY

Though most people make the trip to and from Teotihuacán in a day, staying the night can give you a little more time to explore the archaeological site—and, if you're an early riser, the opportunity to get there right as the gates open, when there are few people in the park. A decent option for an overnight is the **Hotel Villas Arqueológicas Teotihuacán** (tel. 55/5836-9020, WhatsApp tel. 55/4536-6226; www.villasteo.com; US$80-100), located on the ring road south of the ruins. The rooms are out of date and a bit dark, but the lovely grounds make up for those shortcomings. There's a big swimming pool in the central patio, a nice restaurant on-site (the weekend brunch buffet is particularly good), huge lawns, and a small playground for children. There's also a small ruins site on the property. It's less than 1 km (0.6 mi) from entrance 1, but if you don't want to walk, there are often taxis waiting just outside the main entrances.

## PRACTICALITIES

The **Teotihuacán archaeological zone** (Ecatepec Pirámides Km 22+600, Municipio de Teotihuacán, Estado de México; tel. 594/956-0276; www.teotihuacan.inah.gob.mx; 8am-5pm daily; US$5, free under age 13, students, teachers, seniors, and people with disabilities) has five entrances, three on the west side and two on the east. They are each adjoined by a parking lot (US$3 per car), and they all have public restrooms. The traditional place to start your tour is at the southern entrance (no. 1), visiting the Ciudadela before heading north along the Calzada de los Muertos to the pyramids. Buses drop you off here. For a shorter tour, the second entrance is just in front of the Pirámide del Sol.

Wear good walking shoes for exploring the site. A hat, sunblock, and water are musts. If you want to experience the site in relative peace, arrive early, when the ticket-takers open the gate. The tour buses start arriving around 10am. Weekends are the busiest, especially Sunday, when admission is free for Mexican nationals.

## TRANSPORTATION

The ruins lie about 45 km (28 mi) northeast of Mexico City. **Autobuses Teotihuacán** (tel. 55/5767-3573; www.autobuses teotihuacan.com.mx) buses depart the Terminal Central del Norte (Eje Central Lázaro Cárdenas 4907; www.centraldelnorte.com) every 15 minutes 6am-7pm daily and return every 15 minutes from the ruins to the terminal until 8pm. The trip to Teotihuacán takes about an hour. Ask for the bus to Los Pirámides, not Teotihuacán, or you may end up in the town of the same name. It costs about US$6 round-trip. If you want to skip the bus, most hotels can help you arrange a local taxi or tour guide to take you to the pyramids and back, or you can book directly with **Taxis Radio Union.**

Double-decker sightseeing tour bus company **Turibus** (tel. 55/5514-1165, ext. 2; www.turibus.com.mx; US$50, includes admission to the archaeological site) operates daily transport to and from Teotihuacán; the full 11-hour pyramids tour includes lunch, a stop at an artisan workshop, and a stop at the Basílica de Santa María de Guadalupe, but you can choose the shorter Teotihuacán Express tour to skip the basilica and lunch (2 departures daily). **Capitalbus** (WhatsApp tel. 55/6676-8033 or 55/5208-2505; https://capitalbus.com.mx; US$50) offers a similar day trip to Teotihuacán and the basilica.

# Puebla and Vicinity

The big and beautiful city of Puebla remains largely off the beaten track for most foreign visitors, despite its fine architecture, celebrated cuisine, and wonderful traditions in art and craftwork. More old-fashioned than Mexico City, it has a family-oriented downtown district filled with funky small businesses, a more visibly Catholic population, and air clean enough to provide intermittent glimpses of the volcano Popocatépetl rising to the west.

Many people come to Puebla to eat, and with good reason. Though famous poblano dishes like chiles en nogada and tinga are prepared throughout the country, they rarely reach the sublime perfection achieved in their native home, and street snacks here are

# On the Road to Puebla: Twin Peaks

Popocatépetl and Iztaccíhuatl

Twin volcanoes rising between Puebla and Mexico City, **Popocatépetl** and **Iztaccíhuatl** are the most recognizable and striking natural landmarks in the region. Often shortened to Popo and Izta, the volcanoes' Nahuatl names mean "the smoking mountain" and "the white woman," respectively, and they were the subject of great fascination and various legends in pre-Columbian Mexico. Today, these beautiful peaks are the crown jewels of a national park, Parque Nacional Izta-Popo, a surprising refuge of natural beauty located in the middle of the most densely populated region in Mexico.

A symmetrical cone and the second-highest peak in Mexico, Popo has become all the more picturesque, but perhaps a touch more troublesome, since it woke from a decades-long slumber in 1994. In 2000, the largest eruption in 1,200 years occurred on the mountain, and it remains one of Mexico's most active volcanoes, frequently spewing smoke and ash into the air. Craterless Izta, just 16 km (10 mi) north, lies dormant beside it.

Both Popo and Itza are blanketed with pine and oak forests as well as alpine prairie at lower elevations. Izta has permanent glaciers at its peaks, a rarity in Mexico; only the country's highest mountain, the Pico de Orizaba, also claims them. The glaciers have been diminishing rapidly and are expected to disappear altogether. The wilderness surrounding the volcanoes was among the earliest designated nature preserves in the country, receiving national park status from President Lázaro Cárdenas in 1935.

## Downtown Puebla

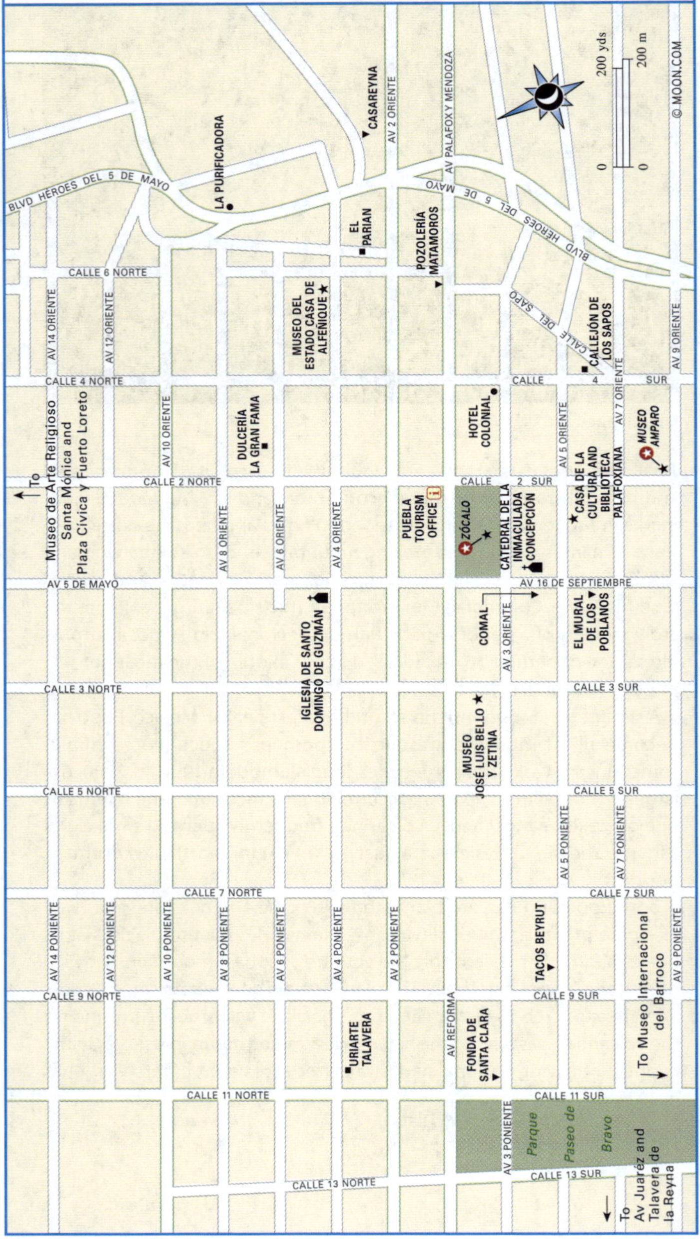

both uniquely prepared and utterly delicious. At the same time, many visitors will find the city's architecture and history to be just as rich and enthralling as its culinary traditions. Puebla has a long and important history in Mexico. Founded in the early colonial era, it's one of the few cities in Mexico that wasn't built directly atop an existing native community, and its beautifully preserved downtown is filled with some of the most impressive colonial churches, palaces, and ex-convents in the country, replete with ornate gold-leaf trimmings, magnificent stonework, and Puebla's distinct signature, Talavera tile.

## SIGHTS

### ⭐ Zócalo

The Zócalo (Av. Palafox y Mendoza and 16 de Septiembre) is Puebla's main public plaza, facing the cathedral and bordered on three sides by 16th-century portales (arcades). Once a bustling marketplace, it is today a nice park, with towering trees and lots of benches, surrounded by sidewalk cafés, restaurants, shops, and newspaper stands. It's always bustling with activity and a great place for sipping a coffee or simply enjoying quality people-watching.

### Catedral de la Inmaculada Concepción

On the south side of the Zócalo, Puebla's Catedral de la Inmaculada Concepción (Calle 16 de Septiembre and Av. 5 Ote.; tel. 222/232-2316; 8am-8pm daily; free) is one of the most beautiful churches in Mexico, first begun in 1575 by Francisco Becerra and completed almost a century later,

Puebla's bustling Zócalo

in 1664. The tile-domed facade, adjoined by the two highest church towers in the country, is a mix of medieval, Renaissance, and baroque styles. Inside you'll even notice a few neoclassical touches in Manuel Tolsá's marble and onyx altar.

### Casa de la Cultura and Biblioteca Palafoxiana

Formerly the archbishop's palace, the building that is today home to the Casa de la Cultura (Av. 5 Ote. 5; tel. 222/232-4647; 9am-8pm Mon.-Fri., 10am-5pm Sat.-Sun.; free) was originally constructed in 1597. Today, the building is a cultural center with exhibition spaces, a cinema, and a café, as well as the home of the Biblioteca Palafoxiana (10am-5pm Tues.-Sun.), the first and oldest library in the Americas. In 1646, Bishop Juan Palafox y Mendoza donated the first 5,000 volumes to the library, including works of philosophy, theology, and history, some printed as early as the 15th century.

### Iglesia de Santo Domingo de Guzmán

Three blocks north of the plaza on Cinco de Mayo lies what remains of the fine baroque Dominican monastery Iglesia de Santo Domingo de Guzmán (Calle 5 de Mayo and Av. 6 Ote.; tel. 222/268-7232; 8am-2pm and 4:30pm-8pm Tues.-Sun.; free), constructed in the mid-16th century and consecrated in 1690. Inside the spacious, highly ornamented church, the exceptional **Capilla del Rosario** stands out, with walls that are covered with gilded floor-to-ceiling carvings, tiles, and cherubs.

### ✪ Museo Amparo

The Museo Amparo (Calle 2 Sur 708; tel. 222/229-3850; www.museoamparo.com; 10am-6pm Wed.-Sun., 10am-9pm Sat.; US$2) is an excellent anthropology and art museum with a gorgeous rooftop café located in two adjoining colonial-era buildings three blocks from the Zócalo. The museum's permanent collection contains more than 2,000 pieces of pre-Columbian and colonial art, including outstanding artifacts from the Maya, Olmec, Zapotec, and Mixtec cultures, as well as paintings, pottery, crafts, and furniture created in Puebla during the viceroyalty. Though best known for its permanent collection, the museum also hosts nice temporary exhibits, often exploring themes in modern and contemporary art.

the roof café at the Museo Amparo

### Museo José Luis Bello y Zetina

José Luis Bello, a wealthy poblano businessman, spent his riches on elegant furnishings and art from Mexico, Europe, and Asia, including porcelain, glass, Talavera ceramics, wrought iron, religious vestments, and clothing. Today, the Museo José Luis Bello y Zetina (Calle 5 de Mayo 409; tel. 222/232-4720; www.museobello.org; 10am-4pm Tues.-Sun.; free) displays that massive collection in a historic building that was once part of Puebla's large Dominican convent.

### Museo del Estado Casa de Alfeñique

The intricate baroque facade of Museo del Estado Casa de Alfeñique (Av. 4 Ote. 416; tel. 222/232-0458; 10am-5pm Tues.-Sun.; US$3) is a classic example of the alfeñique architectural style, named for a white sugar candy made in Puebla, which the trim on this building resembles. Built in 1790, it now houses the state museum, with old manuscripts related to Puebla history, ethnography on different Indigenous groups in the state, and colonial clothing. It's worth the entrance fee to see the beautiful interiors.

### Museo de Arte Religioso Santa Mónica

Museo de Arte Religioso Santa Mónica (Av. 18 Pte. 103; tel. 222/232-0178; 10am-5pm Tues.-Sat.; US$4) was founded as a convent in 1610. The building was converted to a religious art museum and taken over by INAH, the National Institute of Anthropology and History, in 1940, exhibiting work by many well-known colonial-era artists divided over two stories of exhibition spaces. Just as interesting, the museum offers a look at the living quarters and daily life of the nuns who once lived here.

### Plaza Cívica and Fuerte Loreto

To the north of the Centro Histórico, Puebla's civic center is adjoined by the historic military Fuerte Loreto (Fort Loreto) and the **Museo de la No Intervención** (Calzada de los Fuertes s/n, Centro Cívico 5 de Mayo, Zona Histórica de los Fuertes; tel. 222/234-8513; 10am-5pm Tues.-Sat.; US$4, free Sun.), located on the site of the famous Battle of Puebla, in which local troops defeated French invaders, celebrated annually on May 5—or, as it is better known, Cinco de Mayo. The fort is a lovely place to spend an afternoon, with plenty of public spaces and great views of the city below.

### Museo Internacional del Barroco

In 2016, the city of Puebla inaugurated the Museo Internacional del Barroco (Vía Atlixcáyotl 2501, Reserva Territorial Atlixcáyotl; tel. 222/326-7130; 10am-7pm Tues.-Sun.; US$5), a museum dedicated to baroque art and the architecture of Puebla. The collection is fairly modest; the biggest reason to visit is the museum's striking contemporary design by Pritzker-winning Japanese architect Toyo Ito. The museum is about 7 km (4.3 mi) outside the city center; the easiest way to get there and back is with ride-hailing app Uber.

## RESTAURANTS

Just across the street from the city cathedral, the bustling two-story eatery **Comal** (Calle 16 de Septiembre 311-b; tel. 222/688-4888; 8am-midnight daily) is a colorful and contemporary spot to try excellent versions of poblano staples like enmoladas, pipián, memelas, cemitas, and chiles en nogada, along with a craft beer or a glass of mezcal. Try the trio of moles on enchiladas for a taste of Puebla's diverse flavors. For the high quality of the food and service, the prices are surprisingly accessible—which means there is often a wait for a table.

A sophisticated, upscale spot preparing creative poblano cuisine, **El Mural de los Poblanos** (Calle 16 de Septiembre 506; tel. 222/225-0650; www.elmuraldelospoblanos.com; 8am-midnight daily) serves regional dishes made with local ingredients. Everything on the menu, from the creative soups to the range of heirloom moles, is served with unique style and pretty, inventive presentations. Appropriately, they also have a great list of small-batch mezcal and Mexican artisanal beer.

One of the nicest places for a traditional meal is the lobby

Comal

restaurant in the **Hotel Colonial** (Calle 4 Sur 105; tel. 222/246-4612; 7am-10pm daily), which offers a daily three-course comida corrida (lunch special) for a reasonable price. The menu changes daily but almost always includes the option of ordering the restaurant's delicious mole poblano with chicken breast or thigh. The pretty dining room, illuminated by a skylight, is popular with local families and can get quite crowded on the weekend.

Simple yet remarkably good, **Pozolería Matamoros** (Calle 6 Nte. 1; tel. 222/947-3822; 12:30pm-8:30pm Thurs.-Tues.) is just a few blocks from the main square. The namesake dish—a rich hominy soup called pozole—is excellent, but the menu also includes a number of poblano specialties, like chalupas (hand-rolled corn cakes topped with red or green salsa, shredded chicken, and diced onions).

The elegant restaurant **Casareyna** (Privada 2 Ote. 1007; tel. 222/232-0032, ext. 406; 8am-10pm daily), located on the ground floor of the Casareyna hotel, serves mole poblano that is widely cited as among the best in the city, and locals flock here for chiles en nogada in the late summer, when this dish is in season. These two dishes are standouts, but don't let that limit your order: The restaurant's menu of poblano cuisine is, across the board, creative yet traditional, and it is all nicely matched to the intimate stone-walled interior dining room. Make a reservation for lunch on the weekend.

Tacos árabes are a fusion of Mexican and Middle Eastern traditions, and they are a specialty in Puebla: crispy spit-roasted pork served in a pita, sometimes with jocoque, a tangy strained-yogurt spread. One of the best places to try these uniquely delicious tacos (or, if you're vegetarian, an excellent falafel wrap) is casual late-night spot **Tacos Beyrut** (Av. 5 Poniente 718; tel. 222/232-3040; www.tacosbeirut.com; 6pm-11pm Mon.-Sat.).

The legendary **Fonda de Santa Clara** (Av. 3 Pte. 307; tel. 222/232-7674; https://fondadesantaclara.com; 8:30am-7pm daily) is a traditional poblano restaurant serving regional food like mixiotes, tingas, and mole in a delightfully old-fashioned dining room decorated with Puebla's famous Talavera tile. Many people come to try the chiles en nogada, one of Puebla's signature dishes and one of the restaurant's specialties.

## SHOPS

The city and surrounding state of Puebla are well known for fine artisanal products and craftwork, which include sculpted onyx, papel amate (handmade bark paper), papel picado (decorative cut-paper flags), handmade furniture, wool rugs, silverwork, and, most famously, Talavera pottery, which is principally made in the city of Puebla and nearby Cholula.

To browse a selection of handicrafts from Puebla and beyond, stroll the outdoor market **El Parian** (Calle 6 Nte., between Av. 2 Ote. and Av. 6 Ote.; 9am-7:30pm daily), where rows of craft shops are housed in a former 18th-century clothing warehouse. Just a few blocks from the Zócalo, the market's specialty is Talavera, and there are numerous stalls selling colorful painted wares of varying quality and prices, from huge urns to little keepsakes and tiles.

Puebla is famous throughout the country for its traditional

El Parian market in Puebla

# Puebla: A Culinary Capital

a traditional poblano sandwich

Puebla has a remarkable culinary tradition, noted for its complex flavors and for its use of centuries-old heirloom recipes. Uniting pre-Columbian and Spanish ingredients and preparations with a touch of French and Middle Eastern influence, food in Puebla is delicious and very much a part of the cultural experience of visiting the city.

## MOLES

Moles—thick, heavily spiced sauces—are prepared throughout the country, with many famous versions produced in the state of Oaxaca. According to legend, however, mole was first created by the nuns of the Convento de Santa Rosa in Puebla during the 16th century.

Puebla's signature version of the dish, **mole poblano,** usually combines dozens of ingredients, including chocolate, dried chili peppers, onion, garlic, peanuts, raisins, cinnamon, coriander, peppercorns, and sesame seeds. In Puebla, you'll find mole piled onto sandwiches, slathered over turkey, or stuffed into tamales.

Variations on mole are served in restaurants throughout the city. **Pipián,** sometimes called mole verde, is a flavorful sauce made with green pumpkin seeds and spices, ground till smooth; it is also considered a specialty in Puebla, though you'll see it prepared in the traditional cui-

handmade candies. In the Centro, old-fashioned sweet shops, or dulcerías, line Avenida 6 Oriente between 5 de Mayo and 4 Norte. One of the most historic spots is **Dulcería La Gran Fama** (Av. 6 Ote. 208; tel. 222/242-2565; www.lagranfama.com; 9am-8pm Mon.-Sat., 10am-6pm Sun.), which carries traditional sweets from the

sine of other regions, like Yucatán. Pipián rojo is a variation, made with tomatoes and dried chilies.

## OTHER POBLANO SPECIALTIES

Popular throughout Mexico, **chiles en nogada** are a highly distinctive poblano creation. Traditionally prepared during the late-summer pomegranate harvest season and served as a part of the Independence Day holidays in September, a chile en nogada is a large green poblano pepper stuffed with beef or pork, almonds, fruit, and spices, which is then bathed in a creamy walnut sauce and showered with pomegranate seeds. Another regional dish, **tinga poblana** is slow-cooked shredded pork in a stew of chipotle chilies and vegetables. It is usually served with tortillas and rolled into tacos.

## QUICK BITES

Some wonderful quick bites and street foods are also typical to Puebla. A popular appetizer or snack, **chalupas** are small handmade corn tortillas that are deep fried in manteca (lard) or hot oil, then doused in spicy salsa and topped with shredded pork and onions. Puebla's version of the torta is the **cemita,** a sandwich made on a sesame-studded roll also called a cemita. Cemitas are piled with meat, string cheese, lettuce, tomato, and onion, then garnished with pápalo, a fragrant Mexican herb. Another poblano sandwich, the **pelona** is served on a soft, lightly fried bun, layered with beans, meat, and cheese. **Tacos árabes** are Middle Eastern-inspired tacos made with spit-roasted meat served in a warm pita and topped with lime and chipotle salsa.

## DULCES

Puebla is also famous throughout the country for its traditional dulces (sweets). Among the most typical sweets in Puebla are starchy treats made with **camote** (sweet potato). Sweet potatoes are cooked, sweetened, and flavored, then rolled into soft cigar-shaped tubes. Also typical to Puebla are **macarrones,** a type of dulce de leche (milk caramel), and **mueganos,** a fudge-like cake made with flour, eggs, butter, and unrefined sugar. Sweets made with pumpkin seeds are a regional specialty; try **tortitas de Santa Clara,** a small cookie topped with pumpkin-seed cream, or **jamoncillo,** a fudge-like treat garnished with nuts. Many of these sweets (like much of Puebla's famous food) were originally created by nuns, who sold candies and rompope (eggnog) to support their convents, as they continue to do today.

---

region, including camotes (a flavored sweet-potato candy), tortitas de Santa Clara (a round pumpkin-seed-cream-topped cookie), dulce de leche (milk candy), and much more. Many of these unique treats have been made in Puebla since the colonial era.

Perhaps the most famous—and certainly the most

historic—Talavera shop in Puebla is **Uriarte** (Av. 4 Pte. 911; tel. 222/232-1598; http://uriartetalavera.com.mx; 10am-7pm Mon.-Sat., 10am-6pm Sun.), originally founded in 1824. Uriarte's delicately painted pottery, including dishes, trays, tea sets, urns, tiles, and more, is all handmade and very high quality; if you buy more than you can pack in your suitcase, they can help arrange shipping.

Interesting vintage pieces (and occasionally some priceless antiques) show up in the weekend flea market along the street known as the **Callejón de los Sapos** (Calle 6 Sur between Av. 5 Ote. and Calle 3 Sur; 10am-5pm Sun.). Here you'll find everything from old maps and silverwork to jewelry and vintage magazines, as well as the occasional religious artifact or saint—which will come with a hefty price tag. The numerous permanent shops along the alleyway offer some very nice collections of Mexican antiques.

You'll have to travel a bit outside of the central area to visit the factory store of **Talavera de la Reyna** (Lateral Sur Recta a Cholula 3510; tel. 222/225-4058; http://talaveradelareyna.com.mx; 10am-7pm Mon.-Fri., 9am-3pm Sat., 11am-3pm Sun.), another very high-quality artisanal producer of Talavera. At their Cholula-based factory, these artisans sculpt, glaze, and paint everything by hand, creating gorgeous traditional as well as more modern designs.

## WHERE TO STAY

A block from the plaza and across from a picturesque little square, the well-priced **Hotel Colonial** (Calle 4 Sur 105; tel. 222/246-4612; www.colonial.com.mx; US$65) is very convenient for exploring downtown and has, as the name suggests, a lovely historic colonial ambience. The rooms are fairly large and comfortable, though most are also creaky and dated. It's a popular spot with European travelers.

Designed by architect Ricardo Legorreta, **Casareyna** (Privada 2 Ote. 1007; tel. 222/232-0032; www.casareyna.com; US$90-100) is a gorgeous hotel that brings the architect's signature modern vision to several renovated historic buildings on the southeastern edge of the Centro Histórico. The spacious, quiet rooms all have Saltillo tile floors, king beds, and high ceilings. Upstairs, the rooftop pool deck is a nice place to relax in the afternoon, and the in-house restaurant is excellent; a small breakfast is included in the rates.

Puebla's chicest accommodations are at **La Purificadora** (Callejón de la 10 Nte. 802, Paseo

Casareyna

San Francisco, Barrio Alto; tel. 222/309-1920; www.lapurificadora.com; US$140-260), a hotel from the same group that operates Hotel Hábita, Downtown Hotel, and Condesa DF in Mexico City. Blending 19th-century architecture with modern design, the guest rooms have wood floors, fluffy white bed linens, and lots of natural light.

## INFORMATION AND SERVICES

The **Puebla tourism office** (Av. Palafox y Mendoza 14; tel. 222/122-1100, ext. 6418; 10am-6pm daily) in the Zócalo can offer maps and information on upcoming festivals, art exhibits, and other municipal goings-on in Puebla city and state.

## TRANSPORTATION

First- and second-class buses depart Mexico City's Terminal de Autobuses de Pasajeros de Oriente, or TAPO (Calzada Ignacio Zaragoza 200) for Puebla almost constantly, day and night, with lines ADO, Cristóbal Colón, and Estrella Roja offering first-class service to **CAPU** (Calle 11 Nte. and Blv. Atlixco; www.capu.com.mx), a large bus terminal north of the city center in Puebla. The trip takes 1.5-2 hours, depending on traffic, and runs around US$10-15 one-way, depending on the bus line and class of service.

A slightly more expensive but more convenient option is to take **Ebus** (tel. 222/273-8341; http://ebus.mx; US$22 one-way) from Mexico City's central neighborhoods to the smaller and more central **Terminal de Autobuses Puebla 4 Poniente** (Av. 4 Pte. 2110, Col. Amor; tel. 222/273-8300) in Puebla. There are several daily departures from the Ángel de la Independencia on the Paseo de la Reforma and from the World Trade Center (Montecito 38, Nápoles), just off Insurgentes, in the Nápoles neighborhood. Tickets are about US$22 one-way. If the Ebus website doesn't accept your reservation, give them a call to reserve a ticket; the buses fill up.

**Estrella Roja** (tel. 222/273-8300; www.estrellaroja.com.mx) runs an hourly express bus direct from both Terminal 1 and Terminal 2 of the Mexico City airport to CAPU and to the Terminal de Autobuses 4 Poniente. **ADO** has direct service buses, roughly hourly, from Terminal 1 of the Mexico City airport to the Terminal de Autobuses Puebla 4 Poniente.

By car, the easiest way to get to the exit to Puebla is to take Pino Suárez and Tlalpan south, turn off on the Viaducto Miguel Alemán heading east, and follow the signs to Puebla. Returning to the city, paradoxically, it's a bit of a trick to find the entrance to the Viaducto, whereas following Izazaga and then Fray Servando into the city center is fairly straightforward. The toll road to Puebla costs US$5 and allows you to avoid all the curves and slow trucks on the free highway.

# NEAR PUEBLA

## Zona Arqueológica de Cholula

What appears to be a large church-topped hill in the center of Cholula is actually the largest pyramid in the continent by volume, with a base measuring 450 m (1,477 ft) on each side. Construction on this massive structure began in the 3rd century BCE and continued for almost 1,000 years. The pyramid was first thoroughly explored in 1931, revealing altars with offerings, floors, walls, and buried human remains. You can visit the pyramid and part of the excavation site at the Zona Arqueológica de Cholula (Av. 8, Nte. 2, San Andrés Cholula; tel. 222/247-9081; 9am-6pm Tues.-Sat.; US$5). To get to the beautifully gilded **Capilla de la Virgen de los Remedios** (8am-4pm daily), first built in 1594 and rebuilt after an earthquake in the mid-19th century, follow the steep path to the

view of the church-topped pyramid in Cholula

top of the hill. On clear days, views of Popocatépetl are spectacular.

Estrella Roja operates multiple direct buses (US$13) between Mexico City's TAPO and the Cholula bus terminal, but it's generally most convenient to get to Cholula via Puebla. Minibuses leave central Puebla from Avenida 2 Poniente at Calle 3 Sur. The trip costs about US$2. A taxi or rideshare from the centro costs around US$10 and takes about 30 minutes, depending on traffic.

# Background

## The Landscape

| | |
|---|---|
| The Landscape | 299 |
| History | 304 |
| Government and Economy | 318 |
| Local Culture | 320 |
| The Arts | 325 |

### GEOLOGY

Mexico City is located in the Valley of Mexico, an alpine basin surrounded by volcanic mountains, which measures a considerable 2,200 m (7,220 ft) elevation at its lowest point. The valley is on the southern edge of a great plateau known as the Mexican Altiplano, which extends from the United States border to the Trans-Mexican Volcanic Belt, just south of Mexico City. Several of

Mexico's highest peaks—including the famous twin volcanoes of Popocatépetl (5,465 m/17,931 ft) and Iztaccíhuatl (5,230 m/17,160 ft)—rim the valley to the south and southeast.

The Valley of Mexico was once covered by a series of broad, shallow, brackish lakes, which have been largely drained in the past 500 years; today, much of the city is built atop spongy dry lakebed. The unstable earth makes the city more susceptible to damage during seismic tremors. Earthquakes are frequent throughout the region, largely generated by the subduction of the Cocos tectonic plate beneath the North American plate, on Mexico's Pacific coast. Because of the interaction between earthquake wave movement and the valley's weak subsoil, Mexico City sometimes feels the effects of a coastal quake more than places closer to the quake's actual epicenter. Such was the case in the deadly 1985 earthquake, the epicenter of which was more than 160 km (100 mi) away.

Contributing to seismic activity, the Trans-Mexican Volcanic Belt remains active, with eruptions from nearby volcanoes sending tremors (as well as toxic dust) through the capital. The main culprit is Popocatépetl, the most active volcano in the region, which has had several notable eruptions since the 1990s, requiring the evacuation of people living in its foothills. In July 2013, the volcano spewed enough dust and ash that airlines had to cancel their flights for 24 hours.

## HYDROLOGY

Before the Mexica arrived in the Valley of Mexico and began the centuries-long project of damming its lakes, the water level fluctuated dramatically throughout the year, depending on rainfall. In the late 15th century, Nezahualcóyotl, the poet-king of Texcoco, oversaw the construction of a massive dike dividing Lake Texcoco into two halves, one holding saltwater and the other fresh, as a means of controlling floods. In Tenochtitlan, a system of canals was built for drainage control and transportation, while drinking water was brought in from Chapultepec.

As part of his final assault on the Mexica in 1521, Cortés ordered the breaching of Tenochtitlan's dams in an attempt to destroy the city with floodwaters. After the Mexica defeat, the Spaniards left the dike in ruins when they rebuilt the city, and as a result saw their new colonial capital flooded repeatedly. It was not until 1900, with the construction of the Gran Canal de Desagüe (Great Drainage Canal) under President Porfirio Díaz, that the waters of Lake Texcoco were finally emptied.

Currently the only natural bodies of water in the valley are small

---

**Previous:** stairs behind Basílica de Santa María de Guadalupe in northern Mexico City.

tracts of Lake Xochimilco in the south and the remnants of Lake Texcoco northeast of the city, in the state of Mexico. The rivers that once flowed into the valley from the western mountains—such as Río Mixcoac, Río de la Piedad, Río Tacubaya, and Río Churubusco—still exist but are canalized and sealed under major avenues, eventually draining into one of the five canals on the east side of the city, which in turn flow out of the valley to the northeast.

The soggy earth below the city has contributed to the capital's rapid sinking: In the Centro Histórico, you may notice old stone buildings are cracked or tilting, some to the point of becoming uninhabitable. Some neighborhoods have dropped an estimated 7.5 m (25 ft) in the last century alone! Air quality is also affected; the dried lakebeds in the northeast part of the valley create swirling clouds of dust that are swept up into the atmosphere and moved to the southwest directly across the city by the prevailing winds, worsening the air pollution.

# CLIMATE

Altitude tempers Mexico City's tropical location, creating a remarkably pleasant climate almost all year-round. During the spring and fall, daytime temperatures are usually 22-23°C (72-73°F), dropping to 10-12°C (50-54°F) in the evening. The short winter season runs December-February, and the weather is cooler throughout those months, especially at night. April-early June are typically the warmest months, when the temperature slowly climbs until the rainy season begins. In 2024, the temperature in May hit a once-unthinkable 34.3°C (93.7°F), a record for the region.

As in most of central Mexico, Mexico City's climate can be divided into two distinct seasons: the dry season, which runs November-May, and the shorter rainy season, late June-October. During the rainy season, flash floods, furious downpours, and even hailstorms pummel the capital in the afternoon and evening. In most cases, these storms rarely last longer than an hour or two, and they help moderate the heat of the summer.

# ENVIRONMENTAL ISSUES

Mexico City's 20-million-plus population has had a substantial impact on the environment. There is a growing environmental consciousness in the capital, and there have been some modest improvements in recent decades, but environmental problems remain one of the most substantial issues facing the city.

## Air Quality

A semiopaque haze of yellowish smog lingers above Mexico City most days, blocking the view of the surrounding mountains. The city's well-publicized air pollution problems hit an all-time high in the late

## September 19: A City Changed

### SEPTEMBER 19, 1985

At 7:18am on September 19, 1985, Mexico City trembled violently for more than three full minutes when an 8.1 magnitude earthquake rippled across the region. The water-rich sediment below the streets in Mexico City is highly susceptible to movement, and the ground trembled so violently that it led to a phenomenon called soil liquefaction. This created waves of movement that were, ominously, particularly traumatic to taller buildings.

In those three minutes, hundreds of buildings came crashing to the ground while drainage pipes and gas mains burst beneath the streets, contaminating the water supply and causing fires and explosions throughout the city. The death toll was massive, though never definitively determined, with estimates ranging from at least 10,000 to more than 35,000. Tens of thousands more were injured and over 100,000 left homeless. Exacerbating the situation, important medical centers were among the 3,000-plus buildings that were seriously damaged during the quake. Just a day later, a massive aftershock of almost equal magnitude amplified the destruction.

The federal and municipal governments were overwhelmed by the scale of the tragedy, and the people of Mexico City became important first responders, with civilians risking their lives to dig through the rubble of fallen buildings to find survivors. Citywide, people offered homes to neighbors, distributed food, and helped to bring order to the devastated city.

The earthquake of 1985 left a lasting mark on Mexico City. It is the subject of books and essays, including *No Sin Nosotros* by Carlos Monsivais and *Nada, Nadie* by Elena Poniatowska, both preeminent Mexico City writers.

---

1980s and early 1990s; though the city has made progress in improving the environment, air quality is an ongoing problem in the capital. The winter months are the worst, when there are fewer and lighter air currents.

Automobile traffic is the number-one contributor to air quality problems in the greater Mexico City metropolitan region. To help address air quality, the local government has implemented several programs, including tighter vehicle emissions checks, reforestation projects, and a program to limit driving, called "Hoy No Circula," which restricts the number of cars on the road.

Mexico City surveys its Metropolitan Air Quality Index (Índice Metropolitana de Calidad del Aire, or IMECA) every day, measuring the city's levels of ozone, carbon monoxide, carbon dioxide, lead, sulfur, and other contaminants. You can track the daily

## SEPTEMBER 19, 2017

Every September 19 at 11am, in commemoration of the 1985 earthquake and to test the city's first-response system, there is an official earthquake safety drill throughout Mexico City. On September 19, 2017, the drill was performed with particular solemnity, as an 8.1 magnitude earthquake had recently hit the Mexican coast near Oaxaca, shaking the capital violently and destroying coastal towns along the Isthmus of Tehuantepec.

Incredibly, just a few hours after the drill, a 7.1 magnitude earthquake hit central Mexico, with an epicenter just 120 km (75 mi) outside the city. Schools, offices, and apartment buildings in the Roma, Condesa, Del Valle, Tlalpan, Iztapalapa, Coyoacán, and Xochimilco neighborhoods collapsed during the quake, while thousands more structures were declared uninhabitable in the days that followed, leaving many people homeless.

As in 1985, the most important first responders were the people of Mexico City, who organized rescue efforts in fallen buildings (successfully pulling many survivors from the rubble), delivered supplies across the city via bicycle brigades, and operated emergency shelters and collection centers around the clock. Many of the young people who enthusiastically volunteered during the aftermath of the earthquake were the sons and daughters of the very same people who volunteered after the 1985 quake.

## SEPTEMBER 19, 2022

On September 19, 2022, a 7.6-magnitude earthquake struck central Mexico again; though the shaking in Mexico City was considerable, there was no damage or deaths reported in the capital. Like the 2017 earthquake, the tremor started shortly after the citywide earthquake drill, while commemorations for the people lost in previous quakes were still underway.

---

IMECA readings in most local newspapers or online.

## Water

Water is one of the biggest challenges facing modern Mexico City. For the past century, the capital's tremendous demand for water has been largely fed by local underground aquifers. In recent years, drought has drastically reduced the water tables, which are already being tapped for more water annually than can be replenished by rainfall. Additional water is pumped in from the Lerma and Cutzamala Rivers and reservoirs in the state of Mexico, though these sources are also being affected by lower-than-average rainfall attributed to climate change. Poor infrastructure is an unfortunate contributor to the problem; it is estimated that up to 40 percent of the city's water supply is lost through leaky pipes before it reaches household taps.

Not only is the Mexico City water table dropping, but water shortages are increasing all around central Mexico. About 20 percent of Mexico City's residents do not have consistent access to tap water, with some residents relying almost entirely on water delivered by truck. A reforestation program along the banks of the dwindling Lago de Texcoco has helped to cut back on dust and to recycle carbon dioxide, and it may also speed efforts to reclaim more rainwater in the lake basin.

# History

## PRE-COLUMBIAN HISTORY
### Early Civilizations

More than 30,000 years ago, the majority of the North American continent was covered in sheets of ice. Amid this forbidding landscape, the first human settlers are believed to have migrated from Siberia to North America via a narrow land bridge across the Bering Strait. These first people were followed by another wave of migrants, likely of Asian descent, who eventually migrated to the southern reaches of the Andes Mountains of South America.

Eventually, tribes of hunter-gatherers began to organize into communities—there is evidence of living sites dating back over 20,000 years—in a region known as Mesoamerica, a culturally linked swath of territory that covers southern Mexico, Belize, Guatemala, Honduras, El Salvador, and Nicaragua. Although the American population was now physically isolated from Eurasia, they independently developed farming techniques, with maize cultivation dating back 9,000 years.

### The First Inhabitants of the Valley

Groups of nomads arrived in the Valley of Mexico sometime around 20,000 BCE. Over the next several thousand years, the valley's population relied on gathering fruits and grains, until agricultural societies established themselves in the 3rd millennium BCE.

Agriculture created profound changes in social organization. Between 1500 and 650 BCE, the villages around the valley's lakes grew. The first full-fledged city to develop was Cuicuilco, arrayed around a pyramid site located at what is now the junction of Insurgentes Sur and Periférico Sur. By 100 BCE a second city was growing at Teotihuacán in the north. Cuicuilco had already begun to decline when its existence was dramatically cut short when Volcán Xitle exploded and covered Cuicuilco with beds of lava.

## Teotihuacán and the Classic Period

Characterized as an era of great human advancement, the Classic period in Mesoamerica began about 250-300 CE. During the early Classic period, an unknown people founded the city of Teotihuacán in the Valley of Mexico. Teotihuacán's largest structure, the 70-m (230-ft) Pyramid of the Sun, was completed around 100 CE, though the city reached its peak several hundred years later. With an estimated population reaching 150,000 (and possibly more), Teotihuacán's influence reached throughout Mesoamerica. It was overtaken and destroyed around 800 CE, though its lofty pyramids remain standing today.

As Teotihuacán declined, the great Maya and Zapotec people flourished in the south of Mexico, from 200 to 1000 CE. Though their city-states and vast empires had little direct influence on the Valley of Mexico, the Maya aesthetic and philosophical legacy, as well as their skill in astronomy and mathematics, had a notable impact throughout the region.

## The Toltecs and the Post-Classic

After 1000 CE, Maya and Zapotec cities began to decline, as new tribes descended from the north. Among these, a bellicose people known as the Toltec dominated central Mexico about 800-1000 CE, controlling trade routes from the huge city-state of Tollan, now called Tula, in present-day Hidalgo. The Toltecs controlled the Valley of Mexico, and their reach extended as far north as Zacatecas and as far south as Guatemala. Similarities in the architecture of post-Classic Maya cities and Tula have also prompted debate about the interaction between these peoples, suggesting that the Toltec may have been involved in the building of great post-Classic cities like Chichen Itzá.

The Toltec civilization never reached the influence achieved by Teotihuacán and began to decline after 1200 CE. After suffering successive invasions from the Chichimeca tribes to the north, Tula was eventually abandoned.

## The Mexica and La Gran Tenochtitlan

After the decline of Tula, there was increased migration into the Valley of Mexico. In 1250, the powerful cities of Azcapotzalco, Culhuacán, and Texcoco controlled much of the area when a nomadic northern tribe known as the Mexica (pronounced meh-SHEE-ka) arrived in the valley. According to legend, these people originally came from the city of Aztlán, thought to be on the coast of modern-day Nayarit; for that reason, historians began calling them the Aztecs, although the Mexica people never used that name themselves.

After years of enslavement and attacks on their settlements, the Mexica eventually founded a city on an uninhabited island not far from the shore in Lake Texcoco, which they named Tenochtitlan. According to legend, the Mexica knew that they were meant to settle the island when they saw an eagle perched on a cactus with a snake in its beak (a rendering of that vision is at the center of the Mexican flag today). Courageous warriors, the Mexica eventually gained dominance over the valley, vanquishing their chief rivals, the Tepanecs, with the assistance of the great Nezahualcóyotl of Texcoco, and establishing a strategic triple alliance with the cities of Texcoco and Tlacopan under their fourth emperor, Itzcóatl.

In the generations following Itzcóatl's rule, the Mexica started to rewrite their own history, identifying the Toltecs as their spiritual ancestors and downplaying their nomadic past. Moctezuma I, who took power in 1440 after Itzcóatl's death, embarked on an expansionist program that brought much of the Valley of Oaxaca and the Gulf Coast regions under Mexica control. During the next generations of Mexica rulers, almost all of central Mexico fell under their sway, with the exception of a few regions that maintained their independence, notably the Tlaxcaltecas and Chollulans to the east. By the time Moctezuma Xocoyotzin, or Moctezuma II, took power, in 1502, the Mexica were the ruling power in Mesoamerica.

As the center of the empire, the city-state of Tenochtitlan grew rich and splendid, demanding lavish tributes of food, clothing, tools, and jewelry from the hundreds of cities it controlled. Upper-class Mexica dressed in embroidered tunics decorated with feathers, and their boys were sent to schools called calmécac. Children of regular civilians were also sent to vocational schools, to learn the craft of their community, in addition to natural history and religion. Adjacent to Tenochtitlan, and eventually linked to it by continual landfill projects, the smaller island of Tlatelolco was the empire's principal market center, ruled by its own line of kings.

Tenochtitlan itself was large, orderly, and clean. Laid out in an organized grid pattern, it was crisscrossed by a system of canals, which allowed for drainage during the flood season and also provided the principal means of transportation to and from the mainland via canoe. At the center of the city was a stepped pyramid-temple, today called the Templo Mayor, which was the principal religious monument in the city. Indeed, religion was central to life in Tenochtitlan. Huitzilopochtli, the god of war, and Tlaloc, the god of rain, were central figures in their pantheon. The Mexica fed Huitzilopochtli's favor by performing human sacrifices in their temples—a practice common throughout Mesoamerica but brought to new heights in Tenochtitlan. The Mexica often sacrificed prisoners of war brought home from their many battles, with massive sacrifices taking place on festival days.

# SPANISH CONQUEST AND THE COLONIAL ERA

## The Conquest

After Christopher Columbus's 1492 voyage across the Atlantic, Iberian conquest of the Americas swiftly began. The Spaniards first took control of several Caribbean islands, principally Hispaniola and Cuba, where the native population was enslaved and largely died out after a few generations, owing to disease and depression. During that time, several Spanish envoys discovered the existence of richer "islands" to the east, populated by civilizations more advanced than those in the Indies. Rushing to gain control of these new territories, Cuban governor Diego Velázquez chose a young Spaniard named Hernán Cortés from Medellín, Spain, to lead a reconnaissance expedition to the Mexican coast.

Cortés accepted the post, amassing a huge group of volunteers to accompany him on the voyage. Sensing Cortés's growing power and insubordination, Velázquez attempted to cancel Cortés's appointment, but Cortés sailed anyway, bringing 11 ships and hundreds of men with him. They landed first on the coast of the Yucatán peninsula, then traveled north along the Gulf Coast, first stopping in Tabasco and then modern-day Veracruz, where he met with messengers of Moctezuma II.

After sinking his ships and thereby forcing dissenting Spanish soldiers to join the conquest, Cortés made his way to Tenochtitlan, gathering Mexica enemies as his allies along the way. Moctezuma had already received detailed reports about the Spanish arrival, and descriptions had led him to fear Cortés was the embodiment of the god Quetzalcóatl. When the Spanish arrived in Tenochtitlan, Moctezuma allowed them to enter the city as protected guests.

Several weeks went by without event, but tensions brewed. When Cortés returned to the Gulf Coast to fight off a brigade of soldiers sent by Velázquez, Pedro de Alvarado was left in charge, and he led a misguided massacre of 200 Mexica nobles at the festival of Tóxcatl. Cortés returned, but the situation between the Spanish and the Mexica was now irreparable. During this time, Moctezuma was also killed under unknown circumstances while being held hostage by the Spanish. Trying to escape under the cover of darkness, the Spanish lost hundreds of soldiers to angry Mexica attackers while trying to flee the city in an event remembered as the Noche Triste (Night of Sorrows).

Playing on the widespread resentment of the Mexica throughout the region, the Spanish recruited help from many tribes near Tenochtitlan and regrouped their forces. The Spanish were further assisted by the smallpox virus, which they had unwittingly introduced to the Americas. In a matter of weeks, thousands of native people fell sick and died, including Moctezuma's successor, Cuitláhuac.

After extensive preparation, the Spanish launched a waterborne attack on Tenochtitlan in 1521. Months of conflict ensued, concluding with a siege of the city. Led by Moctezuma's cousin, Cuauhtémoc, the Mexica resisted the Spanish, even as they ran low on both food and water supplies. Finally, Cortés and his military forced the Mexica to flee to the adjoining community of Tlatelolco, where they were overcome. The Spanish razed Tenochtitlan and built a new city on its ruins. Victorious, the Spanish named their new city Mexico, capital of New Spain. In 2021, Mexico City observed the 500th anniversary of the founding of the modern city.

## New Spain

Under the direction of Alonso García Bravo, a new Spanish city was constructed, borrowing much from Tenochtitlan's highly organized street plan. The first viceroy of Mexico, Don Antonio de Mendoza, took his post in 1535.

The conquest and colonization were brutal for native people, both physically and culturally. Where they encountered resistance, the Spanish used ruthless tactics to subdue native tribes. Many Indigenous people were enslaved, while others succumbed to foreign disease. As a result of these changes, the native population dropped significantly during the early years of New Spain.

Fifteenth-century Spain was a deeply Catholic place, entrenched in the Inquisition at the time Cortés attacked Tenochtitlan. Converting the native population to Catholicism was a top priority for the Spanish crown (and a justification for colonization), and as early as the mid-1520s, missionaries had founded settlements in Mexico City and in the surrounding communities.

In addition to seeking converts, the Spanish came to Mesoamerica in search of wealth. To encourage settlement, the crown doled out land grants throughout the territories, and Spanish families established large haciendas, clearing the native land for agriculture and cattle grazing. Having admired the gold and silver jewelry worn by Mexica nobles, the Spanish aggressively sought precious metals. Fortuitously, a Spanish expedition discovered a large silver vein outside the modern-day city of Zacatecas in 1546. Several more bountiful silver veins were discovered shortly thereafter.

The discovery of silver gave the colonies massive trading power with Europe. The immense quantities of silver mined in New Spain passed through Mexico City, where Spanish merchants had an official monopoly on all trading in the colony. The city grew immensely wealthy and opulent, known throughout Europe as la ciudad de los palacios (the city of palaces). With the decline of the silver industry in the late 17th and early 18th centuries, Mexico City's economy stagnated.

Throughout the colonial era, society was highly stratified: Spaniards born in Spain were afforded the highest place in society and were consistently appointed to the most important political posts. Mexican-born people of Spanish heritage were referred to as criollos and, despite their common heritage, had a lower social and political standing than the Spanish. Mestizo people of mixed ethnic heritage held a far lower place in society, only above the abysmal position of Indigenous workers and slaves.

# INDEPENDENT MEXICO
## The War of Independence

After close to 250 years of Spanish rule in the Americas, Bourbon king Charles III ascended the Spanish throne. A believer in "enlightened absolutism," he made dramatic changes to the governance of New Spain. Undermining the colony's economic autonomy, he established royal monopolies on seminal industries like tobacco, gunpowder, and mercury (needed for silver extraction). He also forbade church loans, which were a major source of credit within Mexican communities. Finally, he expelled the highly popular Jesuit order from Mexico. For many Mexicans—especially those who had already come to resent the colony's strict hierarchies and distant authority—these changes bred deep resentment.

Mexico's war for independence began on September 16, 1810, when Catholic priest Miguel Hidalgo y Costilla gave his famous grito de la independencia (cry of independence) from a church in Dolores, Guanajuato, where he and a group of criollos led the insurrection. After Hidalgo's capture and assassination, José María Morelos took charge of the army. He in turn was captured and executed. The battles continued for almost a decade until the government of Ferdinand VII was overthrown in Spain. As a result of the change in Spanish governance, Colonel Agustín de Iturbide, a fierce royalist, switched sides to join the Mexican army. With Iturbide at the helm, Mexico achieved independence with the Treaty of Córdoba in 1821. Mexico City, home of wealthy nobles, remained a royalist holdout during the struggle, firmly opposed to independence.

## Early Independent Mexico

The end of the war was the beginning of a century of political unrest and instability in Mexico. After signing the Treaty of Córdoba, Mexico took its first steps toward establishing autonomy. Twenty-four states were named in the First Mexican Empire, with independence leader Agustín de Iturbide crowning himself emperor of Mexico. In 1824, Mexico City was officially designated the seat of the federal government.

Just eight months after Iturbide

## Virgen de Guadalupe: A María for the People

It was not long after the Spanish conquest of Mexico when, on December 12, 1531, the image of a dark-skinned Virgin Mary appeared to Juan Diego Cuauhtlatoatzin, speaking to him in his native Nahuatl language and asking him to build a shrine in her honor on the hill at Tepeyac, previously the site of a Mexica pyramid dedicated to the goddess Tonantzin. Church authorities initially ignored Juan Diego's entreaties, but the Virgin appeared to him again, instructing him to gather roses in his cloak and carry them to the bishop.

image of the Virgen de Guadalupe in Basílica de Santa María de Guadalupe

According to oral histories of the event, Juan Diego returned to the bishop and opened his cloak before the assembled clergymen; inside, there was a detailed image of the Virgin whom Juan Diego had described. The bishop was dazzled, declaring it a miracle, and construction of the church at Tepeyac began. Today, Juan Diego's cloak hangs in the modern Basílica de Santa María de Guadalupe, bearing the famed image of the Virgen de Guadalupe.

took control of the government, Vicente Guerrero and Antonio López de Santa Anna led a successful revolt against the government. They established the first Mexican republic, and another hero of the War of Independence, Guadalupe Victoria, became the country's first president. Amid turmoil, Vicente Guerrero assumed the post of president when Guadalupe Victoria stepped down, though the conservative forces of General Anastasio Bustamante quickly ousted him.

### Mexican-American War

In 1831, Antonio López de Santa Anna was elected president. During this time, the United States was aggressively expanding westward, and US citizens had begun to settle in Texas. When Mexico's constitution centralized power and abolished slavery in 1835, Texas declared independence. In response, Santa Anna sent troops to Texas. He sustained a major victory at the Alamo, but the brutality of the fighting galvanized Texans against the Mexican president. After numerous confrontations, the Texan army overpowered Santa Anna's forces.

On June 16, 1845, the United

The story of a Nahuatl-speaking Mary is believed to have been a watershed moment for Christianity in the Americas, inspiring mass conversion to Catholicism in Mexico City. Thereafter, miracles were repeatedly attributed to the Virgin's influence, and the Virgen de Guadalupe became a symbol of the colonies. During the Mexican War of Independence, famous insurgent Miguel Hidalgo used a banner with the image of the Virgen de Guadalupe as a flag to lead the Mexican army into battle against the Spanish.

While the power of the image is immense, the truth of the origin story is debated. Little is known about the life of Juan Diego, and neither the Virgen de Guadalupe nor Juan Diego are mentioned in the surviving early colonial accounts from Mexico City. Some historians question if Juan Diego existed at all. On the other hand, there are numerous curiosities on the cloak itself. According to some studies, the 47 stars in the image represent the exact constellations seen over Mexico on the night of the winter solstice in 1531. The pigments are also of unknown origin and unusual for the time period in which the narrative took place. And it is remarkable that the shroud has managed to remain so beautifully preserved over nearly 500 years on display—including almost a century of being subjected to flash photography.

Today, the shrine to the Virgen de Guadalupe is the second-most-visited Catholic pilgrimage site in the world, after the Vatican, with an estimated 6 million people visiting each year (including 300,000 visitors arriving on her feast day, December 12). Saint Juan Diego was canonized by Pope John Paul II on July 31, 2002, as the first Indigenous American saint.

---

States annexed Texas, though the state's independence was never formally recognized by the Mexican government. When a skirmish broke out between Mexican forces and the US military along the Texas border, President James Polk asked Congress to declare war. Aggressively recruiting new soldiers to join the effort, the United States advanced into Mexico under General Winfield Scott. After battles through the north, the US launched a maritime attack on the city of Veracruz, then captured the important central city of Puebla, from which Scott's army launched an offensive on the capital. After numerous battles, Scott took control of Mexico City during the Battle of Chapultepec, when American forces invaded the castle on the Cerro de Chapultepec and raised their flag over the city.

The capital of Mexico was temporarily relocated to Querétaro, where Santa Anna signed the infamous Treaty of Guadalupe, which ceded half of Mexico's territory to the United States, including California, New Mexico, Arizona, Texas, Colorado, and Nevada.

## Reform and French Rule

Santa Anna returned to power after the war, but he was overthrown in 1855 by a Zapotec lawyer named Benito Juárez. Among his most significant acts, Juárez abolished church property and amended the constitution to officially recognize freedom of religion. Juárez's presidency was repeatedly threatened by conservative and royalist forces, though he is remembered today as one of Mexico's most just and visionary leaders.

Juárez had a great impact on the layout and power structures in Mexico City. When he took the presidency, much of the Centro Histórico was controlled by large convents, including San Agustín, San Francisco, Santo Domingo, and La Merced. After seizing church properties under the Reform Laws, city officials demolished large parts of these religious compounds and repossessed their land. Remnants of the old convents still stand, but none are fully intact today.

Failing to oust liberals from power, conservative leaders conspired with the government of France to overthrow Juárez's government. France invaded Mexico under Napoleon III and, after a disastrous defeat in Puebla, came back to successfully overwhelm Juárez's forces. The French established the Second Mexican Empire, placing Emperor Maximilian I of Austria in charge. During his brief rule, Maximilian and his wife, Carlota, claimed the Castillo de Chapultepec as their residence, redesigning it in a grand European style. To link the new palace with downtown, the Paseo de la Reforma (originally the Paseo de la Emperatriz), now the city's broadest boulevard, was laid out.

In 1867, there was yet another successful uprising by the liberals; Maximilian was executed in Querétaro. Benito Juárez returned to the presidency, and he remained in power until his death in 1872.

## MODERN MEXICO CITY
### The Porfiriato

Not long after Juárez's successor, Sebastián Lerdo de Tejada, had won his second election, army general Porfirio Díaz took office in a coup. A hero in the war against the French, Porfirio Díaz was a liberal from Oaxaca, but his politics changed in office. He became a powerful and conservative political leader with a strong military outlook. Fascinated by European aesthetics, he spent lavishly on city infrastructure and architecture in the European style.

Under Díaz, Mexico City began to expand beyond the Centro Histórico. The first neighborhoods established outside downtown were Guerrero and San Rafael, north and west of the Alameda, in the 1850s and 1860s, followed by the development of the San Cosme and Santa María la Ribera farther west, and later the Juárez and Cuauhtémoc on either side of the newly chic Paseo de la Reforma. The Colonia Roma, just to the south, followed.

Díaz held the presidency for 26 consecutive years, a period known as the Porfiriato. Under Díaz's dictatorship, Mexico entered into an era of relative stability, though the regime's despotic tendencies did not play out positively for the majority of Mexicans. While the country's wealth increased, social conditions for the poor worsened under Díaz's iron-fisted control.

## The Mexican Revolution

After almost 30 years of the Porfiriato, wealthy politician Francisco I. Madero announced his presidential candidacy, in opposition to Díaz. President Díaz jailed him, and in return, Madero declared a revolt against the Díaz government on November 20, 1910, now remembered as the Day of the Revolution.

The Mexican Revolution was helmed by some of Mexico's most colorful personalities. Leading the división del norte (northern division), the wily and charismatic bandit Pancho Villa recruited thousands to the revolutionary cause. From the state of Morelos, Emiliano Zapata was a middle-class landowner who joined the revolution to promote land reform among peasants. Zapata rode to war dressed as a traditional Mexican charro (cowboy), with a wide-brim sombrero and thick mustache. He is still revered for his populist politics and his strong commitment to rural people and land rights.

Within six months, the people's army defeated Díaz's military. Madero initially took the presidency, but Victoriano Huerta ousted Madero in a coup. In response, Venustiano Carranza, Álvaro Obregón, Pancho Villa, and Emiliano Zapata led yet another revolt against Huerta's government. Villa and Zapata toppled Huerta's regime in August 1914.

Venustiano Carranza made a bid for the presidency, initially opposed by both Villa and Zapata. However, Carranza was able to win a broad base of support by promising constitutional reform. He oversaw the writing of the Constitution of 1917, which included land, law, and labor reforms. Carranza was eventually forced out of power by General Álvaro Obregón.

## Post-Revolutionary Mexico City

The post-revolutionary period was a time of great progress and cultural and intellectual achievement in Mexico. During Obregón's presidency, José Vasconcelos served as the secretary of public education, overseeing the establishment of the National Symphonic Orchestra as well as the famed Mexican mural program. Music and cinema flourished during the 1930s and 1940s, with Mexican movies outselling Hollywood films during World War II. During and after the Spanish Civil War, many European intellectuals took up residence in Mexico, adding to the thriving art and cultural community. Always the center of the republic, Mexico

City was at the heart of this cultural movement, its artists, writers, thinkers, musicians, and actors gaining national and worldwide fame.

In a watershed moment in Mexican politics, Lázaro Cárdenas was elected to the presidency in 1937. Unlike his predecessors, Cárdenas enacted land reform and redistribution as laid out in the Constitution of 1917. In a move that would serve as a model for other oil-rich nations, Cárdenas expropriated oil reserves from the private companies that had been running them. He established Petróleos Mexicanos (Pemex), concurrently founding the National Polytechnic Institute to ensure a sufficient engineering force in the country.

## Expansion and Post-World War II Boom

Mexico City's population exploded during the 20th century. In 20 years alone, the population doubled, from 906,000 in 1920 to 1,757,000 in 1940. To cope with its new residents, the city expanded in all directions, with little planning. The government turned a blind eye to the impromptu settlements set up by rural immigrants, which would eventually become entire cities in their own right, and freely gave out permits to build new, upscale neighborhoods for the wealthy.

The construction of the new national university complex in the early 1950s, along with the expansion of Avenida Insurgentes to connect it to the city center, led to the buildup of the entire southwestern quadrant of the city in just a few short years. Wide-open fields south of the Roma were quickly converted into the Del Valle and Nápoles neighborhoods. In the early postwar years the formerly outlying villages of Mixcoac, San Ángel, Tacuba, Tacubaya, and Coyoacán were formally incorporated into the city limits. To the north, industrial areas grew quickly. When the middle-class suburb Ciudad Satélite was built with great optimism in the late 1950s, it was surrounded by open land; in the years that followed, the city swallowed it completely.

The rural immigrants flooding into the city didn't have money to buy property or houses, and so they simply erected shantytowns in the less desirable eastern side of the valley, once under the waters of Lake Texcoco. Over the years, these ciudades perdidas (lost cities) have become permanent cities. The classic ciudad perdida is Ciudad Nezahualcóyotl, which saw its population increase from 65,000 in 1960 to 650,000 in 1970 to over 1 million by the 1990s, making it one of the largest cities in the country.

## The 1960s and the Tlatelolco Massacre

Mexico City was selected to host the 1968 Olympic Games. For Mexico's government, the Olympic Games were a major financial investment, as well as an important

a memorial to the massacre of 1968 in Mexico City's Zócalo

opportunity to boost the nation's economy and bring Mexico to the world stage. Mexican students saw the international publicity as an opportunity to draw attention to Mexico's one-party-rule government. There were widespread protests against the government in the months preceding the opening ceremony, many drawing tens of thousands of protesters.

Ten days before the Olympic Games were set to begin, thousands of students marched in protest to the Plaza de las Tres Culturas in Tlatelolco. The gathering was meant to be peaceful, but armed military troops were sent in, firing indiscriminately on the crowd. While the government stated that only four students had been killed, eyewitnesses saw hundreds of bodies. The official events were never fully uncovered, yet the massacre permanently tarnished the government's reputation with the people of Mexico City.

## Economic Crisis, NAFTA, and the Zapatista Movement

In the early 1980s, falling oil prices and high worldwide interest rates created a recession in Mexico. President Miguel de la Madrid was forced to drastically cut government spending, the economy stagnated, and unemployment soared. The situation worsened for the capital after a massive earthquake on September 19, 1985. At magnitude 8.1, the quake shook Mexico City for three full minutes, during which time hundreds of buildings collapsed to the ground and at least 10,000 people were killed, though some estimates put the number of fatalities much higher.

Economic recovery began under the next president, Carlos Salinas de Gortari, who renegotiated the country's external debts and embarked on a policy of trade liberalization. In 1994, Mexico signed on as a member of the North American Free Trade Agreement (NAFTA). Under NAFTA and its 2020 update, the United States-Mexico-Canada Agreement (USMCA), Mexico's economy has continued to grow annually, and trade between USMCA nations has more than tripled.

The same morning that NAFTA went into effect, a small Indigenous army called the Ejército Zapatista de Liberación Nacional (Zapatista Army of National Liberation), or EZLN, took armed control of several cities in the southernmost state of Chiapas. Known as the Zapatistas (in a nod to Revolution hero Emiliano Zapata), this small but well-organized group of largely Indigenous revolutionaries declared war on the Mexican government, citing the years of poverty and oppression suffered by the country's native people. In response to the uprising, the Mexican government dispatched thousands of troops to Chiapas, pursuing the EZLN into the southern rain forests, where they suffered heavy casualties.

This rebellion was small in scope but wide-reaching in consequences, inspiring support for Indigenous causes throughout Mexico—and the world. The army's unofficial leader, Subcommandante Marcos, became a national spokesperson for the Indigenous cause and, along with a convoy of EZLN leadership, met repeatedly with Mexican government leaders. In 2000, they marched peaceably to Mexico City, where they met with the federal government and were greeted by thousands of supporters.

## PRI Opposition: The PRD and The PAN

In 1988, leftist politician Cuauhtémoc Cárdenas, son of post-Revolution president Lázaro Cárdenas, split from the monolithic ruling Partido Revolucionario Institucional party and announced his candidacy for president against Carlos Salinas de Gortari. Cárdenas was defeated in a highly suspect election, during which the voting systems failed to function for several hours. He was later elected mayor of Mexico City, bolstering the notion that Mexico was ready for a change from the one-party system that had ruled since the early 20th century.

In the elections of 2000, popular support began to rally around the tall, mustachioed Vicente Fox Quesada, a former Coca-Cola executive. Campaigning on a ticket of change, Fox won a much celebrated victory over PRI candidate Francisco Labastida. Fox's National Action Party (Partido Acción Nacional; PAN) did not control the Congress, however, and Fox's presidency was marked by inefficiency. Fox's PAN successor, President Felipe Calderón, was elected in 2006, taking the office after winning by just one percentage point over the Party of the Democratic Revolution (Partido de la Revolución Democrática; PRD) candidate, Andrés Manuel López Obrador, in an election that was mired by controversy.

During his presidency, Calderón declared a war on drugs as a major spike in drug-related violence plagued much of northern Mexico, causing widespread instability and fear along the border with the United States, among other areas. Capitalizing on dissatisfaction with the PAN and the violence in Mexico, the PRI regained control of the executive branch with the election of Enrique Peña Nieto, former governor of the state of Mexico, to the presidency. Like his predecessor, Peña Nieto defeated PRD candidate López Obrador, and protests against his legitimacy, though less widespread, were also fierce.

## Ayotzinapa

Violence, organized crime, and corruption continued to plague Mexico throughout Peña Nieto's presidency, with journalists, activists, and ordinary citizens the targets of extortion, murder, and disappearance. On September 26, 2014, university students from the Ayotzinapa teachers college in the state of Morelos—an activist educational institution dedicated to teaching and advocating for the rural poor—boarded buses to Mexico City, where they planned to attend a political protest commemorating the 1968 student massacre in Tlatelolco. In circumstances that have never been fully uncovered, their buses came under armed attack by police and organized crime in the city of Iguala. Six students died and 43 went missing without a trace.

Despite widespread public outrage and years of demonstrations, both national and international, there has never been a full account of what happened. The events of Ayotzinapa became a galvanizing moment in Mexican history, sparking massive public protest against Peña Nieto's government and human rights abuses in Mexico. For more information about this pivotal event in recent Mexican history, in 2022 Reveal from the Center for Investigative Reporting and Adonde Media produced a three-part podcast, "After Ayotzinapa," that chronicles the tragedy, the national reaction, and the investigation that followed, as well as the relationship between Ayotzinapa and the US war on drugs.

## The Era of Morena

During his candidacy and controversial loss in the 2012 presidential elections, former Mexico City head of government and two-time PRD presidential candidate Andrés Manuel López Obrador founded a new leftist opposition party, Movimiento Regeneración Nacional, or Morena. López Obrador, popularly known as AMLO, entered the 2018 presidential race as Morena's candidate and won the presidency. During his presidency, López Obrador initiated a series of dramatic social and political changes that are referred to by Morena as the "Cuarta Transformación," or the fourth transformation, which include a raise in the minimum wage and expanded pensions for the elderly. Notably, people living in poverty in Mexico decreased from 52.2 million in 2016 to 46.8 million in 2022.

In 2018, climate scientist Claudia Sheinbaum, who was the secretary of the environment during AMLO's term as head of government in Mexico City, won the election to become the head of government in the capital, establishing Morena's newfound dominance in national politics. In 2024, Sheinbaum was the first woman elected president of Mexico, winning close to 60 percent of the vote. At the same time, Morena won the governorship in 21 of Mexico's 28 states, making it the dominant party nationally.

# Government and Economy

## GOVERNMENT
### The Federal Republic
As laid out in the Constitution of 1917, Mexico is a democratic republic. It is divided into 31 individually governed states, plus one distrito federal (federal district) in Mexico City. The federal government is divided into three branches: executive, legislative, and judicial. State governments are similarly divided into three branches and are elected locally.

### La Ciudad de México
After independence, Mexico City was declared the seat of the national government. Though technically federal land, the Distrito Federal was divided into independent municipios throughout the post-Independence era. President Álvaro Obregón abolished the municipios altogether, dividing the city into delegaciones and uniting political power into a single body run by the federal government. Thereafter, the head of government of Mexico City was appointed directly by the president of the Mexican republic.

Since the late 1990s, Mexico City is run by an assembly and jefe del gobierno (head of government, similar to a mayor). The jefe del gobierno post has always been filled by leftist politicians, first PRD and then Morena. Though they are not without controversy, the party's progressive, populist politics have made some notable changes to the city, such as the introduction of the new aboveground bus system called Metrobús, the development of a financial assistance program for single mothers and other vulnerable groups, and the restoration of much of the Centro Histórico and Chapultepec. Socially leftist government led to the legalization of both same-sex marriage and abortion in Mexico City in the past decade.

In early 2016, the government announced that the Distrito Federal would now officially be named Ciudad de México, and that the city would be granted greater autonomy and more state-like powers, including the creation of a local congress and the drafting of a city constitution.

### Political Parties
#### Movimiento Regeneración Nacional (Morena)
The Movimiento Regeneración Nacional, or Morena, was founded by then-presidential candidate Andrés Manuel López Obrador

and his supporters in 2011 in response to corruption within the PRD party. It was officially registered as a political party in 2014 and quickly became a major national force, with candidates taking the presidency and the head of government in Mexico City in 2018. The most left-leaning of the major parties, Morena advocates environmental stewardship and human rights, including LGBTQ+ rights and the decriminalization of abortion, and opposes neoliberal economic policies.

### Partido Revolucionario Institucional (PRI)

Although the Institutional Revolutionary Party no longer maintains unilateral power in Mexican politics, it remains one of the most important political parties in the country. After its losses in 2000, it regained majority in the legislature in 2003 and retook the presidency in 2012. The PRI was traditionally considered a leftist party, espousing many of the socialist viewpoints common to Latin American governments. Over time, it has become more centrist, especially in its new role as an opposition party.

### Partido Acción Nacional (PAN)

The National Action Party is a traditionally conservative party, established in the 1930s to protect the rights of the Catholic Church. Economically, the PAN generally supports a market economy and free trade, and socially, they also toe a traditionally conservative line, opposing both same-sex marriage and abortion. The PAN grew strong among conservative voters in northern Mexico, and PAN candidates won the national presidency in 2000 and 2006.

### Partido de la Revolución Democrática (PRD)

Until the founding of Morena, the Party of the Democratic Revolution was the most leftist of the major political parties in Mexico. The PRD grew out of the leftist opposition to the PRI, originally led by Cuauhtémoc Cárdenas. The party maintains an important presence throughout the country. It gained a national reputation through leadership in Mexico City, where PRD heads of government have instituted strong urban-planning programs.

### Other Parties

Aside from the three major political organizations, smaller parties in Mexico include the Labor Party and the Green Party, which also have representation in the Congress. In many cases, these smaller political organizations will work together with one of the three major parties to back a candidate.

## ECONOMY

Mexico City produces over 20 percent of Mexico's entire gross domestic product. Since the 1950s, Monterrey and Guadalajara have been developing industrial bases of their own, and in more recent decades, cities such as Puebla, Querétaro, Aguascalientes, Tijuana, and Toluca have been rapidly industrializing as well. But Mexico City completely controls the financial sector, as it's home to Bolsa Mexicana de Valores (the Mexican stock exchange) and all major banks and insurance companies. It also plays a big role in the service economy and is the headquarters of all of the dominant media and communications conglomerates.

## The Informal Economy

As they have for generations, many new immigrants to the city begin their new urban lives hawking their modest wares from any street corner not already occupied by another seller. Driven in part by a desire to clean up the downtown area, city authorities have begun regular patrols to evict unlicensed vendors in the city's central districts. In addition to ambulantes (street vendors), there are thousands of housekeepers, nannies, cooks, chauffeurs, and other household employees working throughout the city as a part of the informal economy.

## Poverty

Mexico is a wealthy and economically powerful nation with abundant natural resources. Yet wealth is poorly distributed throughout the population, and vast extremes in the standard of living define the modern social landscape. Mexico City resident Carlos Slim was named the world's wealthiest person by *Forbes* magazine in 2010, yet 10 percent of Mexicans do not have access to sufficient food or medical care. According to CONEVAL (National Council for the Evaluation of Social Development Policy), a little over 36 percent of the population nationally lives in poverty. Mexico City, like the rest of the country, is a place of great extremes. You will see fashionable people dining in restaurants on a Monday afternoon, while children beg for change at a nearby traffic stop.

# Local Culture

## POPULATION

Accurate population statistics for Mexico City are difficult to obtain. According to the official 2020 census conducted by the National Institute of Statistics and Geography (Instituto Nacional de Estadística y Geografía; INEGI), there are 9,209,944 people living in Mexico City proper. If you extend the range to the entire metropolitan zone (which includes many densely populated areas of the state of Mexico adjacent the city, like the million-plus municipalities of Ciudad Nezahualcóyotl and Ecatepec de Morelos), the number is much higher. According to the Population Division of the Department of Economic and Social Affairs at the United Nations, the entire Mexico City metropolitan region has an estimated population of 21,581,000 inhabitants, making it the fifth-largest city in the world, just behind São Paulo.

Mexico City's growth has slowed considerably since the 1970s, when its population was expanding at an average rate of 4.5 percent per annum. Throughout the 2000s, the city's population grew negligibly (and more slowly than the countrywide growth rate of 1 percent), and the most recent census numbers even show more people emigrating from the city than immigrating to it. In general, the population growth of the past 30 years has been in the outer edges of Mexico City, while the population of the inner core has been declining steadily.

## Class and Ethnicity

A large and multiethnic country, Mexico has suffered from racial and class divisions throughout most of its history. In the colonial era, Mexican society was highly stratified: The most privileged class was the peninsulares, pure-blooded Spaniards born in Spain, followed by criollos, pure-blooded Spaniards born in Mexico. Mestizos, of mixed Indian-Spanish heritage, and indios (Indigenous people) were afforded a lower social status and little political power.

Today, the vast majority of Mexicans are mestizo, or mixed race. Genetic studies have confirmed that most Mexicans are predominantly a mix of Spanish and Indigenous American heritage; however, mestizo implies a mixed ethnic background, and it may include other ethnicities. To a smaller extent than in the United States or the Caribbean, some enslaved Africans were brought to New Spain during the colonial era, and they also mixed with the population. Mexicans of strictly European heritage, about 10 percent or less of the population, are generally Spanish descendants, though there have been other waves of European migrants to Mexico, including Irish, German, and French, among others.

In the country at large, about 8-10 percent of the population identifies as Indigenous, with around 6 percent speaking a native language. Nahuatl, the modern version of the language spoken in the Valley of Mexico before the Spanish conquest, is the most widely spoken Indigenous language in Mexico. Fewer than 2 percent of people in Mexico City speak a native language.

## Indigenous People and Cultures

An estimated 30 million people were living in Mesoamerica when the Spanish arrived in the 15th century. Immediately following the conquest, the native population was drastically reduced, both through violence and through diseases introduced by European settlers. Though many ethnic groups disappeared entirely, a significant Indigenous population has survived to the present day, with the largest communities living in Oaxaca, Chiapas, Yucatán, Quintana Roo, Hidalgo, Puebla, and Morelos. About 6.7 million people in Mexico speak an Indigenous language, and many communities in remote or rural areas have maintained native customs, craftwork, and dress.

Mexico City draws a large number of Indigenous immigrants, though their presence is largely subdued. You will rarely see people dressed in traditional clothing or speaking native languages, though there are some historic Nahuatl-speaking communities in the state of Mexico. For more information about Mexico City's Indigenous communities, the Asamblea de Migrantes Indígenas de la Ciudad de México (Assembly for Indigenous Migrants to Mexico City) hosts educational events, cosponsors conferences, and gives workshops, including classes in native languages, in support of native people living in the capital (http://indigenasdf.org.mx).

While most Mexicans are fiercely proud of the advanced societies of pre-Columbian Mexico, native people have been highly marginalized since the beginning of the colonial era. Today, predominantly Indigenous communities suffer from a lack of basic resources, education, and infrastructure. They are at a further disadvantage from a deeply embedded racism that has been perpetuated since the colonial area. In 2023, an estimated 65 percent of Indigenous people lived below the poverty line.

## Women

In Mexico, women and men share equality under the law. Second-wave feminism arrived in Mexico in the 1950s and 1960s, and there are numerous nonprofit organizations working to improve conditions for women, socially and politically. In 1994, the EZLN's rebel army included male and female soldiers and commanders and listed women's rights within its agenda for social justice.

There has traditionally been a large gender gap in Mexico's workforce, but economic realities, social changes, and increased education have changed the situation in recent decades, with women taking jobs in all sectors of society, from the small entrepreneur who cleans homes to the president of the nation. At the same time, women earn less than men across the board and continue to play a larger role in the household.

## LGBTQ+ ISSUES

Mexico is a generally accepting society, and most people are unlikely to raise a fuss about someone else's business. At the same time, the Catholic Church has traditionally opposed gay and lesbian relationships, making it less acceptable for LGBTQ+ people to come out within conservative Catholic households. Today, as in many aspects of society, Mexican attitudes toward LGBTQ+ people are becoming more liberal. In the capital, same-sex marriage was legalized in 2008, and gay couples may legally adopt children. Popular support for marriage equality is split, with about half the country backing it.

Generally speaking, the gay community is more visible and comfortably accepted in Mexico City than in most parts of Mexico. More and more, it is common to see same-sex couples holding hands while walking down the street or snuggling on a park bench. Annual LGBTQ+ pride events in June are massively attended.

## RELIGION

After Cortés vanquished the city of Tenochtitlan, the Spanish razed the Mexica temples and built Catholic churches atop their remains. Coming from a deeply religious atmosphere in Spain, colonial missionaries were active throughout the New World, establishing an abundance of churches, Catholic schools, and hospitals. Throughout Spanish rule of Mexico, the Catholic Church was one of the country's biggest landowners and a major player in politics. There were massive conversions among the Indigenous population to Catholicism, which are said to have spiked after the apparition of the Virgen de Guadalupe in Mexico City in 1531. Today, according to INEGI, close to 85 percent of Mexicans identify as Catholic.

The Catholic Church continues to hold a very important place in Mexican society, even for those who aren't actively religious. Throughout the country, Catholic schools are among the best and most popular options in private education, while Catholic mass is the traditional celebration for life's milestones: baptism, important birthdays, marriage, and death. Catholic holidays are widely and exuberantly celebrated, with the entire country taking a vacation for Holy Week and Easter.

One religious icon common to all of Mexico is the Virgen de Guadalupe. Worship of the image began in the early colonial era, after Juan Diego Cuauhtlatoatzin was said to have witnessed a dark-skinned Virgin Mary in a series of three visions at Tepeyac, a hill in northern Mexico City. Today, many Mexican churches are named for Our Lady of Guadalupe, who has become fused with Mexican identity. The official feast day for Guadalupe, December 12, is widely celebrated in Mexico City and throughout the country. Juan Diego, the Mexica man who saw the vision of the Virgen de Guadalupe, was declared a saint in 2002.

### Other Religious Groups

Mexicans who don't identify as Catholic are generally Protestants and Evangelicals, who number at about 7.5 percent of the population. The country also has a small historic Jewish community. The majority of Jewish immigrants arrived in Mexico from Syria, the Balkans, and Eastern Europe at the end of the 19th century and beginning of the 20th century. Today, an estimated 90 percent of the 40,000-50,000 Mexican Jews live in Mexico City, with notable communities in the Condesa, Polanco, and Santa Fe, among other areas.

## LANGUAGE

Mexico is the largest Spanish-speaking country in the world. English is widely spoken in the service industry, though visitors should take the time to learn at least enough Spanish to conduct everyday transactions, like ordering food in restaurants or paying for a bus ticket.

A distinctive aspect of Mexican Spanish is the great number of words incorporated from Indigenous Mexican tongues, particularly Nahuatl, the language spoken by the Mexica. Among notable examples, the word *chocolate* comes from the Nahuatl word *chocolatl*. *Coyote* is a derivation of the term *coyotl*, also from the Nahuatl. Both of these words have also been transferred from Nahuatl to English. In Mexico, many indigenous plants or animals, like the guajolote (wild turkey) and mapache (raccoon), are still more commonly referred to by their Indigenous names. In addition, Mexico retained many Indigenous place-names after the conquest. Tlatelolco, Mixcoac, Chapultepec, Tacubaya, and Tlalpan are all neighborhoods in Mexico that have Castellan versions of the Nahuatl place-name—not to mention the name México itself, which took its name from the Mexica people of Tenochtitlan.

Mexican Spanish, and especially Mexico City Spanish, is extremely rich with slang expressions, unique tones of voice, and hilarious wordplay, and it is immediately recognizable to Spanish speakers from any other country, both because of its distinct character and also because of the prevalence of Mexican television and movies throughout Latin America.

# The Arts

Mexico has rich and varied traditions in music, literature, visual arts, architecture, and film, as well as robust traditions in popular art, textiles, craft, and clothing. Both traditional and contemporary forms are celebrated in Mexico City, with fine art museums, popular art museums, concert halls, galleries, and festivals enthusiastically attended by locals.

## FILM

Although Mexicans have been making films since the genre was invented, the 1930s and 1940s are known as the golden age of Mexican cinema. During this era, Mexican directors prolifically produced feature films, even surpassing Hollywood in international success during World War II. The glamorous and charismatic film stars of the golden age—Mario Moreno Cantiflas, Tin-Tan, Dolores del Rio, Pedro Infante, and Maria Felix, among others—are some of the country's most beloved personalities. In the 1940s and 1950s, Spanish filmmaker Luis Buñuel made many of his most celebrated films in Mexico, including *Los Olvidados*. Mexican film output began to decline by mid-century, although a few experimental young filmmakers contributed to the country's canon, including Arturo Ripstein and Mexico-based Chilean-French filmmaker Alejandro Jodorowsky.

In the 21st century, Mexican film and filmmakers have made a prominent resurgence. In 2000, Alejandro González Iñárritu's widely acclaimed *Amores Perros* was heralded as the beginning of a new era in Mexican filmmaking, focused on gritty modern themes. The following year, Alfonso Cuarón's film *Y Tu Mamá También* was nominated for several Golden Globes and Academy Awards. Cuarón and González Iñárritu, like many of Mexico's filmmakers and actors, work extensively in Hollywood; González won Best Director at Cannes for his 2006 release *Babel,* while Cuarón took home the same prize for *Gravity* in 2014. Another lauded director from Mexico, horror film director Guillermo del Toro, won major accolades for 2008's *El Laberinto del Fauno (Pan's Labyrinth)* and 2017's *The Shape of Water.*

In 2018, Alfonso Cuarón put Mexico City in the spotlight for his Oscar-winning movie *Roma,* a tribute to his childhood, featuring many scenes in the city's Roma, Condesa, and San Juan neighborhoods, including extensive footage of the house at 22 Tepeji in the Colonia Roma, located directly across from Cuarón's childhood home.

## POPULAR ART AND CRAFTS

Mexico has celebrated traditions in popular art and handicrafts, or artesanía. Most Mexican craftwork relies on centuries-old techniques that unite pre-Hispanic and Spanish aesthetics. Among other disciplines, Mexico is famous for textiles, weaving, embroidery, ceramics and pottery, blown glass, baskets, woodworking, toymaking, hammered tin, lacquered wood, shoemaking, and tooled leather.

Like most aspects of Mexican culture, traditional handicrafts are highly specific to the region in which they are produced. In Puebla, for example, the Spanish introduced tin glazes and kiln-firing to skilled Indigenous potters. The resulting blend of traditions created a novel version of Spain's decorative Talavera ceramics, but with more color and whimsy. In Tonalá, Jalisco, artisans create an entirely different line of burnished and painted pottery, much of which can be used for cooking. In Mexico City, traditional craft shops and museums, like the Museo de Arte Popular, celebrate these wonderful traditions.

## LITERATURE

Although the Nahuatl-speaking people in modern-day Mexico City did not have a written language, poetry and song were the basis of a widespread literary tradition that existed in Mesoamerica before the arrival of the Spaniards. Writing in the beautiful Nahuatl language, the poet-king of Texcoco, Nezahualcóyotl, was a prolific crafter of verse, with many poems written by or attributed to him surviving today. Codices, pictorial manuscripts drawn on handmade bark paper, were made throughout Mesoamerica, both before and after the arrival of the Spanish.

After the conquest, Mexican-born writers made distinguished contributions to literature in Spanish. Baroque dramatist Juan Ruiz de Alarcón and writer Carlos de Sigüenza y Góngora were two important literary figures during the colonial era, but they are both surpassed in reputation by the beloved baroque poet Sor Juana Inéz de la Cruz. *Respuesta a Sor Filotea* (Reply to Sister Philotea), in which she defends a woman's right to education, is a classic.

During the 20th century, Mexico's national character was more strongly reflected in its literary traditions. Writers like Rosario Castellanos, Nellie Campobello, and Juan Rulfo began to describe a distinctly Mexican environment, exploring the country's identity and consciousness. Rulfo's most famous work, *Pedro Páramo,* influenced writers not only in Mexico but in all of Latin America. Carlos Fuentes's 1958 novel *Where the Air Is Clear* is one of the most emblematic books about the city.

In the 1990s, Mexico City-born poet and essayist Octavio Paz received the Nobel Prize in literature. His meditation on the Mexican people, *The Labyrinth of Solitude,* is his most famous work, though he is also remembered as a poet. His wife, Elena Garro, was also a celebrated journalist, novelist, and playwright. Mexico City was also home to many famed expatriates from Latin America, notably celebrated Colombian writer Gabriel García Márquez and Chilean Roberto Bolaño, whose novel *Los Detectives Salvajes* offers a wonderful portrait of the city's subcultures.

In Mexico City, there is a long tradition of writers who chronicle city life. Among the most influential was Salvador Novo, an essayist and historian who also distinguished himself by being openly gay in the more conservative climate of the early 20th century. Another keen observer of Mexican society, Carlos Monsiváis, was a famed chronicler of the city whose collection of essays, *Rituales del Caos,* is a Mexico City classic. Journalist, essayist, and novelist Elena Poniatowska has written many books about Mexican history, culture, and people in the 20th century, in addition to being a frequent op-ed contributor to Mexico City's newspapers. A new generation of Mexican writers has begun to leave a mark on the literary scene, many based in Mexico City, including famous authors like Fernanda Melchor, Jorge Volpi, Guadalupe Nettel, Valeria Luiselli, Yuri Herrera, Álvaro Enrigue, and Cristina Rivera Garza, among many others.

## MUSIC AND DANCE

Native Mesoamerican, African, and European musical traditions all contributed to the development of unique music and dance traditions in Mexico. Folk musical styles, or sones, developed in various regions, with diverse rhythms and instrumentation. From these sones, various genres of Mexican music flourished. Such song forms, like son jarocho from the state of Veracruz and huapango from the Huasteca region, are still very popular throughout the country.

Mariachi, Mexico's best-known musical ensemble, is characterized by its brassy sound and robust vocal style, as well as its impressive visual presentation. Dressed in formal charro suits and large sombreros, mariachi bands usually feature a lineup of violins, trumpets, guitars, bass guitars, and jaranas (a slightly larger five-string guitar). Mariachi music is a fixture at special events, like weddings or birthday parties, throughout Mexico. Mariachis generally play rancheras, traditional Mexican ballads, often covering nostalgic or patriotic themes. This song style became very popular in the late 19th and early 20th centuries, and again flourished in the 1940s and 1950s.

One of Mexico's most popular and distinctive genres, norteño music grew out of the traditional conjunto norteño, an ensemble noted for its inclusion of the bajo sexto (a 12-string guitar) and the button accordion, an instrument that was introduced by German immigrants to northern Mexico. European styles, like polka and waltz, also influenced norteño music. Similar to norteño, the popular banda style incorporates more brass sounds. Norteño and banda groups, like the world-famous Los Tigres del Norte, have a massively popular following in both Mexico and the United States.

## VISUAL ART AND ARCHITECTURE

Though most pre-Columbian cities were abandoned or destroyed by the 16th century, their ruins offer a glimpse into the accomplished architecture, city planning techniques, and artistic achievements of early Mesoamerica. The most distinctive features of Mesoamerican cities are the stepped temple-pyramids, seen in the Valley of Mexico at sites like Teotihuacán, which are often surrounded by wide public plazas and palaces.

As the Spanish began to colonize the Americas, they built new cities in the European style. Catholic missionaries and Jesuit educators were active throughout the country, and wealthy benefactors helped support their efforts by funding massive religious projects. Baroque art and design, which originated in Italy, formed the dominant aesthetic during the colonial era. Inside chapels, religious oil paintings and elaborate retablos (altarpieces) show enormous creativity and skill on the part of Mexican artists. Among the most famous names of the era, artist Miguel Cabrera contributed hundreds of religious paintings to chapels in Mexico City, Guanajuato, and other colonial capitals.

The French occupation and the ensuing dictatorship of Porfirio Díaz also left a mark on the country's architecture, especially in the capital. Emperor Maximilian oversaw the construction of the Paseo de la Reforma in Mexico City, a large and central avenue that was designed to resemble a Parisian boulevard. During his decades of presidency, Porfirio Díaz followed in the emperor's footsteps, investing in buildings, monuments, and sculptures that would transform Mexico City into a European-style capital, which also included neoclassical buildings.

At the same time President Díaz was constructing marble monuments, a new and more national strain of art was emerging in Mexico. The wildly original printmaker José Guadalupe Posada produced political and social satire in lithography, woodcut, and linocut for local publications, often depicting Mexican aristocrats as calaveras (skeletons). His wry wit and whimsical aesthetic would become synonymous with Mexico, and today, his pieces are often used as illustration during Day of the Dead.

After the Revolution of 1910, art, culture, and intellectual thought flourished in Mexico. Through progressive movements in government, the folk arts began to receive institutional support, while a new, government-sponsored public murals program brought artists Diego Rivera, José Clemente Orozco, and David Alfaro Siqueiros to a greater public and international fame. American photographer Edward Weston spent extensive time living and working in Mexico, not long before Manuel Álvarez Bravo began photographing nationalistic scenes in Mexico, rising to international prominence. A fixture in Mexico City's political circles, Frida Kahlo was another expressive oil painter of the post-revolutionary era; she became internationally renowned for a series of powerful self-portraits.

Today, Mexico has a vibrant and flourishing contemporary art scene. Collectors have also been important in stimulating Mexico's art scene, particularly Eugenio López Alonso, the owner of the Colección Jumex, a vast and important collection of Latin American and contemporary art.

# Essentials

Getting There .......... 330
Getting Around ........ 334
Visas and Officialdom .. 342
Conduct
 and Customs ........ 346
Health and Safety ...... 349
Travel Tips ............. 354
Information
 and Services ......... 356

## Getting There

### AIR
**Aeropuerto Internacional Benito Juárez de la Ciudad de México (AICM)**

**The Aeropuerto Internacional Benito Juárez de la Ciudad de México** (MEX; tel. 55/2482-2424 or 55/2482-2400; www.aicm.com.mx), abbreviated as AICM, is on the east side of the city near Lake Texcoco. Both domestic and international flights arrive and depart from

the two main wings, Terminal 1 and Terminal 2, each used exclusively by different airlines. The terminals are about 3 km (1.8 mi) apart and not connected by walkways. A light-rail track connects the terminals in case you end up on the incorrect side of the airport, though you must have a boarding pass to be allowed to board the train; buses also run between the terminals, and they are open to everyone. Before leaving for the airport, check with your carrier to see which terminal your airline operates from.

Though it rarely gets much attention, inside the Sala B in Terminal 1, there is a mural by Mexican artist Juan O'Gorman illustrating the history of flight, from a Mexica nobleman eyeing the wings of a bat with curiosity to the Wright brothers and Charles Lindbergh.

## Aeropuerto Internacional Felipe Ángeles (AIFA)

In 2022, President Andrés Manuel López Obrador inaugurated the new **Aeropuerto Internacional Felipe Ángeles** (NLU; https://aifa.aero), abbreviated as AIFA, 20 km (12 mi) from the city center in the community of Santa Lucía in the state of Mexico, with the intent to reduce the congestion at AICM, which has long been running at maximum capacity. At press time, Mexican carriers Volaris, Viva, and Aeroméxico operate many domestic flights out of the airport, as well as a couple of flights to destinations in Texas. A planned light-rail line connecting AIFA to Mexico City's central districts should boost the popularity of the new facility; in the meantime, there are buses departing from central Mexico City to the airport throughout the day (check the website for details).

## Getting To and From Aeropuerto Internacional Benito Juárez
### Taxi and Uber

Registered taxis operate from the airport, with service 24 hours daily year-round. Official airport taxis are more expensive than regular cabs, but they are the only legal taxi option; nonairport taxis are not allowed to pick up passengers within the terminals. Uber can also pick up and drop off from both airport terminals.

There are several registered taxi companies, operating in both Terminal 1 and Terminal 2, that offer flat-rate prices to destinations throughout the city. There is little difference between one airport taxi company and another. You must buy a ticket from one of the booths inside the airport terminal, then take your ticket curbside to the queue of waiting taxis, where attendants will take you to a car and help you load your luggage

**Previous:** Torre Latinoamericana.

(it's customary to offer a small tip to the porters).

Generally, taxis cost about US$15-20 to most central neighborhoods and several dollars more if heading south to Coyoacán or San Ángel.

### Metro and Metrobús

If you're arriving in Mexico City between 6am and midnight and don't have a lot of baggage, you can take the Metro into town from the Terminal Aéreo station on Line 5. The station is just outside Terminal 1, on the Boulevard Puerto Aéreo, at the corner of Avenida Capitán Carlos León González. Follow the signs for the Metro out of the airport; they look like a stylized letter *M*.

The Metrobús also connects to the airport via an extension of Line 4. There are stops for the Metrobús heading into the city center at door 7 in Terminal 1 and at door 2 in Terminal 2. The first major hub on Metrobús Line 4 is the San Lázaro station, which connects to the Terminal Central del Norte bus station, as well as to the Metro. You can also continue on Line 4 to the Buenavista train terminal, which offers connecting service to the Metro, to Metrobús Line 1, or to the suburban trains to the state of Mexico. Metrobús operates roughly 5am-midnight daily.

### Intercity Bus

Several bus companies offer direct routes from the airport to the nearby cities of Toluca, Pachuca, Puebla, Cuernavaca, and Querétaro. They depart from the international wing of Terminal 1 and from the ground floor of Terminal 2. Follow the signs to the ticket counters. Most buses run every half hour or hour throughout the day, with more limited but continuing service at night. Rates and schedules are available on the airport's website (www.aicm.com.mx).

### Driving

The airport is just off the eastern side of the Circuito Interior, an intercity highway that is easily accessible from most major neighborhoods in the center, west, and south of the city. The exits for the airport are clearly marked, but follow signs to make it to the correct terminal. There are parking lots in the domestic and international wings of Terminal 1 and in Terminal 2, with rates of about US$4 per hour and US$25 for 24 hours.

## BUS

For both visitors and Mexicans, buses are the most popular and economical way to travel around Mexico. Dozens of private companies offer service to almost every corner of the country, with literally hundreds of buses leaving from and arriving in Mexico City every hour.

Unless you are going a very short distance, first-class or executive-class bus service is generally faster and more comfortable than second-class service. First-class buses have bigger seats, fewer stops, and in-cabin restrooms—some even offer snacks and drinks for the ride. Second-class buses are 20-40 percent cheaper than first-class buses, and they are generally comfortable and safe. The disadvantage of second-class buses is that they rarely offer direct service between two cities. Instead, they stop at rural towns along their route to pick up and drop off passengers, adding considerably to travel time.

That said, second-class buses can be more convenient for shorter trips, with many bus lines offering frequent and inexpensive service between neighboring towns. In some cases, they are the only option.

## Intercity Bus Stations

There are four major bus terminals in Mexico City, located at the four major exits from the city. Each is accessible by Metro, and some by Metrobús.

For northern destinations, including Querétaro, San Miguel de Allende, Guanajuato, Zacatecas, Chihuahua, Monterrey, and Tijuana, buses depart from the **Terminal Central del Norte** (Eje Central Lázaro Cárdenas 4907). The Terminal Central del Norte is accessible via the Autobuses del Norte station on Metro Line 5.

**Terminal Central Sur Taxqueña** (Av. Taxqueña 1320) is a smaller station serving southern destinations, like Cuernavaca, Acapulco, and Taxco, accessible via Metro Line 2 Tasqueña station. Taxqueña also connects to the Tren Ligero (light rail) to the southern neighborhoods of the city.

**Terminal de Autobuses de Pasajeros de Oriente,** better known as TAPO (Calzada Ignacio Zaragoza 200), offers service to eastern and southeastern cities like Oaxaca and Puebla. To get there, take Metro Line 1 or Metrobús Line 4 to the San Lázaro station.

**Terminal Centro Poniente** (Av. Sur 122) has departures to Toluca, Valle de Bravo, Morelia, Guadalajara, and Puerto Vallarta and is connected to the Observatorio Metro station on Line 1.

When you are arriving by bus, all stations have authorized taxi services operating in the terminal, with fixed rates to different neighborhoods in the city. Only authorized taxis are legally permitted to pick up passengers at a bus station; however, you can get an Uber from any bus terminal if you leave the station and walk out to the curb (often, if you can't locate your car, the driver will call or text you to coordinate).

## Booking Bus Tickets

For trips to major nearby cities such as Puebla, Toluca, or Cuernavaca, buses depart from Mexico City every 20-30 minutes throughout the day, so it's generally unnecessary to make advance reservations for travel. If you are going to destinations with less frequent service or are traveling during the holidays, it's best to get your ticket beforehand.

It is usually easiest to book bus

tickets online, but you can also buy tickets at **OXXO convenience stores** (www.oxxo.com), which has thousands of locations throughout the city. OXXO represents dozens of bus lines, including Primera Plus, ETN, Turistar, Futura, Chihuahuenses, Costa Line, Transportes del Norte, and TAP. The store charges a small commission, payments must be made in cash, and the ticket is nonrefundable—although, in most cases, the tickets are transferrable if you change your departure beforehand.

You can also purchase bus tickets in advance online or by phone. Contact **ADO** (tel. 55/5784-4652; www.ado.com.mx) for Oaxaca, Puebla, Chiapas, Veracruz, Yucatán, and other southern destinations. **Autobuses Pullman de Morelos** (tel. 800/022-8000; www.pullman.mx) runs buses to Cuernavaca and Acapulco. For northern destinations, including Guadalajara, San Miguel de Allende, Guanajuato, Zacatecas, Puerto Vallarta, and more, use **ETN** (tel. 800/800-0386; www.etn.com.mx) or **Primera Plus** (tel. 800/375-7587; www.primeraplus.com.mx).

# Getting Around

Depending on where you're going, there are ample transport options, including buses, microbuses, taxis, Uber, Metro, Metrobús, and light-rail. Getting around Mexico City on public transportation is cheap, efficient, and generally safe. Within each neighborhood, walking is the best way to see everything.

## TARJETA DE MOVILIDAD INTEGRADA (INTEGRATED MOBILITY CARDS)

Since 2019, Mexico City has been working toward consolidating the payment systems for public transportation under the tarjeta de movilidad integrada (integrated mobility card), a reusable and rechargeable plastic "smart card" that is accepted on the Metrobús, Metro, Tren Ligero, Trólebus, and for 1-, 3-, and 7-day Ecobici passes, among other city-run transport systems. Though the program is still being rolled out, eventually it will be the only way to access public transportation in the city.

A tarjeta de movilidad integrada can be purchased at all Metrobús and Metro stations, and costs about US$1. They can be recharged (called a recarga) with anywhere from US$1-30 in credit for rides. The machines accept cash and credit cards, including foreign credit cards, but don't give change.

The tarjeta de movilidad integrada is currently required to ride the Metrobús as well as Lines 1 and 12 of the Metro. At press time, you could still buy individual tickets for a ride at in-station taquillas (ticket counters) on other Metro lines.

## METRO

Mexico City's extensive underground **Metro system** (https://metro.cdmx.gob.mx) is a reliable, ultra-cheap, and safe way to travel both short and long distances. Almost all of the city's central districts have at least one Metro stop in the vicinity, and daytime service on most lines is frequent, with one train arriving minutes after another has departed the station.

Mexico City's Metro is incredibly easy to use. The system's 12 color-coded lines run in a web across the city, intersecting at key points, with each stop marked by a visual icon as well as a name. The direction of the train is indicated by the final station on the line. In the station, signs marked "Correspondencia" indicate the walking route to transfer train lines; to know where to go, look for the name of the final station in the direction you are going.

### Tickets and Hours

At a cost of about US$0.25 per ticket, it is the most inexpensive major urban subway in the world, and the second-busiest, after Tokyo. Transfers between trains are free. Magnetized paper tickets are currently being phased out in favor of the tarjeta de movilidad integrada, which is accepted at all stations. Though the intention is to eliminate paper tickets eventually, most stations still have ticket counters where you can buy a single Metro ride.

The Metro runs 5am-midnight Monday-Friday, 6am-midnight Saturday, and 7am-midnight Sunday.

### Peak Hours and Rain

Riding the Metro can be considerably more difficult when the trains are full. Peak hours vary by line, but most tend to get shockingly crowded at centrally located stations at the beginning and the end of the workday. Sometimes it can be close to impossible to board, and the crowds of waiting passengers on the platform simply watch a series of full-to-the-brim trains pass by. In general, riding the Metro is particularly challenging during the 7am-9am weekday morning rush hour, and in the evenings 5:30pm-7:30pm. Rainstorms can also lead to an overcrowded Metro any time of day.

### Customs and Safety

Unfortunately, getting on and off a train is a bit of a free-for-all, especially during rush hour. Riders are not known for their courtesy when boarding crowded cars, so you need to be proactive if you want to exit. Pickpockets are also not unknown on the Metro, particularly at busy stations. When riding the Metro, keep purses, backpacks, and cameras close to you, and be aware of anything valuable in your pockets, especially when boarding a train or when standing in a crowded car.

There has been a very active pickpocketing ring working at the Pino Suárez Metro stop. Despite word-of-mouth reports and published newspaper stories exploring the problem, the police have been unable to stop the crime.

## Women's Cars

Women traveling alone, both foreign and Mexican, may receive unwanted attention on the Metro. Particularly disturbing, some women are groped on crowded subway cars. To avoid these problems, there are train cars specially designated for women and children under 14 only, generally located at the front of the train.

# METROBÚS

**Metrobús** (www.metrobus.cdmx.gob.mx) is a high-speed bus service that runs on dedicated lanes along major city avenues. For destinations along Insurgentes, including Roma, Condesa, San Ángel, and UNAM, as well as destinations along the Paseo de la Reforma, including the Museo de Antropología and Chapultepec, the Metrobús can be a far more pleasant and convenient option than the Metro.

## Tickets and Hours

You must purchase a tarjeta de movilidad integrada to ride the Metrobús. Cards can be purchased and recharged in any station. The Metrobús runs 4:30am-midnight Monday-Saturday and 5am-midnight Sunday. A single ride is US$0.30.

## Choosing Your Route

Similar to the Metro, the Metrobús runs along color-coded lines, with each stop marked by a visual icon as well as a name. Unlike the Metro, Metrobús routes vary along the same avenue, with buses stopping at different end points and transfer points. For example, on Line 1 along Insurgentes, there are 6 different routes, with some buses running the full route of 46 stations between Indios Verdes and El Caminero, while others stop earlier (at Buenavista, for example) or connect to Line 2 via Tepalcates. There are maps (and police officers) in every station to help you plan your trip. Before boarding, check the final destination of the bus above the windshield to make sure you're on the right bus.

## Peak Hours

Like the Metro, the Metrobús can become intolerably packed during peak hours. Though it is slightly less hectic than the belowground free-for-all, it is nonetheless more comfortable to avoid the Metrobús 7am-9am and 5:30pm-7:30pm.

## Women's Cars

The first car on all Metrobús units is designated for women and children under the age of 14.

# LIGHT RAIL

Some outlying neighborhoods in the north and south are serviced by light-rail lines. In the south, the **Tren Ligero** (www.ste.cdmx.gob.mx) departs from the Tasqueña

Metro station, running to destinations including Estadio Azteca, Huichapan, and Xochimilco 5am-midnight Monday-Friday, 6am-midnight Saturday, and 7am-midnight Sunday; the last trains depart at 11:30pm.

The **Ferrocarril Suburbano de la Zona Metropolitana** (Estación Terminal Buenavista, Av. Insurgentes Norte and Eje 1 Norte; tel. 55/1946-0790) offers frequent passenger train service to the Valley of Mexico, to points between Cuautitlán and the Buenavista train terminal, located at Avenida Insurgentes Norte in Colonia Buenavista (and accessible via Metro Buenavista).

## TAXI

There are three types of taxis in Mexico City: taxis libres, which are hailed on the street; sitio taxis, which are based at a fixed station and can be either called or picked up from their home base; and radio taxis, reached by telephone. By law, all taxis (except for private car services, which sometimes operate from high-end hotels) are equipped with taxímetros (taximeters).

### Taxis Libres

Metered taxis libres roam the streets picking up passengers. Most are painted white and pink, per city regulation, though you'll still see some red-and-gold (the previous color scheme) sedans circulating as well. Taxis hailed on the street in Mexico City have a shaky reputation, with reason. Though not particularly common, taxis libres have been involved in armed muggings and kidnapping of both foreigners and locals. In almost any circumstance, it is better to take a registered taxi, either a sitio or a radio taxi.

In the case that you do take a street taxi, check that the driver has a taximeter and tarjetón (identification card) in the window with a license number, keep the window rolled up and doors locked, and give clear directional instructions to the driver. Be sure the driver turns on the meter as soon as you start driving.

Street taxis charge US$0.80 (about 9 pesos) as a base rate, then about a peso per 250 m or 45 seconds—roughly US$0.40 per km (US$0.64 per mi). After 11pm and until 6am, taxis are legally allowed to charge an additional 20 percent on the fare.

### Sitio, Radio, and Hotel Taxis

Safer alternatives to street cabs are the city's sitio (pronounced SEE-tee-yoh) taxis and radio taxis, which operate with a fleet of registered drivers. You'll find sitios all over the city, except in the Centro Histórico, though their prevalence has waned considerably since the introduction of ride-hailing services like Uber.

Sitios often have a curbside kiosk nearby where dispatchers log the taxis in and out, though some do not. Sitios are legally allowed to charge a slightly higher price than libres, with a base fare of about US$1.50 and an additional US$0.50 per km (US$0.80 per mi). There are sitios at all four major bus terminals in Mexico City, as well as a number of sitios operating at Benito Juárez International Airport. Radio-dispatched sitios, or radio taxis, reached by telephone, with service to and from anywhere in the city, are considered the safest way to travel. Radio taxis charge a base rate of about US$2.50 and about US$0.60 per km (US$1 per mi) or 45 seconds. A few good options for citywide travel are Radio Union, with one base of operations at Colima and Avenida Cuauhtémoc in the Roma Norte (tel. 55/5514-7709), and Taxi Mex (tel. 55/7059-9854; www.taximex.com.mx), also with a kiosk in the Roma Norte on Colima and Avenida Oaxaca.

In addition to city-licensed taxis, most hotels work with private car services; these are the most expensive cabs by far, usually charging a flat rate between destinations, though they are safe and can be very comfortable. The cars are usually unmarked four-door sedans, and the drivers often speak some English. Some are licensed tour guides as well, who will offer a flat rate for a day trip to places like Teotihuacán or Xochimilco with tour services included.

## RIDE-HAILING SERVICES

**Uber** (www.uber.com) operates in Mexico City, and is generally a safe, pleasant, and inexpensive way to get around. Uber charges a flat rate between destinations and often arrives within minutes. In order to use the service, you need to use the Uber app on your phone, which is connected to a credit card. Download it, and make sure you have roaming capabilities on your phone.

## BUS

In addition to the Metro and Metrobús, there are several types of buses in the city, from large city buses to smaller microbuses called peseros. In general, visitors to the city will not need to use regular city buses to reach destinations in the central districts, but they can sometimes come in handy if you are traveling to destinations in greater Mexico City.

To find the right bus for your destination, start by looking at the placards posted in the front window. Usually, only the end of the route is listed (along with, in some cases, major destinations along the way), so you most likely will have to ask drivers where they stop. At the end of each Metro line, huge corrals of peseros and smaller VW bus combis depart for destinations around the edge of the city.

## CAR

Driving in Mexico City can be a challenge at first, particularly because of the city's size and circuitous topography. Not to mention, maddening traffic jams can halt your progress for hours on end.

Fortunately, chilangos, though perhaps a little heavy-footed on the gas, aren't particularly reckless drivers. Armored cars, city buses, and taxis can occasionally be aggressive (practice defensive driving!), but those who have driven in other large chaotic cities will find Mexico City negotiable with the proper maps or GPS navigator in tow.

If driving, choose your hours carefully. Mornings (8am-10am) can be very congested, while midday traffic is usually reasonable until around 4pm. During the week, late afternoon and early evening are the worst, particularly on the main commuter routes in and out of the city and in the Centro. Traffic begins to dissipate around 9pm or earlier in the city center. The worst traffic of all occurs on Friday afternoon, and even worse still if it's a viernes quincena, a Friday that coincides with the twice-monthly payday. Unpredictable demonstrations in various parts of the city—but particularly on Paseo de la Reforma, on Paseo Bucareli, and in the city center—also regularly tie up traffic, as does the weekly closing of Paseo de la Reforma on Sunday for cyclists.

## Navigation

As might be expected, learning your way around an urban area of several million inhabitants can be a bit confusing, but being familiar with a couple of major avenues can help you stay oriented. Avenida Insurgentes is the longest boulevard in the city and a major north-south route crossing Mexico City. To the northeast, Insurgentes takes you to the exit for Pachuca and Teotihuacán, while to the south it continues past San Ángel to UNAM and the exit to Cuernavaca and Acapulco. Paseo de la Reforma is a broad avenue punctuated by large traffic circles (called glorietas) running northeast-southwest from the exit to Toluca to the Basílica de Santa María de Guadalupe.

The city is circled by two ring highways, the inner Circuito Interior and the outer Periférico. The Circuito makes a complete loop, although it changes names (including Río Churubusco, Patriotismo/Revolución, and Circuito Interior) along the way. There are no freeways passing through the center of town, so the city has developed a system of ejes viales (axes), major thoroughfares that cross the city, with traffic lights somewhat timed, either east-west or north-south. Ejes are numbered and given a reference of norte (north), sur (south), oriente (east), or poniente (west). Other important roads that are not technically ejes are the east-west Viaducto Miguel Alemán and the south-to-center Avenida Tlalpan, both of which are major two-way arteries.

In addition to a good GPS system, the best tool for drivers is the *Guía Roji*, a bright red book of maps and indexes of the city. It can be found in Sanborns department stores, as well as at many street corner newsstands, for about US$20.

## Hoy No Circula

Mexico City's Hoy No Circula (No Circulation Today) program has made strides in reducing automobile emissions in the Valley of Mexico. All 16 boroughs in the capital and 18 municipalities in Mexico state participate in the program, which prohibits cars from driving on certain days of the week, based on the last letter of their license plate. Foreign-registered cars are not exempt from the program, nor are cars from other states of the republic. Failure to comply can result in hefty fines and often towing and impoundment of your car. Even for foreigners, there is no opportunity to claim ignorance; every driver has the responsibility to comply with the restrictions.

The rules are subject to change, and may be extended in the case of heavy air pollution. Be sure to check www.sedema.cdmx.gob.mx for updated information.

The schedule is as follows for license plates registered in Mexico City or the state of Mexico. Driving is prohibited 5am-10pm for cars with the following license plates:

- **Monday:** No driving if the final digit is 5 or 6, yellow sticker.
- **Tuesday:** No driving if the final digit is 7 or 8, pink sticker.
- **Wednesday:** No driving if the final digit is 3 or 4, red sticker.
- **Thursday:** No driving if the

Bucarelli Fountain in a traffic circle on the Paseo de la Reforma

final digit is 1 or 2, green sticker.
- **Friday:** No driving if the final digit is 9 or 0, and those with letters only or temporary plates, blue sticker.
- **Saturday:** On the 1st and 3rd Saturday of the month, no driving for cars with hologram 1 if the final digit is 1, 3, 5, 7, or 9. On the 2nd and 4th Saturday of the month, no driving for cars with hologram 1 if the final digit is 0, 2, 4, 6, or 8. Cars with hologram 2 are not permitted to drive on any Saturday.
- **Sunday:** In most cases, all vehicles may drive. Check www.sedema.df.gob.mx for updated information.

Local cars are required to have a decal bearing a 0, 1, or 2. A 0 or 00 means the car is exempt from any days off, regardless of the license number, because it has passed emissions tests. A 1 hologram requires the car to not circulate on one day, regardless of the conditions; and a 2 means the car cannot circulate on two days of the week.

For **cars with foreign plates,** or for cars registered in states other than the state of Mexico or Mexico City, there are additional restrictions. The rules are as follows:

- No driving on one weekday, as corresponds to the final number on your license plate (as listed above).
- No driving 5am-10pm on any Saturday.
- No driving 5am-11am Monday-Friday.

Foreign-registered cars are not required to have decals, though like local cars, they may apply for exemption from the Hoy No Circula rules by passing emissions tests and receiving a "0" or "00" hologram from Centros de Verificación (Verification Centers) run by the Secretaría del Medio Ambiente del Gobierno (the Environment Secretariat).

On rare occasions, such as for Christmas holidays, cars from outside Mexico City may be exempt from the circulation rules. Other times, when pollution levels are high, additional restrictions may be added to the program. Full schedules and rules are available (in Spanish) at the Environmental Secretariat's website: www.sedema.df.gob.mx.

## Officials

Traffic cops, or transitos, respond to traffic accidents and issue citations for moving violations. When you're driving in Mexico, the transit cops may stop you. However, if your car is in Mexico legally, the papers are in order, and you haven't broken the law, it should be a fairly easy interaction. If you did break the traffic rules in some way, you will be issued a citation and fine, which you will pay in the transit office.

Another official service on the streets of the city is Apoyo Vial (Road Support), men and women in bright yellow uniforms driving motor scooters. Funded jointly by the city and federal governments, Apoyo Vial helps out with emergency breakdowns, traffic accidents, and directing traffic in congested areas. Their services are free.

## Car Rentals

There are many car rental offices throughout the city and in the airport, as well as in the lobbies of some of the bigger hotels. In general, rental car prices are much more expensive in Mexico than in the United States. Mandatory insurance packages (which you are required to buy when you go to pick up the keys, even if they don't appear in an online booking) can triple the price of the rental. All told, a small car with unlimited mileage will run US$50-80 a day, sometimes less if you shop around. International companies operating in Mexico include **Avis** (www.avis.com.mx), **Budget** (www.budget.com.mx), and **Dollar** (www.dollarmexico.com.mx).

Some local rental companies offer cars at lower prices than the international agencies. A good option is **Casanova Renta de Automoviles** (Patriotismo 735, Col. Mixcoac; tel. 55/5563-7606 or 800/227-2668; www.casanovarent.com.mx; 8am-6pm Mon.-Fri., 8am-1:30pm Sat.), offering no-frills cars for 20-30 percent cheaper than big car rental companies. Be sure to reserve ahead of time, as their good prices mean that they often sell out of options, and be sure to check with them about requirements to rent, which may include a proof of residence in Mexico City.

# Visas and Officialdom

## TOURIST PERMITS AND VISAS

Immigration paperwork is fairly straightforward for residents of most countries, whether they are planning a short-term or long-term stay in Mexico. For more detailed information, visit the website of the **Secretaría de Relaciones Exteriores** (www.sre.gob.mx/en) or the **Instituto Nacional de Migración** (www.inm.gob.mx).

### Entry Requirements

No advance permission or visa for travel to Mexico is required for the citizens of about 40 countries, including the United States, Canada, most of Europe and Latin America, New Zealand, and Australia. Citizens of these countries need only a valid passport to enter Mexico. A **tourist permit** will be issued to visitors of these countries at the point of entry.

### Tourist Permits

Visitors who do not require a visa to visit Mexico are granted a six month travel permit, officially known as the forma migratoria multiple (FMM) but unofficially referred to as a "tourist card," at the airport or border. Mexico is currently phasing out paper FMMs. If arriving by air, you will receive a stamp in your passport with the number of days you're allowed or be directed to the self-service kiosks, where you will be issued an FMM form electronically. If driving, stop at the immigration office at the border to get a paper tourist card. No matter how you enter, you must present a valid FMM at departure.

Tourists are allowed to remain in Mexico without a visa for 180 days annually. In most cases, you will receive the full 180 days when you enter (and you can request the full amount of time, if you need it). If you get fewer than 180 days and need to extend your time, you can do so free of charge at any immigration office.

If you lose your tourist card while you are in Mexico, you can report it at an immigration office and pay a fine to replace it, or you can wait and pay the fine at the airport. If you choose to do the latter, leave ample extra time to check in and visit immigration before your flight.

### Children Traveling Alone

Children under the age of 18 entering Mexico unaccompanied by either parent must present a letter translated into Spanish and notarized by a Mexican embassy or consulate that gives the consent of both parents for the trip. The letter should include the dates of travel, the reason for the trip, airline information, and the name of the child's official guardian. The US State Department further recommends that unaccompanied minors travel with a copy of their birth certificate or other documents that prove their relationship. In cases of divorce, separation, or death, the minor should carry notarized papers documenting the situation.

Rules regarding minors were originally established to help combat human trafficking and are therefore rather strict. Current information on minors traveling to Mexico can be obtained from the Mexican Embassy (http://embamex.sre.gob.mx/eua) in the United States.

### Tourist Visas

If you do not live in one of the 40 countries exempt from visa requirements, it is necessary to apply for a tourist visa in advance of arrival in Mexico. If you apply in person at a Mexican consulate, you can usually obtain a tourist visa on the day of application, although for some countries it can take a couple of weeks. Legal permanent residents of the United States, regardless of nationality, do not need visas to visit Mexico for tourism.

### Business Visas

Citizens of USMCA (United States-Mexico-Canada Agreement)

partners are not required to obtain a visa to visit Mexico for business purposes. Business travelers must solicit a business permit, or FMM, at the point of entry; it's valid for 30 days. To ratify your FMM, you must present proof of nationality (a valid passport or original birth certificate, plus a photo identification or voter registration card) and proof that you are traveling for "international business activities," usually interpreted to mean a letter from the company you represent, even if it's your own enterprise. Those who arrive with the FMM and wish to stay over the authorized period of 30 days must replace their FMM with a temporary resident visa form at an immigration office in Mexico.

Citizens of non-USMCA countries who are visiting for business purposes must obtain an FM3 visa endorsed for business travel, which is valid for one year. Visitors to Mexico coming as part of human rights delegations, as aid workers, or as international observers should check with a Mexican embassy about current regulations.

## Overstays

If you overstay your visa, the usual penalty is a fine of about US$50 for overstays up to a month. After that the penalties become more severe. When crossing a land border, it's rare that a Mexican border official asks to see your FMM or visa. Regardless, the best policy is to stay up to date with your visa.

## Nonimmigrant Visas (Residente Temporal)

Far and away the most popular visa option for foreign residents of Mexico is the residente temporal, or temporary resident visa. There are several categories, but all of them classify holders as nonimmigrant residents of Mexico. These are the type of visa issued to most retirees, employees, and business owners. The benefit is that it allows you to come and go from Mexico as you please, and there is no minimum residency requirement.

You must apply for a visa at the Mexican consulate in your home country. The applicant must submit a proof of citizenship (passport), proof of residence, three months of bank statements, a proof of income, and five color photos measuring 2.3 by 3 cm (0.3 by 1.2 in), three of the photos looking directly at the camera and two in profile.

## Student Visas

Students who will be in Mexico for fewer than six months can use a tourist visa for the length of their stay. No special visa is required. Those planning to study in Mexico for a longer period of time may need to apply for a student visa, which is a variation of the temporary resident visa (application procedures are roughly analogous).

# CUSTOMS
## Basic Allowances

Customs, or aduana, allows visitors to Mexico to enter the country with personal items needed for their trip, as well as duty-free gifts valued at no more than US$500. Personal effects may include two photographic or video cameras and up to 12 rolls of film, up to three cellular phones, and one laptop computer. The full list of permitted items is available at the Customs Administration, or **La Administración General de Aduanas** (www.aduanas.gob.mx). Most animal-derived food products are not permitted, including homemade foods, pet food or dog treats, fresh or canned meat, soil, or hay. Other food products are permitted.

If you are arriving by air, you will be given a customs declaration form on the airplane and will pass through the customs checkpoint right after immigration. Here, luggage is often passed through an X-ray machine, and passengers may be detained if a possible contraband item is detected. Random inspections may also take place.

There are severe penalties for carrying firearms into Mexico. Also note that narcotics are heavily regulated in Mexico, so if you have a prescription for painkillers or other controlled substances, carry what you'll need for personal use, along with an official note from your doctor. Sudafed and all pseudoephedrine-based decongestants are illegal in Mexico, so leave those at home.

Customs regulations can change at any time, so if you want to verify the regulations on a purchase before risking duties or confiscation at the border, check with a consulate in Mexico before crossing, or check on the customs website (in Spanish): www.aduanas.sat.gob.mx.

## Pets

Mexico, the United States, and Canada share land borders, and therefore, as long as a cat or dog is in good health, there are no quarantine requirements between those countries. If you are bringing a cat or dog to Mexico, the animal must be accompanied by a certificate of health, issued by a licensed international veterinarian no more than 10 days before arrival in Mexico, and proof of a current rabies vaccination. Further, rabies vaccinations must be issued at least 15 days before entry but can be no more than a year old. If you're not coming from the United States or Canada, you must also present proof that the animal has been treated for worms and parasites. Bring a copy of your pet's vaccination record; customs officials may request it. If your pet does not meet health standards, it may be detained at the airport.

## EMBASSIES AND CONSULATES

Most foreign embassies are located near the city center, with the majority of embassies concentrated in the Polanco and Cuauhtémoc neighborhoods, including the **United States Embassy** (Paseo de la Reforma 305, Col. Cuauhtémoc; tel. 55/5080-2000; http://mexico.usembassy.gov), the **Canadian Embassy** (Schiller 529, Col. Bosque de Chapultepec; tel. 55/5724-7900; www.canadainternational.gc.ca), the **Australian Embassy** (Ruben Dario 55, Col. Polanco; tel. 55/1101-2200; www.mexico.embassy.gov.au), and the **British Embassy** (Río Lerma 71, Col. Cuauhtémoc; tel. 55/1670-3200; www.gov.uk/government/world/mexico). If you have trouble with the law while you are in Mexico or your citizenship papers have been lost or stolen, you should contact your embassy right away.

## POLICE

Officers in blue fatigues patrolling streets or parks are a part of the Protección Civil (Civil Protection), the local police force. In Mexico City, they are generally around to keep the peace in public spaces, as well as to respond to emergencies, break-ins, or other complaints. The police officers stationed in the Centro Histórico or along the Paseo de la Reforma are generally happy to answer questions or give directions to tourists as well.

# Conduct and Customs

## BUSINESS AND ETIQUETTE
### Terms of Address

Mexicans are generally polite and formal when interacting with people they do not know well. When speaking to an elder or to someone with whom you will have a professional relationship, it is customary to use the formal pronoun usted instead of the informal tú. If you are unsure which pronoun a situation requires, you can always err on the side of caution by using usted with anyone you've just met.

It is also common practice to speak to someone you've just met using a polite title, such as señor for a man, señora for a married or older woman, and señorita for a young woman. When speaking with a professional, Mexicans may also use the person's professional title, such as doctor/doctora (doctor), arquitecto/arquitecta (architect), or ingeniero/ingeniera (engineer).

### Greetings

When greeting someone in Mexico, it is customary to make physical contact, rather than simply saying "hello." A handshake is the most common form of greeting between strangers, though friends will usually greet each other with a single kiss on the cheek. The same gestures are repeated when you say goodbye. When greeting a group of people, it is necessary to greet and shake hands with each person individually, rather than address the group together.

If you need to squeeze past someone on a bus or reach over their shoulder at the market, it is customary to say "con permiso" (with your permission). If you accidentally bump into someone (or do anything else that warrants a mild apology), say "perdón" (sorry).

## Time and Appointments

Mexico has a reputation for running on a slower clock. Certainly, there is less urgency in Mexico, and it is not considered excessively rude to arrive tardy to a social engagement. However, when it comes to doctor's appointments, business meetings, bus schedules, or any other official event, punctuality is just as important in Mexico as it is anywhere else.

## Table Manners

When you are sharing a meal, it is customary to wish other diners "buen provecho" before you start eating. Buen provecho is similar to the well-known French expression bon appétit. If you need to leave a meal early, you should excuse yourself and again wish everyone at the table "buen provecho." As in most countries, when sharing a meal, it is customary to wait for everyone to be served before starting to eat.

## Tipping

In a restaurant, waitstaff receive a tip of 10-20 percent on the bill, though foreigners are generally expected to tip on the higher end of the scale. In bars, a 10 percent tip is standard.

Tips for hotel housekeeping are optional according to Mexican custom—some guests tip, and some don't, and it is less common in budget hotels. However, it is becoming more standard—and it's always appreciated. It is customary to tip porters at an airport or hotel several dollars per bag, or about US$5-10, depending on how far you are going and the size of your load. In nicer hotels, it is necessary to give a higher tip.

Though it is not necessary to tip a taxi driver when traveling within city limits, tips are always graciously welcomed. At gas stations, a small tip of about US$1-4 is customary for gas station attendants (all gas stations are full service in Mexico).

In supermarkets, the baggers generally work for tips and do not receive a salary from the store. Let them bag your groceries, then tip anywhere from US$0.50-2.

## Bargaining

When shopping, it is not common practice to bargain or ask for lower prices on goods in shops and stores in Mexico City. Some vendors may offer a small discount for bulk purchases or for cash payments, but these are offered at the shop owner's discretion. Don't expect employees at a brick-and-mortar store to bargain on prices.

In an artisan or craft market, such as the Mercado de la Ciudadela or the Bazaar Sábado in San Ángel, or at an antiques market like La Lagunilla or the Saturday market on Avenida Cuauhtémoc, prices for goods may be more flexible. It is customary to ask the vendor for the price of the item (they are rarely marked with price tags), and the vendor may then offer you a lower price as you think it over. This is particularly true for large purchases. In general, these discounts are not significant (don't expect to pay half of the price initially quoted) and aggressive haggling is not common, nor is it particularly fruitful. If you do wish to bargain on a price, do so politely.

Do not bargain at food markets, even if you are buying a substantial quantity. Usually, the prices at food markets are low to begin with, and few vendors can afford to drop their prices further.

## Smoking

Smoking tobacco (including electronic cigarettes) is prohibited in restaurants and bars throughout Mexico City. Though many people still smoke, they are required by law to smoke outside (patios, sidewalk seating, and open-air terraces located inside restaurants are all places where smoking is permitted). When the antismoking laws first went into effect, tough fines on establishments violating the policy helped ensure its widespread adoption throughout the city. However, as time passed, many establishments opened open-roofed segments of their restaurants or allowed patrons to smoke near entryways, leading to more lax rules.

## Dress

Mexicans are not particularly concerned with how visitors dress, and the more formal attire that was once common in the capital has become far less prevalent today. The one place where a minor dress code still applies is in Catholic churches: upon entering a church or chapel in Mexico, visitors are expected to remove their hats.

## Business Hours

Standard business hours are 8am-5pm or 6pm Monday-Friday, with lunch breaks taken 1pm-3pm. Banks are usually open 9am-5pm Monday-Friday, though hours may be longer and include Saturday at some branches. Though lunch breaks are common in a corporate environment, many small business owners will work in their shop from morning to night, without so much as a coffee break.

No matter what hours are posted for small businesses, the actual opening and closing times may vary. This is also true for tourist information offices. Banks usually follow their posted hours to the minute.

# Health and Safety

## FOOD AND WATER
### Food Safety
Getting sick from a serious foodborne illness or parasite isn't particularly common in Mexico City, especially if you take some precautions when eating. However, some travelers do experience gastrointestinal distress or diarrhea while visiting Mexico.

Changes in the food you eat and the water you drink, changes in your eating and drinking habits, and a new overall environment can cause unpleasant diarrhea, nausea, and vomiting. Because it often affects Mexico newcomers, gastrointestinal distress is called turista (tourist) in Mexico, and "traveler's diarrhea" in English. In many cases, turista can be effectively treated with a few days of rest, liquids, and antidiarrhea medication, such as Pepto Bismol, Kaopectate, or Imodium.

To avoid turista, eat and drink with moderation, and go easy—at least at first—on snacks offered by outdoor street vendors or market stands, where food is exposed to the elements. It's always a good idea to choose street stands where you see a lot of other clients, which is a good indication of the food's quality. Some people consume street food from all over the city with no incident; others become ill after eating in markets or on the street. Use your discretion.

If the symptoms are unusually severe or persist for more than a few days, see a doctor. It could be a case of amoebic or bacterial dysentery. Most hotels can arrange a doctor's visit.

### Water Quality
Mexican tap water is treated and potable, yet it is generally considered unsafe for drinking, in part because of the unknown condition of most buildings' plumbing and water tanks. Hotels and restaurants serve only purified drinking water and ice. Bottled water, like all bottled beverages, is readily available and safe for drinking; however, since April 2024, all restaurants are required by law to bring you a glass of filtered water if you ask for it, without requiring you to purchase water. You can also make tap water safe for drinking by boiling it for several minutes to kill any bacteria or parasites.

## ALTITUDE SICKNESS
At 2,250 m (7,380 ft), Mexico City is at high elevation. Some visitors experience mild altitude sickness shortly after arrival. Symptoms include headache, shaky stomach, breathlessness, and general malaise. The body needs time to acclimate to the change in barometric pressure and lesser amounts of oxygen, and the air pollution can exacerbate the symptoms. If you feel ill, take it easy for a while: no running, no climbing pyramids, no alcohol.

Some people find it takes two or three days to fully adjust to the elevation when flying in from places at or near sea level.

## DEHYDRATION

At high elevation, it's important to drink plenty of water and other fluids to avoid dehydration. Alcohol and caffeine increase your potential for dehydration. Symptoms of dehydration include darker-than-usual urine or inability to urinate, flushed face, profuse sweating or an unusual lack thereof, and sometimes a headache, dizziness, and general feeling of malaise.

## EARTHQUAKES

Earthquakes are common in Mexico City, and occasionally deadly. In the wake of the massive 1985 quake, building codes were updated and many unsafe structures were demolished. In fact, Mexico has some of the strictest seismic building codes in the world, making most newer buildings very safe, even during big earthquakes. That said, tens of thousands of older structures are not up to code and remain vulnerable to damage or collapse during a quake, as was demonstrated during the devastating 7.1 magnitude earthquake in 2017.

When checking into your hotel or apartment rental, it's a good idea to ask about emergency exits and evacuation plans. In some cases, it is safest to evacuate to the street when you hear the seismic alarm or feel tremors; in other cases it is safer to stay put, especially if you are on the 4th floor or above. If you are outside, stand in the middle of an intersection (you'll likely see many other people gathered there), away from tall buildings.

After the trembling has stopped, go outside until your hotel or building has had a preliminary structural inspection. Do not light cigarettes or candles, even if the power goes out, and remain alert to the smell of gas leaks.

## INFECTIOUS DISEASE

No vaccines are required for travel to Mexico City, though it's always a good idea to be up to date on routine vaccines. Some doctors recommend the hepatitis A vaccine for travel to Mexico. Hepatitis A affects the liver and is contracted from contaminated food or water. Symptoms may resemble the flu, though they are severe and may last several months. Typhoid is also contracted through contaminated food or water, though it's more of a concern in rural areas.

To date, the mosquitoes that carry the Zika virus and the mosquitoes that carry dengue are not found in Mexico City, owing to the city's high altitude and climate.

## COVID-19

At the time of writing in the fall of 2024, Mexico City had mostly stabilized from the effects of the coronavirus pandemic, but the situation is constantly evolving. Now more than ever, Moon encourages

## The Seismic Alarm

Though highly susceptible to earthquakes, Mexico City is not on a fault line. In most cases, earthquakes originate from faults along the Pacific coast, with seismic waves traveling hundreds of miles to reach the capital. As a result, there is often a substantial minute-or-more delay between the time an earthquake begins off the coast and when its tremors can be felt in Mexico City.

Using this delay to its advantage, Mexico City initiated the **Sistema de Alerta Sísmica Mexicano (Mexican Seismic Alert System),** a citywide earthquake warning system, which is linked to a series of seismic sensors along the Pacific coast and in the state of Guerrero. Whenever the sensors detect a tremor of magnitude 6 or higher, a pulsating siren sounds on loudspeakers throughout the city. The siren, though distinctive, can sound a bit like a home or car alarm, so pay attention if you think you hear it. In addition to the siren, a voice repeats the words alerta sísmica (seismic alert). You can listen to the sound of the seismic alarm online to familiarize yourself with it.

Many of Mexico City's residents also use seismic alarm apps on their smartphones, which operate using the same model as the municipal system. You can install these apps on your phone, then modify them to only sound an alarm when earthquakes reach a certain intensity. The most popular options are SkyAlert and Alerta Sísmica DF, both available for iOS and Android.

Though the alarm system is a lifesaving innovation, note that when an earthquake's epicenter is closer to the capital, the alarm system may not sound in time for you to safely evacuate your building. On September 19, 2017, most of the capital's residents only heard the alarm after the ground had already begun to shake.

---

readers to be courteous and ethical in their travel. Get vaccinated if your health allows, make an effort to follow all Mexican health protocols and customs, and if possible, test regularly before, during, and after your trip.

It is currently not necessary to provide proof of vaccination or a negative COVID test result to enter Mexico. You may still be asked to wear a mask in some establishments, or when riding in a taxi or Uber. Note that passengers traveling to Mexico on Mexican airlines, like Aeroméxico, are required to follow Mexican guidelines for masking while on board, regardless of their country of origin.

**Farmacias de Ahorro** (www.fahorro.com) or **Farmacias San Pablo** (www.farmaciasanpablo.com.mx), both large pharmacy chains, can administer and provide certified results of COVID antigen tests. At-home test kits are generally not available in Mexico.

Facial coverings, including N95 and KN95 masks, are widely available from street vendors and at almost any pharmacy, including the pharmacies listed above.

More information about the current situation, as well as lists of COVID test providers, can be found at the US Embassy in Mexico's website (https://mx.usembassy.gov) or at local consulate sites.

## MEDICAL ASSISTANCE

The quality of basic medical treatment, including dentistry, is high in Mexico City. Large hotels usually have a list of recommended physicians in the neighborhood. Polanco is the best area for private medical clinics, where a consultation will run US$25-60. Another good option is to call the Centro Médico ABC (tel. 55/5230-8000 or 55/5230-8161), which has a referral service for quality doctors of different specializations.

### Emergencies

In case of emergency, dial **911** from any telephone to reach an emergency dispatcher.

### Doctors and Hospitals

**Centro Médico ABC** (Calle Sur 136, No. 116; tel. 55/5230-8000 or 55/5230-8161; https://centromedicoabc.com), at the corner of Avenida Observatorio, south of Bosque de Chapultepec in Colonia Las Américas, is considered one of the best hospitals in the city, and prices are accordingly high.

Another well-regarded hospital is **Hospital Español** (Ejército Nacional 613, Polanco; tel. 55/5255-9600; www.hespanol.com).

## PRESCRIPTIONS AND PHARMACIES

Visitors to Mexico are permitted to carry prescription medication for preexisting conditions among their personal effects. Generally, they can bring no more than a three-month supply of medicine with them, and it should be accompanied by documentation from a doctor. (There can be strict penalties, including incarceration, for tourists who are suspected of drug abuse.) Most common over-the-counter medication is available in Mexico. Drugs in Mexico are regulated and safe; there are also generic brands.

If you need to purchase prescription medication while you are in Mexico, you can visit a doctor, who will write you a prescription. If you'd like to take your meds home, rules for export depend on your home country.

There are pharmacies, or farmacias, throughout the city. Many are open 24 hours daily. All Sanborns department stores have an in-house pharmacy.

## CRIME CONCERNS

Until the 1980s, Mexico City was known as one of the safest large cities in the Americas. The image suffered a reversal after the economic crisis of 1994-1995, when the peso plummeted, unemployment soared, and robbery and kidnapping became more common. Fortunately, the city has become much safer, and with reasonable precautions, most visitors will feel entirely comfortable throughout their stay.

## Precautions

In most cases, crime in Mexico City is economic—in other words, theft, break-ins, mugging, and pickpocketing are the most common problems. Crime can occur anywhere in Mexico City, even in affluent neighborhoods, but you can reduce the dangers by traveling by day or on well-lit roads, keeping an eye on your wallet and camera in crowded subway cars or busy markets, carrying a cell phone, and always taking registered taxis.

There have been rare but very troubling cases of taxi-related muggings and kidnappings, wherein taxi drivers shuffle unsuspecting passengers down dark side streets, where they are assaulted and robbed. To avoid taxi-related crimes, take registered taxis, called sitios, or get a car with a ride-hailing app like Uber. There are safe, registered taxi stands in the airport, in bus terminals, and in every major neighborhood, and dozens of independent companies that will pick you up anywhere in the city.

After dark, you should be more cautious, especially when walking through unpopulated areas. The Centro Histórico is now patrolled by police officers in the evening, but it is best to stick to the areas to the west of the Zócalo, along the Alameda Central, or near the pedestrian street Regina if you are going out at night. After dark, avoid walking alone through the Doctores, Guerrero, and the areas around Plaza Garibaldi until you are better acquainted with the city. In the Roma, Condesa, and Polanco neighborhoods, there is less crime in the evening, especially in popular areas where crowds of diners and partygoers make the streets safe for walking. Nonetheless, it is wise to be on guard in the evenings, no matter where you are, and to avoid deserted streets or very late hours.

It's a good idea to carry limited cash and credit cards—no more than you need for an outing—when moving about the city, and don't wear ridiculously expensive-looking clothes or jewelry. Keep money and valuables secured, either in a hotel safe or safe deposit box, and lock the doors to your hotel room and vehicle.

When using ATMs as a source of cash, do so during the day or in well-lit, well-trafficked places. One reliable option is to use the Inbursa ATMs located inside Sanborns department stores. In general, don't change too much money at once.

Finally, if confronted by someone intent on robbing you, don't resist. Violence is usually a problem only if you don't cooperate.

# Travel Tips

## STUDYING IN MEXICO
### Spanish Language and Mexican Culture

Mexico City is an excellent place to study Spanish, even if it hasn't traditionally been a popular choice with language learners. One of the major advantages of studying Spanish in Mexico City is having the opportunity to interact with a largely Spanish-speaking population on a daily basis.

One of the best options is the prestigious Universidad Nacional Autónoma de México's **Centro de Enseñanza Para Extranjeros** (Center for Instruction for Foreigners; https://cepe.unam.mx), or CEPE, which offers blocks of intensive introductory, intermediate, and advanced Spanish-language classes, as well as culture and history courses. The programs enjoy a very good reputation and are divided among six departments: Spanish, art history, history, social sciences, literature, and Chicano studies. UNAM also runs special training programs for teachers of Spanish as a Second Language (SSL). For all courses, tuition is reasonable, and CEPE can arrange housing either with local families or in dormitories.

## ACCESS FOR TRAVELERS WITH DISABILITIES

Although the government has made some efforts to improve the situation, Mexico City is not an easy place for travelers with disabilities, particularly people with a limited range of movement. Many of the old colonial-era structures that house hotels, restaurants, and museums do not have ramps or wheelchair access, nor do they have elevators inside the building. Using the Metro system can also be a challenge as not all stations have elevators; check www.metro.cdmx.gob.mx to review facilities at each station.

That said, there have been some positive developments in the city. The newer Metrobús system is a big improvement on the Metro, with ramps leading into all stations, audio-signaled pedestrian crossings, and information printed in Braille. Many public museums and cultural centers have added ramped entrances. With a little advance planning, visitors can also find a number of hotels and restaurants that have made special accommodations for visitors with disabilities.

## TRAVELING WITH CHILDREN

Mexico City is a surprisingly kid-friendly, family-oriented place. There are plenty of great activities for kids in the city, from the wonderful children's museum in Chapultepec park to the colorful Ballet Folklórico performances at the Palacio de Bellas Artes. Most restaurants welcome children, and you will see plenty of other kids touring museums and cultural centers with their parents. A few hotels do not allow children under a certain age, but others are more than happy to accommodate children with foldout beds in the rooms. The Hotel Catedral in the Centro or the Hotel Stanza in the Roma, which adjoins a large playground, don't charge extra for children under age 12, making them an economical choice for families traveling together. Children under age 5 ride for free on the Metrobús.

## WOMEN TRAVELING ALONE

Women traveling alone will generally feel safe and comfortable in Mexico City, though they should take the same safety precautions they would in any large city. Mexico is a social place, and unaccompanied women may be approached by men when dining alone at a restaurant or having a beer in a cantina—or even wandering through a museum. Generally, these interactions will not escalate. In the rare case that you do feel unsafe, look for a nearby police officer or enter a well-lit restaurant or business.

## LGBTQ+ TRAVELERS

LGBTQ+ visitors will find a generally accepting, cosmopolitan environment in the capital. There is a large and visible gay population in the city, with an ever-increasing acceptance of diverse sexuality, gender expression, and queerness. Although many Mexico City residents are still relatively conservative, the attitude throughout the city is definitively one of tolerance; it is not uncommon to see same-sex couples holding hands or kissing in public.

## TRAVELERS OF COLOR

In Mexico City, like all of Mexico, most people are from a mixed-ethnic heritage, predominantly a mix of Spanish and Indigenous American. On the whole, other ethnic groups are in the minority and less visible in Mexico City, especially outside the city's central neighborhoods like the Roma, Condesa, and Centro Histórico.

Mexico City has become increasingly diverse in the past two decades. There has been a notable influx of Indigenous, mixed-race, and Afro-Latino people from Central America. There are large Korean and Japanese communities in the city, as well as a large and multiracial expatriate community from the United States living in the Roma, Condesa, Juárez, Santa María, and other central neighborhoods. South Americans and Europeans also have a long presence in the city. Owing to the increasing diversity, travelers of color will generally not stand out or receive unwanted notice in Mexico City, and most will find the city is a welcoming and friendly place for people of color. That said, Mexico has a long history of racial inequality running all the way back to the conquest and enslavement of the native people by the Spanish. Issues of racial discrimination and prejudice persist, which travelers may or may not witness or experience.

In some cases, Mexican customs and attitudes toward race may differ from what you've experienced in your home country. One noticeable example of this is that terms that would be considered derogatory in the United States are still somewhat commonly used (without derogatory intent) in Mexico—for example, addressing or referring to someone Black or dark-skinned as negrito, and addressing someone who is Asian (of any background) as chinito.

# Information and Services

## MONEY
### Currency

The unit of currency in Mexico is the peso, which comes in paper denominations of 20, 50, 100, 200, and 500. Coins are available in denominations of 50 centavos and 1, 2, 5, 10, and 20 pesos. The $ symbol denotes prices in pesos. While it's highly unlikely you'll ever confuse dollar and peso prices because of the differing values, you should ask when in doubt.

### Paying in Dollars

Restaurants and other commercial establishments in Mexico City may accept US dollars as well as pesos. Note, however, that if you pay in dollars, the vendor determines the exchange rate, which may not always be in your favor.

### Sales Tax

An impuesto al valor agregado (IVA, or value-added tax) of 16 percent is tacked onto all goods and services, including hotel and restaurant bills as well as international phone calls. Hotels may add an additional 2 percent lodging tax. Most budget hotels include the IVA and hotel tax in their quoted prices.

### Changing Money
#### ATMs

The best way to get pesos is with an ATM card; they are accepted in cajeros automático (ATMs) in all Mexican and foreign-owned banks and invariably offer the best and most up-to-the-minute exchange rate. Some charge a rather hefty handling fee, however, so pay attention when clicking through the screens.

When using your ATM card, always choose an official bank (like Banamex, Santander, Scotiabank, Inbursa, Banorte, HSBC, or BBVA Bancomer). Recently, there have been reports that ATM and credit card numbers have been stolen and used for illicit withdrawals in Mexico. If you are dealing with an official bank rather than a stand-alone ATM, it will be easier to get the money credited back to your account in the unfortunate case that your number is used fraudulently.

### Banks

While banks are the best place to withdraw money from an ATM, they will no longer change dollars or other foreign currency into pesos unless you are an account holder. In most cases, you will need to visit a casa de cambio (see below) if you are carrying cash.

### Casas de Cambio

In most cases, the only place to change cash is at a casa de cambio, or private money-changing office. Nowadays, these are far less common as most travelers carry ATM cards, but you can still see them in the airport and in popular tourist neighborhoods like the Centro Histórico, the Zona Rosa, and the Condesa.

If you're going to change money at an exchange house, it pays to shop around for the best rates, as some places charge considerably more than others. The rates are usually posted; compra, always the lower figure, refers to the buying rate (how many pesos you'll receive per dollar or other foreign currency), while vende is the selling rate (how many pesos you must pay to receive a dollar or other unit of foreign currency).

## MAPS AND TOURIST INFORMATION
### Maps

Most tourist-information kiosks offer small foldout maps of the city that point out noteworthy sites. You can pick them up for free at any tourist information booth you see. Google Maps and Waze provide accurate directions in Mexico City.

### Tourist Information

Mexico City has its own tourist office, the **Secretaría de Turismo de la Ciudad de México** (Av. Nuevo León 56, 9th Fl., Col. Condesa; tel. 55/5286-9077; www.turismo.cdmx. gob.mx). For the most part this is an administrative office, so if it's information you need, you're better off visiting one of the several tourist suboffices (módulos de información turística) around the city and at the airport. These small offices usually stock a variety of free brochures, maps, hotel and restaurant lists, and information on local activities.

## TIME, POWER, AND MEASUREMENTS
### Time

Mexico City time coincides with central standard time in the United States in winter and mountain daylight time in summer, six hours ahead of universal time (UTC-6). Since 2022, Mexico does not participate in daylight saving time.

Time in Mexico is commonly expressed according to the 24-hour clock, from 0001 to 2400 (one minute past midnight to midnight).

## Electricity
Mexico's electrical system is the same as that in the United States and Canada: 110 volts, 60 cycles, alternating current (AC). Electrical outlets are of the US type, designed to work with appliances that have standard double-bladed plugs.

## Measurements
Mexico uses the metric system as the official system of weights and measures. This means the distance between Nogales and Mazatlán is measured in kilometers, cheese is weighed in grams or kilograms, a hot day in Monterrey is 32°C, gasoline is sold by the liter, and a big fish is 2-m (3-ft) long.

# COMMUNICATIONS AND MEDIA
## Postal Service
**Correos de Mexico** (www.correos demexico.gob.mx), Mexico's national postal service, is known to be both erratic and slow. It can be reliable, if sluggish, for simple communications, like postcards. However, larger and more valuable items are at risk of loss. If something absolutely must arrive in the hands of the recipient, you should pay more for a private service.

The Mexican post office offers a more reliable express mail service called Mexpost. International rates are relatively high, but it is a good option for mailing communications within Mexico. The most atmospheric place to send a postcard is doubtlessly the grand old **Palacio Postal** (Tacuba 1; 9am-6pm Mon.-Fri.), which also has Mexpost services.

## Courier Services and Shipping Companies
In most cases, you will have better luck shipping packages with private companies. They offer more reliable and faster (though also more expensive) ways to send letters and packages within Mexico and internationally. DHL (https://dhl.com), UPS (www.ups.com), FedEx (www.fedex.com), and Mexican-owned Estafeta (www.estafeta.com) all offer national and international expedited shipping.

The courier **Estafeta Mexicana** (Av. Insurgentes 105-9, Col. Juárez; tel. 55/5511-0206; and Chilpancingo 62, Col. Hipódromo Condesa; tel. 55/5270-8300; www.estafeta.com) is an official agent of the US Postal Service, which makes for reliable lower-priced service to the United States.

Although these companies have branches throughout the city, some convenient locations include **DHL** (Madero 70, Col. Centro; tel. 55/5345-7000; https://dhl.com), **FedEx** (Av. Paseo de la Reforma 296, Col. Juárez; tel. 55/5228-9904; www.fedex.com), and **UPS de México** (Inside PakMail, Patriotismo 8, Condesa; tel. 800/7433-877; www.ups.com).

## Telephone Services
Landlines are becoming increasingly uncommon in Mexico, as many people switch to the relative

ease and lower upfront costs of cellular telephones. If you need to make local calls while you're visiting, many hotels will include calls to Mexico City landlines in the cost of a room. Because much of Mexico's cellular phone service operates on a different system, called El Que Llama Paga (Whoever Calls, Pays), calling a cell phone will incur an additional charge.

### International Calls

To direct-dial an international call via a landline, dial 00 plus the country code, area code, and number. Note that long-distance international calls are heavily taxed and cost more than equivalent international calls from the United States or Canada. Confirm prices with your hotel before dialing internationally.

The cheapest way to make long-distance international calls is via the internet, using Skype or some other service, although most US and Canadian carriers offer economical short-term service for visitors to Mexico.

### Foreign Cell Phones in Mexico

Most cell phone plans offer daily or monthly international service, and some carriers include calling and texting in Mexico in their unlimited plans. If you have an unlocked phone, you can buy a SIM card to use in Mexico. Once you have a Mexican chip, you can buy credit for your phone and make local calls. There are cell phone outlets throughout the city that will be happy to help you get it set up; you can set up a contract or you can have credit charged directly to your phone at the register in OXXO or other convenience stores.

### Email and Internet Access

Today, most hotels, coffee shops, and restaurants offer free wireless internet connections to patrons. If you bring your computer, tablet, or smartphone, you should have no problem connecting it while you are in Mexico City.

If you'd prefer to travel without your laptop, cybercafés are an excellent and inexpensive alternative. Scattered throughout the city, these public computer terminals charge by-the-hour or by-the-minute rates to use the internet on shared computers. It rarely comes to more than a few dollars per hour, and most have printing and scanning services.

## Media

### Newspapers

Among the national Spanish-language dailies, *Reforma* and *El Universal* are the two most popular mainstream papers. *La Jornada* is a highly political, leftist paper beloved by students and intellectuals, while *El Financiero* generally covers business and politics.

### Magazines

In Spanish, *Proceso* (www.proceso.com.mx) is a political magazine known for its crack reporting. Its stories on Mexican politics are often excellent. Two glossy weekly magazines are *Milenio,* which also has good international news stories, and *Cambio.*

For cultural events, nightlife, dining recommendations, fashion, and lifestyle-related stories, pick up a copy of the long-running magazine *Chilango,* sold at most newsstands. *Time Out México* also has excellent cultural listings; copies are free and distributed throughout the city. For more serious coverage of the arts in Mexico, including reviews and criticism, pick up a copy of *La Tempestad* or *Revista Código,* both in Spanish.

*Revista de la Universidad de México* is a must-read for the city's intellectuals, published by UNAM's cultural division.

### International Publications

Newsstands in Mexico tend to be limited to national publications, though most airports and some bookshops will carry a wider range of imported titles like *Vanity Fair, Time, The Economist,* and other general interest magazines. The department-store chain Sanborns has a large newsstand, with dozens of national titles and many English-language titles as well.

### Television

There are six broadcast networks in Mexico, four run by media conglomerate Televisa and two by TV Azteca. Channels run by Televisa and TV Azteca broadcast a mix of morning shows, news programs, sports, and American television series (usually dubbed into Spanish), as well as widely popular telenovelas, or soap operas.

There are two excellent public television channels in Mexico City: the widely viewed Canal Once (Channel 11) and the Mexico City-based Canal 22 (Channel 22). These channels offer special programming on culture, politics, travel, and anthropology, in addition to airing high-quality movies and documentaries. There is also children's programming in the mornings.

### Radio

Mexico City has a long history of excellent radio and boasts hundreds of AM and FM stations. Radio Universidad, 96.1 FM and 860 AM, is run by UNAM and has excellent educational and musical programming. Formato 21 is another good radio station with news 24 hours daily at 790 AM.

# Index

## A
Acapulco: 62 132
accessibility: 354
air travel: 330–331
Alameda Central: 16, 86–111, 93–94; map 88–89
Alameda de Santa María: 120–121
altitude sickness: 349–350
Ángel de la Independencia: 122–123, 124
Antiguo Colegio de San Ildefonso: 61
Antiguo Palacio del Ayuntamiento de Coyoacán: 231
archaeological sites: 64–65, 66–68, 90–91, 279, 280–286, 298
architecture: 182–183, 328–329
Arena Coliseo: 83
Arena México: 108
arts and culture: 79–81, 104–107, 132–134, 158–165, 198–199, 238–242, 255–258, 325
ATMs: *see* money
Autódromo Hermanos Rodríguez: 260
Aztlán Parque Urbano: 167

## B
Ballet Folklórico de México de Amalia Hernández: 94, 107
banks: *see* money
Baños de Moctezuma: 150
Barrio Chino: 95
Basílica de Santa María de Guadalupe: 248
Biblioteca Central: 250
Biblioteca de Arte: 180
Biblioteca Palafoxiana: 290
Biblioteca Vasconcelos: 121
biking: 136, 167–168
Bosque de Chapultepec (Primera Sección and Segunda Sección): 166
Bosque de Chapultepec (Tercera Sección and Cuarta Sección): 166–167
business hours: 19, 190, 262–263
bus travel: 332–334, 338

## C
cafés: 214–215
Calzada de los Muertos (Avenue of the Dead): 281
Canals at Xochimilco: 251
cantinas: 74–75, 77, 101, 127, 131, 195, 196, 216–217, 236
Capilla de la Purísima Concepción: 231–232
Capilla de las Capuchinas: 251–252
Capilla de la Virgen de los Remedios: 298
Capilla del Rosario: 290
Capilla de Santa Catarina: 229
car travel: 338–342
Casa de Cultura Jesús Reyes Heroles: 229
Casa de la Cultura: 290
Casa de la Malinche: 232
Casa de la Primera Imprenta de América: 80
Casa del Lago: 258
Casa del Lago Juan José Arreola: 158–159
Casa Gilardi: 163–164
Casa Guillermo Tovar de Teresa: 199
Casa Lamm: 180
Casa Luis Barragán: 151
Casa Pedregal: 250–251
Casa Wabi: 133
Castillo de Chapultepec and the Museo Nacional de Historia: 149–150
Catedral de la Inmaculada Concepción: 289
Catedral Metropolitana: 65–66
CENART (Centro Nacional de los Artes): 239–240
Cencalli: La Casa del Maíz y la Cultura Alimentaria: 159
Centro Cultural de España: 61, 65
Centro Cultural Digital: 132
Centro Cultural Universitario Tlatelolco: 91
Centro de la Imagen: 107
Centro Histórico: 16, 50–85; map 52–53; neighborhood walk 54–58
Centro SCOP: 208–209
chapulines: 154
Chapultepec and Polanco: 140–171; map 142–143; neighborhood walk 144–147
children, traveling with: 33–37, 354–355
chinicuiles: 155
Ciclotón: 136
cinema: 158, 238, 258, 325
Cineteca Nacional: 158, 238
Cineteca Nacional: 158
Ciudadela (The Citadel): 281
classical music: 107, 199, 239, 242, 258
community centers: 200
Complejo Cultural Los Pinos: 159
concert venues: 158, 255

361

Conjunto Urbano Nonoalco Tlatelolco: 182–183
consulates: *see* embassies
Coyoacán: 17, 220–243; map 222–223; neighborhood walk 224–227
crafts: 326
crime: 352–353
Cuicuilco: 251
cultural centers: 132, 158–159
culture: *see* arts and culture
customs: 344–345
cycling: *see* biking

# D

dance: 107, 199, 239, 242, 258, 327–328
day trips: 278–298; map 280
dehydration: 350
Desfil de Alebrijes Monumentales: 135
Desfile Cívico Militar Revolución Mexicana: 135
Día de la Independencia: 82
Día de Nuestra Señora de Guadalupe: 259–260
Diego Rivera: 60, 68, 104, 255
disabilities, travelers with: 354
disease: 350

# E

earthquakes: 350, 351
economy: 319–320
Edificio Basurto: 182
elotes: 99
embassies: 345–346
environmental issues: 301–303
Equal Bicigratis: 135
escamoles: 155
Espacio Escultórico de la UNAM: 256–257
Estadio Azteca: 261
Estadio Ciudad de los Deportes: 218
Estadio Olímpico: 250
Estadio Olímpico Universitario: 261
etiquette: 346–348
events: *see* festivals and events
Ex-Teresa Arte Actual: 80–81

# F

festivals and events: 24–25, 82–83, 134–135, 259–260
film: *see* cinema
Filmoteca UNAM: 258
Fonoteca Nacional: 238–239
food: 48–49, 98–99, 154–155, 186–187, 294–295; *see also* Restaurants Index, specific place
food safety: 349
Foro Lindbergh: 181
Foro Shakespeare: 199
Foro Valparaíso: 81
Frontón México: 137
Fuerte Loreto: 291
Frida Kahlo: 228, 255

# GH

G.56: 161
Galería de Arte de la SHCP: 79
Galería de Arte Mexicano: 160
Galería Hilario Galguera: 133
Galería OMR: 198
galleries: 79, 132–133, 160–161, 198
government: 318–319
Greater Mexico City: 18, 244–263; map 246–247
guided tours: 21, 24
Hemiciclo de Benito Juárez: 94
history: 304–318
hospitals: 352
Huerto Roma Verde: 200
huitlacoche: 155

# IJK

Iglesia de la Santísima Trinidad: 68
Iglesia de Nuestra Señora de Loreto: 62
Iglesia de San Jacinto: 250
Iglesia de Santiago Tlatelolco: 91–92
Iglesia de Santo Domingo de Guzmán: 290
Instituto Italiano di Cultura: 230
Insurgentes Sur-Narvarte: 204–219; map 206–207
itinerary ideas: 26–47
jai alai: 137
Jaliscience: 251
Jardín Centenario: 231
Jardín Hidalgo and Antiguo Palacio del Ayuntamiento: 231–232
Juárez, Benito: 94, 312
Kahlo, Frida: 228, 255
Kurimanzutto: 160

# L

La Alameda de Santa María: 120–121
Labor: 160–161
Laboratoire: 161
Laboratorio de Arte Alameda: 105
La Ciudadela (The Citadel): 281
LAGO/ALGO: 159
La Jaliscience: 251
landscape: 299–304

language: 324
La Teatrería: 199
La Titería: 242
LGBTQ+ travelers: 322-323, 355
light rail: 336-337
literature: 326-327
live music: 77-78, 102, 131-132, 197, 217-218, 236
local culture: 320-324
lucha libre: 83, 108-109
Lunario: 158

# MNO

Marcha del Orgullo LGBTI CDMX (LGBTI Pride March): 134
Memorial de: 68 91
Mercado de la Merced: 70
Mercado de la Paz: 251
Mercado Sonora: 70
metro: 332-336
Metrobús: 336
money: 356-357
Monumental Plaza de Toros México: 219
Monumento a Colón: 125
Monumento a la Revolución Mexicana: 121
Monumento a Los Niños Héroes: 151
murals: 40
Museo Amparo: 290
Museo Anahuacalli: 255
Museo Archivo de la Fotografía: 79-80
Museo Caja de Agua: 90
Museo Casa Estudio Diego Rivera: 255-256
Museo Casa Leon Trotsky: 228
Museo de Arte Carrillo Gil: 257
Museo de Arte Moderno: 162-163
Museo de Arte Popular: 106
Museo de Arte Religioso Santa Mónica: 291
Museo de El Carmen: 249
Museo de Geología: 120
Museo de Historia Natural and Museo Jardín del Agua: 164-165
Museo de la Ciudad de México: 68-69
Museo de la No Intervención: 291
Museo de la Secretaría de Hacienda y Crédito Público: 65
Museo del Estado Casa de Alfeñique: 291
Museo del Estanquillo: 80
Museo del Juguete Antiguo: 198
Museo del Objeto del Objeto (MODO): 199
Museo del Palacio de Bellas Artes: 95
Museo del Sitio: 61
Museo del Sitio de la Cultura Teotihuacana: 281-283
Museo del Sitio y Centro de Visitantes Chapultepec: 150
Museo del Tequila y El Mezcal: 104
Museo Experimental El Eco: 133-134
Museo Franz Mayer: 105-106
Museo Frida Kahlo: 228-229
Museo Internacional del Barroco: 291-292
Museo José Luis Bello y Zetina: 291
Museo Jumex: 161-162
Museo Kaluz: 105
Museo Memoria y Tolerancia: 106-107
Museo Mural Diego Rivera: 94, 104-105
Museo Nacional de Antropología: 148-149
Museo Nacional de Arquitectura: 95
Museo Nacional de Arte: 59
Museo Nacional de Culturas Populares: 239
Museo Nacional de la Estampa: 106
Museo Nacional de la Revolución: 122
Museo Nacional de San Carlos: 133
Museo Soumaya: 161
Museo Tamayo: 164
Museo Universitario Arte Contemporáneo (MUAC): 257-258
Museo Universitario de Ciencias y Artes CU: 250
Museo Universitario del Chopo: 134, 258
Museo Vivo del Muralismo: 60
museums: 79-81, 104-107, 133-134, 161-165, 198-199, 238-239, 255-256
music: 327-328
neighborhood walks: Centro Histórico 54-58; Chapultepec and Polanco 144-147; Coyoacán 224-227; Paseo de la Reforma 116-119; Roma and Condesa 176-179
Noche de Museos 81
Nuestra Señora de Guadalupe del Buen Tono: 96
Olivia Foundation: 198
markets: 216-217

# PQR

Palace of Quetzalpapalotl: 284
Palacio de Bellas Artes: 94-95, 107
Palacio de Cultura Citibanamex: 63
Palacio de los Deportes: 255
Palacio Nacional: 65, 68
Palacio Postal: 59
plátanos machos: 98-99
pambazos: 98

Papalote Museo del Niño: 165
parks: 135, 165-167, 243, 260
Parque Ecológico de Xochimilco: 257
Parque Ecológico de Xochimilco (PEX): 260
Parque España: 181
Parque Hundido: 209
Parque Lincoln: 165-166
Parque México: 181
Parroquia de San Agustín de las Cuevas: 251
Parroquia de San Juan Bautista: 231
Parroquia y Ex-Convento de San Juan Bautista: 231
Paseo de la Reforma: 16, 112-139; map 114-115; neighborhood walk 116-119
Paseo Dominical Muévete en Bici: 137
passports: 17, 342
Patio of the Jaguars: 284
people-watching: 24
pharmacies: 352
Pino Suárez Metro Station: 65
Pirámide de la Luna (Pyramid of the Moon): 284
Pirámide del Sol (Pyramid of the Sun): 283-284
planning tips: 16-25
Plaza Cívica: 291
Plaza de la Constitución: 251
Plaza de las Tres Culturas: 90
Plaza de San Juan: 96
Plaza de Santo Domingo: 60
Plaza Garibaldi: 92
Plaza Loreto: 62
Plaza Río de Janeiro: 180
Plaza San Jacinto: 249-250
Plaza Santa Catarina: 229-230
Plaza y Capilla de la Conchita: 231-232
police: 346
Poliforum Siqueiros: 208
postal services: 358
Proyectos Monclova: 160
markets: 111
Puebla and Vicinity: 286-298; map 288
pulque and pulquerías: 102, 103, 131
quelites: 154-155
quesadillas: 99
recreation: 83, 108, 135-137, 165-168, 200, 218-219, 243, 260-261
Rectoría: 250
Rectoría San Francisco Javier and Plaza Romita: 180
religion: 323-324
rental cars: *see* car travel
reservations: 18

RGR: 161
Rivera, Diego: 60, 68, 104, 255
Roma and Condesa: 172-203; map 174-175; neighborhood walk 176-179

# S

Sala de Arte Público David Alfaro Siqueiros: 164
Sala Nezahualcóyotl: 258
Semana Santa: 259
September 19: 302-303
Sinagoga Histórica Justo Sierra: 62
shopping: 46-47; *see also* Shops Index, specific place
smoking: 348
souvenirs: 240-241
spectator sports: 83, 108, 137, 218-219, 260-261
studying: 354

# T

tacos: 186-187
tamales: 99
taxi: 337-338
Teatrería: 199
Teatro de los Insurgentes: 209
telephone services: 358
Templo de Quetzalcóatl: 281
Templo de Santa Teresa La Nueva: 62
Templo Mayor: 65, 66-68
Templo San Hipólito: 92-93
Templo y Convento de Regina Coeli: 69
Templo y Plaza de Santo Domingo: 60
Tenochtitlan: 64-65
Teotihuacán: 279, 280-286; map 282
theater: 107, 199, 239, 242, 258
tianguis: *see* markets
Tianguis Cultural del Chopo: 134
tipping: 347
Titería: 242
Tlalpan: 251
tlacoyos: 98
Torre Latinoamericana: 62-63
tortas: 98
tourist information: 357
tourist permits: *see* visas
transportation: 17-18, 330-342
travelers of color: 355-356
travel tips: 354-356

# UVWXZ

Universidad del Claustro de Sor Juana: 69-70
Verbena Navideña: 82-83

Virgen de Guadalupe: 310–311
visas: 342
visual art: 328–329
Viveros de Coyoacán: 243
volcanoes: 287
walks: *see* neighborhood walks
water safety: 349
women travelers: 322, 355

Xochimilco: 256–257
Zócalo: 63–65, 289
Zona Arqueológica and Museo del Templo Mayor: 65, 66–68
Zona Arqueológica de Cholula: 298
Zona Arqueológica Tlatelolco: 90–91
Zona Rosa: 123
Zsona MACO: 259

# Restaurants Index

Al Andalus: 75–76
Alma Negra: 215
Arroyo: 254
Auna: 153
Au Pied de Cochon: 190
Auténtica Cabaña: 285
Azul Histórico: 71–72
Balcón del Zócalo: 72
Bar La Ópera: 74
Barraca Valenciana 234
Beatricita: 126
Botánico: 192
Buna: 215
Café Avellaneda: 214
Café de Tacuba: 71
Café El Jarocho: 234–235
Café El Popular: 72
Café Jekemir: 215
Café La Habana: 96
Café Nin: 129
Camino a Comala: 214
Cantón Mexicali: 188–189
Cardenal: 72–73
Cardinal: 214
Carnitas El Cherán: 97
Casa del Pan Papalotl: 232
Casa de los Tacos: 234
Casa de Toño: 127
Casareyna: 292
Casino Español: 76
Chiandoni: 214
Chilpa: 184
Chocolatería La Rifa: 130
Churrería El Moro: 76–77
Cicatriz Cafe: 129
Ciena: 192
Cocuyos: 75
Comal: 292
Comal Oculto: 153
Comedor Jacinta: 152
Contramar: 188

Corazón de Maguey: 233
Coyota: 127
Cuadrilátero: 97
Danzantes: 233–234
Danubio: 75
Desastre Libros y Café: 215
Don Toribio: 72
Ehden: 75
Especial de Paris: 130
Esquina del Chilaquil: 185
Farmacía Internacional: 100
Fogones: 184
Fonda: 99.99 212
Fonda de Santa Clara: 293
Fonda Margarita: 211
Fugaz: 192
Gracias Madre Taquería Vegana: 184–185
Gruta: 284
Guzina Oaxaca: 152
Hidalguense: 183
Hostal de los Quesos: 213
Hotel Colonial: 292
Huequito: 97–98
Jardín del Pulpo: 235
Kuinitos: 127–128
Loosers: 181–182
Makan: 100
Mari Gold: 153–154
Máximo Bistrot Local: 191–192
Mendl: 192–193
Mercado Coyoacán: 235
Mercado San Juan: 101
Merendero Las Lupitas: 232
Mi Compa Chava: 188
Mictlan Antojitos Veganos: 211
Mi Gusto Es: 213–214
Molino El Pujol: 183–184
Mano Jardín: 235
Montejo: 210–211
Mural de los Poblanos: 292
Nadefo: 128

Neveria Roxy: 193
Nicos: 253–254
Orale Arepa: 156
Orinoco: 185
Panadería Rosetta: 193
Panchos: 155
Paradero Conocido: 97
Parados: 188
Parnita: 182
Pastelería Ideal: 76
Paxia: 73–74
Pialadero de Guadalajara: 125–126
Pigeon: 191
Pizza Félix: 189
Pozolería Matamoros: 292
Pujol: 152–153
Quintonil: 153
Rincón Tarasco: 213
Rokai and Rokai Ramen: 128
Roldán 37: 74
Rosetta: 189
Salón Corona: 74–75
Salón Ríos: 127
San Ángel Inn: 254
Sanborns: 73
Sanborns de los Azulejos: 71
Sartoria: 189
Secina: 210
Siembra Taquería: 156
Supplì: 101
Tacos Beyrut: 293
Tacos Chupacabras: 234
Tacos Domingo: 100
Tacos El Güero (Tacos Hola): 185
Tacos Los Condes: 212
Tacos Manolo: 212
Tamales Doña Emi: 185
Tamales Madre: 124–125
Tetetlán: 254
Tlayudas: 211
Turix: 154–155
Vilsito: 212–213
Zéfiro: 74

# Nightlife Index

Bipo: 236
Bodeguita en Medio: 197
Bósforo: 102
Café de Nadie: 193
Cananea: 130
Centenario: 107 235
Covadonga: 195
Coyoacana: 236
Faena: 77
Fiebre de Malta: 130–131
Fifty Mils: 131
Gin Gin: 157–158
Hostería La Bota: 77–78
Jazzatlan Capital: 197
Jazzorca: 217–218
Kaito: 215
Licorería Limantour: 194
Marrakech Salón: 78
Mezcalero: 236
Oropel: 195
Páramo: 194
Parker & Lenox: 131–132
Petanca Roma Club: 197
Pulquería La Joya: 131
Pulquería Las Duelistas: 102
Revuelta Queer House: 195
Riviera del Sur: 195
Salón España: 77
Salón Los Angeles: 102
Salón Paris: 131
Sunday Sunday: 78
Sungay Brunch: 132
Ticuchi: 157
Tío Pepe: 101
Tlecan: 195
Valenciana: 216–217
Vicio: 236
Zinco Jazz Club: 77

# Shops Index

Bazaar Sábado: 263
Bazar Reto: 243
Blue Demon Jr. Galería: 110
Callejón de los Sapos: 296
Canasta: 202
Carla Fernández: 138

Casa Bosques: 201
Casa del Obispo: 262–263
Central de Abasto de la Ciudad de México: 261–262
Centro Cultural Elena Garro: 243
Centro de Antigüedades Plaza del Ángel: 138
Chic by Accident: 202
Ciudadela Centro Artesanal: 110
Delirio: 202–203
Dulcería de Celaya: 84–85
Dulcería La Gran Fama: 294
Expendio Doméstico: 169
Fábrica Social: 138–139
FONART: 169
Happening Store: 201–202
Ikal: 170
Juárez Shopping District: 138
Lago: 170–171
Laguna: 203
Lagunilla: 109
Librería Rosario Castellanos: 201
Mercado de Cuauhtémoc: 200–201
Mercado de Jamaica: 261
Mercado de Medellín: 203
Mercado San Juan: 110
Mercado Sonora: 85
Nacional Monte de Piedad: 83
180°: Shop 201
Onora: 168
Parian: 293
Péndulo: 171
Remigio: 83–84
Sombreros Tardan: 84
Talavera de la Reyna: 296
Tane: 171
The Shops at Downtown: 85
Tianguis Cultural del Chopo: 139
Uriarte: 296
Uriarte Talavera: 168

# Hotels Index

Alcobas: 273
Camino Real Polanco México: 274
Casa de los Amigos: 272
Casa González: 272–273
Casa Jacinta: 276
Casa Nima: 275
Casa Pani: 272
Casita del Patio Verde: 276–277
Casareyna: 296
Círculo Mexicano: 269
Condesa DF: 275
Diplomatico: 276
Downtown Hotel: 269–270
Four Seasons Hotel: 273
Gran Hotel de la Ciudad de México: 270
Hotel Catedral: 269
Hotel Colonial: 296
Hotel Hábita: 273
Hotel Isabel: 270
Hostel Mundo Joven Catedral: 269
Hotel Stanza: 275
Hotel Villas Arqueológicas Teotihuacán: 285
Ignacia Guest House: 275
InterContinental Presidente Mexico City: 273–274
Patio: 272
Purificadora: 296–297
Red Tree House: 276
Wyndham Garden Polanco: 274
Zócalo Central: 270

# Photo Credits

All photos © Julie Meade except page 1 © Zsuriel | Dreamstime.com; page 2 © (bottom) Agcuesta | Dreamstime.com; page 4 © Arkadij Schell | Dreamstime.com; page 6 © Elovkoff | Dreamstime.com; page 8 © Ibrester | Dreamstime.com; page 10 © (top) Kmiragaya | Dreamstime.com; (bottom) Marketanovakova | Dreamstime.com; page 12 © (top) Andre Nery | Dreamstime.com; page 13 © Jesus Eloy Ramos Lara | Dreamstime.com; page 14 © (top) Xhico | Dreamstime.com; page 19 © Kmiragaya | Dreamstime.com; page 24 © (top) Byelikova | Dreamstime.com; page 26 © Javarman | Dreamstime.com; page 27 © (bottom) Noamfein | Dreamstime.com; page 29 © Wirestock | Dreamstime.com; (bottom) Chon Kit Leong | Dreamstime.com; page 30 © Photosimo | Dreamstime.com; page 31 © (top) Diego Grandi | Dreamstime.com; page 33 © Agcuesta | Dreamstime.com; page 34 © (bottom) Natalia Golovina | Dreamstime.com; page 35 © (top) Lucidwaters | Dreamstime.com; page 36 © Aurora Esperanza Ángeles Flores | Dreamstime.com; page 37 © (top) Jesus Eloy Ramos Lara | Dreamstime.com; page 40 © Helen Chen | Dreamstime.com; page 42 © (bottom) Witold Ryka | Dreamstime.com; page 51 © (top left) Michele Ricucci | Dreamstime.com; page 59 © Alexandre Fagundes De Fagundes | Dreamstime.com; page 66 © (top) Jiawangkun | Dreamstime.com; page 67 © (bottom) Chon Kit Leong | Dreamstime.com; page 70 © Rafael Ben-ari | Dreamstime.com; page 71 © Amith Nag | Dreamstime.com; page 73 © Arlette Lopez | Dreamstime.com; page 82 © (bottom) Arlette Lopez | Dreamstime.com; page 87 © (top right) Konstantin Kalishko | 123rf.com; page 91 © (top) Sailingstone Travel | Dreamstime.com; page 92 © Rafael Ben-ari | Dreamstime.com; page 93 © (bottom) Girnyk | Dreamstime.com; page 94 © (bottom) Renan Greinert | Dreamstime.com; page 101 © Marketanovakova | Dreamstime.com; page 103 © Dencurrin | Dreamstime.com; page 104 © (bottom) Angela Ostafichuk | Dreamstime.com; page 108 © Outline205 | Dreamstime.com; page 113 © (top right) Alejandro Vázquez | Dreamstime.com; page 118 © (top) Elovkoff | Dreamstime.com; page 119 © Jose Antonio Nicoli | Dreamstime.com; © Kmiragaya | Dreamstime.com; page 121 © Rmarxy | Dreamstime.com; page 123 © (bottom) Kmiragaya | Dreamstime.com; page 134 © Lucie Ericksen; page 135 © Alfredo Hernández Ríos | Dreamstime.com; page 140 © Elovkoff | Dreamstime.com; page 141 © (top left) Aleksandra Lande | Dreamstime.com; (top right) Miguel Aco | Dreamstime.com; page 146 © Guillermo Carbajal | 123rf.com; page 147 © (bottom) Jesús Eloy Ramos Lara | Dreamstime.com; page 148 © (bottom) Javarman | Dreamstime.com; page 158 © Atosan | Dreamstime.com; page 164 © Coralimages2020 | Dreamstime.com; page 172 © Wirestock | Dreamstime.com; page 173 © (top right) Kmiragaya | Dreamstime.com; page 186 © Marcos Castillo | Dreamstime.com; page 204 © Julie Meade; page 205 © (top left) Daniel Gomez | Dreamstime.com; page 218 © (bottom) Ulrike Stein | Dreamstime.com; page 220 © Kmiragaya | Dreamstime.com; page 221 © (top left) Lucie Ericksen; (top right) Jiawangkun | Dreamstime.com; page 225 © Demerzel21 | Dreamstime.com; page 230 © Aurora Esperanza Ángeles Flores | Dreamstime.com; page 240 © Bernardojbp | Dreamstime.com; page 244 © Jesus Eloy Ramos Lara | Dreamstime.com; page 245 © (top left) Carlos Sanchez Pereyra | Dreamstime.com; page 249 © (top) Oksana Byelikova | Dreamstime.com; page 260 © Cascoly | Dreamstime.com; page 261 © Marcosdominguez | Dreamstime.com; page 262 © (bottom) Angela Ostafichuk | Dreamstime.com; page 264 © Xing Wang | Dreamstime.com; page 266 © Suriel Ramirez Zaldivar | Dreamstime.com; page 281 © (top left) Gerasimovvv | Dreamstime.com; (top right) Aleksandar Todorovic | Dreamstime.com; page 285 © (bottom) Wilsilver77 | Dreamstime.com; page 286 © Lucie Ericksen; page 287 © Lucie Ericksen; page 289 © Arturoosorno | Dreamstime.com; page 295 © Kmiragaya | Dreamstime.com; page 301 © Carlos Araujo | Dreamstime.com; page 312 © Jesus Eloy Ramos Lara | Dreamstime.com; page 332 © Michele Ricucci | Dreamstime.com; page 342 © (bottom) Atosan | Dreamstime.com

# Gear up for a bucket list vacation

# or plan your next beachy getaway!

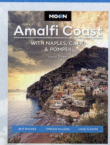  
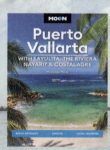  
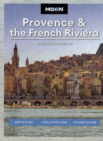  

# MOON ROAD TRIP GUIDES

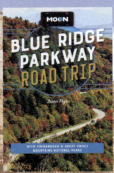

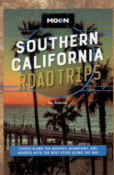
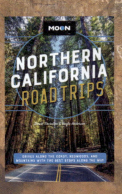
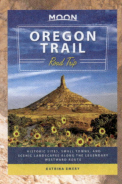

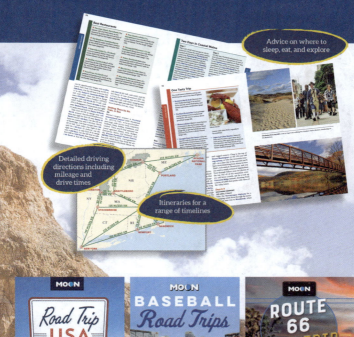

- Advice on where to sleep, eat, and explore
- Detailed driving directions including mileage and drive times
- Itineraries for a range of timelines

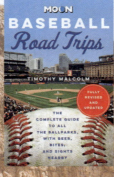
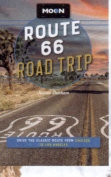
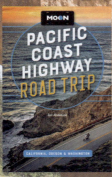
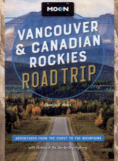
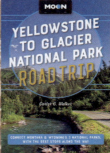

Liked this book? Travel deeper with more & Beyonds from Moon:

Barcelona
Budapest
Copenhagen
Florence
Lisbon
Marrakesh
Milan
Prague
Venice

## OR TAKE THINGS ONE STEP AT A TIME

*Moon's pocket-sized city walks with fold-out maps are the perfect companion!*

# MAP SYMBOLS

| | | | | | | | |
|---|---|---|---|---|---|---|---|
| ≡ | Major Hwy | | Pedestrian Friendly | ------- | Trail | ········· | Ferry |
| = | Road/Hwy | | Tunnel | ⊥⊥⊥⊥⊥ | Stairs | -·-·-·- | Railroad |

- ■ **Sights**
- ■ **Restaurants**
- ■ **Nightlife**
- ■ **Arts and Culture**
- ■ **Recreation**
- ■ **Shops**
- ■ **Hotels**

- ⊛ City/Town
- ◉ State Capital
- ○ National Capital
- ✪ Highlight
- ★ Point of Interest
- • Accommodation
- ▼ Restaurant/Bar
- ■ Other Location

- ▲ Mountain
- ✦ Unique Feature
- 🌊 Waterfall
- ♠ Park
- ⌂ Archaeological Site
- TH Trailhead
- P Parking Area

# CONVERSION TABLES

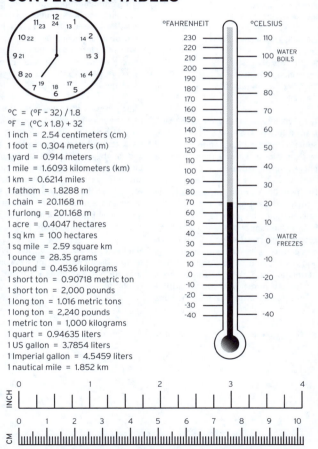

°C = (°F - 32) / 1.8
°F = (°C x 1.8) + 32
1 inch = 2.54 centimeters (cm)
1 foot = 0.304 meters (m)
1 yard = 0.914 meters
1 mile = 1.6093 kilometers (km)
1 km = 0.6214 miles
1 fathom = 1.8288 m
1 chain = 20.1168 m
1 furlong = 201.168 m
1 acre = 0.4047 hectares
1 sq km = 100 hectares
1 sq mile = 2.59 square km
1 ounce = 28.35 grams
1 pound = 0.4536 kilograms
1 short ton = 0.90718 metric ton
1 short ton = 2,000 pounds
1 long ton = 1.016 metric tons
1 long ton = 2,240 pounds
1 metric ton = 1,000 kilograms
1 quart = 0.94635 liters
1 US gallon = 3.7854 liters
1 Imperial gallon = 4.5459 liters
1 nautical mile = 1.852 km

**MOON MEXICO CITY**
Avalon Travel
Hachette Book Group, Inc.
555 12th Street, Suite 1850
Oakland, CA 94607, USA
www.moon.com

Editor: Devon Lee
Managing Editor: Courtney Packard
Copy Editor: Christopher Church
Graphics and Production Coordinator: Darren Alessi
Cover Design: Toni Tajima
Interior Design: Megan Jones Design and Darren Alessi
Map Editor: Karin Dahl
Cartographer: Karin Dahl
Proofreader: Brett Keener
Indexer: Courtney Packard

ISBN-13: 979-8-88647-130-4

Printing History
1st Edition — 2000
9th Edition — August 2025
5 4 3 2 1

Text © 2025 by Julie Meade & Avalon Travel.
Maps © 2025 by Avalon Travel.
Some photos and illustrations are used by permission and are the property of the original copyright owners.

Hachette Book Group, Inc. supports the right to free expression and the value of copyright. The purpose of copyright is to encourage writers and artists to produce the creative works that enrich our culture. The scanning, uploading, and distribution of this book without permission is a theft of the author's intellectual property. If you would like permission to use material from the book (other than for review purposes), please contact permissions@hbgusa.com. Thank you for your support of the author's rights.

Front cover photo: Mexican Stock Exchange Building © Thom Lang/Getty Images
Back cover photo: Museo Soumaya © Margarita Ray | Dreamstime.com

Printed in China by RR Donnelley Dongguan

Avalon Travel is a division of Hachette Book Group, Inc. Moon and the Moon logo are trademarks of Hachette Book Group, Inc. All other marks and logos depicted are the property of the original owners.

All recommendations, including those for sights, activities, hotels, restaurants, and shops, are based on each author's individual judgment. We do not accept payment for inclusion in our travel guides, and our authors do not accept free goods or services in exchange for positive coverage.

Although every effort was made to ensure that the information was correct at the time of going to press, the author and Hachette Book Group, Inc. do not assume, and hereby disclaim, any liability to any party for any loss or damage caused by any information or recommendations contained in this book, including any errors or omissions regardless of whether such errors or omissions result from negligence, accident, or any other cause.

Hachette Book Group, Inc. is not responsible for websites (or their content) that are not owned by Hachette Book Group, Inc.